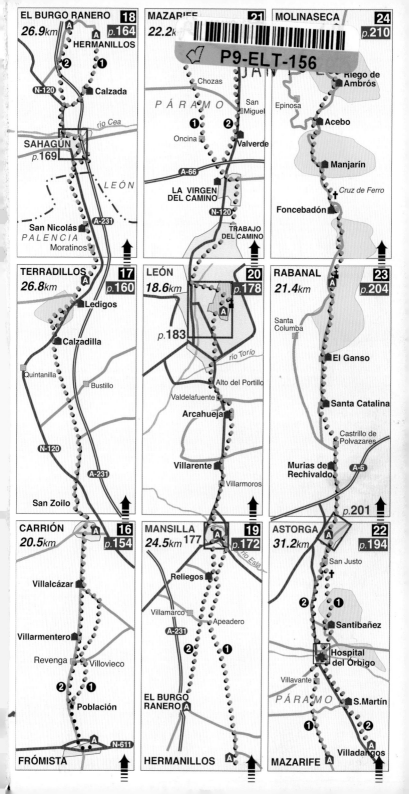

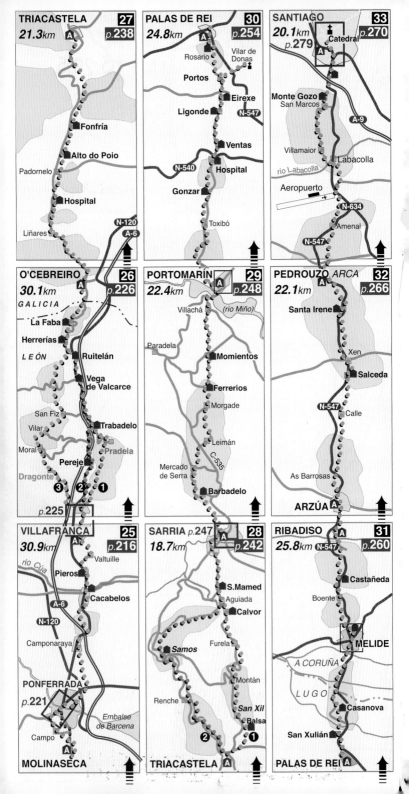

TRIACASTELA `27`
21.3km p.238

Fonfría
Alto do Poio
Padornelo
Hospital
Liñares

O'CEBREIRO `26`
30.1km p.226

GALICIA
La Faba
Herrerías
Ruitelán
LEÓN
Vega
de Valcarce
San Fiz
Vilar
Trabadelo
Moral
Pradela
Pereje
Dragonte
3 **2** **1**
p.225

VILLAFRANCA `25`
30.9km p.216

río Cúa
Valtuille
Pieros
Cacabelos
A-6
N-120
Camponaraya
PONFERRADA
p.221
Campo
Embalse
de Bárcena
MOLINASECA

PALAS DE REI `30`
24.8km p.254

Rosario
Vilar de
Donas
Portos
Eirexe
Ligonde N-547
Ventas
Hospital
N-540
Gonzar
Toxibó

PORTOMARÍN `29`
22.4km p.248

Villachá (río Miño)
Paradela
Momientos
Ferreiros
Morgade
Leimán
C-535
Mercado
de Serra
Barbadelo

SARRIA p.247 `28`
18.7km p.242

S.Mamed
Aguiada
Calvor
Furela
Samos
Montán
Renche
San Xil
Balsa
2 **1**
TRIACASTELA

SANTIAGO `33`
20.1km p.279

Catedral
Monte Gozo
San Marcos
A-9
Villamaior
Labacolla
Aeropuerto río Labacolla
N-634
Amenal
N-547

PEDROUZO *ARCA* `32`
22.1km p.266

Santa Irene
Xen
Salceda
N-547
Calle
As Barrosas
ARZÚA

RIBADISO `31`
25.8km N-547 p.260

Castañeda
Boente
MELIDE
A CORUÑA
LUGO
Casanova
San Xulián
PALAS DE REI

A PILGRIM'S GUIDE TO THE

Camino de Santiago

St. Jean · Roncesvalles · Santiago

The Way of St. James
The ancient pilgrim path also known as *Camino Francés*

John Brierley

*A Practical & Mystical Manual
for the Modern Day Pilgrim*

© John Brierley 2003, 2006, 2007, 2008, 2009, 2010, 2011, 2012, 2013

First published as A Pilgrim's Guide to Camino Francés in 2003
This new fully revised **10th** edition published in **2014**.

ISBN 978-1-84409-624-4

British Library Cataloguing-in-Publication Data.
A catalogue record for this book is available from the British Library.

All photographs © John Brierley 2014
Author photograph Gemma Brierley
All maps © John Brierley 2014

Printed and bound in the European Union

Published by
CAMINO GUIDES
An imprint of Findhorn Press Ltd
117-121 High Street
Forres IV36 1AB
Scotland

Tel: +44(0)1309-690582
Fax: +44(0)131-777-2711

Email: info@findhornpress.com
www.findhornpress.com
www.caminoguides.com

CONTENTS:

A ACKNOWLEDGEMENTS:

This guidebook has been a lifetime in the making and a decade in the mapping. It is an on-going journey with many deep valleys and high peaks. Countless individuals have crossed this path and each one, in their own way, has helped to shape it. This is no less true today as I finalise this latest update of the original guide. So, apart from my earlier mentors and helpers, I want to thank the many Friends of the Way *Amigos del Camino* and the various associations whose voluntary efforts to waymark the route means that, today, we need only the barest details to get us safely to our destination. And finally I acknowledge Elías Valiña Sampedro of O Cebreiro whose vision set in motion the revitalisation of the modern camino de Santiago. I heard his call and was inspired.

And a special thanks to pilgrims who took the time to feedback comments and suggestions, many of these have now been incorporated in this latest guide such as bedbug infestation and treatment. Just before an earlier edition went to the print I received an email asking why I was endorsing 'cheap' air travel to and from Santiago when it was so costly on the environment. Details have been included on how you can offset damaging greenhouse emissions and travel *carbon-neutral*, whether this be by air, rail or bus. My conscience is also clear because I know that walking the caminos can be a powerful catalyst for positive change so that the means (of getting there) fully justifies the end (expanded awareness). A central tenet of these guides is that pilgrimage starts the moment we become conscious that life itself is a sacred journey, carrying with it the responsibility to act accordingly.

And finally, I thank you, fellow pilgrim, for travelling the path with me. Let us remind each other that every step is a prayer – for good *or* ill – so let us manifest goodwill in all our thoughts, words and actions.

Buen Camino John Brierley

NOTE TO THE 10th EDITION:

The route still remains largely unchanged since the previous 9th edition was published but the addition of several new pilgrim hostels and hotels built in time for the last Holy Year has helped to relieve some of the pressure on accommodation. Some existing hostels have also seen an upgrading of facilities offered particularly the addition of washing *and* drying machines *secadoras*, the latter can be a real boon in wet weather.

The biggest change continues to be the rise in the number of pilgrims travelling the camino – reaching 192,488 last year (over ¼ Million in the 2010 Holy Year *Año Santo*). Inevitably this puts a strain on resources and some hostels at bottleneck locations were *completo* by noon, before they were even officially due to open! This is no reason *not* to go during the extended summer period but we need to be flexible on where to sleep and have enough energy in reserve to search out alternatives if necessary. The one piece of advice that I would pick out from the first edition and underline is simply this, *'There are no guarantees in the life of a pilgrim and we are well served by developing an attitude of gratitude for all learning experiences found along the path.'*

A snapshot of modern Spain has been included at the end of the historical sketch to provide a cultural and political context for pilgrims visiting Spain for the first time. As an aide-mémoire essential Spanish *Español* words are shown in italics with the exception of camino that has now effectively become anglicised. A self-assessment questionnaire has also been included to help formulate and, hopefully, answer some of the deeper questions that often bubble to the surface when we clear space and head off along a path of enquiry.

INTRODUCTION:

Welcome to The Way of St. James *el camino de Sant Iago*. Unlike many other routes to Santiago de Compostela, the waymarking on the French Way *camino francé*s is now very extensive. The familiar yellow arrow *flecha amarillo* will become a source of great comfort to you along the way – popping into view just when you think you are lost. This said, an accurate map and guidebook is useful to help you plan your itinerary and excursions and to put you back on the path when your mind wanders and your feet follow!

I generally found guidebooks were either too big (and full of information that I could gather elsewhere along the way) or too small (with inadequate data). There was also a wide variation in the distances provided, exacerbated by the total absence of details of the start and end point for measurements, 'Burgos 12 km' is meaningless without specifying *where* in Burgos – the new pilgrim hostel is 7.8 km from the start of the city environs, a very long way at the end of a day's walk! But what inspired me to write *another* guidebook was the almost universal absence of any reference, yet alone waymarks, to the *inner* path.

I urge you to find a spiritual purpose for taking this journey. If you have difficulty with this term, find one more meaningful to you, and check out your local bookstore – you'll find a wealth of literature on the subject. The words 'significant journey' threw up 63 million suggestions on my web browser – so you get the idea! But attend to this promptly so that you have time to mull over your motivation *before* you travel. A core question arises; what turns a walking holiday into pilgrimage? When you receive an answer you may find a fundamental change in how you approach the journey – from intentionality down to what you put in your backpack. The strategy is not to feel pressurised to follow any particular 'way' – you will know when something rings true for you – learn to trust your resonance. Some suggestions are listed in the bibliography.

I have endeavoured to find a balance between the *inner* and *outer* journey by paying equal respect to both. That is why these guides are subtitled *a practical and mystical manual for the modern day pilgrim*. That we might find a place to lay our weary head at the end of the day but also, and crucially, that we might feel supported and encouraged to dive into the mysteries of our individual soul awakenings, without which all journeying is essentially purposeless. Along every path of enquiry there comes a point that requires a leap of faith, where we have to abandon the security of out-dated dogma handed down to us over millennia. When we reach that point we have to let go of the safety of the familiar and dive into the unknown, with nothing but our faith to support us.

The traditional pilgrim way is on foot. You can also obtain a certificate of completion *compostela* by going on bike or horseback but you may miss some of the beauty of the outer landscape and the spirit of the inner journey. Pilgrimage takes the time it takes. Travel alone if at all possible – this way you are more likely to meet the local villagers and shepherds and absorb their wisdom and local lore. You will learn the native language as you go and you will also meet other fellow pilgrims along the way. But above all, you may meet your *Self* and find that you are never alone – and that is surely a primary purpose of pilgrimage and of life itself.

This guidebook is dedicated to awakening beyond human consciousness. It was born out of a mid-life crisis and the perceived need for a time to reflect on the purpose and direction of life. We have a sacred contract, a divine function and reason why we came here. Pilgrimage provides an opportunity to delve deeper into that purpose and the time to re-orientate our lives towards its fulfilment. We have been asleep a long time, but alarm bells are ringing for young and old and there are signs that we are collectively waking up. The Call of the Camino is being heard all around the world – the call to move beyond that which separates us and to find that common bond, that spiritual thread which binds us together and, by extension, connects us to the Source of all that is. There is a yearning to break free from our self-imposed imprisonment and isolation so eloquently captured in the words of Christopher Fry in A Sleep of Prisoners:

> Thank God our time is now when wrong
> Comes up to face us everywhere,
> Never to leave us till we take
> The longest stride of soul folk ever took.
>
> Affairs are now soul size.
> The enterprise is exploration into God.
> Where are you making for?
> It takes so many thousand years to wake,
> But will you wake for pity's sake?

May your journey along your chosen path be blessed – rough or smooth, long or short – whichever route you take, know that you are loved and your destination is assured. God speed *Ultreia!*

❶ Travel – A Quick Guide:

• **When?** Spring is often wet and windy but the route is relatively quiet with early flowers appearing. Summer is busy and hot and hostels often full. Autumn often provides the most stable weather with harvesting adding to the colour and celebrations of the countryside. Winter is solitary and cold and some hostels will be closed.

• **How long?** The route is divided into 33 stages each one corresponding to an average days walk – but find your own pace and overnight at intermediate hostels as required. Clear the decks and allow some spaciousness into your life – 5 weeks is ideal but join or leave the route to fit in with your schedule.

❷ Preparation – *Outer*: what do I need to take *and* leave behind.

• Buy your boots in time to walk them in before you go.
• Pack a Poncho, Spain can provide downpours at any time of year.
• Bring a hat, sunstroke is painful and can be dangerous.
• Look again if your backpack weighs more than 10 kilos.

  What *not* to bring:
• Get rid of all books (except this one – all the maps you need are included.)
• Don't take 'extras', Spain has shops if you need to replace something.
• If you want to deepen your experience, leave behind:
   – your *camera* – you'll be able to live for the moment rather than memories.
   – your *watch* – you'll be surprised how quickly you adapt to a natural clock.
   – your *mobile phone* – break the dependency and taste the freedom.

❸ Language learn it now, *before* you go.

❹ Pilgrim Passport, Protocol & Prayer

• Get a *credencial* from your local confraternity – and join it.
• Have consideration for your fellow pilgrims and gratitude for your hosts.
• May every step be a prayer for peace and an extension of loving kindness.

❺ Preparation – *Inner*: why am I doing this?

Take time to prepare a purpose for this pilgrimage and to complete the self-assessment questionnaire. Start from the basis that you are essentially a spiritual being on a human journey, not a human being on a spiritual one. We came to learn some lesson and this pilgrimage affords an opportunity to find out what that is. Ask for help and expect it – it's there, now, waiting for you.

Whatever you do – for heaven's sake don't forget to start.

B **BEGINNING** – *Before you go*: This section has more detailed notes on preparation. Once you have finalised your packing consider cutting out these pages along the dotted line to leave extra space for your *credencial* or other personal papers – every ounce needs to be accounted for!

When to go? If you like peace and quiet, the **spring** months of March and April will provide fewer other pilgrims and tourists. Hostels will be opening and flights and ferries should be operating, at least on a limited basis. You will be accompanied by early spring flowers and cool conditions for walking, although the nights are likely to be cold and rain plentiful, especially in the mountain areas and Galicia. Pack additional wet gear and warm fleeces.

The **summer** months can be very hot and accommodation, even water, in short supply. July and August are bedlam and, if this coincides with a Holy Year (any year when St. James Day, 25th July, falls on a Sunday) it can turn into a nightmare for those wanting an introspective time. These 2 months alone account for almost half of all pilgrims arriving in Santiago for the whole year. May, June and September are also becoming very busy.

The **autumn** season from late September through October often provides more stable weather than spring, the fierce heat of summer is over, the snow hasn't yet arrived and most hostels are still open. If you are an experienced walker, the depths of **winter** can provide some of the most mystical experiences. There may be fewer flights and many hostels will be closed, but I have never wanted for a bed or floor to sleep on at this time of year. Costs will be lower and you'll have much of the camino to yourself. Bring warm waterproof clothes and remember that daylight hours are restricted, so the daily distance that you can cover is reduced.

The **weather** in northern Spain, particularly Galicia, is very unpredictable. The **summer** months may see temperatures soar to over 32 Celsius (90 Fahrenheit) and the nights are often uncomfortably warm. Sun protection is vital, especially on the high plateau *Meseta* much of which has no shade of any kind. Plenty of water is essential to replace fluids lost through physical exertion and the heat. In **winter** the higher ground can be blocked with snow with temperatures dropping below freezing. At the shoulder seasons, you can expect anything in between. The worst weather I ever experienced was in May when it rained nonstop in Galicia for 9 days, accompanied by fierce storms and low temperatures – by contrast, early November was warm and dry. So be prepared for any eventuality. **Daylight hours** can be important when planning each day's stage. In the summer you have all the hours God made and certainly more than you could walk! In mid winter, your daylight is reduced to 8 hours.

When does everyone else go? The following graphs might help your decision. Whilst clearly not everyone arriving at Santiago will report to the pilgrim office or collect a *compostela* the latest figures available (2012) give an indication of general trends. 70% of all pilgrims arrive in Santiago via the *camino francés* (down from 95% 8 years ago) and 41% arrive in July and August. However most start in Galicia, the majority in Sarria (40,734 – 21%) which entitles pilgrims to a compostela being just over 100 km from Santiago so the Galician stages are particularly busy. The next major gateway to the Camino is St. Jean Pied de Port (22,214 – 11%) and Roncesvalles (10,406 – 5%).

The number of pilgrims has increased fivefold over the past decade with pilgrims from 138 nationalities collecting a compostela during 2012 (49% Spanish). The first graph shows the number of pilgrims collecting a compostela over a 12-year period. Holy Years (in yellow) increases the numbers on the route and the visit by Pope Benedict during the Holy Year in 2010 saw the number pass ¼ Million for the first time in the modern history of the camino. The next Holy Year *Año Santo Jacobeo* will not be until 2021.

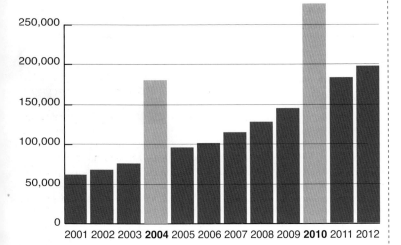

The next graph is based on average monthly figures. July and August traditionally account for nearly half of all pilgrims arriving in Santiago. The latest statistics available for 2012 (May with 21,766) indicate a doubling of the 2011 figures!

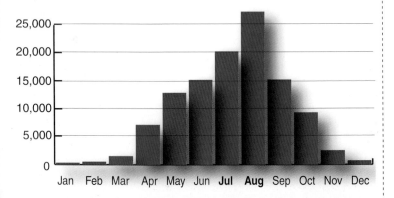

How long does it take? This depends on many factors such as level of fitness, which varies between individuals and within individuals (your biorhythms don't just affect mood swings!). When you add in variations in weather, detours (planned and otherwise) and different motivation and time constraints all this results in a heady mix of possibilities. I once met a manic pilgrim in Finisterre who had just arrived from Seville. He had walked 1,000 kilometres in a staggering 19 days that's over 50 km per day! He just had time to proudly show me his *credencial* to 'prove' the fact, before heading off down the hill again! It appears that many people allow completion of the journey in the minimum time to become the main focus. You are the only one who can evaluate your purpose and, if sporting achievement is yours, so be it, but it is unlikely to be a pilgrimage.

Statistics are limited, but my sense is that most people take 4 weeks to walk the entire *Camino Francés*. This fits (just) into a month-long holyday period with a day either side to fly in and out. These 30 days represent something of a minimum and would require averaging 28 kilometres a day with no detours, no rest days, no strains or sprains and no alternative travel plans. By the time you have found a bed, had a shower, massaged your feet, washed your socks, had a meal… there will be little time to attend mass, meditate, write-up your spiritual journal, reflect on your purpose…

Find your own pace but the one described here will allow you to reach Santiago *gracefully* in 5 weeks. This allows for an average of 24 kilometres a day for 33 days with 2 rest days. I like the idea that I walk one day for every year that Christ lived on earth. It connects me to a bigger picture and slows the pace to allow the inner alchemy of introspection to work. Pilgrimage takes the time it takes – 6 weeks (40 days and 40 nights) invites a deepening of the experience and would allow for the inclusion of the pilgrimage to Finisterre returning to Santiago via Muxía (see *Camino Finisterre*) and still provide time to integrate lessons and insights learnt along the way. Others start along one of the waymarked routes that commence further back in France (see map inside back cover) and there is now a waymarked route all the way from Budapest (via Hungary, Austria, Switzerland, France)! However, many people work within a 2-week framework and so will need 2 or 3 trips to complete the entire camino. The commencement of daily budget flights from the UK to midpoints such as Santander and Valladolid make access to Burgos and León an easy option and rail and bus connections within Spain are reliable and inexpensive.

In reality we have all the time in the world, but most of us don't believe it (especially our employers, employees, partners and peers). Come back to the 'real world' is a phrase that is often heard – and where, in heaven's name, might that be? And even if we know we have all the time there is, if we are honest perhaps we are afraid to take the time to reflect on our life and its direction. I know people who have cleared the decks and opened up a whole summer for pilgrimage, only to return within days, terrified of having time to contemplate their lives and the changes that any soul-searching might prescribe. Pilgrimage, like life, is experienced on many different levels. What makes sense for one may seem strange to another. We each have our reason for going. Whatever you do, don't put off starting as it might prove to be a major turning point in your life.

How to get there – *and back*: (See **map** on inside back cover for airports and ferry terminals). Note that schedules and prices are liable to change and reduced services can be expected during the winter months.

Carbon Neutral Travel: All travel has an impact on the environment; none more so than air travel. We can, however, minimise the damaging emissions of greenhouse gases by offsetting the amount produced in what is effectively a carbon sink. <www.climatecare.org> will calculate the amount of emissions produced by air, rail or car from your departure point and what you would need to contribute to offset this. A return flight London to Santiago will produce 0.33 tonnes of CO_2 – rail reduces this by around $2/3^{rds}$ but the stakes go up if you're coming from the west coast of the USA or Canada where you produce 2.04 tonnes (based on 80% seat occupancy). Carbon offsets don't solve the problem but help orientate us towards finding solutions. The key aspect here is about raising awareness – not about producing guilt trips. In these harsh economic times the cancellation of flights by airlines that haven't enough passengers booked to make the flight economic is an increasing trend. *The following schedules are liable to change at short notice – stay flexible!*

From the UK by Air: The easiest way to get to St. Jean de Pied de Port is to fly to **Biarritz**. Ryanair and Easyjet both have a direct service from London. These schedules usually allow time to catch the airport coach (regular departures; journey time ½ hour) to Bayonne *Baion* rail station in time to get the mountain railway to St. Jean. The scenic rail journey takes 1½ hours with a 5 minute walk into the town centre. Alternatively consider taking a taxi direct from the airport to St. Jean, a distance of 55 km and check out any other passengers with scallop shells who might share the cost or contact Express Bourricot © +33 559 373 628 a pilgrim travel company adjoining the pilgrim office in St. Jean who will collect. **Bilbao** with rail or bus connections to Bayonne (or Pamplona for Roncesvalles) has direct flights from London (and some regional airports) with Ryanair, EasyJet, Vueling, BA & Iberia. Other access points along the camino with direct Ryanair flights from the UK include **Madrid**, **Valladolid** and **Santander** with easy onward bus or rail connection to Logroño, Burgos or León. Easyjet fly London to Oviedo (Asturias) with easy access to León. **From Ireland by Air:** Ryanair fly Dublin (+ Knock) to Biarritz also Madrid and Santander. Aer Lingus fly Dublin to Bordeaux, Bilbao or Madrid. Iberia has an extensive service to regional airports. **From USA and Canada:** Madrid or Paris offer the best onward connections.

Bus: National Express/Eurolines London to Bordeaux depart 14:00 arrive 10.45 next day with onward travel by bus or rail. **Rail:** Raileurope/Seat61 show daily schedule London – Bayonne (via Eurostar Paris) and TGV taking around 10 ½ hours (e.g. 09:12—19:46). **Ferry:** P&O sail Portsmouth to Bilbao – journey time 36 hours. **Car Hire**: It is very competitive *within* Spain and this makes a good option for onward travel especially when car sharing. However, a pick-up in one country with a drop-off in another is usually prohibitively expensive.

From the rest of Europe: There are extensive and inexpensive rail and bus connections from all parts of Europe. The budget airlines have also extended their networks within Europe – check out appropriate sites.

Returning from Santiago: Increased services by rail, bus and air have made departure from Santiago easier and in some cases cheaper than previous years. Travel costs vary widely but increasing competition between national and budget airlines has helped to minimise the hike in oil costs. Generally the sooner you commit to going the cheaper the ticket – but staying flexible on a return date can sometimes be rewarded with a last-minute promotional fare. Galicia has 3 international airports at Santiago, A Corunna & Vigo although a question mark now hangs over whether Galicia can justify 3 airports in such close proximity.

•**Air** *Ryanair* fly direct from Santiago to London, Frankfurt and Milan and a wide selection of cities within Spain (with possibility of onward connections). *Easyjet* now fly from Santiago to London Gatwick and Geneva. *Vueling (Click Air)* fly direct to Paris and Zurich. *Air Berlin* has flights to major destinations throughout Europe from Santiago or via their hub in La Palma Majorca. *Aer Lingus* fly Santiago – Dublin (summer schedule) and *BA* and *Iberia* and other major airlines offer regular services throughout the year via connecting airports in Spain, mainly Madrid. There are direct daily bus links from Santiago to Porto and Lisbon airports, which widens the possibilities of return flights.

•**Rail** – you can book online through Spanish rail network RENFE (in English) www.renfe.es/horarios/english or Rail Europe www.raileurope.co.uk/ •**Bus** you can book online with Alsa / National Express for connections throughout Europe www.nationalexpress.com (click on Spanish services). •**Ferry** The advantage of sailing home is that you get a chance to acclimatise slowly – Santander & Bilbao  offer regular sailings to the U.K. Check with Brittany Ferries (Portsmouth to Bilbao and Santander - Plymouth to Santander). •**Car Hire** If you can find other passengers to share the cost then this is often a relatively cheap and convenient way to travel on to such places as Santander or Bilbao and flying or sailing home from there.

TRAVEL NOTES:

_____
_____
_____
_____
_____
_____
_____
_____
_____
_____
_____
_____
_____
_____
_____
_____
_____
_____
_____
_____
_____

Pilgrim Passport *credencial* **and Protocol:** In order to stay at pilgrim hostels and to receive a *compostela* (certificate of completion of pilgrimage to Santiago) you need to provide proof that you have walked the route (at least the last 100 km from Sarria). This is done by having a pilgrim passport *credencial* impressed with a rubber stamp *sello* primarily by the wardens *hospitaleros* in the pilgrim hostels but you can also have it stamped at cathedrals, churches, hostels, bars and town halls along the way.

You can obtain a pilgrim passport or record before travelling from the Confraternity of St. James in London or possibly from a local Confraternity in your country of origin (see useful addresses at the back) alternatively you can obtain a *credencial* on arrival at the pilgrim office in St. Jean Pied de Port / Roncesvalles (or Sarria as a last resort). Every effort should be made to join and support the work of the Confraternities who do so much to prepare and maintain the route and its facilities. Apply in good time (an internet application may speed processing.)

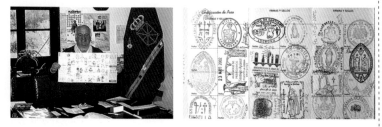

Pilgrim Hostels: *hostales, refugios* or *albergues de peregrinos* are reserved exclusively for pilgrims on the camino. They are provided throughout the route at convenient 10 – 20 km intervals (frequently less, never more) and all are on, or immediately adjacent, to the camino. This includes youth hostels *albergues juvenil* that are generally available to pilgrims holding a *credencial*. Accommodation is usually in bunk beds with additional overflow space on mattresses *colchonetas* on the floor *suelo*.

Bedbugs *chinches* are an increasing source of concern and any accommodation where people live in close proximity has added risks. Bedbugs live in mattresses etc., feeding at night, so until the accommodation is treated the problem remains. Carrying a pre-treated pillowcase and bed sheet (e.g. LifeAventure 3X) can be a useful preventative measure. If affected (3 or more bites in a row is a good indication) you need to [1] immediately advise the establishment of the problem and also the next hostel(s) so that they can take preventive measures. [2] wash and/or tumble dry all clothes at highest settings for 2+ hours and [3] Seek medical attention in severe cases (Hydrocortisone). Advice is often contradictory so seek help from those who have experience of the problem. Tourist offices may be able to help and vinegar is reported to reduce itchiness.

Hostels are generally open from March (Easter) through to October. Many now stay open all year (subject to closing for holidays such as Christmas or maintenance) and these are indicated where known but even those listed as closed may be open and vice-versa – be prepared for the unexpected. With increasing demand new hostels are opening every year and existing ones extending their season and the greater problem is finding accommodation in the summer rather than the winter! Names and telephone numbers have been included for emergency use (busy wardens will not thank you for idle requests) and to aid pilgrims travelling off-season to establish whether or not a hostel is open. It is generally not possible to book pilgrim hostels in advance.

Albergues fit into one of 6 main categories – the shortened form appears on the maps *Priv.* + *N° of bunk beds* ÷ *N° dormitories [20÷2] additional private rooms +*. *Prices can change at short notice and are provided as a guide. Some include breakfast and this is shown € incl.*

❶ *Muni*. **Municipal** hostel *albergue municipal* a basic hostel with limited facilities owned and maintained by the local authority. The warden *hospitalero/a* often lives next door (average cost €5). In this category are the Galician government hostels *Xunta. albergues Xunta de Galicia* (€6).

❷ *Par*. **Parish** hostel *albergue parroquia* these are generally owned by the local diocese and run by the parish priest. Some offer a regular pilgrim mass and they tend to be more informal and relaxed than municipal hostels with a communal meal and blessing. Generally welcoming but basic (av. cost €5 or *donativo*).

❸ *Conv*. **Convent or Monastery** hostel *monasterio o convento* (*mosteiro* in Gallego) it is often difficult to differentiate between a monastery (community of monks) and a convent (community of nuns) as the Spanish word *monasterio* or *convento* applies to both. *Convento* on its own is a monastery (monks) while *convento de monjas* (nuns) is a convent! The atmosphere in each is often markedly different so check the details provided (av. cost €5 or *donativo*).

❹ *Asoc*. **Association** hostels are owned and run by local Spanish or other national confraternities, sometimes in conjunction with the local authority. They tend to be particularly well equipped for the needs of the pilgrim and are generally staffed by former pilgrim volunteers (av. cost €7).

❺ *Priv.**(star) **Network** hostel *red de albergues* are private hostels that have formed themselves into a loose association. They are often owned and maintained by an individual but are increasingly being handed over to a management group engendering greater confidence in on-going availability. They have a similar sense of brotherhood/sisterhood as in confraternity hostels but often provide additional facilities such as washing/drying machines, internet access, dinner and breakfast and many have single/double rooms for higher price (€10+).

❻ *Priv*. **Private** hostels *albergues privado* are similar to the network hostels (above) but with no overall code or regulations. They tend to be more flexible than other hostels (commercial realities) with a full range of facilities and many have washing *and* drying machines and more flexible opening hours (€10+ additional private rooms, where available, from €20+)

Opening Hours: vary but are generally cleaned and ready again from around midday to welcome pilgrims. A few still open later although private hostels tend to open earlier. Many hostels have a policy of holding places for those travelling by foot until around 18:00, cyclists not being admitted until after that time. Hostels generally close their doors and turn off lights around 22:00. The morning routine will find early birds discreetly, or noisily, leaving their beds from 05.30 with the main rush hour between 06:30 and 07:30. Most hostels close for cleaning at 08:30 when the last stragglers will be sent on their way.

Any special arrangements, such as the provision of breakfast, will generally be notified on arrival but it is good practise to scan any notice boards. Opening times for tourist offices and museums are generally from 10:00–13:00 and again after *siesta* from 16:00–19:00. Shop hours are generally a bit longer. Note that many public buildings, including churches, are ***closed on Mondays***.

Warden *hospitalero/a* every hostel has at least one person whose job it is to ensure that the place is open at the appropriate time in the day and doors are locked and lights turned off at night. Resident *hospitaleros* are generally voluntary, live in the hostel itself and have probably walked the route in previous years and therefore know the needs of their fellow pilgrims. Non-resident wardens will live locally (often adjoining) and can provide reliable local information such as where to shop, restaurants, times of Mass, etc. Non-resident wardens are generally on hand between 16:00 and 20:00 to allocate bed spaces, collect the overnight charge and to stamp *credenciales*.

Facilities and levels of cleanliness vary widely, but hot showers are now standard everywhere. Don't forget that hot showers do not mean limitless hot water. If you are last in a group early in the afternoon, the water may have run cold. Conversely if you are last in during the evening it may have heated up again! There is a welcome increase in the number of hostels now providing automatic washing machines *lavadora* rarer but often more practical is the addition of a clothes-dryer *secadora* (not to be confused with the less useful spin-dryer *centrífuga*) – it can rain for days on end and a *secadora* can make an big difference to personal comfort (note machines are often out of order). Most hostels provide a kitchen with cooker, pots, pans and (some) basic cutlery and the majority have a sitting room or lounge that often serves as the dining area.

Standards – earlier versions of this guide had a 'scallop shell' grading system but standards and facilities offered are changing constantly so grading can often set up false expectations. Galicia is trying to introduce a rating system e.g. 2 stars[**] awarded to hostels which have a bed to shower/toilet ratio of 10:1 or less (that's considered good!). However, you will find an objective note of facilities offered which includes the number of bed spaces (usually bunks) and the number of rooms. Simple division will indicate how many roommates you are likely to be sharing with – up to 110 beds in one dormitory (Roncesvalles) *[110÷1]*! and down to 2 *[60÷30]* (Azofra). A + sign indicates additional private rooms may also be available (in addition to dormitory accommodation).

Gratitude for mercies small and large is a trait to be developed by all genuine pilgrims. This is nowhere more apparent than in the offering and acceptance of a place for the pilgrim to lay his or her head. Tired at the end of a long day or caught out in a storm *tormenta* any port may well induce a feeling of profound gratitude for the humblest of abodes and the most casual of welcomes – this is entirely as it should be.

The best way to establish the standard of a hostel is from the welcome you receive at the door and from comments made by fellow pilgrims in the *guest book*. There is an erroneous belief that all 'true' pilgrims must stay at the pilgrim hostels. Mediaeval pilgrims used every available bed regardless of whether or not it was an official *hospital de peregrino*. Indeed, medieval merchants and innkeepers were dependent on the custom of the pilgrims for their livelihood and it is no different today. Yes, by all means stay in the recognised hostels and meet up with fellow pilgrims and share news, but don't become reliant solely on these hostels. Spread your inner and outer wealth!

Hotels: If the hostels are full **alternative accommodation** is generally available in the immediate area. These also vary widely in facilities offered and priced (generally per room – not per person) accordingly. The Spanish tourist board categorises all 'official' accommodation. and **'r'** in each category denotes *residencia* (no dining facilities beyond breakfast). In practise the main defining feature in cost is the number of stars awarded. The cost of accommodation also varies between seasons (add 25% during peak holidays) and regions (add 25% in cities). Some smaller hotels and hostels, particularly in rural areas, offer a pilgrim discount but ask at reception *before* booking.

During off-season the price of a room can often be less than that officially displayed. At the lower end (from €15) we find simply beds *camas* and guest houses known variously as *fondas*, *hospedajes* or *hospederías* without any star category. Moving up the scale (from €25) are *pensiónes* **P** and *hostales* **Hs** with one or more stars and the smaller rural *hoteles* **H**. In the middle bracket (from €40) are up-market B&B's usually presented at a high standard and known variously as rural houses *casa rural* **CR**, rural tourism *turismo rural* **TR** or agricultural tourism *agrícola turismo* **AT**. *Then come the hotels from 1 star in rural areas* **H*** *(€20+) up to 5 stars* **H******* *in the city (€150+).*

Costs: allow a basic €25 a day to include €5 for overnight stay at a municipal hostel and the remainder for food and drink. Some hostels provide a communal supper (dependent on the warden *hospitalero*) for a small contribution and many have a basic kitchen where a meal can be prepared. Alternatively most locations have one or more restaurants to choose from and many have a special 'pilgrim menu' for a fixed price of around €10. If you want to indulge in the wonderful gastronomy of Spain and sample its finer wines then expect to double this basic cost. A few parish hostels still use a donation basis with the underlying philosophy: *leave us what you can and if that is only your prayers that will be sufficient.* We must be careful not to abuse this trust in our individual circumstances – unless you are a genuine mendicant, plan to leave at least 5 euros towards basic costs of maintenance. Private hostels average around €10–€15 per night but often provide additional facilities such as internet access, washing / drying machines and dining facilities (supper and breakfast at extra cost).

Payment: all pilgrim hostels, most small pensions, rural B&B's *casa rurales* and local shops operate on a **cash only basis**. That being said, even the smallest town and many of the villages have automatic cash dispensing machines *cajeros automáticos* that accept most international bank debit or credit cards. Traveller's cheques are difficult to exchange and also rely on inconvenient bank opening hours. Consider settling your bill the night before if you plan an early departure.

Eating out: A basic pilgrim menu or *menú del dia* starts from around €8. Once you go off the set menu costs rise out of all proportion. *Tapas* (small snacks available from many bars and cafés throughout the day) or the more generous *raciones* are appetising but expensive. Vegetarians have a really hard time as Spain, which is firmly carnivorous, has little understanding of the needs of the *vegetariano/a*. Vegetable soup is often made on meat stock and don't be surprised to find chunks of ham in your cheese omelette unless you are *very* specific! Breakfast equates to *café* and *croissantes*. Another cultural challenge posed to northern European and North American pilgrims are meal times. Lunch *almuerzo* (or simply *comer*) is the main meal and rarely ends before 15:00 and dinner *cena* doesn't usually start before 20:00. It helps to think laterally (*tapas*), to speak clearly (*en español*) and to prepare meals of your choice and time in the hostels from provisions bought in the local shop *mercado*.

Respecting nature: Litter is becoming a real problem. Please don't leave waste behind you. Orange peel takes several years to decompose plastic bottles 450! Carry a container to take your waste away – toilet tissues are the biggest offenders *www.shewee.com* has an absorbent pouch and urinating device for women hikers. *Walk the path so that no one can tell that you have passed by.* A rewarding discipline is to collect some rubbish along the way each day with the intention of leaving the path *better* than you found it. If a sense of superiority arises, visualise yourself cleaning up the mess that you left behind at other times in your life when you were, perhaps, less aware. It only requires a few un-aware pilgrims to create the problem... and only a small band of conscientious ones to alleviate it! You might also like to try a psychic cleansing after experiencing any negativity in your own thoughts or in any interaction that you witness en route that is unloving. Simply shake out the negativity from your mind and invite loving thoughts to replace them. These simple practises will help to keep both the physical and psychic environment clean.

Respecting fellow pilgrims: facilities such as showers and kitchens have a limited supply of hot water and utensils and these facilities, especially during the summer months, can be stretched. Be aware of your own needs but also of the needs of others and try and find a balance that feels right. If you have arrived early and bagged the best bed keep an eye on who comes in later – if you are on a bottom bunk and someone arrives late with a damaged knee you could move to a top bunk. Observe your reactions but don't judge yourself. There is already enough guilt in the world to engulf it and we certainly don't need more! Awareness is the starting point for change.

PREPARATION – *OUTER:*

Physical – what shape is the body in? Any reasonably fit person can accomplish this journey without undue stress. Some years ago I walked from Seville to Santiago (1,000+ km) with a Japanese grandfather who celebrated his 80th birthday en route. However, if you have recently had an illness or are otherwise concerned about your state of health then go and have a medical check up. It generally takes the body a week to adjust fully to the regular walking with full backpack. Give body, mind and soul time to acclimatise. Don't push yourself at the beginning – remember that most injuries, such as strained tendons and blisters occur in the early days.

It is always advisable to put in some physical training before you go. I would be surprised if more than 10% of pilgrims actually act on this advice. If you are one of the 90% who haven't then *please* heed the advice to take the first week slowly. I know many pilgrims who have had to deal with the mental, let alone physical, anguish of having to pull out of the pilgrimage because they did too much in the early days. Lightweight walking poles, if used properly, can greatly reduce wear and tear on the body. If you don't have a pair (one in each hand creates better balance and is twice as effective) consider buying a set. They are likely to prove a good investment for this walk – and future ones!

A related matter is the weight you carry, both your backpack and body weight. If you are 2 stone overweight and are going to be carrying an additional 2 stone on your back, the resultant stress factor is likely to show up in cracks, literally, in the body (1 stone = 14 pounds = 6.4 kilograms). While you will inevitably lose weight on the journey, try and reduce before you start out. Pilgrimage is a great metaphor for life. What are you carrying that is unnecessary? *"From contentment with little comes happiness."* African proverb.

Equipment and Clothing: *Think quality not quantity*

Your pilgrimage starts at the planning stage. So start by invoking the highest for your journey and bring awareness to what you buy. There is so much exploitation of human and natural resources supported by our unconscious consumerism. Become informed and use your voice and money to support those companies who genuinely try to make a positive difference in the world. To walk a pilgrim path for peace in gear produced from exploitative business practises or oppressive regimes is not congruent – we must make very effort to *walk our talk*.

What to bring? You will bring too much; everyone does! Be prepared to give away, leave behind or post back items you don't need and notice which option you choose, why and at what stage of the journey. Aim to carry no more than 10% of body weight with an ***upper limit of 10 Kilos (22 lbs)***. Whatever you carry your knees and feet will absorb most of the shock and will be the first to buckle if you carry more than essentials. Buy materials that are essentially: (a) lightweight and non-bulky (b) that wick away moisture from your skin (c) are easy to wash and quick to dry.

Essential equipment from the feet up includes:

walking shoes / boots: They should provide good ankle support, be breathable, lightweight and yet have strong soles for the rough ground you will encounter. Heavyweight boots are not necessary but consider trail shoes with waterproof lining if travelling in the winter season. **Sandals** or other lightweight shoe for use in the evening while your walking shoe dry out and have a chance to breathe.

socks: bring several pairs as it is a good idea to change socks and massage your feet half-way through the day (even if you don't think they need it).

trousers, skirts and shorts: for most of the year shorts are ideal and your legs will dry out much more quickly than fabric if you walk into a rain shower. Rural Spain remains very traditional – a sarong is ideal for women to wrap around bare legs when visiting churches, etc., and also cool and easy to wash and dry.

fleece: a lightweight fleece is useful – you will need to increase the thickness the closer into winter that you plan to travel. If you intend travelling in mid-winter you will need proper thermal clothing and a sleeping bag for the subzero temperatures that you may encounter, particularly on the higher ground where you can expect snow and ice.

waterproofs: even allowing for obvious seasonal changes the weather in northern Spain, particularly in Galicia, is notoriously unpredictable (see Weather). There are many lightweight rain and wind-proof jackets and trousers, Paclite® by Burghaus are ideal, but expensive. A cheaper option is a plastic poncho that covers not only the body but the backpack as well. This can be rolled out during rain showers and the loose fitting nature of the poncho means you don't get *too* much build up of sweat as with most tight fitting plastic or nylon garments. A popular model is the Altus available from www.barrabes.com or pilgrim shops.

hat: in the summer months your main consideration will be protection from the sun. Wear a wide brim hat to protect your head and neck and any other exposed areas. Sunstroke can be painful and, in extreme cases, dangerous.

rucksack: 50 litres should be ample, avoid large capacity bags (70 +litres) as you may be tempted to fill it with unnecessary items. An essential element is the waist strap that must allow you to adjust and carry the weight on your hips – *never* off your shoulder. You will need dry bags (not plastic bags which can actually pool water!) to ensure dry kit at the end of a wet day. If you are not using a poncho then a backpack cover is also recommended for heavy downpours.

sleeping bag: essential for all pilgrim hostels. If you are travelling in the summer months a lightweight 1 or 2 season bag will suffice. A zip will allow you to open it up in very hot conditions. Most hostels, especially in the mountain areas, have blankets.

first aid: All hostels are obliged to carry first aid boxes and there are innumerable chemists *farmacia* along the way. However, some essentials should be carried with you. While prevention is better than cure, unless you are well seasoned you will get blisters! Each to their own, but *Compeed®* is readily available, easy to apply and acts as a second skin. Whatever you bring apply it as soon as you feel a hot spot developing (don't wait until it has developed into a full blister). Many make the mistake of loosening shoes to relieve the pressure but this can aggravate the friction – the cause of the problem in the first place. Make sure your footwear fits snugly.

Other essentials are plasters and antiseptic ointment for cuts and pain relief tablets such as Paracetamol for toothache etc. and Ibuprofen for relief of muscular pain. Bring a high factor sun protection and apply regularly or, alternatively try Calypso or P_{20}® by Riemann which binds to the skin and only needs to be applied once each day. You will also need lip protection and after sun lotion. Be sure to bring an adequate supply of any prescribed medication, e.g. inhalers for asthmatics, as these may be difficult to obtain en route without prescription. Elasticised tubing can help support a sprained knee or ankle.

For the **homoeopathically** inclined, essentials might include: Arnica for muscular sprains and bruising, Calendula for cuts and Combudoron for insect bites. For those using chemically based products, bring equivalent treatments.

toiletries: Apart from the usual take a small scissors with needle and thread for draining blisters and essential repairs.

water container: many people prefer carrying two ½ litre bottles rather than a bulkier 1 litre that can be harder to pack and unpack. **Water is essential** and evidence supports the view that a minimum 2 litres a day can significantly reduce  fatigue, blisters and other common ailments of long distance walking as well as avoiding dehydration. There are drinking fonts *fuente* [F] all along the way – fill up at every opportunity especially in high summer when drinking fonts can dry up. Non-tap water is often OK to drink but not guaranteed *sin garantia* – check with locals if in doubt. You may notice a difference between the quality of water around the main cities with their chemical additives, so empty and refill from the purer waters of the mountains and rural villages whenever possible.

Optional Extras:

walking poles: while not essential, they are highly recommended and will greatly reduce the impact on your body (around 25% if used properly). They will steady you over rough patches and may create confidence when facing the innumerable dogs that dot the countryside. Take two to avoid becoming lopsided and try and get ones with the handles angled to avoid wrist strain. Most pilgrims opt for a wooden staff collected along the way and that is certainly better than nothing.

sleeping mat: very useful if you want the freedom of experiencing life under the stars and increasingly necessary if you are travelling in the busy season as it allows you more options – there will always be a floor somewhere! *Therm-a-Rest®* is the most comfortable but is heavier and more expensive than a basic foam-style mat.

cooking utensils: many hostels have basic kitchen equipment. However, if you intend cooking regularly it is advisable to bring your own utensils and cutlery. A small plastic container with lid will make it easier to carry soft fruit (such as tomatoes) and sandwiches.

camping equipment: there is no need to carry a tent; however, if you enjoy and are experienced in the outdoors you will know what to bring. Campsites en route are few and far between and most hostels don't have facilities for tents.

books: be *very* selective as books add enormously to weight and you'll be surprised how little time you have for reading. Try bringing something inspirational and uplifting that you can read over again such as a compendium of your favourite poems. Historical notes and more detailed information on the many artistic treasures to be found along the way are often issued free of charge from tourist offices or as part of the price of an entry ticket.

camera: a *compact* camera may allow you to share some of your experiences with friends and family on your return. But don't forget that you can't photograph an *inner* experience, so don't set up a disappointment for yourself! A well-known travel author, writing in *The Times* states, *Photographing local people is selfish. It takes much and gives little.* The camera not only creates a physical barrier but also insulates the photographer from the reality of the experience. I have taken several thousand slides for this guidebook and regret any offence I may have caused – but perhaps they will suffice for your purposes also.

binoculars: a *compact* set will enable you to pick out the detail of some of the many fine monuments and buildings along the way. It might also help to identify alternative paths and help pick out directional signs, etc. I would prefer to take a pair of binoculars to a camera, but better still:

monocular: weighs less than half that of a pair of binoculars. It is easy to use, won't go out of focus and fits easily into a pocket. It might be a compromise for leaving behind the camera and binoculars.

mobile phone: consider leaving it behind – your experience, and that of your fellow pilgrims, will be enhanced by so doing. Break the dependence.

A checklist with Spanish translations is provided on the next page to help strengthen your vocabulary and assist you to buy or replace items along the way.

This is not necessarily a recommended list, as this will vary through the seasons. Highlight your essential items and then tick them off as you put them into your backpack. (see also *Basic Pilgrim Phrases*).

Checklist:	*Lista:*
Clothes:	*Ropas:*
hat (sun)	*sombrero*
sunglasses	*gafas de sol*
shirt(s)	*camisa(s)*
T-shirt(s)	*camiseta(s)*
travel vest	*chaqueta de viaje*
jacket –	*chaqueta –*
waterproof	*chubasquero*
breathable	*transpirable*
underpants	*calzoncillos*
shorts	*pantolones cortos*
trousers	*pantalones largos*
handkerchief	*pañuelo*
socks	*calcetines*
Shoes:	*Zapatos:*
boots (mountain)	*botas (de montaña)*
shoes (walking)	*zapatos (de andar)*
sandals (leather)	*sandalias (piel)*
Size:	*Tamaño:*
larger	*mas grande*
smaller	*mas pequeño*
cheaper	*mas barato*
more expensive	*mas caro*
model	*modelo*
Essential documents	*Documentos esenciales:*
passport	*pasaporte*
pilgrim record	*credencial de peregrino*
wallet / purse	*monedero / cartera*
cash	*dinero en efectivo*
credit card	*tarjeta de crédito*
travel tickets	*pasaje de viaje*
diary	*diario*
emergency addresses	*dirección de emergencia*
phone numbers	*números de teléfono*
Backpack	*Mochila*
rain cover	*protección de mochila*
sleeping bag	*saco de dormir*
towel	*toalla*
water bottle	*botella de agua*
penknife	*navaja*
Toiletries:	*Artículos de tocador:*
soap	*jabón*
shampoo	*champú*

tooth brush	*cepillo de dientes*
toothpaste	*dentífrico*
hair brush	*cepillo de pelo*
comb	*peine*
sink stopper	*tapón de fregadero*
shaving cream	*espuma de afeitar*
razor (blades)	*maquinilla de afeitar*
face cloth	*guante de aseo*
sun cream (lotion)	*crema solar (loción)*
after sun cream	*leche solar (after sun)*
moisturiser	*crema hidratante*
toilet paper	*papel higiénico*
tissues	*pañuelos de papel*
sanitary pads	*salva-slips*
tampons	*tampones*

First Aid Kit: ***Botiquín***

painkiller	*analgésico*
aspirin / paracetemol	*aspirina / paracetamol*
plasters	*esparadrapo*
blister pads	*apósito para ampollas*
compeed-*second skin*	*compeed-segunda piel*
antiseptic cream	*crema antiséptica*
muscular ache (ointment)	*pomada para dolores musculares*
homeopathic remedies	*remedios homeopáticos*

Medicine (prescription):   ***Medicina (prescripción):***

asthma inhaler	*inhalador para el asma*
hay fever tablets	*medicina para las alergias*
diarrhoea pills	*pastillas para la diarrea*
other (doctor)	*otros (médico)*

Accessories: (optional)   ***Accesorios: (opcional)***

walking poles	*bastones de caminar*
pilgrim shell	*concha de peregrino*
monocular	*catalejo*
binocular	*prismáticos*
camera	*cámara*
torch	*linterna*
wrist watch	*reloj de pulsera*
alarm clock	*despertador*
poncho	*poncho*
sleeping mat	*esterilla*
clothes pegs	*pinzas para la ropa*
clothes line (cord)	*cuerda para tender ropa*
earplugs (against snoring)	*tapones para los oídos (ronquidos)*
cutlery	*cubiertos*
knife	*cuchillo*
fork	*tenedor*
spoon	*cuchara*
mug / cup	*taza / vaso*

LANGUAGE *LENGUAJE:*

The Spanish are proud of their national identity and language, particularly in rural areas. It is a matter of extreme discourtesy to assume that everyone will automatically speak English. To walk into a shop or to stop and ask directions in anything other than the native language of the area you are travelling through is clearly insensitive. It behoves pilgrims to have at least a few basic phrases and to make the time to learn and use them. English is **not** widely spoken in the countryside. Ideally get a language CD a month or two *before* you travel and spend a few minutes each day practising this lovely lyrical language – the third most widely spoken in the world. Be sure to take a small dictionary and phrase book with you. Below you will find some basic pilgrim words and phrases that may not be included in a general phrase book.

As all place names and directions will, of course, be in Spanish (or Galego when in Galicia) all maps have been prepared accordingly. Some common phrases and words have also been scattered around the text as a reminder that you are a guest in someone else's country. For the real novice, I have included words that have a similar resonance between English and Spanish. This should enable you to more readily bring to mind the required word, even if it isn't exactly *exactamente* the word that a professional translator might have used. An example is vigilance! with the Spanish counterpart ¡*Vigilancia!* One might more properly use the word danger *peligroso* but this bears no resemblance to the English word at all. For those of you who are *elocuente,* please *omitir* the following *sección!* Spanish is placed in italics immediately following the English word or phrase. You will make progress if you follow these fundamental conventions *convenciónes fundamentales:*

Nouns are either masculine or feminine. Most are obvious, some are not. Trial and error is a way forward, with words ending in *e* favouring the masculine and those in *a* the feminine. The *el* or *la,* plural *los* or *las* and add *s* or *es* at end of the word. The man *el hombre,* the men *los hombres,* the woman *la señora,* the women *las señoras.* **Vowels** are articulated at the end of the word. Melide, pron: Meh-**lee**-deh. U is pronounced as in oo – one *una* pron: **oo**-na. **Emphasis** is on the penultimate syllable unless otherwise denoted with an accent. Nájera, pron: **Ná**-kher-a, *not* Ná-**kher**-a.

Consonants are similar to English excepting: 'c' is pronounced th as in then. Centre *centro* pron: **then**-tro – 'd' at the end of a word is pron: th as in path. You *usted,* pron: *oo-***steth**. Note here the emphasis is on the last syllable, an exception to the rule! – 'g' and 'j' have a guttural kh sound similar to a Scottish loch: urgent *urgente* pron: *er-**khen**-tay* or garden *jardín* pron: *khar-**deen*** (note emphasis on last syllable because it has an accent) – 'h' is always silent. Hotels *hoteles* pron: *oh-**tel**-es.* –'ll' is pronounced with a yeh sound / full *lleno* pron: **yeh**-*no.* –'ñ' is pronounced as in onion / tomorrow *mañana* pron: *man-**yahn**-ah.* –'qu' is pronounced as in k for key / fifteen *quince* pron: **keen**-*thay.* –'v' falls between v and soft b sound / journey *viaje* pron: *bhee-**a**-khay.*

Verbs are more complex but follow 3 basic forms: [1] those ending in *-ar* as in *hablar* to speak. I speak *hablo,* you speak *hablas,* he/she speaks *habla,* we speak *hablamos,* you all speak *habláis,* they speak *hablan.* [2] those ending in *-er* as in *comer* to eat. I eat *como,* you eat *comes,* he/she eats *come,* we eat *comemos,* you all eat *coméis,* they eat *comen.* [3] those ending in *-ir* as in *vivir* to live. I live *vivo,* you live *vives,* he/she lives *vive,* we live *vivimos,* you all live *vivís,* they live *vivan.*

Basic Phrases: so here are a few simple phrases to get you going. A new language can't be learnt in a day; but it is really important that you *try* whenever the opportunity arises – everyone loves a trier.

Greetings / *Saludos*

Yes / *Sí*   No / *No*
Please / *Por favor*   Thanks / *Gracias*

How are things? / *Qué tal?*   Have a good trip / *Buen viaje*
Hello! How are you? / *Hola! Cómo está?*
Good day / evening / night *Buenos días / Buenas tardes / noches*
What a splendid day / *Qué día mas espléndido!*
Goodbye! Until later / *¡Adiós! Hasta luego*

Welcome / *Bienvenida*

What's your name? / *¿Cómo te llamas?* My name is ... / *Me llamo ...*
Where do you live? / *¿Dónde vives?*   I live in London / *Vivo en Londres*
Are you English? / *Eres Inglés(a)*   I'm Irish / *Soy Irlandes(a)*
I'm single / *Estoy soltero(a)*   I'm married / *Estoy casado(a)*
I have 2 sons / *Tengo dos hijos(as)*   I have no children / *No tengo hijos*
I'm here on holiday (pilgrimage) / *Estoy aquí de vacaciones (peregrinación)*

Excuse me! / *¡Disculpe!*   Pardon? / *¿Perdone?*

What did you say / *¿Cómo dice?*   It's not important / *No importa*
Do you understand? / *¿Entiende?*   I don't understand! / *¡No entiendo!*

I speak very little Spanish / *Hablo muy poco español*
Do you speak English? / *¿Habla usted Inglés?*
How do you pronounce that? / *¿Cómo se pronuncia eso?*
Please write it down. / *Escríbamelo, por favor*
What does this mean? / *¿Qué significa esto?*

Where is it? / *¿Dónde está?*

Here / *Aquí*   There / *Allí*
On the left / *a la izquierda*   On the right / *a la derecha*
Outside the bank / *Fuera del banco*   Beside the cafe / *Al lado del café*
Near the centre / *Cerca del centro*   Opposite the market / *Enfrente del mercado*

Where are you going? / *¿A dónde vas?*
Where is the pilgrim hostel / *¿Dónde está el albergue de peregrinos?*
Where are the toilets / *¿Dónde están los servicios?*
Where can I change some money? / *¿Dónde se puede cambiar dinero?*
Where do I get the taxi to the airport? / *¿Dónde se coge el taxi al aeropuerto?*
How do I get to the centre of León? / *¿Cómo se va al centro de León?*

What time is it? / *¿Qué hora es?*

It's midday / *Es mediodía*   Five past one / *Es la una y cinco*
Ten past two / *cuatro y dos*   Half past three / *Tres y media*
Quarter past four / *cuatro y cuarto*   Twenty to five / *cinco menos veinte*
Quarter to six / *seis menos cuarto*   Five to seven / *siete menos cinco*
Today / *Hoy*   Yesterday / *Ayer*
Tomorrow / *Mañana*   Day after tomorrow / *Pasado mañana*
Last week / *la semana pasada*   This month / *este mes*
Next year / *al año que viene*   Every year / *todos los años*

What day is it today? / *¿Qué día es hoy?*
Lunes / Martes / Miércoles / Jueves / Viernes / Sábado / Domingo
What is today's date? / *¿Qué fecha es hoy?*
It's April 10th / *Estamos a diez de abril*
Saturday, September 25th / *sábado, veinte cinco de septiembre*
spring / *primavera*   **summer** / *verano*
autumn / *otoño*   winter / *invierno*
enero / febrero / marzo / abril / mayo / junio / julio / agosto / septiembre /
octubre / noviembre / diciembre

Room / *Habitación*
Do you have any vacancies? / *¿Tienen alguna habitación libre?*
I'd like a room for one night / *Quería una habitación para una noche*
There's a problem with the room / *La habitación tiene un problema*
It's too hot (cold) / *Hace demasiado calor (frío)*
There is no hot water / *No hay agua caliente*
Where can I wash my clothes / *¿Dónde puedo lavar mi ropa?*

Doctor / *Médico*   **Dentist** / *Dentista*
I need a dentist (doctor) / *Necesito un dentista (medico)*
Where is the health centre? / *¿Dónde está el centro de salud?*
I have blisters / *Tengo ampollas*
I have a tendinitis / *Tengo tendinitis*
My leg/knee/foot/toe...hurts / *Mi pierna/rodilla/dedo del pie...me duele*
My ankle is swollen / *Mi tobillo está hinchado*
My lower back is in spasm / *Mi espalda tiene una contractura*
Where is the pharmacy? / *¿Dónde está la farmacia?*

Food / *Comida*   **Menu** / *Menú*
breakfast / *desayuno*   lunch / *la comida*
savoury snack / *tapas*   dinner / *cena*

meat / *carne*   **fish** / *pescado*
beef steak / *bistec*   trout / *trucha*
fillet steak / *filete*   salmon / *salmón*
pork / *cerdo*   sole / *lenguado*
lamb / *cordero*   hake / *merluza*
veal / *ternera*   prawns / *gambas*
chops / *chuletas*   squid / *calamares*
ham / *jamón*   mussels / *mejillones*
chicken / *pollo*   seafood / *mariscos*

vegetables / *verduras*   **(tomato) salad** / *ensalada (de tomate)*
desert / *postres*   fruit / *fruta*
sandwich / *bocadillo*   cheese / *queso*
red wine / *vino tinto*   **white wine** / *vino blanco*
water / *agua*   milk / *leche*
I am hungry / *Tengo hambre*
What time is dinner (breakfast) / *¿A qué hora es la cena (el desayuno)?*
Is there a vegetarian restaurant? / *¿Hay un restaurante vegetariano?*
What's today's menu / *¿Cuál es el plato del día?*
Do you have a menu in English / *¿Tiene un menú en Inglés?*
This food is cold (too hot) / *La comida está fría (muy caliente)*
Where can I find a shop to by food? / *Dónde puedo encontrar una tienda para comprar comida?*

Train / *Tren*   **Bus / *Autobús***

Have you a timetable? / *¿Tienen un horario?*
What time do we get to León? / *¿A qué hora llegamos a León?*
How much is a single (return) ticket? / *¿Cuánto cuesta el billete de ida (y vuelta)*

I want to cancel my reservation / *Quería anular mi reserva*
When does the museum open? / *¿Cuándo abre el museo?*
When does the bus arrive at Arcos? / *¿Cuándo llega el autobús para Arcos?*
When is the next train to Bilbao? / *¿Cuándo sale el próximo tren para Bilbao?*

Shoes / *Zapato*   **Size / *Talla***
I take size 8 / *Calzo el cuarenta*
footwear / *calzado*   shoelace / *el cordón*
shoemaker / *zapatero*   shoeshop / *zapatería*

Clothes / *Ropa*   **Size / *Talla***
I take size 40 / *Mi talla es la 40*
Have you a bigger (smaller) size? / *Tiene una talla mayor (menor)*
big / *grande*   small / *pequeño(a)*
(See under check list for other items)

Books: (limited)   ***Libros: (cupo lim.)***
spiritual texts   *textos espirituales*
inspirational quotations   *citas inspiradoras*
poetry   *poesía*
phrase book –   *libro de frases –*
   Spanish   *Español*
   French   *Francés*

Map / *Mapa*   **Plan / *Plano***
option / *opción*   crossing / *cruce*
castle / *castillo*   church / *iglesia*
chapel / *ermita*   cathedral / *catedral*
wayside cross / *cruceiro*   drinking font / *fuente*
bridge / *puente*   rise or height / *alto*
park / *parque*   town square / *la plaza de la ciudad*
town centre / *centro de ciudad*   ruins / *ruinas*
river / *río*   street / *calle* (written c/)
sun rise /*salida del sol*   sun set / *puesta del sol*
waymarking / *indicador*   yellow arrow / *flecha Amarillo*

_____

_____

_____

_____

_____

_____

_____

_____

_____

_____

_____

_____

_____

_____

THE CAMINO – PAST, PRESENT & FUTURE

The Past – *The Changing Course of History*

•Pleistocene Age c. 1,000,000 B.C.

The earliest human remains ever discovered in Europe are to be found on a small hill directly on the camino (see stage 12 – Atapuerca). So we follow in the footsteps of our ancestors who have been accorded the scientific name *Homo Antecessor* and dated to over 900,000 years B.C. In recognition of the unique part Atapuerca plays in our understanding of the way of life of the first human communities the site was accorded World Heritage status by UNESCO in 1998.

•Late Palaeolithic period c. 10,000 B.C.

During this period we see the arrival of hunter-gatherer clans *Homo sapiens* from central Europe. They settled along the north-western fringes of Spain in the Cantabrian Mountains where we can still find some of the best examples of their rock art in the cave dwellings at Altamira. These have been described as the 'Sistine Chapel of the Paleolithic period' and led the site to be added to the UNESCO World Heritage list in 1985. (The caves are situated 30 km west of Santander.)

•Megalithic period c. 4000 B.C.

This period is best known for the building of great *mega* stone structures sometimes referred to as Dolmens or Mamoas. They are the early 'cathedrals' of our ancestors and were aligned to the winter solstice sun and connected to sun worship. Some of the best examples can be found along the *camino* in Galicia. This megalithic culture was deeply religious and left a powerful impact on the peoples who followed.

•Early Celtic period c. 1,000 B.C.

Central European Celts settled in north-western Spain and Portugal, inter-marrying with the Iberians and giving rise to the Celtiberian tribes. Remains of their Celtic villages *Castros* can be seen dotted around the remote countryside, especially in Galicia, but examples also exist along other parts of the camino. These fortified villages were built in a circular formation usually occupying some elevated ground or hillock. The extensive mineral deposits of this area gave rise to a rich artistic movement and bronze and gold artefacts of this period grace many museums.

•Early Roman period c. 200 B.C.

The Roman occupation of the Iberian peninsular began around the 2nd century B.C. The Romans were attracted by the rich mining potential of the area. Decimus Junius Brutus was the first Roman general to break the fierce resistance of the Celtiberian tribe known as the Lusitani who occupied the area around the Miño valley. Brutus fought his way to the end of the world *finis terrae*, a place of immense spiritual significance at that time.

•Early Christian Period c. 40 A. D.

While there may be no historical evidence to support the contention that St. James preached in Galicia, there is some anecdotal testimony to that effect. It appears that some years after Christ's crucifixion St. James sailed to Galicia (probably Padrón and Finisterre) and commenced his ministry amongst the pagan population there. It is reasonable to assume that he and his followers would have known about the importance of Finisterre as one of the foremost places of Druidic ritual and initiation. It was common practice for the early Christian church to seek out such sites on which to graft its own message. It appears that St. James' mission met with only limited success and he returned to Jerusalem where he was summarily beheaded by Herod in 42 A. D. Following his martyrdom, St. James disciples brought his body back via Padrón in order to be buried at World's End *Finis Terre.* The legendary Queen Lupa conspired with the Roman Legate based at Dugium (present day Duyo in Finisterre) to destroy St. James body and that of his disciples (see *A Pilgrim's Guide to the Camino Finisterre*). In a story reminiscent of the Biblical Red Sea flight into freedom, they managed to escape with the bridge over the river Tambre collapsing just after they had passed over. Libredon (now Santiago) was not far away and it was here they finally laid St. James body to rest. This period marks the beginning of the San Tiago story in Spain but the mists of time grew over these remarkable events, until they finally disappeared from collective memory. This period also saw the martyrdom of the Gnostic master Prescillian who lived in Galicia and some legends suggest was buried in Libredon.

•The Middle Ages c. 476 – 1453

The decline and fall of the **Roman Empire in Spain** was hastened by the barbarian invasions and the arrival first of the Franks and Suevi tribes and then of the Visigoths from Gaul, although their chaotic influence was felt most acutely in Toledo. Incessant internal squabbles resulted in one faction seeking, rather unwisely, support from the Muslim community in Morocco, who duly obliged, arriving in rather larger numbers than anticipated! Islam had spread at breathtaking speed across northern Africa and less than 80 years after Muhammad's death in Medina in 632 the Moorish conquest of the southern Iberian peninsular, spearheaded by Tariq of Tangier in 711, was virtually complete.

The relatively benign rule of the Moors (the name given to the Arab and Berber settlers from Morocco) appears to have been much more favourable than life under the Visigoths. The latter had initiated the first expulsion of Jews from the peninsular while the Moors allowed complete freedom of religious and artistic expression. Indeed the **western Islamic empire**, centred at Córdoba, was amongst the most tolerant and enlightened administrations to be found anywhere in the known world at that time. *Mozarabic* was the name given to freely practising Christians under Moorish rule and this period saw a great flowering of the sciences, art and architecture in Spain. Some of the finest example of the Mozarabic style (Christian churches built using the typical Moorish horseshoe arch) can be seen at San Miguel de Escalada near León and at Santo Tomás de las Ollas in Ponferrada.

While this period was not without resistance to Muslim domination, alarm bells began to ring when they advanced northwards and in 778 Charles the Great *Charlemagne* crossed the Pyrenees to stop their advance at Zaragoza and greatly upset the volatile Basques by breaching the walls of Pamplona on his return (having given assurances that the town would not be damaged) setting in motion the famous battle of Roncesvalles and the defeat of the rear-guard of the army under the command of his nephew Roland. This in turn spawned the epic poem of chivalry *La Chanson de Roland*. The story of El Cid a century later has a similar chivalric vein (see under Burgos).

The Santiago story re-emerges in 813 when a shepherd named Pelayo was drawn to a field in Libredon by a 'bright light' or star. Thus we have, the field *compos* of the stars *stella* of Saint James *Sant Iago*, which gives us *Santiago de Compostela*. Other accounts suggest the name comes from the Latin for burial *componere,* as there was evidence of a Roman cemetery on this spot built over earlier Celtic remains. Either way, the Bishop of Iria Flavia (Padrón) *Theodomirus* seized the moment and 'confirmed' the discovery of the tomb of the Apostle and so the story of St. James was resurrected in perfect timing to spearhead the re-conquest *reconquista* of Spain for Christianity, starting with the battle of Clavijo in 844 to the decisive victory at Las Navas de Tolosa in 1212 and each time St. James appeared at the crucial moment to turn the tide of battle.

Thus we have the image of St. James the Moor-slayer **Santiago Matamoros**, depicted as the knight in shining armour astride a white charger decapitating Moors with his sword. On the strength of these successes, St. James became the patron saint of Spain, a position that he enjoys to this day. The first written record of pilgrimage to Santiago also belongs to this period when Bishop Gotescalco journeyed here in 950 and in 1072 Alfonso VI abolished tolls for all pilgrims travelling up into Galicia through Val Carce.

Between the 12th and 14th centuries Santiago de Compostela grew in importance and prestige, at times even eclipsing the pilgrim routes to Rome and essentially taking over from the pilgrimages to Jerusalem once the crusades had collapsed and the Holy Land was lost to the Christian cause and no longer accessible. It is remarkable that tens of thousands of pilgrims chose to suffer the hazards of this route every year during the Middle Ages. A combination of the relative accessibility of the route and the miracles associated with the relics of the Saint beneath the magnificent cathedral were certainly contributing factors in its popularity. The *Camino de Santiago* was now firmly established and from this period we see the gentler image of St. James the Pilgrim **Santiago Peregrino** portrayed all along the route with staff, bible, wide brim hat to keep off the sun and scallop shell *concha*. The *concha* survives as the single identifying symbol of the pilgrim to Santiago, hence the term *concheiros* to distinguish them from *romeros* and *palmers* which were applied to pilgrims going to Rome and Jerusalem respectively. One of the great exponents of the camino in the 12th century was Pope Calixtus II who instigated the privileges of the Compostelan Holy Years. It was at this time that the French priest Aymeric Picaud from Parthenay-le-Vieux near Poitou travelled the pilgrim road. He recorded his experiences in detail in 5 volumes that became known as the ***Codex Calixtinus*** in honour of the incumbent Pope. Book 5 is known as the Book of St. James *Liber Sancti Jacobi* and is essentially the first travel guide to the camino dividing it into 13 stages commencing at Saint-Michel by St. Jean Pied de Port.

The increasing activity gave rise to many religious and chivalrous orders dedicated to the protection of the pilgrim and the furtherance of the aim of the Crusades to re-establish Christianity now diverted away from the Holy Land and specifically towards Spain. While there has been extensive research into the Camino de Santiago and the background events that helped to shape the physical route we walk today, its esoteric heritage is less well documented. For many, the Knights Templar with their links to the contemporary Western mystery tradition became a corner stone in this 'hidden' heritage of the camino. Their secret initiation rites and Gnostic (as opposed to literalist) interpretations of biblical events coupled with their rising influence throughout the Western world, became a threat to the power base of the Papacy and the Catholic Monarchies and led to their eventual downfall. Pope Gregory and King Philip of France joined forces and on Friday 13th October 1307, **Jacques de Molay**, the Grand

Master of the Order, and the majority of the Knights Templar were arrested and subsequently put to death. The legacy of this massacre lives on in our collective folk memory as the reason why Friday 13th is considered unlucky. With the demise of the Knights Templar there disappeared one of the original protectors of both the outer pilgrim pathway and its inner mysteries. One of the bestpreserved Templar castles lies directly on the camino at Ponferrada (pictured).

Much of the property and commanderies of the Knights Templar along the camino were transferred to the **Hospitallers of St. John** who already had a strong presence in Spain. This illustrious order influenced the development of many of the towns and cities we travel through today, such as Pamplona, Burgos, León, Santiago, not to mention the many villages and hamlets that maintained pilgrim *hospitals* to house and protect the pilgrims that travelled this route and the many other caminos that snaked their way across Spain to Santiago. In this way the caminos provided a framework for the re-emergence of Catholicism throughout Spain.

•The Catholic Monarchs 1479 – 1808

Spain's 'Golden Age' sprang from the union of Isabel I of Castile and Fernando V of Aragón. Isabel *la Católica* is widely regarded as the most influential ruler in Spanish history. She oversaw the *reconquista* and the collapse of Islam and Moorish rule in Iberia. More notoriously, Isabel instigated the Inquisition and ruthlessly stamped out all 'heretical' sects, expelling the Jews from Spain in the process. She then set about financing and promoting the 'discovery' of the new world and the plunder of its ancient riches. 1492 marked both the Discovery of the Americas by Columbus and the final re-conquest of Granada under her rule. She must have regretted marrying off her daughter, Catherine of Aragon, to Henry VIII but would, no doubt, have been pleased that her grandson Charles V became Holy Roman Emperor and married, rather more fortuitously, Isabel of Portugal. This deft move added the considerable wealth of Portugal to her overseas dominions and an already impressive list of assets.

The only surviving (legitimate) child from the marriage of Charles and Isabel acceded to the throne in 1556 becoming Felipe II of Spain (and Philip I of Portugal) and effectively the first King of a united Hispanic peninsular. This marks the high point of Spanish influence abroad. Things began to go downhill from here on, starting with the ill-advised Spanish support of Mary Queen of Scots claim to the English throne and the ensuing ill-fated Armada in 1588. The power and influence of the monarchy continued its downward spiral over the next century and in 1700 Felipe V came to the Spanish throne, starting the War of the Spanish Succession between the Bourbon dynasty of France and Charles of Austria whose claim to the Spanish throne was supported by the British. Spain suffered badly in this long drawn out dispute, losing Gibraltar in the process.

•The Peninsular War and the First Republic 1808 – 1810

Events turned from bad to worse with the arrival of Napoleon's army in 1808 and the abdication of King Carlos IV. Spanish resistance was supported by British troops under Sir John Moore and the French were finally ejected and in 1810 a newly formed Parliament *Cortes* prepared a constitution. This first effort at parliamentary rule was short lived and was quickly followed by the Carlist Wars and a series of military coups lasting for another century.

•The Franco Years 1936 – 1975

In 1936 General Franco seized power leading to the one of the bloodiest civil wars in history. The Republican northeast enlisted thousands of volunteers in the International Brigade but was no match for the Nationalist army in the southwest under Franco that had the support of Nazi Germany and Fascist Italy. The ensuing carnage on all sides is hauntingly portrayed in Pablo Picasso's painting *La Guernica*. Monuments to the dead of the Civil War are found all along the camino and its legacy still casts a shadow over Spain.

•Modern Spain 1975 – 2013

Franco's carefully groomed successor, Admiral Carrero Blanco, was assassinated by Basque separatists in 1970 and on Franco's death in 1975, King Carlos nominally succeeded and appointed political reformist Adlofo Suárez to form a government. This proved widely popular with the people but the liberal approach of Suárez was not supported by the military. The Suárez government drew up a new constitution and in 1978 Spain became a full democracy under a cumbersome and decidedly expensive system of self-rule with its 17 autonomous communities *autonomías* (the larger ones are subdivided into provinces) which each elect representatives to the central government based in Madrid. The camino passes through 4 of these *autonomías* viz: Navarra, La Rioja, Castilla y León (Burgos, Palencia and León provinces) and Galicia (Lugo and la Coruña provinces). The only hiccup in this progress towards democracy was a military coup in 1981 but Spain regained her composure and democracy was swiftly re-established and the Franco years put firmly behind.

In 1982 the socialist party (PSOE) won a sweeping victory under Felipe González who successfully steered Spain into full membership of the EEC in 1986. In 1996 José María Aznar, leader of the right wing *Partido Popular* (PP), came to power but in 2002 the oil tanker Prestige ran into a storm off Finisterre and the ensuing ecological catastrophe sank not only the livelihood of scores of Galician fisherman but, in time, the right wing government as well. The disregard for the environment displayed by the President of Galicia and the Spanish environment minister resulted in a popular cry up and down the country of 'never again' *nunca mais*. It only took the government's deeply unpopular support of the invasion of Iraq coupled with the retaliatory Madrid bombings in March 2004 to put the socialist's back in power under the youthful leadership of José Luis Rodríguez Zapatero. The new government set in motion an immediate change in foreign policy and, more controversially, a sudden but decisive shift from a conservative Catholic to a liberal secular society that led to a newspaper headline, *Church and State square up in struggle for the spirit of Spain.* The Euro crisis in 2011 led to a crushing defeat of the Socialists and a return to the conservative PP under Mariano Rajoy who was elected on a promise to reduce Spain's public deficit... and seemingly immune to all these social and political upheavals, the camino quietly goes about her gentle spirit of transformation.

• **The Present:** *Breakdown and Breakthrough:*

Two centuries of rampant materialism have resulted in a spiritual aridity unparalleled in human history. Statistics reveal a collapse in church attendance matched by a significant fall in the numbers entering the priesthood. Recent surveys indicate that Spain, until recently seen as a deeply religious society, now has less than 20% of its population actually practising Catholicism.

Yet here is the rub – in this same period the numbers entering the Camino de Santiago have soared and the pilgrim figures have risen tenfold in a decade. How do we interpret these trends? There seems little doubt that there is a great thirst for genuine spiritual experience and a deep desire to refresh and enliven our religious life. It has been suggested by a leading Christian moderator that we have become bored and disillusioned with the religion we have been fed since childhood and this is leading to a collapse of formalised religious practice.

• **A Future Perspective:** *A New Age of Pilgrimage:*

There are many explanations for the anomalies and sweeping changes confronting us today. Each of us will read the signs and interpret these to develop our own future scenarios. I favour the emerging concept of a new and unprecedented flowering of human consciousness that is so positive and profound that we have no collective idea where it will lead us. We have become so spiritually dehydrated that we are now desperate to drink directly from the Divine Well itself and our thirst will no longer be slaked by drinking from a substitute or tainted source. We are awakening to a new spiritual age – one less dependent on an outer authority and more attuned to the God within. Conjecture is rife, but we cannot deny the statistics that point, on the one hand, to collapse and, on the other hand, to renewal. While the death of the old can be alarming the birth of the new is always exciting. Something is undoubtedly 'astir in the land' and what we are witnessing is, perhaps, a collective emergence to a new spiritual reality directing our lives. Of course, the more cynical might point to tourism, now the single largest industry in the world, as the reason for the sudden rise in the interest in the Camino de Santiago. Truth is relative and human nature such that we each will tend towards a theory that reinforces our individual belief systems.

Today, Santiago flourishes as a centre of both tourism and pilgrimage, but the ancient path itself is less susceptible to commercialisation. *El Camino* is rousing itself from centuries of slumber and its potential to exert a positive influence on the changes confronting us at every turn along the way is enormous. The spirit of St. James and the camino is alive and well and ready to assist each one of us in formulating a new and positive future quite unlike anything we have manifested in the past. 'Time for Change' was Barack Obama's platform – ours too.

PREPARATION – *INNER*: *Why am I doing this?*

A majority of those setting out on the *Camino de Santiago* give a religious or spiritual reason for going, yet few appear to undertake any conscious inner preparation for the journey. It is so easy to allow the demands of our secular life to rob us of time for such preparation. We take our tired bodies and neglected souls and dump them at the start of the camino and trust that all will be well. And of course, all will be well and our physical and spiritual muscles will become rejuvenated – it's just that warm-up exercises will maximise the benefits and speed our rate of recovery. A pilgrim travels on two paths simultaneously and must pay attention to both. When we place ourselves on the pilgrim path we sow the intention to stretch and expand soul consciousness so that we can lift ourselves out of the mundane in order to journey back to God or whatever name we give to that nameless Source from whence we came.

And how, in this busy secular world of ours, do we prepare for such a journey? A useful guideline is to spend at least as much time on inner preparation as general logistics. This way we balance the inner and outer realities and give equal account to both. Spirit seeks to inform all those who sincerely ask the deeper questions behind our existence. These questions may arise from some crisis; diagnosis of a life threatening disease, death of a loved one, loss of employment, marital breakdown or just deep dissatisfaction with life for no apparent reason. All of these events can awaken in us a desire to understand the context as well as the content of our lives. Existential loneliness will not disappear by finding or replacing partners, changing jobs, moving house. Of course, in discovering who we are these outer circumstances may change but it is our ability to observe the changing dramas of our life, and the life of others around us, against a larger backdrop that will bring a united purpose to all our journeying.

We all have different psychological, spiritual and emotional needs and pathologies. While pilgrimage can be a way of breaking through resistances (releasing blocks and realising insights as to what prevents us being all that we truly are) it is wise to start off with a relatively balanced state of mind. If you feel you need psychotherapy, counselling or other help, seek it. It will be disturbing enough when previously dearly held belief systems start to break down. A mental and emotional check up might be useful, even necessary, before you start embarking on an inner quest.

When asked to describe a personal experience of the sacred, an overwhelming majority refer to a time alone in nature, 'A sunrise over the sea; animal tracks in fresh powder snow; a walk under the full moon'. It was not the sun or the moon that created any shift in perception but they acted as a reflection of a larger perspective, a distant memory of something holy – something bigger than, and yet part of, us. This is where the camino can provide such a powerful reminder of the sacred in our lives and the desire to reclaim our spiritual inheritance.

As we set out towards the fabled city of Santiago we need to be mindful, as *A*

Course In Miracles suggests, that the true temple is not a structure at all. Its true holiness lies at the inner altar around which the structure is built – yet the real beauty of the inner temple cannot be seen with the physical eye. An emphasis on beautiful structures can be a sign of unwillingness to exercise spiritual vision. As we walk through the *landscape temple* that is the *camino* and through the towns and cities spread out along the way, we pass some of the most physically striking religious buildings to be found anywhere in this world. But let us not confuse the messenger with the message and so help each other to search out and find that elusive *inner altar*.

Risks: Apart from the obvious precautions, especially in the larger towns and cities, it is hard to conceive of a safer environment within which to reflect on life and its direction. The people along the camino have been welcoming pilgrims for centuries. The needs of medieval pilgrims were looked after by *hospitallers*, today they are called *hospitaleros* which is a much more welcoming word than the English equivalent of warden. And this distinction goes to the heart of the camino. Countless millions have walked this path with a high purpose in mind and many of these seekers return to serve the on-going needs of the pilgrim. That elevated intentionality and goodwill is embedded in this route and available to each of us as we pass along it.

There are of course exceptions to every rule. We live in a fearful world and this is nowhere more obvious than in Spain where military and armed police presence is noticeable everywhere you go and many homes have guard dogs. However, we need to put crime in perspective and realise that our privilege to have the freedom, time and money to be able to walk a pilgrim path can be resented by a tiny minority who see pilgrims as a legitimate target for rich pickings. We need to remind ourselves that an attack is really a cry for help and calls for understanding and a loving response, not a counter-attack. If you find yourself becoming fearful for yourself or your belongings, you might find the following words of *William Ward* a source of encouragement:

To laugh is to risk appearing a fool
To weep is to risk being called sentimental
To reach out to another is to risk involvement
To expose feelings is to risk exposing your true self
To place your ideas and dreams before a crowd is to risk their loss
To love is to risk not being loved in return
To live is to risk dying
To try is to risk failure.

But risks must be taken
Because the greatest hazard in life is to risk nothing.
The people who risk nothing may avoid suffering and sorrow,
But they cannot learn, feel, change, grow or really live.
Chained by their servitude they are slaves who have forfeited all freedom.
Only a person who risks is truly free.

SELF-ASSESSMENT *INNER WAYMARKS*

This self-assessment questionnaire is designed to encourage you to reflect on your life and its direction. View it as a snapshot of this moment in the on-going journey of your life. In the busyness that surrounds us we often fail to take stock of where we are headed and our changing roles in the unfolding drama of our life story.

You might find it useful to initially answer these questions in quick succession as this may allow a more intuitive response. Afterwards, you can reflect more deeply and check if your intellectual answers confirm these, change them or bring in other insights. You can download copies of this questionnaire from the *Camino Guides* web site – make some extra copies so you can repeat the exercise on your return and again in (say) 3 months time. This way you can compare results and ensure you continue to follow through on any insights that came to you while walking the camino.

❐ How do you differentiate pilgrimage from a long distance walk?

❐ How do you define spirituality – what does it mean to you?

❐ How is your spirituality expressed at home and at work?

❐ What do you see as the primary purpose of your life?

❐ Are you working consciously towards fulfilling that purpose?

❐ How clear are you on your goal and the right direction for you at this time?

❐ How will you recognise resistance to any changes that might be necessary?

❐ When did you first become aware of a desire to take time-out?

❐ What prompted you originally to go on the camino?

❐ Did the prompt come from something that you felt needed changing?

❐ Make a list of what appears to be blocking any change from happening.

❐ What help might you need on a practical, emotional and spiritual level?

❐ How will you recognise the right help or correct answer?

❐ What are the joys and challenges in working towards your unique potential?

❐ What are your next steps towards fulfilling that potential?

How aware are you of the following? Score yourself on a level of 1 – 10 and compare these scores again on your return from the camino.

❐ Awareness of your inner spiritual world

❐ Clarity on what inspires you and the capacity to live your passion

❐ Confidence to follow your intuitive sense of the right direction

❐ Ability to recognise your resistance and patterns of defence

❐ Ease with asking for and receiving support from others

MAP LEGEND *OUTER WAYMARKS*

This guidebook provides you with essential information in a concise format. The maps have been designed so you can instantly see how far it is to the next café or place of interest etc. without having to scale the distance. All pilgrim hostels are clearly shown (with the number of bed-spaces in brackets) and the location of alternative accommodation is also provided. Distances on the maps correspond to those in the text and are generally spaced at around 3 km intervals corresponding to approximately 1 hour of walking at an average pace. For clarity and accuracy each stage begins and ends at the front door of a clearly specified pilgrim hostel.

Waymarks: Thanks to the voluntary efforts of the various associations and 'friends of the way' – waymarking is now so thorough that we need only the barest information to get us safely to the end of each stage along the way. If you get 'lost' it is invariably because you have let your mind wander and your feet have followed! – stay present and focused especially at points shown with an exclamation mark [!]. If you find yourself temporarily off-course be careful when asking directions as locals are not generally familiar with the waymarked paths but may direct you along the public roads – it is often best to re-trace your steps until you pick up the waymarks again. A sun-compass has been provided on each map as an aid to orientation. In all cases where there are alternative routes I have recommended 'the path less travelled' – my criteria is always to minimise the amount of time spent on asphalt which is so hard and tiring underfoot.

Should you become lost you will find a '**sun compass**' to help re-orientate you. Even in poor weather we can generally tell the direction of the sun so, for example, if you are walking from St. Jean to Roncesvalles you are heading south/west and the morning sun will be on your left (east). At midday the sun will be straight ahead (south) and by late afternoon it will be on your *right>* (west). If you find yourself in the late afternoon with the sun on your *<left* – stop and re-assess as you may be following some other track *back* to St. Jean. Those of us who decide to leave our wristwatch at home

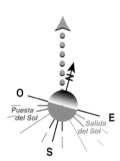

the sun will also become our natural clock. It is surprising how quickly we get to know the time of day by the length of our shadow and our body will ring an alarm bell when it is time to eat or drink. The sun can also help us shift our human egoic tendency of self-aggrandisement towards greater humility by realising the relative insignificance of our physical existence. We like to identify ourselves as being at the centre of the universe and say that the sun rises in the east because that is our experience but it is entirely wrong – it is of course the earth turning on its axis that turns us towards the sun in the morning and away from it at night. This is more than mere semantics. The idea that the sun was the centre of our solar system was a heresy as Galileo discovered to his cost.

Familiarise yourself with the map symbols and note: [1] the **recommended** route generally follows the most natural pathway and is indicated by a line of yellow dots ● ● ● ● – symbolic of the yellow arrows that will be your friendly guide throughout the journey. Distances along this recommended route are shown in **blue.** [2] **Alternative** routes that are mostly by road are marked with **grey** dots ● ● ● ● symbolising the greyness of the asphalt and distances provided are also coloured **grey** and the text appears on a grey background.

[3] **Alternative** scenic routes (more remote and sometimes with local waymarks only) are shown with green dots ● ● ● ● indicating the natural landscape they travel through and the text appears on a green panel. [4] **Detours** are shown with **turquoise** dots ● ● ● ● and the text appears on a turquoise panel.

Each day's stage is measured from the front door of one albergue to the next, i.e. daily distances are between sleeping accommodation. Intermediate hotels or hostels are also shown, those directly on the route in a solid panel and those *off* route with a border only. The number of available beds is also shown [in brackets]. The maps have been designed to show relevant information only and are therefore not strictly to scale – instead accurate distances are given between each point marked on the map and this corresponds to the text for ease of reference. Distances in between these points are shown bracketed in the text as follows: **[1.0 km]** plus **[0.2 km]** add up to the boxed figure in blue 1.2 km Note <left means *turn* left – (left) means *on* your left – right> *turn* right etc.

❓ Indicates an option – recommended routes usually follow the less travelled tracks so as to minimise the time spent on asphalt. The main (N-*National*) roads are shown in red, symbolic of their added danger and volume of traffic. Every effort has been made to minimise exposure to these 'red' routes and extra care is needed on the few stretches where they simply cannot be avoided. ❗Indicates either a dangerous stretch of road, a steep descent or an area where the waymarks are not clear. Use the 'sun compass' to help orientate yourself through cities and other poorly waymarked areas.

Text and place names on the maps are generally in Spanish *Castellano*. However, on entering Galicia, place names are provided in *Galego* unless they appear 'on the ground' in Spanish. The Church of St. John may, therefore, appear as *Igreja San Juan* or *Igrexa San Xoán*. Villages in Spain, particularly Galicia, tend to straggle without any defined centre and even the local church is frequently located outside the actual town. Distances are usually measured to the albergue or other clearly defined feature, such as a drinking font [F] *fuente*.

Contour guides are shown for each day's walk. This will give you a thumbnail sketch of the day's terrain and help you prepare for the uphill stretches and anticipate the downhill ones. They are drawn to an exaggerated scale to emphasise steep inclines.

Equivalent distances are given for each stage adjusted for height using the common factor of 10 minutes for every 100 metres climbed and then applied to the slower (leisurely) pace of 20 minutes per kilometre. For example: Total (cumulative) climb during the day of 600 metres is equivalent to an extra 3 kilometres (time and energy expended) calculated as follows: 600 (metres) ÷ by 10 = 60 (minutes). 60 ÷ 20 (minutes per km) = 3 (km). **Note: 1 km = 0.6 mile.**

Based on the following chart a very fit (fast) walker can accomplish up to a ***maximum*** of 40 ***adjusted*** kilometres in an 8-hour day. This drops to 35 km for an average walker and 25 km for a leisurely pace.

Fitness Level	kph	minutes/km	25km	30km	35km	40km
			The above distances (kilometres) will take the following time (hours)			
Fast walker	5 kph	12 min's/km	5.0	6.0	7.0	8.0
Average pace	4 kph	15 min's/km	6.3	7.5	8.6	—
Leisurely pace	3 kph	20 min's/km	8.3	—	—	—

■ **Average pace** depends on many other factors, apart from gradient. Awareness of the following additional factors will help you plan your itinerary. **Time of day will also affect your speed and endurance.** Ideally start each day early and either (a) finish by lunchtime or (b) plan a midday stop, rest in the shade, and continue on when the worst heat of the day is over.

■ **End of day pace** will produce the biggest variations. On the longer stretches you may find your pace slowing considerably and you should allow *half* the normal pace (*double* the time) in calculating whether to continue onwards at the end of a long day. *(Pilgrims tend to only query measurements for the last section of a day that they feel must be longer than that published! That is why it is misleading to publish time rather than distance for any section).*

Traversing cities along the route. The more time you spend on the quiet country sections the greater is likely to be your vulnerability to the noise and bustle of the cities. If you are travelling as a solo contemplative pilgrim you might plan your itinerary to walk through the city on the relatively traffic free Sunday or during siesta times. Waymarking in cities has to compete with consumer advertising, traffic lights and other distractions, so allow time to retrace steps if you take a wrong turning.

Traffic can be dangerous and draining. Spanish driving is no safer than in any other country (some would maintain it's worse!). Regarding the energy drain often experienced as a result of the noise and air blast or suction, especially of large articulated trucks, it can help to understand the dynamics of subtle (and not so subtle) energy. One way of working with this is to try 'singing' into the roar as it passes you by. As you hear traffic approaching, start humming your favourite tune. As it draws nearer raise your volume until, at the moment of passing, your roar matches that of the vehicle's engine. This is one simple method of, at least, dispersing any possible negative inner and outer vibrations! You can also use the sudden roar of a car passing at speed (or the sudden bark of a dog) as an alarm call – a rude awakening and reminder of your purpose for being on pilgrimage. Whatever reaction you have, try and stay focused and shake out any negative or angry reactions immediately they arise.

Senda: These modern gravel paths represent a sort of soulless modern 'autopista for pedestrians'. They are shown on the maps on a grey path (as opposed to earth green) to denote their confusion between path and road (being neither one or the other). They run alongside the public road and are 'softening' with time.

Future Scenarios: Over the past few years, bus loads of tourists on 'pilgrim' holidays have begun to appear along the route. Some, doubtless well meaning charity organisations also organise bus tours that threaten to overload the capacity of the camino to cope gracefully. I have recently been forced off the path by 4 wheel drive 'pilgrim safaris' from a UK adventure holiday company – a humbling but not particularly edifying experience! *Mickey Mouse* dressed as a pilgrim complete with staff has already appeared around Sahagún, one of the worst effected areas. Perhaps León will develop a pilgrim theme park that might, ironically, reduce numbers on the camino itself. We need to stay vigilant and give feedback to local authorities, travel and charity organisations of any concerns we might have and remind ourselves that, during the medieval period, the camino was able to cope with twice the present number of annual pilgrims.

Map symbols used in this guide:

Total km — Total distance for each day's stage

△ — Adjusted for climb (100m vertical = additional 0.5km)

(850m) Alto ▲ — Contours / High point of each stage

< Ⓐ Ⓗ > — Intermediate accommodation

◄ 3.5 — Precise distance between points (3.5 km = ± 1 hour walking)

—●150m > / ^ / < — Interim distances •150 metres turn right / straight on (s/o) / left

||||||||||||||||||| — Path or track (*green*: symbolising natural pathways)

||||||||||||||||||| — Gravel track *senda* (*grey*: symbolising artificial pathways)

▬▬▬▬▬▬ — Secondary road (*grey*: asphalt)

▬N-11▬ — Main [N-] road (*red*: additional traffic and hazard)

═A-1═ — Motorway (*blue*: conventional motorway colour)

❽ ❽ ⊙ — Option Point / Extra vigilance required / Roundabout

● ● ● ● ● — Main (recommended) route (*yellow*: maximising pathways)

● ● ● ● ● — Alternative road route (*grey*: more asphalt)

● ● ● ● ● — Alternative scenic route (*green*: more remote / less waymarks)

● ● ● ● ● — Optional detour *desvío* to point of interest (*turquoise*)

❓ ❌ — Option *Opción* / Crossroads *Cruce* or Junction

++++++++●— — Railway / Station

▪ ▬ ▪ ▬ ▪ — National boundary / Provincial boundary

〜 〜 — River / Stream

⬭ ⬭ — Sea or river estuary / Woodland

Ⓣ ↑ ✝ — Church / Chapel / Wayside cross

⤬ ↑ ☥ — Picnic area / Windmill / Radio mast

Ⓕ ☕ 🏪 — Drinking font *(Fonte, Fuente)* / Café bar / Mini-market

🄸 🏨 — Tourist Office / Manor house

✚ ✉ ⛽ — Hospital / Post office / Petrol station

✈ ⇌ 🚌 — Airport / Rail / Bus station

↡ ❖ XᵗʰC — Viewpoint / Ancient monument / 10ᵗʰ Century

Ⓐ❶ Ⓙ — Pilgrim hostel(s) *(Albergue)* / Youth hostel *(Juventude)*

Ⓗ Ⓟ Ⓒ — Hotel / Pension / Country B&B *(Casa rural)*

Ⓗ Ⓐ Ⓙ — *(off* route accommodation)

[32] — Number of bed spaces (usually bunks)

[÷4]+ — ÷ number of rooms / **+** additional private rooms

Par. — Parroquial hostel (church parish) € donation

Conv. — Convent or monastery hostel €5+

Muni. — Municipal hostel €5+

Xunta — Galician government *(Xunta)* hostel €6

Asoc. — Association hostel €7+

Priv. (*) — Private hostel (private network with star *) €10+

▭ — Town plan with page number

(Pop. – Alt. m) — Town population and altitude in metres

▨ — City suburbs (*grey*)

— Historical centre *centro histórico* (*brown*)

33 STAGE SUMMARY – ROUTE MAPS & TOWN GUIDES

St Jean Pied de Port – Santiago de Compostela 789.1 km (490.3 miles)

Page	Map	Km	From	To	*Town Plan*
			NAVARRA --		
48	01	25.1	St Jean	Roncesvalles	*St Jean p.45*
56	02	27.4	Roncesvalles	Larrasoaña	
62	03	20.9	Larrasoaña	Cizur Menor via	*Pamplona p.69*
72	04	19.0	Cizur Menor	Puente la Reina	*Puente la Reina*
80	05	21.9	Puente la Reina	Estella	*Estella p.86*
88	06	21.1	Estella	Los Arcos	*Arcos p.96*
94	07	28.6	Los Arcos	Logroño	*Logroño p.100*
			LA RIOJA --		
102	08	30.1	Logroño	Nájera	
108	09	21.0	Nájera	Santo Domingo	
114	10	22.9	Santo Domingo	Belorado	
			CASTILLA Y LEON *(BURGOS)* ---------------------		
120	11	24.3	Belorado	St Juan Ortega	
126	12	25.6	St Juan Ortega	Burgos	*Burgos p.133*
136	13	21.0	Burgos	Hornillos	
142	14	20.2	Hornillos	Castrojeriz	
			CASTILLA Y LEON *(PALENCIA)* ------------------		
148	15	25.2	Castrojeriz	Frómista	
154	16	20.5	Frómista	Carrion 'Condes	
160	17	26.8	Carrion 'Condes	Terradillos	
164	18	26.9	Terradillos	Hermanillos via	*Sahagún p.169*
			CASTILLA Y LEON *(LEÓN)* ------------------------		
172	19	24.5	Hermanillos	Mansilla	*Mansilla p.177*
178	20	18.6	Mansilla	León	*León p.183*
186	21	22.2	León	Mazarife	
194	22	31.2	Mazarife	Astorga	*Astorga p.201*
204	23	21.4	Astorga	Rabanal	
210	24	26.5	Rabanal	Molinaseca	
216	25	30.9	Molinaseca	Villafranca via	*Ponferrada 221*
226	26	30.1	Villafranca Bierzo	O'Cebreiro	*Villafranca 225*
			GALICIA *(LUGO)* ------------------------------------		
238	27	21.3	O'Cebreiro	Triacastela	
242	28	18.7	Triacastela	Sarria	*Sarria p.247*
248	29	22.4	Sarria	Portomarín	
254	30	24.8	Portomarín	Palas do Rei	
260	31	25.8	Palas do Rei	Ribadiso (Arzúa)	
			GALICIA *(LA CORUÑA)* -----------------------------		
266	32	22.1	Ribadiso	O' Pino/Arca	
270	33	20.1	Arca (Pedrouzo)	Santiago	*Santiago p.279*

ST. JEAN PIED de PORT *(pop. 1,800 – alt. 170m)***:** The ancient capital of the Basque region of Basse-Navarre retains a delightful medieval atmosphere in its narrow streets. The Basque language has also been preserved so signs and place names may appear in French or Basque (and across the border in Spanish or Basque). This attractive town nestles in the foothills of the Pyrenees at the 'foot of the pass' *pied de port* to Roncesvalles (Ronceveaux in French). A population of 1,800 serves the many tourists, hill walkers and pilgrims that converge on this small enclave in the summer months. Activity gravitates towards the central square *Place du-Gaulle* where the efficient tourist office © 0559-370 357 is located along with a range of hotels and cafés where you can wine and dine amongst the traffic fumes or…

Explore the historic walled town where the pilgrim office and hostels are located. St. Jean Pied de Port has become the principal gateway to the camino and the traditional starting point for pilgrims from all over the world with the exception of those in Spain, where the main starting point is Roncesvalles (for the whole route) or Sarria in Galicia which is just over 100 km from Santiago and the minimum distance required to qualify for a compostela.

**Porte St. Jacques
and Municipal Pilgrim Hostel**

❏ **Monuments historiques:** A basic tour starts with a visit to the medieval *rue de la Citadelle*. This is a continuation of the Way of St. James through France *Chemin de Saint Jacques* and part of the camino itself. From this ancient cobbled main street there are several access points to the old ramparts. At the very top of the town is St. James Gate ❶ *Porte St Jacques* *XVthC* (UNESCO World Heritage status) through which pilgrims arriving from Le Puy, Vezelay and Paris, via Ostabat, enter the town. From the *Porte St Jacques* a steep climb takes us to the imposing ❷ *Citadelle* (Table d'Orientation) with a fine view over the old town and the Pyrenees over which we will pass tomorrow. *[A steep climb down on the eastern boundary (269 steps!) brings us to the narrow Porte de l'Echauguette that opens onto the river Nive – see below].* Continuing down the rue de la Citadelle we pass the Prison of the Bishops ❸ *La Maison des Evêques XVIthC* museum displaying artefacts from the Camino de Santiago. Just below we find the pilgrim office *Accueil pèlerins* at no 39. Further on down (right) is rue de France leading to one of the 4 medieval gates to the town ❹ *Porte de France* and rue Eglise leading to ❺ *Porte de Navarre*. At the bottom of the street (left) we arrive at The church of Our Lady at the End of the Bridge ❻ *Notre Dame du Bout du Pont XIVthC* – a fitting place, perhaps, from which to bless the beginning of your journey and that of your fellow pilgrims who will pass under her protective arch *Porte Notre Dame* on the way out in the morning. From the church you can take a peaceful 1 km circular detour up river, past the wooden footbridge, to the Roman bridge *Pont Eyeraberri*. Cross over and return via the Pelota court *Frontón* and the Spanish Gate ❼ *Porte D'Espagne* leading into the rue d'Espagne back to the Porte Notre Dame (See town plan).

Pilgrim Passport – you can obtain a *Carnet de Pelerin / Credencial del Peregrino* from the pilgrim office open 07:30–22:00 (closed lunch). It will provide general information on the first leg of the route, some idea of local weather conditions and can check availability of accommodation (+key for albergue 1).

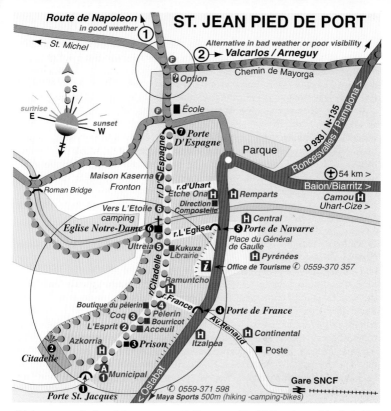

ST. JEAN PIED DE PORT

■ **Accommodation** / *Logements*. © France +33. ■ *Tourisme* 14 place De Gaulle © 0559-370 357. ❑*Accueil pèlerins* pilgrim office 39 rue de la Citadelle © 0559-370 509 *(pilgrim passport /carnet/ credencial)*.

■ *Albergues:* ❶Municipal *Asoc.[24÷3]+* N°55 Rue de la Citadelle adj. Porte St Jacques 24 beds €8 incl. (open all year–check in at *Accueil*). ❷L'Esprit du Chemin *Asoc.[18÷4]* © 0559-372 468 N°40 opp. pilgrim office €8, dinner available + picnic for next day. Adj. at N°36 is ❸Au Chant du Coq *Priv.[15]* © 0674-310 283. ❹L'auberge du pèlerin *Priv.[43÷4]* © 0559-491 086 adj. Ramuntcho at N°25 €16. ❺Gîte Ultreïa *Priv.**[15÷4]+ © 0680 884 622 adj. church at N°8 €15. ❻Le Chemin Vers L'Etoile *Priv.[20÷5]+* © 0559 372 071 N°21 rue d'Espagne (adj. L'Atelier du Chocolat) €15 incl. ❼Maison Kaserna *Par.[12÷1]* © 0559-376 517 N°43 rue d'Espagne € donativo / communal meal.

■ *Hotels €60-80:* The only hotel in the old town is •**Ramuntcho** H** © 0559-370 391 rue de Citadelle, 24 located on the corner of rue de France with dining room where you can eat *al fresco* on the balcony. •**Gîte d'Étape Etchegoin** © 0559-371 208 Rue d'Uhart, 9 also dormitory rooms. •**Les Remparts** H** © 0559-371 379 Place Floquet,16. •**Etche Ona** H** © 0559-370 114 Place Floquet,15. •**Central** H** Place du Général de Gaulle, 1 © 0559-370 022. •**Itzalpea** H** © 0559-370 366 Place du Trinquet, 5. •**Continental** H** © 0559-370 025 on Av. Renaud (on the road to rail station). At the top end of the square (and price bracket) •**Les Pyrénées** H****© 0559-370 101 from €160.

■ See p.17 for average cost of hostels and p.19 hotels – within Spain.

■ *Pilgrim facilities on rue de Citadelle: Express Burricot (N°31)* transfer of backpacks. *Boutique du pélerin (N°32) pilgrim maps & accessories + internet open 07:00 until 19:00 daily. Librairie Kukuxka (N°3) books and maps. Direction Compostelle Place de Floquet* © 0559 491 277 *pilgrim accessories.*

Choice of routes: This first stage is one of the more strenuous and is a veritable baptism of fire into *El Camino* and Spain. Don't worry; millions of pilgrims have gone before you to pave the way! You do, however, have a choice of 2 different routes to reach Roncesvalles and your choice will be dependent on 2 main considerations: [a] prevailing weather conditions and [b] your personal level of fitness and experience. Whichever route you take is likely to be taxing as we stretch both physical and spiritual muscles that have, perhaps, become somewhat atrophied over time with our increasingly sedentary and secular lives. This stage represents one of the steepest ascents of the whole pilgrimage. However, the climb is rewarded with the great panorama of the Pyrenees. So have all your gear, food and water prepared for an early morning start so you can sleep soundly during the night holding your inner purpose for this journey, rather than your worldly goods, clearly in mind. If that purpose remains obscure – ask for clarity now.

❶ **Route de Napoléon: 25.1 km** *(adjusted for climb 32.0 km allowing for a cumulative ascent in the day of 1,390m equivalent to an extra 6.9 km of time and effort expended over and above that required for a level walk).* This is the longest and most arduous route but the most beautiful and spectacular. It was the way favoured by the great French general to get his troops in and out of Spain during the Peninsular War and by medieval pilgrims anxious to avoid the bandits hiding in the trees surrounding the lower route. It is the recommended route in good weather and it makes the most of the early morning sun, which doesn't penetrate into the Valcarlos valley (alternative route) until later in the day. The steep climb up onto the high plateau is rewarded with wonderful views back over St. Jean de Pied Port. The last section up through the Col de Bentartea and Col de Lepoeder is entirely on natural pathways.

[1a] A little known (and used) variant on route [1] is the GR65 from Mayorga on the outskirts of St. Jean. This alternative adds 1 km to the recommended route that it re-joins at the 1,000m contour close to the Pic d'Orisson. While it avoids most of the asphalt section of the D428 it is poorly waymarked and it is easy to get lost along the remote mountain paths. If you are an experienced hill walker and want to use this route obtain the IGN 1:25 map 1346 OT available in St. Jean or any good map shop – otherwise stick to the main route.

Likewise, unless you are an experienced hill walker, you should not tackle the recommended route: [a] in winter when daylight hours are greatly diminished and weather more extreme, or [b] during any other season if the weather looks bad or is forecast to deteriorate. Note that during late autumn and early spring there are frequent snow showers and these can obliterate the waymarks. At any time of year hill fog can cause poor visibility. Fog should be distinguished from early morning mist, which usually burns off in the first few hours long before you reach the high plateau and have to leave the relative security of the road. If you are unsure or anxious, enquire at the pilgrim office as they have access to local weather forecasts and regular updates. Guidebooks are duty bound to sound cautionary notes! Be sensible, but know that any reasonably fit person can cover the ground and is likely to have a peak experience in so doing. Remember to take food and water with you, as there are no facilities (beyond Orisson) and drinking fonts are few and far between. If the weather is very unsettled then it might be preferable to stick to the rigours of the N-135.

❷ **Valcarlos route: 24.0 km** *(adjusted for climb 28.9 km allowing for a cumulative ascent in the day of 990m, equivalent to an extra 4.9 km).* Charles' Valley *Valcarlos* was the way chosen by the Holy Roman Emperor Charlemagne to get his troops in and, somewhat disastrously, out of Spain. You cannot avoid the main road completely, but you can save 6 km of it before Arneguy and a further 10 km of it after Valcarlos. This alternative route runs parallel to the main road and follows quiet country lanes into Arneguy. However, the waymarking is not so clear and there are several side roads that could delay you unless you stay alert and vigilant. 6 km after Valcarlos a path leaves the road and climbs directly to the Ibañeta pass through a mixture of pine and beech trees. This is a very steep pathway but it eliminates the innumerable bends on the main road.

A variant on route ❷ is to follow the main road all the way to Roncesvalles 27.5 km, adjusted for climb 32.0 km (allowing for a cumulative ascent in the day of 890m equivalent to an extra 4.5 km). The road route is the longest and goes through the villages of Arneguy and Valcarlos with their shops, bars and hotels. However, this is a main route into Spain and is designated an N *(nacional)* road and is not recommended. Today, the road carries an ever-increasing amount of tourist traffic and is noisy and dangerous particularly in wet or windy conditions. Note that apart from the noise and danger of traffic it can also be very chilly in the early morning, as the sun does not penetrate the deep-sided valley until later in the day.

Preparations for next day – Outer: As you will need to leave early in the morning to get to Roncesvalles, you should shop for lunch the evening before as there are limited facilities on both routes and shops won't be open when you leave at first light in the morning. An exception is the *Boutique du pélerin,* which opens at 07.30. The rue d'Espagne has several food outlets including *Alimentacion* (opposite patisserie *Barbier Millox*) and a supermarket *Le Relais des Mousquetaires* on the corner of the rue d'Uhart and just before Porte d'Espagne is the *Boulangerie Iriart* (opens around 7 a.m.) Fill your water flask before you leave town and top up as you pass drinking fonts en route.

Preparations for next day – Inner: Take time now, again, to reflect on the purpose of your pilgrimage. Try the church for some quiet space or take a walk along the river. Look again at your personal journal or self-assessment notes and ponder on the journey of your life that has brought you this far – reflect on your purpose for now. You may yet meet Jesús Jato, but in the meantime you can walk with his words in your heart *El Camino es tiempo de meditación interior, no itinerario turístico.*

REFLECTIONS:

❑ **Personal Journal:** *"... The stress of arriving at St. Jean combined with the urge to begin the pilgrimage resulted in a false start. I walked for several hours before I realised that my mind was anywhere but present to the sacred journey I was embarking on. I had fallen straight back into my familiar mode of active doing and the simple act of Being was lost to me. In my haste and confusion I had forgotten to pause and to dedicate this first leg of the journey to my purpose – 'to find and inhabit that place within me that touches God'. Tears welled up from deep within me at this prompt from my guides, 'Start anew', they urged...*

...It was hard to retrace my steps but I knew that it was meaningless to continue in this frame of mind. Lost in the busyness of both past and future, I had forsaken the present, the only place I could find what I was looking for. I write these notes on a tiny balcony directly above the camino with the church tower just visible against the darkening sky. Tomorrow I will follow my inner guidance and start afresh..."

❏ **A journey of a thousand miles begins with a single step**. *Lao Tzu*

---

01 **789.1** km (490.3 miles) to Santiago de Compostela

ST. JEAN PIED-DE-PORT (Pays Basque) – RONCESVALLES (Navarre)

[1] Recommended route (weather permitting)
Via Route de Napoléon / Col de Loepeder /

▦▦▦▦	Path / Track	--- --- 12.4 ---	*49%*
▬▬▬	Quiet Road	--- --- 12.7 ---	*51%*
▬▬▬	Main Road	--- --- 0.0	
Total km	**Total distance**	**25.1 km** (15.6 ml)	

 Adjusted for climb 32.0 km (accrued ascent 1,390m = 6.9 km)

Alto ▲ High point: Col de Loepeder 1,450m (4,757 feet)

< 🅰 🏠 > **Intermediate Accommodation:** Huntto **5.6** km & Orisson **8.0** km

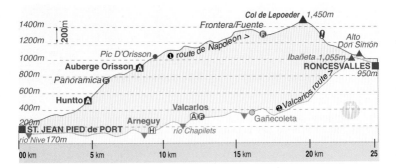

❶ **Recommended *Route de Napoléon*:** A strenuous uphill walk is rewarded with stunning views in all directions (provided we are spared the hill fog). The first part, as far as *Huntto*, is through steeply wooded countryside that gives way to open hill and moorland, interspersed with some woodland (mostly beech) on the Spanish side. While the uphill section will stretch the cardiovascular muscles, injury is more likely on the steep downhill stage into Roncesvalles when mind and muscles will be tired – stay very focussed.

The Practical Path: While we start with one of the more demanding walks of the entire route, you will doubtless be full of energy and the sense of adventure ahead. Don't let euphoria force a pace in these early days that you and your feet have not adequately trained for – walk lightly and easily within your physical capabilities. The hospitals and health clinics of Logroño, only 160 km away specialise in treating foot and leg injuries sustained by over-eager pilgrims some of whom are forced to abandon the journey at this early stage. If you are with a companion(s) then find your own walking speed and don't allow yourself to be forced into someone else's stride. You can always catch up later and in the meantime you will make new friends and experience the rich camaraderie that develops along the way. For general emergencies (medical, police etc.) ✆ 112.

❏ **The Mystical Path:** A sharing from the heart can be reflected in a simple smile. If the eyes are the windows of the soul, then words are often the blinds that shut out the light. Will you see the collection of handcrafted crosses by the

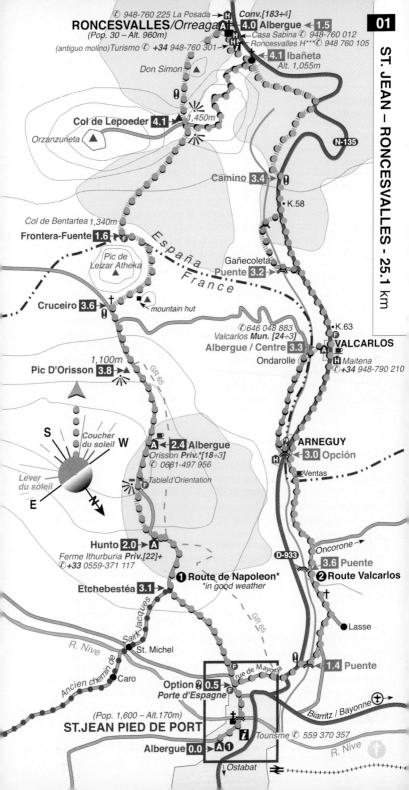

© 948-760 225 La Posada → **H**   *Conv.[183÷4]*
RONCESVALLES/*Orreaga* **A H** **4.0** Albergue ← **1.5**
(Pop. 30 – Alt. 960m)   **H** ← *Casa Sabina* © 948-760 012
(antiguo molino)Turismo © **+34** 948-760 301   **H** ← *Roncesvalles H****** © 948 760 105

Don Simon ▲   **4.1** Ibañeta
    Alt. 1,055m

Col de Lepoeder **4.1** →   *1,450m*
Orzanzurieta ▲

    N-135

    Camino **3.4**

    • K.58

Col de Bentartea 1,340m
Frontera-Fuente **1.6** → **F**   *España*
    France
Pic de   Gañecoleta
Leizar Atheka ▲   **Puente** **3.2** →
    ▲ *mountain hut*

Cruceiro **3.6** †   © 646 048 883   • K.63
    Valcarlos **Mun.** *[24÷3]*   **F**
    Albergue / Centre **3.3** → **A**   **VALCARLOS**
    Ondarolle ©   **H** *Maitena*
Pic D'Orisson **3.8** ▲ *1,100m*   © **+34** 948-790 210

    GR 65
Coucher
du soleil   **A** ← **2.4** Albergue
S   *Orisson* **Priv.*** *[18÷3]*
    © 0681-497 956
W   **F** *Table d'Orientation*
Lever
du soleil   **P** **ARNEGUY**
E   **H** ← **3.0** Opción
    ■ *Ventas*

Hunto **2.0** → **A**
Ferme Ithurburia **Priv.** *[22]+*   *Oncorone* →
© **+33** 0559-371 117   **D-933** **3.6** Puente

❶ Route de Napoleon*   **❷ Route Valcarlos**
    **in good weather*   †
Etchebestéa **3.1** →   • *Lasse*
    GR 65
R. Nive   *Saint-Jacques*
Ancien chemin de   St. Michel
    • Caro   **1.4** Puente
    rue de Mayorga
Option **0.5** → **F**   *Biarritz / Bayonne* ⊕
Porte d'Espagne   †   **i** *Tourisme* © 559 370 357
(Pop. 1,600 – Alt.170m)   *R. Nive*
ST.JEAN PIED DE PORT
Albergue **0.0** → **A** **❶**
↓ *Ostabat*

remote boundary marker and will you stop awhile to reflect on the truth behind this symbol? What else will your awareness reveal to you along the way that you can share with your fellow pilgrims when you reach Roncesvalles?

❑ **Personal Reflections:** *"... The deep sense of peace that surrounds me is in stark contrast to the stress I felt when I first set out. It had taken me awhile to realise it was All Saints Day – an auspicious start to my journey and a moment of tenderness as I recalled burying my father in Spanish soil on this very day all those years ago. I record these thoughts in the silence of my own company, surrounded by empty chairs and empty tables. I am the only pilgrim in this enormous building but I am not alone as the ancient Celtic prayer reminds me, 'Christ before me. Christ behind me. Christ all around me... Christ within me."*

Fauna and flora: Take time to take in the magnificence of the natural landscape that surrounds you. Watch out for the Griffon Vultures that soar in the mountain thermals alert for any signs of a sheep or other animal about to expire and become its staple carrion. These majestic birds have a wingspan up to 2.5m (8 feet) and there are 1,800 pairs in the region, the biggest concentration in the world. We will also see a variety of birds of prey including the Kite and Buzzard or the smaller and swifter Sparrow hawk and Falcon. This area is an important flight path for many species of migrating bird, all of which has spawned an ornithological information centre at Ibañeta. You may also encounter a rare Pyrenean chamois or wild horse on the hill and almost certainly see many of the hill ponies running free (distinguishable by their neck halters). The black-faced sheep roaming the high pasture are *Manech* bred for the quality of their milk and its award winning *Ossau Iraty* cheese. Depending on the season, you will see many varieties of wild flowers of every hue and colour including orchids, violas, narcissus and the ubiquitous pale blue irises that carpet the path all along the camino from here to the 'end of the world' at *finis-terre*.

Leaving the pilgrim office and central albergue in St. Jean we turn down the cobbled rue de la Citadelle passing the parish church *Notre Dame du Bout du Pont* [F] (left) and pass through the archway and over the river Nive. This is the lowest point of the first stage at 170m above sea level. By this afternoon we will have climbed to 1,450m through the Col de Lepoeder! *(As we look back from the bridge we will find the Virgin and Child watching over us as we take our first steps on the journey).* Proceed up the cobbled rue D'Espagne to:

0.5 km **Porte D'Espagne–Option** *Opción* [?] Ancient gateway to Spain and the point at which we decide which route to follow. Drinking font *Fuente* [F] (left). *For the **alternative road** route via Valcarlos and Puerto de Ibañeta continue up for 100m past the school and turn right> into Chemin de Mayorga. This avoids the busy roundabouts in St. Jean. The Chemin de Mayorga is also the access point to the variant [1a] via the GR65 (see route map).*

For the **recommended way ❶** via Route de Napoleon over the Col de Lepoeder continue straight on passing [F] (right) – fill up if you haven't already. Ignore signs to St. Michel and continue up into the Chemin de Saint Jacques (*Jondoni Jakobe Bidea* in Basque) along the minor road D-428 veering <left at Villa Etchea Kalavainea and continue up to grove of chestnut trees at junction:

3.1 km **Etchebestéa** (no sign) but here the road from St. Michel (Stage I of the Codex Calixtinus) joins from the left. *This was the ancient route taken by pilgrims coming from France.* Keep straight on uphill on the asphalt road (ignoring any woodland paths) to:

2.0 km Huntto •Albergue Ferme Ithurburia *Priv.[22÷4]+* © 0559-371 117 where Mme. Ourthiague offers a variety of meal options with 22 pilgrim bed spaces from €14 +priv. rooms (open all year). ½-board €32. Shortly afterwards **[0.3 km]** turn <left onto grass track to re-join road **[1.1 km]** with [F] (right) and viewing table and rest point (left). Continue along asphalt road for **[1.0** km] to:

2.4 km Orisson •Auberge *Priv.*[18÷3] © 0559-491 303 network* hostel. Open all year with 18 beds in 3 dormitories and good facilities. No kitchen but popular bar and restaurant with panoramic viewing platform ½-board only – €31. *[Note that the next albergue is: Roncesvalles – 17.1 km].* [F] (left) We now break through the 1,000m level to arrive at:

Auberge d'Orisson

3.8 km Pic D'Orisson (1,100m) with its statue of the Virgin *Vierge d'Orisson / Vierge de Biakorri* (left 100m – see photo previous page) set against an impressive backdrop of the surrounding mountains and valleys. *(Note Marian shrines to Our Lady appear all along the route and are one of the most common symbols of devotion on the camino).* Nearby are the ruins of the ancient Chateau Pignon and this remote area once had a medieval pilgrim hostel. Continue on the asphalt road to the turn off (right) to Arneguy D-128 **[1.7 km]**. Keep straight on/left here for another **[1.9 km]** and turn off right> by memorial cross [!].

3.6 km Cruceiro a modern wayside cross and memorial leads us onto a rough grass track that cuts through a gap in the ridge ahead (*Pic de Leizar Atheka* and *the Col de Bentarte*). We *must* leave the road at this stage. *(If the weather has deteriorated and you are not confident of proceeding, your options are: return to Auberge Orisson, St Jean or take the D 128 to Arneguy. In an emergency there is a tiny mountain hut 50m (right) just through the gap ahead).* Pass through the gap in the ridge **[0.5 km]** (mountain shelter right) onto a woodland path turning <left at wire fence **[0.6 km]** along a heavily eroded gully passing a stone marker (No. 199) to a cattle grid **[0.5 km]** that marks the Spanish border.

1.6 km Frontera [F] *Fontaine de Roland* (left) cross over the cattle grid into Spain with a stone border marker (ahead left) confirming that we are now in Navarre. *(Don't stray onto the GR10 the long-distance route over the Pyrenees from the Atlantic to the Mediterranean that crosses the path down to the left)* continue up right> on the GR65 to pass the ruins of an ancient border post (left). The camino now continues in a gentler climb through scattered woodland (mostly beech) up along a wide track until we reach the highest point at:

4.1 km Col de Lepoeder (**1,450 metres**) from here we have our first view southwards over Navarre with the roof of the abbey at Roncesvalles and the town of Burguete in the valley below. [?] **Option:** *(If you are tired or it is getting late (dusk) and/or it is wet and slippery underfoot, you can take the less steep (but longer) option by turning right> downhill on the asphalt road to Ibañeta 4.0 km and a further 1.6 km to Roncesvalles).* Otherwise, keep straight on over the road to the pathway that drops steeply down [!] through magnificent beech woods *bosque de Irati* one of the largest remaining beech forests in Europe, around the conical hill of Alto Don Simón to:

4.0 km Roncesvalles [Orreaga] with •Albergue *[183÷4]* + 2 hotels, monastery, collegiate church, bookshop, museum and tourist office (see details overleaf).

ST. JEAN PIED-DE-PORT – RONCESVALLES
(Pays Basque)   (Navarre)

❷ **alternative road** route *Via Valcarlos*
and the Puerto de Ibañeta
Preferred option in bad or deteriorating weather.

	Path / Track	--- ---	7.3	---	*31%*
	Quiet Road	--- ---	11.4	---	*47%*
	Main Road	--- ---	<u>5.3</u>	---	*22%*
Total km	**Total distance**		**24.0 km** (14.9 ml)		

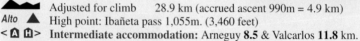

Adjusted for climb   28.9 km (accrued ascent 990m = 4.9 km)
Alto ▲ High point: Ibañeta pass 1,055m. (3,460 feet)
< Ⓐ Ⓗ > **Intermediate accommodation:** Arneguy **8.5** & Valcarlos **11.8** km.

The Practical Path: This is another strenuous uphill climb with less open views but more shelter from wind and rain in the woodland areas. While providing the security of the main road with shops and hotels along the way (Arneguy and Valcarlos) it also contains the hazards and noise of traffic and the harsh asphalt that is so tiring underfoot. Note that almost half the journey is directly on or parallel to the busy National Route N-135.

The variant [2a] is not recommended as it follows the main road all the way to Roncesvalles and you will have asphalt underfoot for the entire distance of 27.5 km (32.0 km when adjusted for the cumulative ascent of 890m). Note: many pilgrims inadvertently take this option as they miss (a) the turn-off right> onto the quieter country lanes just outside St. Jean (b) the scenic routes (green dots) in Arneguy and the turn-off <left above Valcarlos onto the woodland path.

0.0 km St. Jean from pilgrim office and central albergue turn down the cobbled Rue de la Citadelle passing the parish Church of Our Lady at the End of the Bridge *Notre Dame du Bout du Pont* and out under the archway, over the river Nive and proceed up the cobbled rue D'Espagne to:

0.5 km Porte D'Espagne Option [?] This alternative road route via Valcarlos is recommended in bad weather. It is no less strenuous but the woods provide some shelter from rain and wind although the sun doesn't penetrate into the valley until late in the day. To access this route continue up for 100m past the school and turn right> into Chemin de Mayorga (signposted) to join the main road to Pamplona *Pampelune* on the D-933 (the N-135 once you cross the border into Spain).

1.4 km Puente [!] (1.9 km from the centre / albergue) as you leave the suburbs behind the main road takes a sharp left hand bend *down* to a slip road (right) [!] **Be Vigilant** *Vigilante*. Here, barely visible from the road and identified by a **3t** sign (3 tonne weight restriction) with red and white posts, is a short slip road to a concrete bridge over the river Chapitel (sometimes called petite Nive). Many pilgrims plod on along the main road, oblivious of this quieter parallel route.

You now continue on quiet lanes that wind their way up and down the pleasant rolling countryside parallel but away from the dangerous N-135. Veer <left at T-junction **[0.5 km]** continue and turn sharp <left at hairpin bend **[1.9 km]**. We now continue along a steeply undulating road for **[1.2 km]** down towards the main road over stream (bridge to the N-135 left) with sign to Oncorone right:

3.6 km Puente (left) Turn up right> (sign Oncorone) and then down <left and

up again! to finally emerge onto the first short stretch of track where you cross the border into Spain at the modern shopping development *Venta Xabi*. [F] (right) and cafe (left). Continue straight on through the car park (don't cross the river) and take the delightful riverside path all the way into Arneguy and:

3.0 km **Arneguy / Option**. Several hotels and restaurants in Arneguy including •Clementia H** © 0559-371 354. Continue straight on along the main road *or* turn <left over the bridge (back into France!) and take the quieter scenic route via Ondarolle (recommended) to cross the bridge and turn immediately right> up along the far bank of the river all the way into Ondarolle [2.6 km] and turn down right> to re-cross the river and take the steep path up [0.7 km] to:

3.3 km **Valcarlos** *Luzaide* •**Albergue** *[24÷2]* © 646-048 883 municipal hostel below main square €10 incl. (open all year). Continue past the public toilets turn <left on the main road. [F] pilgrim monument opp. the church dedicated to St. James containing the first of many statues to the Saint as slayer-of-the-Moors *Santiago Matamoros*. Other accommodation: •**Maitena** Hs* © 948-790 210 adjoining the square and •**Casa Marcelino** Hs © 948-790 186. The village takes its name from Charlemagne, who camped here on his return home and to lick his wounds after the defeat of his army rearguard and the death of Roland at Ibañeta. [F] (right) as you leave the town [0.5 km]. Stay on the main road for another [2.0 km] and take a new turn off down <left (km.61) for [0.7 km] into:

3.2 km **Gañecoleta** (no facilities) cross the river and take the riverside path cross back again up to the main road [1.3 km] continue up past (km.58) and take the slip road <left [2.1 km] to leave the main road for the last time.

3.4 km **Camino** after [0.4 km] leave the track and take the narrow footpath up right> as it winds through beech and hazel woods to join the main road beside a house & dog kennels *Casa Borda Guardiano* [2.2 km]. Leave the road again after 90m and turn <left and continue through pine plantation for [1.5 km] to:

4.1 km **Puerto Ibañeta** (1,055m) formerly the site of the Church and Hospice of San Salvador built in 1127 to serve pilgrims to Santiago and moved shortly afterwards to Roncesvalles. The pass now has a modern chapel and a stone monument to Roland (*Song of Roland fame, to mark the point at which the wail of his horn* Oliphant *was heard, too late to be rescued by Charlemagne*). There is also a bird observation post with information on the many species and flocks of birds that use this pass on their migrations. Turn <left down by the side of the observation centre along the path for the remaining [1.5 km] through the beech woods to:

1.5 km **Roncesvalles** *Orreaga*

•**Albergue** *Conv.[183÷4]* administered by the collegiate church © 948-760 000 in a new building adjacent to the youth hostel and funded by the Navarre government (2011). The accommodation is spread over 3 floors with bunk beds in cubicles of 4 at €10 (open all year). Excellent modern facilities and open all year (separate building for use in the winter months). Summer overflow in the original medieval hostel *Itzandegia* on the main road with 110 beds in one room!

Albergue Roncesvalles

Admission to the pilgrim hostel and a practical (small) pilgrim passport *credencial del peregrino* can be obtained from the collegiate pilgrim office with entrance under archway at the front of the main building. Open 10:00–13.30 and 16:00–19:00. **Other accommodation:** *adj. monastery* •**Casa Sabina** Hs ℂ 948-760 012 with ind. rooms *from* €40. •**La Posada** Hs ℂ 948-760 225 *from* €45. •**Roncesvalles** H*** ℂ 948 760 105 part of the original monastery building with ind. rooms *from* €60 and the adjoining •**Casa de los Benficiados** ℂ 948 760 105 from €70 double. *Next accommodation: Burgete (3.0 km).*

RONCESVALLES 'valley of thorns' (*Orreaga* in Basque) is still cloaked in its medieval atmosphere and provides another gateway to the camino. This is the major entry point for Spanish pilgrims travelling up via Pamplona and was one of the earliest and most revered pilgrim refuges connecting the Augustinian's with the care of the Santiago pilgrims. Since the 12th century it has received, *'All pilgrims... sick and well. Catholics, Jews, pagans, heretics and vagabonds...'* this open hospitality continues today with one judicial agency offering the opportunity to walk the camino as a way of purging offenders of their misdeeds in lieu of a custodial sentence – finding self respect engendering a reformed life (details of this inspiring *last chance* concept can be found at www.oikoten.be).

The Royal Collegiate Church of Saint Mary *Real Collegiata de Santa María* was built at the behest of the Navarrese King Sancho the Strong *Sancho VII el Fuerte* but was not consecrated until 1219 (after his death). It houses the beautiful 14th century statue of Our Lady of Roncesvalles *Nuestra Señora de Roncesvalles* and runs a bookshop with pilgrim literature, maps and souvenirs and an interesting museum which includes the fine enamel / silver relic known as Charlemagne's chessboard *ajedrez de Carlomagno.* Adjoining the church is the cloisters *claustro* rebuilt in the 17th century after they collapsed under snow! Access is via an inconspicuous door opposite the bookshop. Off the cloisters is the splendid 14th century *Sala Capitular* with its evocative 13th century mausoleum housing the tomb of Sancho VII and his wife Clemencia. The iron chains that Sancho broke in the defeat of the Moors at the famous battle of *Navas de Tolsa* in 1212 are located here and appear in the crest of the Government of Navarra. There is a small admission charge for the museum and cloisters.

Beside the Hostal La Posada is the 12th century Romanesque chapel of the Holy Spirit *Capilla de Sancti Spiritus* otherwise referred to as the *Silo de Carlomagno* and reputed to be the burial place of the slaughtered rear-guard of Charlemagne's army and a medieval pilgrim burial site. Adjoining is the tiny 13th century Gothic chapel of St. James *Capilla de Santiago* whose re-positioned bell (from the chapel at Ibañeta) once guided pilgrims through the swirling mists often experienced around the Ibañeta pass. Adjacent is a monument commemorating the battle of Roncesvalles and the death of Roland in 778.

Lying at an altitude of 950m, Roncesvalles has a resident population of less than 100. The helpful **Turismo** ℂ 948-760 301 is located in an old mill *antiguo molino* behind Casa Sabina. A simple pilgrim dinner is obtainable after mass (book *before* 18:00) at either the Casa Sabina or La Posada and provides an opportunity to meet other pilgrims and share experiences.

Pilgrim Mass: Mon-Fri at 20:00, Sat & Sun 19:00 and festival days 18:00 in the *Iglesia de Santa María* with special blessing for all pilgrims of any faith (check times at the pilgrim office). A pilgrim mass is often available along the camino, generally around 8 p.m. but check availability and times at the hostel.

PROVINCE OF NAVARRA: A fiercely independent mountainous region, its turbulent past has been influenced most notably by the French. Charlemagne's army damaged the walls of Pamplona despite an assurance that the city would not be harmed and so the Basques subsequently massacred the rear-guard of his army at Roncesvalles in retribution – but break no promises here and you will find a generosity of spirit and loyalty second to none. The hospitality of this region is graphically captured in the writings of many foreign authors, notably Ernest Hemingway who stayed for extended periods in Burguete and Pamplona. Fighting bulls and horses are bred in the hills and trout from the mountain streams and local game make up much of the cuisine of this area. Pork products find their way onto most menus with *chorizo* predominating (pork sausage marinated in various local spices, especially paprika) and often found in stews and soups. Vegetarians *vegetarianos* have a hard time here but on the lowlands further west we find widespread asparagus *espárrago de Navarra* and the bright red peppers *pimientas del piquillo* often stuffed with olives and other non-meat delicacies and eaten as snacks *tapas* along with the ubiquitous Spanish omelette *Tortilla de Patatas* made with thinly sliced potato and onion. The Navarrese love a sense of occasion and this is no more apparent than in the running of the bulls held during the festival of San Fermín in Pamplona in early July (to be avoided like the plague if you are on a solitary pilgrimage).

REFLECTIONS: *"I am doing the camino once again, looking for something I left behind or perhaps never found. It's like coming home."* Notes from a returning pilgrim from New Mexico recorded in the Pilgrim book in Roncesvalles. What are your reflections for this opening day?

_____

_____

_____

_____

_____

_____

_____

_____

_____

_____

_____

_____

❏ **Whatever you can do, or dream you can; begin it.**
Boldness has genius power and magic in it. *Goethe*

02 764.0 km (474.7 miles) to Santiago

RONCESVALLES – LARRASOAÑA

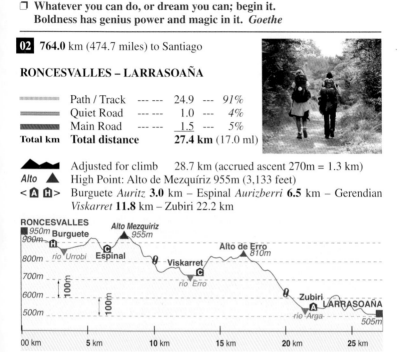

	Path / Track	--- ---	24.9	---	91%
	Quiet Road	--- ---	1.0	---	4%
	Main Road	--- ---	1.5	---	5%
Total km	**Total distance**		**27.4 km** (17.0 ml)		

Adjusted for climb   28.7 km (accrued ascent 270m = 1.3 km)
Alto ▲   High Point: Alto de Mezquíriz 955m (3,133 feet)
<🅰 🏠>   Burguete *Auritz* **3.0** km – Espinal *Aurizberri* **6.5** km – Gerendian
Viskarret **11.8** km – Zubiri 22.2 km

The Practical Path: Take care not to over extend yourself on these first few days of your journey. This second stage leads downhill across the fertile plain of the río Erro that flows southwards to join the río Ebro that we will meet in Logroño. The Alto de Erro forms the ridge that separates the Erro from the Arga river valleys. There is good woodland shade and plenty of drinking fonts along this delightful section of the camino 91% of which is natural pathways running more or less parallel to the N-135 which it crosses at several points. Close gates *cierren el portillo* as you pass through and be careful of the steep descent into Zubiri – the exposed rock makes it very slippery, particularly in wet weather.

– –

■ *Note: If you are feeling tired and it is getting late in the day when you reach Zubiri consider staying here and then Pamplona the following day. It is 5.5 km to the hostel in the Larrasoaña – allow 2 hours for a slower 'end of day pace.'* See p.19 for average costs of hotels within Spain. Prices shown are for comparison purposes only and liable to change.

■ *Decide each stage according to your individual level of fitness and pace. A good alternative for the next 3 stages is:* ❶ *Roncesvalles – Zubiri 22.2 km* ❷ *Zubiri – Pamplona 21.2 km* ❸ *Pamplona – Puente la Reina 24.1 km.*

– –

❏ **The Mystical Path:** Will you notice the *Pasos de Roldán?* The largest of these boulders is said to represent Roland's footsteps. Other legends have this melancholy place as scene of his failed attempt to summon Charlemagne to his rescue. Perhaps, in the silence of your own heart, you may still hear the wail of the Oliphant – symbol of that clarion call to spirit. Will you rest awhile at the old pilgrim well and hear a different horn break the woodland silence, a harsh and urgent note of warning from the fast moving traffic – a reminder to pilgrims that we travel now at a slower pace; one that allows awareness to expand.

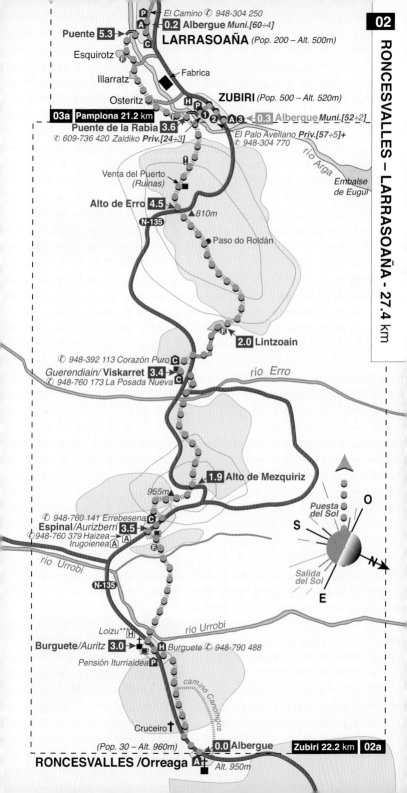

El Camino ℂ 948-304 250

0.2 **Albergue** *Muni.[60÷4]*

Puente **5.3**

LARRASOAÑA *(Pop. 200 – Alt. 500m)*

Esquirotz

Illarratz

Fabrica

Osteritz

ZUBIRI *(Pop. 500 – Alt. 520m)*

03a **Pamplona 21.2 km**

0.3 Albergue *Muni.[52÷2]*

Puente de la Rabia 3.6

ℂ 609-736 420 Zaldiko Priv.[24÷3]

El Palo Avellano *Priv.[57÷5]+*
ℂ 948-304 770

río Arga

Embalse de Eugui

Venta del Puerto
(Ruinas)

Alto de Erro 4.5

▲810m

N-135

Paso do Roldán

2.0 Lintzoain

ℂ 948-392 113 Corazón Puro

Guerendiain/ **Viskarret 3.4**

ℂ 948-760 173 La Posada Nueva

río Erro

1.9 Alto de Mezquiriz

▲955m

Puesta
del Sol

O

S

N

ℂ 948-760 141 Errebesena

Espinal/Aurizberri **3.5**

ℂ948-760 379 Haizea→
Irugoienea

Salida
del Sol

E

río Urrobi

N-135

río Urrobi

Loizu*** H

Burguete/Auritz **3.0** → H *Burguete* ℂ 948-790 488

Pensión Iturrialdea P

camino Canónigos

Cruceiro

(Pop. 30 – Alt. 960m) **0.0** **Albergue**

Zubiri 22.2 km **02a**

RONCESVALLES /Orreaga *Alt. 950m*

❏ **Personal Reflections:** "…a blister has already formed on my left foot to balance the bruise on my right shoulder. Was it arrogance or absent-mindedness that made me ignore the advice to stop and tighten my shoelaces and backpack – 60 seconds of adjustment would have prevented the friction and saved days of unnecessary suffering. I have become so conditioned to travelling in the fast lane, always trying to get somewhere in the shortest possible time, that I forget that the present moment contains the only time there is to actually act – all else is psychological time leading to stress… and unnecessary blisters."

0.0 km **Albergue Roncesvalles** leave the albergue and continue down the N-135 veering off right> at the camino information signboard **[0.2 km]** onto woodland path parallel to the main road (14th century pilgrim cross on far side) and re-join road at the outskirts of Burguete **[2.0 km]** and continue for **[0.8 km]** through suburbs to:

SANTIAGO DE COMPOSTELA 790

3.0 km **Burguete** *Auritz* a traditional Navarese village at the start of which we find •**Hotel Burguete** Hs** ℓ 948-790 005 *from* €49 where Ernest Hemingway used to stay (it still has the piano bearing his signature 25/07/1923). The sombre central square is overshadowed by the *Iglesia de San Nicolás de Barri (a Saint closely identified with the camino and protector of pilgrims; but alas no help to the wise women of the area that were classified as witches and burnt at the stake here in the 16th century.)* Café Frontón serves breakfast to the throng of pilgrims arriving from Roncesvalles (if there are queues consider going on to Espinal or Viskarret), public toilets adjoin. Other central accommodation •**Jaundeaburre** Hs* ℓ 948-760 078) •**Pensión Iturrialdea** P* ℓ 948-760 243 and on the far side of town the up-market •**Loizu** H*** ℓ 948-760 008 ind. rooms *from* €50.

100m past the square turn right> [!] down beside the *Banco Santander* and over the river Urrobi onto a wide farm track. At far end ford a small stream to enter a delightful woodland path to join a new asphalt track [F] left down into:

3.5 km **Espinal** *Aurizberri* traditional village with *Iglesia de San Bartolomé* (left) as we enter. [Note: 200m left •**Albergue** *Haizea* Hs ℓ948-760 399 with bunk beds €15 & •**Albergue** *Irugoienea* Priv.[18÷2]+ ℓ649 412 487]. Continue along main street café/bar *Tobi Onã* in the central square (right). Casa rural •**Errebesena** CR ℓ 948-760 141 [F] (left) and turn off <left **[0.3 km]** onto quiet road which merges into a track and continue for **[1.6 km]** up through young forestry plantation, climbing steps into mature beech woods at the high point 955m and finally down through open fields to:

1.9 km **Alto de Mezquiriz** (Alt. 930m) cross N-135 [!] by stone plaque to the Virgin and Child and continue on the path down steeply through beech woods running above and parallel to the main road (path has been resurfaced and can be slippery when wet so watch your step [!]). Cross the río Erro on stepping-stones before finally crossing the N-135 into:

3.4 km **Viscarret** *Guerendiain Bizkarreta* ancient hamlet and beginning of stage II of the Codex Calixtinus with the 13[th]c Church of St. Peter & popular •*Café Juan* •**La Posada Nueva** CR ℂ 948-760 173 and new (2013) pensión •**Corazón Puro** c/ San Pedro ℂ948 392 113 B&B+dinner in double room €18x2= 36 (5 rooms). On leaving village there is a deceptively good shop (left) after which turn <left onto path and <left again where path meets road through dense woodland and after [**1.2** km] cross over N-135 again and continue for [**0.8** km] into:

2.0 km **Lintzoain** pass pelota court [F] (right) and climb steep narrow defile (recently concreted) into dense mixed woodland. This delightful shaded woodland path continues along a ridge and the *Pasos de Roldán* until we meet:

4.5 km **Alto de Erro** (Alt. 810m) crossover N-135 to camino information signboard (left) and into woodlands passing a former pilgrim inn *Venta del Puerto* (now a ruin and cattle shelter) and descend steep rock outcrop [!] (Dangerous in wet weather) to:

3.6 km **Puente de la Rabia** medieval bridge over the Río Arga *so called because of the legend that any animal led 3 times around the central arch would be cured of rabies. This is also the likely site of a former leprosarium. Chapels and hospices dedicated to San Lazarus were often located at the entrance or exit to towns along the way.* We will cross the river Arga many times over the next few days until we finally leave it at Puente la Reina.

If you are feeling strong *fuerte* continue to the albergue in Larrasoaña (5.6 km) further on. The busy N-135 bypasses this latter historic village which is quieter and more in keeping with the spirit of the camino. This would also allow you more time the following day to explore the historic city of Pamplona before proceeding, perhaps, to Cizur Menor (see next stages). If you are feeling tired or it is late in the day then turn right> over the bridge into the industrial town of:

Zubiri •**Albergue ❶** *Zaldiko Priv.[24÷3]*+ ℂ 609-736 420 private hostel in terraced brick house between the bridge and church. 24 beds in 3 rooms €10 and all facilities + small patio (no kitchen) but nearby bar with pilgrim menú. Continue past the church and turn right> on main road to •**Albergue ❷** *El palo de avellano Priv.[40÷5]*+ ℂ 948 304 770 €15 incl. also doubles €58 and just beyond •**Albergue ❸** *Escuela Muni.[48÷2]* ℂ 628 324 186 on the left 100m [300m from Puente de Rabia]. Basic municipal hostel €8 on the N-135 in a former school building.

Albergue ❶ *Zaldiko*

Albergue ❸ *Escuela*

ZUBIRI: Industrial town (Pop: 400 – alt. 530m) serves the adjacent Magna plant *Magnesitas de Navarra* straddling the N-135. Facilities include grocery shop, bank and panadería centred around the parish Church of St. Stephen *San Esteban* with [F]. Other accommodation: by the bridge •**Zubiaren Etxea** P ℂ 948-304 293 opp. albergue Zaldiko •**Usoa** P* ℂ 948-304 306) and on the main road •**Zubiri** Hs ℂ 948-304 329 and •**Goika** P* ℂ 948-304 067 also pension •**Sna. Bento Barri** ℂ 636134781.

From the medieval bridge *Puente de la Rabia* continue up concrete path [F] (left) and continue over a stream to climb above the bleak Magnesitas industrial complex (down to your right) and through the hamlets of Ostériz, Ilarratz and Esquirroz [F] and covered rest area) and along the Arga river valley to:

5.3 km **Puente Larrasoaña** medieval bridge. (*If you stayed the night in Zubiri and do not plan to visit this historic pilgrim village keep straight on for Pamplona*). Turn right> over the bridge and past the 13ᵗʰ Century Church of San Nicolás and veer <left into the village square with town hall and:

0.2 km **Larrasoaña** •Albergue *Muni.[60÷4]* Ⓒ 605 505 489 popular municipal hostel with 60 places €6 (open all year) with 28 beds in one dormitory

and remainder on mattresses *colchones* in small rooms upstairs and additional space in a converted nearby outbuilding that is brought into service during busy periods. The basic facilities include a small open patio at rear. The extensive church porch also provides a 'floor and roof' in times of need. A warm welcome can be expected from the energetic mayor a true friend of the Way of St. James *amigo del Camino de Santiago*. I walked the way with him and know he has first-hand experience of the needs of fellow pilgrims.

Albergue Larrasoaña

Other accommodation: Pensión •El Camino P* Ⓒ 948-304 250 at the far end of the village in c/San Nicolás, 16 (350m past the main square) also serves as a popular pilgrim meeting point with café-bar and restaurant Casa Salgado serving pilgrim *menú* and breakfast from 07:00. At the other end of town are •El Peregrino P* Ⓒ 948-304 554 and •Bidea P* Ⓒ 948-304 288 c/San Nicolás, 100. Casa Elita, a small food shop is also located in this area.

LARRASOAÑA: This quaint town (Population 200 – Alt. 500m) has retained its close links with the pilgrim's Way. An important pilgrim halt in medieval times with 2 pilgrim hospitals and a monastery (no longer evident) it achieved the status of *Villa Franca* (a settlement of pilgrims arriving from France). Today it continues to welcome pilgrims and provide hospitality in its various hostelries. The town is full of Jacobean symbols and armorial shields on its traditional stone buildings. Soak up the tranquillity before you hit bustle of Pamplona!

Pension *El Camino* & pilgrim Bar

Pension *El Peregrino*

REFLECTIONS: *"Worrying is praying for what you don't want."* Pilgrim
book in Zubiri.

❏ **I am not a human being on a spiritual journey.**
I am spiritual being on a human journey. *Spiritual maxim*

03 **736.6** km (457.7 miles) to Santiago

LARRASOAÑA – CIZUR MENOR

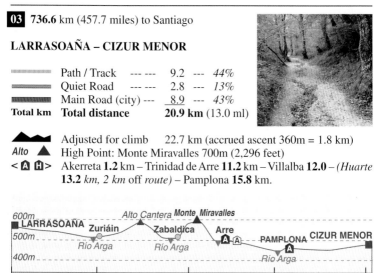

▨▨▨ Path / Track	--- ---	9.2 ---	*44%*
▬▬▬ Quiet Road	--- ---	2.8 ---	*13%*
▨▨▨ Main Road (city)	---	8.9 ---	*43%*
Total km **Total distance**		**20.9 km** (13.0 ml)	

◣ Adjusted for climb   22.7 km (accrued ascent 360m = 1.8 km)
Alto ▲ High Point: Monte Miravalles 700m (2,296 feet)
< ▣ ▣ > Akerreta **1.2** km – Trinidad de Arre **11.2** km – Villalba **12.0** – *(Huarte* **13.2** *km, 2 km* off *route)* – Pamplona **15.8** km.

The Practical Path: The first half of this section is a tranquil walk crisscrossing the río Arga. The latter half is along busy main roads leading into and through the city of Pamplona. There is plenty of shade along the tree-lined riverbanks and a number of drinking fonts along the way. Be prepared for the noise and bustle of city life after the relative calm of the camino. City folk are forever in a rush, so tread warily amongst the traffic and watch your wallet. Pilgrims have reported items stolen from the suburbs of Trinidad de Arre onwards – 'Trust in God, but tether your camel,' feels like balanced advice. Pamplona is also a beautiful city and the camino runs through its historic heart – so you can soak up some of the lively atmosphere and its major buildings by just walking the waymarked route. Many pilgrims make an overnight stop here so they can visit the cathedral, museums and art galleries and explore Pamplona's medieval streets and sample some of its famous cafés and tapas bars.

❏ **The Mystical Path:** Will you notice the ancient stone cross with the delicate relief of St. James as pilgrim atop the scallop shell? It stands sentinel over the magnificent medieval bridge, gateway to this historic city. The sightless eyes have watched countless thousands of pilgrims wend their wary way over these self-same arches. And what of the invisible eye that sees beyond space and time, gateway to the inner realm of spirit. One path is full of distraction, distortion and decay. The other leads to the real world where only truth is visible. Which world you see depends on which you are looking for.

❏ **Personal Reflections:** *"... So many contrasting sensations – the quiet of the countryside, the bustle of the city, the warmth of the sun, the cool of the rain, the perfume of the wild flowers, the acrid smell of burning rubbish, the bright red of the ubiquitous poppy, the dull grey of asphalt road. I sit supported by my rucksack and watch the wild grasses and wheat stalks swaying in the wind. My lunch is laid out before me like a royal feast with local cheese and freshly baked bread acquired from a travelling baker's van. I feel an overwhelming sense of*

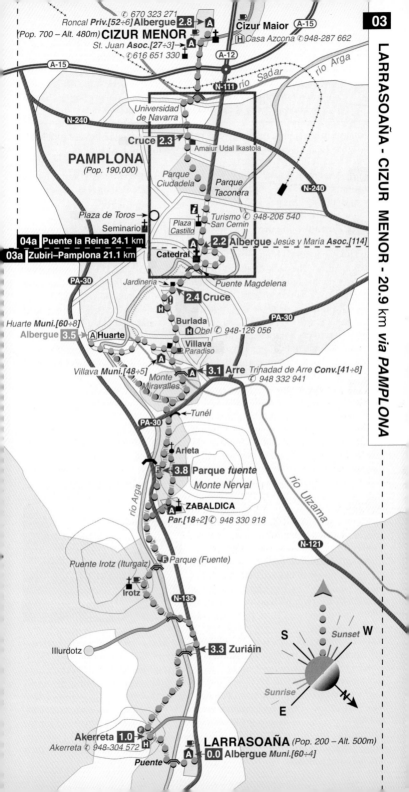

*well-being and, somewhat self-consciously, say out loud that beautiful grace
with which to bless the richness of this day and my simple meal:*

> *The silver rain, the shining sun, the fields were scarlet poppies run
> And all the ripples in the wheat are in the food that I do eat
> So when I sit for every meal and say a grace, I always feel
> That I am eating rain and sun and fields were scarlet poppies run.*

If you have been staying in Larrasoaña return to the medieval **bridge [0.2 km]**:
Turn right> to climb up to the tranquil hilltop **village [0.8 km]** of:

1.0 km Akerreta •Hotel ©948-304 572 beautifully restored Basque house
with rooms from €80. Continue downhill through open country to re-join the
river Arga before crossing into:

3.3 km Zuriáin along the N-135 turning <**left [0.6 km]** (signposted Illurdotz).
Re-cross the river **Arga [0.3 km]** and continue right> between group of houses
(dogs) and abandoned buildings climbing up a narrow quarry path overlooking
the Arga valley. The path drops down through **Irotz** •*Café* and across the river
again over the medieval stone bridge *Puente de Iturgaiz / Irotz* **[1.6 km]** turning
<left along river bank rest area [F] [left] to **Zabaldika** option [right] **[0.7 km]**.
Option Zabaldika ● ● ● ● Cross the N-135 uo to the village **[0.3 km]**
•Albergue *Par.[18÷2]* © 948 330 918 parish hostel 18 beds and communal
meals with prayers *donativo* adj. the 13[th]C *iglesia de San Esteban*. Return to the
N-135 or take the path along *Monte Narval* to rejoin the main route at Arleta.
For the main route continue under the N-135 to picnic site and **park [0.8** km].

3.8 km Parque*fuente* [F] Take the steep path up the side of *Monte Narval* to
Arleta and continue to **underpass [2.1 km]** to climb around the side of pine-
covered *Monte Miravalles* Alto 495m **[0.4 km]** and option 1 [left] to Huarte.
Option Huarte ● ● ● ● first of 2 options to the hostel at Huarte (details next
panel). Reconnect with the main route via river at the Puente de la Magdalena.
For the main route join a disused road that drops down to the magnificent
medieval bridge over the río Ulzama (tributary of the Arga) just above a weir
and here we enter the suburbs of Pamplona in **Villava [0.8** km]:

3.1 km Trinidad de Arre •**Albergue**
Hermanos Maristas **Conv.[34÷4]** © 948
332 941 located behind the basilica church
Convento de la Trinidad adj. bridge.
Check-in at front reception – no urgency,
a pilgrim hospital has existed here since
the 11th century! 34 beds €8 in this quiet
location by the river with peaceful gardens.
Shops and restaurants close by in Villava.

Note: *for the next 9.7 km (until you reach Cizur Menor on the western outskirts)
the camino winds through the busy city of Pamplona (population 190,000) a
vibrant university city built around the historical old town at its centre. The
recommended route will bring you past most of the main sites and is generally
well waymarked but you need to be extra vigilant for the yellow arrows which
now appear on every conceivable surface such as lampposts and pavements
but have to compete with many other signs. You also need to watch out for the
fast moving traffic and your belongings – petty theft has always been a problem
in our unequal society. Medieval pilgrims were sometimes murdered for their
satchels and sandals!*

Turn <left over the bridge at Arre and continue along Calle Mayor in Villava to the Town Hall [**0.5** km] *Casa Consistorial* (flags) and •*Café Paradiso*. 300m Left is the modern hostel •**Albergue** *Villava Muni.[48÷5]* ℂ 948 331 971 on c/ Pedro de Atarrabia €10 beside the rio Ulzama:

Detour Huarte [**3.5** km] ● ● ● ●
Secondary access to the modern hostel at Huarte opposite *Café Paradiso*, turn left past the Frontón and continue s/o over pedestrian bridge (río Ulzama) by Plastico Brello. Veer right and join the main road that runs along the Río Arga. Don't cross the road bridge but turn left (sign Uharte) and follow the river into Huarte up the wide main street to Plaza San Juan. •**Albergue Huarte** *Muni.[60÷8]* located behind the

Albergue Huarte

church (right hand side of main street) municipal hostel ℂ 948-334 413. Open all year with 60 beds (8 rooms) and all modern facilities €10. Return to Villava or continue along the river to rejoin main route at Puente Magdalena.

Continue s/o through the busy suburbs of **Burlada** for [**1.9** km] with various modern hotels and cafés, •**Obelix P*** ℂ 948-126 056 •**La Buhardilla** Hs ℂ 948-382 872 •**Hotel Villava** H*** ℂ 948-333 676. Watch out [!] for waymarks veering diagonally right> by Banco Pastor into C/Larrainzar (*neumaticos* sign) up to main road (traffic lights) with garden centre

2.4 km **Cruce** Cross over to garden centre *Jardineria Arvena*.

For an **alternative road route** turn <left and immediately right> up into Av. de la Baja Navarra passing the huge cross and edifice of the Seminario Diocesano (whose student accommodation is sometime made available to pilgrims during vacations) and turn right> into and through Parque de la Media Luna to re-join the recommended route at the cathedral which is clearly visible at this stage.

For the **recommended route** veer right> and make your way over the pedestrian crossing by garden centre turning <left into c/ Burlada, a quiet road that runs parallel to the river Arga and crosses over it at the evocative medieval bridge ❶ *Puente de la Magdalena XII[th]C* [**1.4** km] a traditional symbol of the camino. [*Note:* Turn left over bridge for 200m to •**Albergue** ❶ *Casa Paderborn [26÷5]* ℂ 948 211 712 located by the river at Playa de Caparroso, 6 and operated by a German confraternity. 26 places in 5 rooms all facilities €4.

Albergue ❶ Casa Paderborn

To proceed directly to the city centre veer right> over bridge, cross the tree-lined Playa Caparroso veering right> around the old city walls entering this historic city over the drawbridge and the splendid ❷ *Portal de Zumalacárregi* [**0.5** km] also called Portal de Francia – a reminder that Pamplona has always opened its doors to pilgrims coming from France since mediaeval times. (Note: immediately inside the city walls there is an option to turn up sharp <left along the ramparts and viewpoint and veer right into the shaded square Plaza San

José to ❸ *Cathedral of Santa María la Real*. An austere Gothic structure with a neoclassical façade. If you are staying the night in the adjacent albergue you can leave your backpack there and return to visit the interior which is much more satisfying than the stark edifice. The 15[th]C alabaster mausoleum of Carlos *El Noble* and his wife Leonor adorns the main nave but pride of place is the beautiful south door ❹ *puerta preciosa* ascribed to Master Esteban who also carved the south door *Puerta de las Platerias* in Santiago Cathedral. The beautiful cloisters, with their fine filigree stonework (see photo above), adjoin the diocesan museum (site of the original Roman citadel). Pamplona's new pilgrim hostel is only 100m down off calle Curia:

The main route (from Portal de Francia) continues s/o into calle Carmen (*antiguo Rua de los Peregrinos*). Here at the start (N°31) is **Albergue** ❷ *Ibarrola Priv. [20÷1]* © 948 223 332 opened in 2012 with its ultra modern interior. €18 incl. Proceed to the cross of 5 roads **[0.2 km]**. To continue through the city centre turn right into c/ de Mercederes or turn <left into c/Curia to visit the cathedral and the main pilgrim hostel **[0.1 km]** passing the pilgrim equipment and map shop *Caminoteca* at N° 15 © 948-210 316.

2.2 km Pamplona *Centro* **Albergue** ❸ *Jesús y María Asoc.[114÷2]* © 948 222 644 part of the austere 17[th]C Jesuit church of *Jesús y María* on c/Compañía (closed Dec, Jan & during festival in July). 114 beds in cubicles €7, built into the side naves with all modern facilities. Good location from which to explore the old town.

Pamplona Albergue ❸ *Jesús y María*

Other hostels (€15+ incl.): •**Hemingway** c/Amaya,26 © 948-983 884. •**Aloha** c/Sangüesa,2 © 648-289 403. •**Xarma** Av. Baja Navarra © 948- 046 449. ❏ **Other Accommodation:** © **Spain +34.** *Turismo* Plaza San Francisco, c/ Eslava, 1 © 848 420 420. In the old city around San Saturnino is a wide selection of small and inexpensive hotels and pensions which includes:
❏ *Hotels:* •**Lambertini** P[*] c/Mercadore, 17 © 948-210 303 •**La Viña** P c/ Jarauta, 8 © 948-213 250 •**Pensión Eslava** P[*] c/Eslava, 13 © 948-221 558 •**Escaray** P c/Nueva, 24 © 948-227 825 •**Pensión Otano** P[**] c/ San Nicolás, 5 © 948-227 036 •**San Nicolás** P[*] c/ San Nicolás, 13 © 948-221 319 •**Don Lluis** Hs c/ San Nicolás, 24 © 948-210 499 •**Aralar** Hs c/ San Nicolás12 © 948-221 116 •**La Montañesa** P[*] c/San Gregorio, 2 © 948-224 380 •**Dionisio** P[*] c/San Gregorio, 5 © 948-224 380 At the far end of c/Mayor (behind the Convento Recoletas) is •**Hotel Eslava** Hr[**] overlooking the tiny *Plaza Virgen de la O* which forms part of the old city walls and leads directly into the spacious Parque Traconera where we find (in the top price bracket) the 4 star •**Iruña Palace** *Tres Reyes* © 948-226 600 and back on Plaza del Castillo the newly refurbished 5 star •**La Perla** [*****]© 948- 223 000 (Hemingway used to stay here).

Calle San Nicolás

During the hectic summer months additional pilgrim accommodation *may* be available at: •**San Saturnino** (city centre). •**Catholic Scouts** (Puente de la Magdalena). •**Seminario Diocesano** Av. de la Baja Navarra •**Ikastola Aimur** sports hall at c/Fuente del Hierro. •**Juvenil** *youth hostel* c/Goroabe, 36.

Pamplona Detours: [1] If you are a Hemingway *aficianado* take a trip down the Paseo Ernest Hemingway to a statue of the author outside the bullring *plaza de Toros*. His novel 'The Sun Also Rises' published in 1926 made *Sanfermines* popular among foreigners so that today it has become one of the best-known fiestas in Spain. Records suggest the festival was started in the 13th century but may have pre-Roman origins and some legends suggest that San Fermín himself was martyred by being dragged

San Fermin – Souvenir shop

by bulls thorough the streets. Alcohol is probably the biggest cause of injury and death today despite rule 6 that states, 'it is not allowed to enter the route in a state of drunkenness or under the effects of drugs'. Return via *calle Estafeta* the famous street through which the bulls run as part of this world-renowned *Encierro* that takes place during San Fermín from July 6th to 14th when the city goes wild, beds are impossible to find and everything costs double.

Detour [2] just off the calle Estafeta is Pamplona's main square *Plaza del Castillo*, a huge open space with covered arcades shading the shops, bars and cafés. Don't miss the magnificent and sumptuous *interior* of the art deco café Iruña. Bar Txoko (top corner - gets the last of the evening sun) have splendid tapas. From the square it is a short walk to the Romanesque Church of St. Nicholas situated half way down the

Plaza del Castillo

bustling and evocative *c/San Nicolás* full of inexpensive *pensiónes* and *tapas bars* or head back to the camino via c/Chapitela into the Plaza Consistorial with the splendid ornamental façade of the town hall dominating the square.

Detour [3] If you want to visit the *Museo de Navarra* turn down right behind the town hall ❺ into c/Santo Domingo and at the far end is the classical facade of the medieval pilgrim hospital, now the Navarrese museum with Roman artefacts from the 1st century. At the start of c/Mayor we arrive at the geographical centre of Pamplona at ❻ San Saturnino a 13th century fortified church also called San Cernín and formerly the main pilgrim hostel on the upper floors. If you are staying in Pamplona this is a good place to take your bearings. Just in front of the church (in the paving slabs) is a plaque marking the well from which San Saturnino baptised the first Christians in

Pamplona Town Hall ❺

the city. The helpful tourist office is nearby (200m) down c/Campana in Plaza de San Francisco at the corner of c/Eslava (see city plan).

PAMPLONA with an ever-expanding population (currently around 200,000) is a vibrant university city that retains its close historical connections with the camino and whose patron Saint is San Fermín. The Roman general Pompaelo reputedly founded the city in the first century B.C. Its long and dramatic history has been closely linked with pilgrims, many of who were enticed to settle in the city under special status. This migration often created petty jealousies between the native inhabitants and the favoured settlers, resulting in the development of separate districts, which later became fortified as open hostilities raged between the inhabitants and their differing cultures. In 1423 King Carlos conceded the Privilege of the Union,

Pamplona Cathedral
Calle Curia *(pilgrim hostel right)*

which extended the special status to all parts of the city and began an era of cooperation. Several other towns and cities along the Way such as at Estella (stage 5) followed a similar pattern of agreement and development. Pamplona marks the beginning of stage III of the Codex Calixtinus.

You could easily spend a day here exploring the many interesting monuments and museums, or… from the cathedral / pilgrim hostel continue back down the c/Curia (opposite the entrance to the cathedral) which leads into c/Mercaderes and up past the Iglesia San Saturnino into the narrow c/Mayor which opens out into the Plaza Recoletas (right) and ❼ Iglesia de San Lorenzo (left) with its chapel to the patron saint of Pamplona, San Fermín.

Museo Diocesano

Here we cross over the busy street into c/Bosquecillo alongside the Parque de la Taconera (right). At the busy junction of Av. de Pio XII and Av. del Ejército veer <left diagonally over the junction (pedestrian crossings) and through the relative calm of the park that surrounds the historic star-shaped citadel ❽ *ciudadela* (left). Halfway round the park watch out for arrows that veer off right> over the c/Vuelta del Castillo into c/Fuente del Hierro •**Fuente del Hierro** P* ✆ 948-178 270 and follow this wide tree-lined modern thoroughfare to:

2.3 km **Cruce** Junction of c/Fuente del Hierro with c/de Iturrama. The school campus of Amaiur Udal Ikastola (right) makes its sports hall available for groups and possibly individual pilgrims to sleep in during the summer months. For additional hotels in this modern area of Iturrama veer right off the main camino and follow the connecting road for 300m that curves around between 2 playgrounds and links up with Av. Pio XII (the Clinica Universitaria and hotel Blanca are visible at this next junction). There are a number of small *pensiónes* in this city area including •**Payvi II & Payvi III** P* ✆ 948-278 508 Av. Pío XII, 30 (adjoining petrol station) and •**Pasadena** P* ✆ 948-177 650 Av. Pío XII, 32.

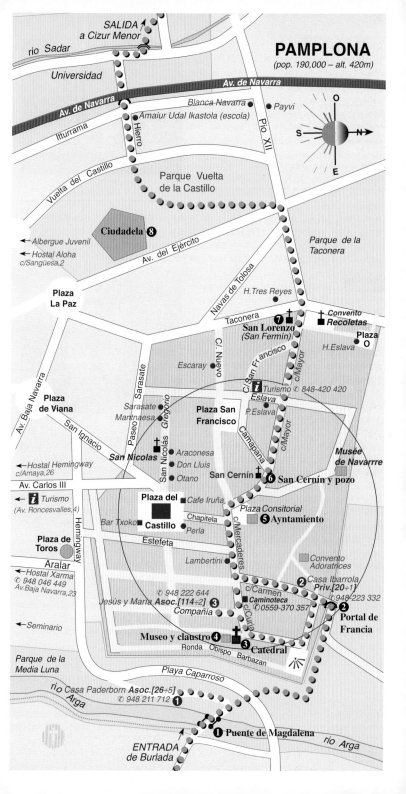

Continuing on from Fuente del Hierro-Iturrama roundabout, pass under the busy Av. de Navarra ring road along the university campus. Here on the left [0.7 km] we can receive 'accreditation' from the university by having our credenciales stamped by the porter. Continue to the roundabout veering right> along main road and <left across the stone bridge over the Río Sadar [0.3 km]. Continue straight on over the Río Elorz [0.4 km] the railway line and the A-15 autopista and uphill along the main road for [1.4 km]

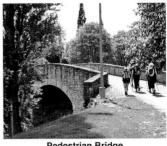

Pedestrian Bridge
Río Sadar

into Cizur Menor and the church of St. John the Baptist (left) and: •**Albergue** ❷ *Sanjuanista Priv.[27÷3]* run by the Knights of St. John of Malta ✆ 616 651 330 adjoining the first church on the left as you enter the town. Open April to September with 27 beds €4 (5 rooms) and basic facilities.

2.8 km Cizur Menor crossroads.
•**Albergue** ❶ *Roncal Priv.[50÷5]* Maribel Roncal ✆ 670 323 271 located just up from the crossroads (below the church of San Miguel). Run by the dedicated Roncal family with 50 beds €10 (5 rooms) with all facilities including a garden offering tranquillity – very popular and fills quickly during the summer season open all year except Nov. (see photo right).

Note: If the albergues are full your options are [a] retrace your steps and find accommodation in Pamplona or its suburbs (a local bus service connects from here to the city centre). [b] Head over to Cizur Maior to the popular Hotel Casa Azcona Av. Belascoaín ✆ 948 28 76 62 or the modern 4 star Marriott hotel •**AC Zizur Mayor** ✆ 948-287 119 or the more modest •**Hostal Nekea** ✆ 948-185 044 Travesia San Francisco, 1 (Directions: head uphill past the church and take the flyover (autopista) [1.0 km] into the busy modern suburb of Cizur Maior. From this point the quickest way back onto the camino is to take the road to Galar. Or [c] continue on to the next albergue in Zariquiegui 6.2 km.

Cizur Menor an affluent dormitory town of Pamplona. It was formerly a commandery of the Order of St. John of Jerusalem and also provided a pilgrim hospice dedicated to Our Lady of Forgiveness *Nuestra Señora del Perdón*, who was, and remains, much venerated in this area. Occupying an elevated site is the 12th century Romanesque church dedicated to the archangel Saint Michael *Iglesia de San Miguel Arcángel*. There are several restaurants (often closed in during week days) a bar and a chemist.

REFLECTIONS: *"The camino already feels like a real pilgrimage and has developed a deeper significance than when I began. I am stronger and have more courage than I thought. I have already been given many blessings and gifts..."* Notes from an Australian pilgrim recorded in the Pamplona albergue.

❐ **Be the change you want to see in the world.** *Mahatma Gandhi*

04 **715.7** km (444.7 miles) to Santiago

CIZUR MENOR - PUENTE LA REINA

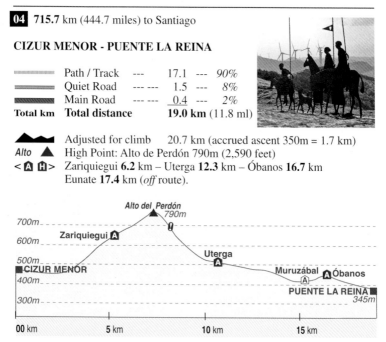

▥▥▥▥	Path / Track	---	17.1 ---	90%
▬▬▬	Quiet Road	--- ---	1.5 ---	8%
▨▨▨	Main Road	--- ---	0.4 ---	2%
Total km	**Total distance**		**19.0 km** (11.8 ml)	

◣◤▲ Adjusted for climb 20.7 km (accrued ascent 350m = 1.7 km)
Alto ▲ High Point: Alto de Perdón 790m (2,590 feet)
<🅰 🇭> Zariquiegui **6.2** km – Uterga **12.3** km – Óbanos **16.7** km
Eunate **17.4** km (*off* route).

```
                          Alto del Perdón
                              ▲ 790m
700m _ _ _ _ _ _ _ _ _ _ _ _ ╱╲ _ _ _ _ _ _ _ _ _ _ _ _ _ _
                        Zariquiegui 🅰  🎏
600m _ _ _ _ _ _ _ _ _ _ _ ╱ _ _ _ ╲ _ _ _ _ _ _ _ _ _ _ _
                       ╱              ╲   Uterga
500m _ _ _ _ _ _ _ _ ╱ _ _ _ _ _ _ _ _ ╲_ 🅰 _ _ _ _ _ _ _ _
    ■CIZUR MENOR ╱                         ╲  Muruzábal 🅰 Óbanos
400m _ _ _ _ _╱_ _ _ _ _ _ _ _ _ _ _ _ _ _ ╲_ _(🅰)_ _🅰_ _ _
   ╱                                           ╲ PUENTE LA REINA■
300m _ _ _ _ _ _ _ _ _ _ _ _ _ _ _ _ _ _ _ _ _ _ _ _ _ _ 345m

00 km        5 km           10 km          15 km
```

The Practical Path: A short stage (*add 5.1 km from Pamplona centre*) with few trees and therefore little shade. Ahead of us lie a range of hills and we have a steep climb up to pass through the middle of the wind turbines *parque ecológico* visible on the skyline ahead at the Hill of Forgiveness *Alto del Perdón.* As we ascend there are wonderful views back over Pamplona and to the south the conical peak of *Higa* at Monreal is clearly visible, behind which are the Sierra de Leyre and the Somport Pass through which the *Camino Aragonés* joins the route at Eunate. As we crest the summit the view west over the Arga valley opens up with the villages we pass through now visible ahead. Be careful on the steep descent – it is easy to twist an ankle on the loose boulders.

❐ **The Mystical Path:** Will you see the beehives? Each home to thousands of bees that collect nectar from the almond blossom and other flowering trees and plants that grace this fertile plain in the springtime. In the winter all is laid bare and the hives lie dormant waiting a time of renewal. Each season dresses the physical landscape in its different hues – what is the season of your *inner* landscape? Is it time to sow new seeds, a time of growth, of harvest or a time of reflection in the deep rich soil of the soul? The seasons turn in an endless cycle of life. After the dark of the winter solstice comes the light of mid summer day and in between these high and low points are the spring and autumn equinoxes when light and dark are perfectly balanced. Have we got the balance right in our life between the busy-ness of the ego and the being-ness of spirit?

❐ **Personal Reflections:** *"... I saw her ahead on the road to Cizur Menor, a diminutive figure walking alone into the dusk. We were both making for the hostel unknowing that Maribel Roncal had closed it that year to take a well-earned rest. Dusk turned to nightfall as we contemplated our options. She was a young mendicant carrying no money and accepting only whatever charity*

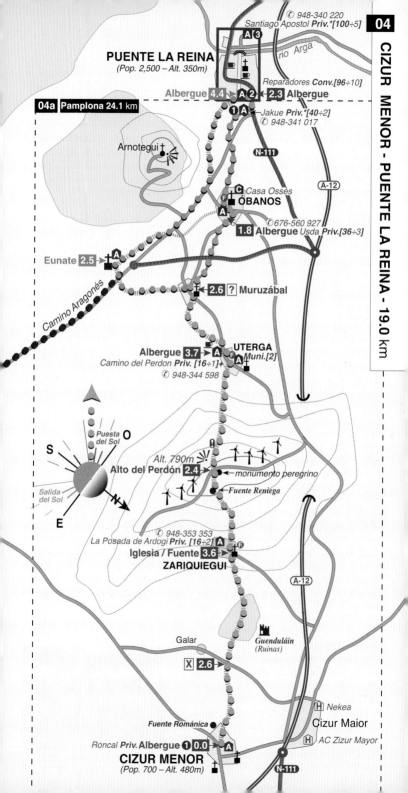

04

© 948-340 220
Santiago Apostol Priv.*[100÷5]

PUENTE LA REINA
(Pop. 2,500 – Alt. 350m)

🅐 3

río Arga

Reparadores Conv.[96÷10]

Albergue 4.4 → 🅐 2 · 2.3 Albergue

04a **Pamplona 24.1 km**

1 🅐 → Jakue Priv.*[40÷2]
© 948-341 017

N-111

Arnotegui †

🄲 Casa Ossès
📻 ÓBANOS
🅐

A-12

© 676-560 927 Albergue Usda Priv.[36÷3]
1.8 Albergue

Eunate 2.5 † 🅐

Camino Aragonés

† 2.6 ? Muruzábal

Albergue 3.7 → 🅐 UTERGA
Camino del Perdon Priv. [16÷1] † Muni.[2]
© 948-344 598

O *Puesta del Sol*

S

Salida del Sol

E

Alt. 790m
Alto del Perdón 2.4
→ monumento peregrino
Fuente Reniega

© 948-353 353
La Posada de Ardogi Priv. [16÷2] 🅐
Iglesia / Fuente 3.6
ZARIQUIEGUI

A-12

Galar

Guenduláin
(Ruinas)

X 2.6

🄷 Nekea

Cizur Maior

🄷 AC Zizur Mayor

Fuente Románica

Roncal Priv. Albergue 1 0.0 🅐
CIZUR MENOR
(Pop. 700 – Alt. 480m) †

N-111

she received along the way. She accepted a simple pilgrim meal at the bar but refused to take any emergency cash. I was the one imprisoned by my fears – my wallet thick with euros and credit cards. She was free, fearless and with an unshakable belief in the goodness of her fellow human beings. Her courage and trust leave me deeply humbled and with a profound sense of unease at my own doubts and limitations…"

0.0 km **Cizur Menor** from albergue ❶ turn right> at the crossroads (if coming from Pamplona continue s/o) and veer right> opposite medieval well, down past pelota court [F] and s/o through modern housing estate to a dirt road which threads its way all the way up to the village of Zariquiegui (below the wind farm on the horizon). The path winds through open arable fields to:

2.6 km **Cruce** cross asphalt road to Galar visible on a knoll up to the left. (*It was over this very ground that Charlemagne's Christian forces defeated Aigolando's Muslim army in the 8th century. Today a more peaceful spot is hard to imagine as we leave the city behind us*). Further on the path crosses a stream as we begin a gentle climb (bypassing the ruins of Guenduláin palace in the woods to the right – visible once we have cleared the trees) to:

3.6 km **Zariquiegui** prominent Church of Saint Andrew *San Andrés* with Romanesque doorway and [F]. 50m up the street opposite •**Albergue** *Priv. [16÷2]* © 948-353 353 private hostel with 16 beds €11 incl. with small bar / basic restaurant and small grocery store. Continue up steeply towards the wind turbines and just below the ridge is the ancient spring (dry) *Gambellacos* [2.2 km]. *Fuente Reniega (renouncement). A medieval pilgrim reached this spot dying of thirst. The devil, disguised as a pilgrim, offered to show him a spring if he would only renounce God. The pilgrim refused and St. James himself miraculously appeared revealing the spring and quenching his thirst with water in a scallop shell. Today, the well is usually dry (a sign, perhaps, of the spiritual aridity of our times) but we can look back over Pamplona and the Pyrenees beyond them and reflect on our own journey to this point. The hum of the wind generators above remind of us the possibilities of creating another, more sustainable future.* A final climb [0.2 km] and we reach the summit:

2.4 km **Alto del Perdón** (altitude 790m) featuring a wrought iron representation of medieval pilgrims, heads bent to the west wind. An information board gives a brief outline of this area and the ecological project (renewable energy) it fosters. Looking ahead are the villages we will pass through spread out below lining the route westwards. The conical peak of Monte Arnotegui with hermitage atop is situated overlooking Puente de la Reina and is just visible ahead on the horizon. Descend [!] carefully over the loose stones and through the scrubland to the rich red earth, vineyards and almond trees below. Here the path winds along a delightful ridge running parallel to a quiet country road that you join at:

3.7 km **Uterga** •**Albergue** ❶ *Muni.[2÷1]+* opposite the fountain [F] is a basic municipal hostel in the main square. Open all year with 1 bunk bed for 2 with floor space (supposedly) for 2 more in 1 very small room with shower & toilet off. No kitchen or other space but well maintained (keep it that way if you are staying). •**Albergue** ❷ *Camino del Perdón Priv.[16÷1]+* (Ana Calvo © 948-344 598 modern private hostel also on c/Mayor and

Uterga – Albergue ❷

open all year with 16 beds €10 + private rooms. Lounge area, no kitchen but bar & restaurant with pilgrim menu. *[Next Albergue: Óbanos – 4.4 km].* If all else fails, the Gothic parish church has a wide porch and the [F] in the centre offers pure fresh water (you might want to empty out the chemical residue from the water of Pamplona and refill here). The quiet country road continues to:

2.6 km **Muruzábal** Church of St. Stephen *San Esteban* with statue of St. James and [F] in the main square with bar and chemist.

Detour ● ● ● ● ● *Eunate (recommended):* This short detour will add 2.8 km to the direct route (around 1 hour including brief stop at Eunate). Directions: at the entrance to the village (opposite the town hall) turn <left past the church and around the back of the houses where the road turns down <left (Eunate is now visible ahead) onto a wide farm track passing a small *Ermita* before crossing the main road onto a tree-lined avenue to **Eunate church.** The beautiful 12th century Romanesque Church of Santa María de Eunate (see photograph below) is one of the jewels of the camino.

2.5 km Eunate Church and Hostel. The church has been linked with the Knights Templar who long defended the pilgrim on the route to Santiago. There is a striking similarity with the church at Torres del Rio (see next stage) with its octagonal form, modelled on the Holy Sepulchre in Jerusalem, and its unadorned interior, a feature also associated with the Knights. But, uniquely, Eunate has a splendid freestanding outer porch with delicate twin pillars that surrounds the church. (Closed on Mondays, but its setting and external cloister is still worth the visit). It has been suggested that Eunate was also a burial place for pilgrims who had succumbed to the gruelling physical hardships experienced along the route. Standing on its own in the simple beauty of the countryside it evokes a powerful reminder of our own journey back to our spiritual source and Home. Guardians *Mariluz* and *Jan* lovingly tend the church and provide taped background Gregorian chant and a pilgrim stamp from their private house adjoining that also acts as a traditional pilgrim refuge •**Albergue** *Priv.[8]* – small private hostel with basic facilities and accommodation for around 8 pilgrims. Continue to Puente la

Reina past the albergue through the picnic site to the main road [1.0 km]. *(An alternative here is to take the road to Óbanos, a distance of 1.1 km from this point, which is clearly visible up ahead and join the waymarked camino from there)* – or turn <left and continue past the road to Arnotegui and turn <left onto track [1.5 km] veering off right [1.6 km] over river to central Albergue [0.3 km]. Total distance from Eunate for both options is 4.4 km.

4.4 km **Puente la Reina - Central Albergue** ❷

For the direct route to Óbanos from Muruzábal continue along the main road turning right> as you leave the village to follow the path parallel to the secondary road, under the new bypass, to the village of Óbanos clearly visible on the pronounced rise ahead of you. Make your way through its sleepy winding streets resplendent with their armorial crests emblazoned in the stone facades for to:

1.8 km **Óbanos Plaza and Albergue** opposite the imposing parish church **[F]** and shaded cloister in this historic village. Here the noblemen of Navarre met in the 14th century in an effort to limit the power of the monarchy. Their motto translates loosely as 'Liberty for people and country.' The impressive neo-Gothic Church of St. John the Baptist *San Juan Bautista* has a splendid retablo and statue of St. James. The skull of St. William is also housed here in a silver reliquary giving zest to the mystical play enacted here every few years: *The Mystery of Óbanos. Legend has it that William (Guillaume) Duke of Aquitaine, killed his sister Felicia in a bout of fury at her refusal to return to court duties after her pilgrimage to Santiago. Riddled with remorse and in repentance Guillaume also took the pilgrimage to Compostela and renounced his nobility for a life of poverty, penitence and prayer. He lived the remainder of his life in the hermitage of Arnotegui just outside the village.*

•**Albergue** *Usda Priv.[36÷3]* ℂ 676-560 927 prominently situated on the corner of the main square at San Lorenzo, 6. 36 beds €8 basic facilities with rear patio and lounge with open fire in the winter. Casa rural •**Osses** CR ℂ 948-344 261 c/San Guillermo, 3. Bar & restaurant Ibarberoa (in street behind the church) and shop (not obvious) in the square. Continue down the hill out of Óbanos across the main road along a track through fields joining the main road at hotel and albergue [1] Jakue for the final stretch to:

Plaza Óbanos & Albergue

2.3 km **Puente la Reina •Albergue** ❷ *Conv.[96÷10]* adjoining main road as you enter the town at c/Crucifijo, 1. Monastery hostal run by the Padres Reparadores ℂ 948-340 050 with 96 beds €5 (10 rooms) in renovated building with all facilities and extensive rear garden (open all year). The route from Óbanos brings you directly to this original pilgrim hostel [1] (where the distances in this guide are measured to). It is conveniently situated opposite the

Albergue ❷ *Padres Repardores*

Church of the Crucifixion ❶ *Iglesia del Crucifijo*, which has undergone no less than 3 name changes and been administered by 3 different Orders. Originally known as the Church of St. Mary of the Meadows *Iglesia Santa María de las Vegas* under the auspices of the Knights Templar, when that order was outlawed it was looked after by the Order of the Hospitallers of St. John and became the Iglesia Santo Cristo. Today, it is named after the unusual 14th century 'Y' shaped Gothic crucifix brought here by medieval pilgrims from Germany. It is now under the care of the Padres Reparadores in the seminary opposite (linked by a stone arch). To access the town, pass under the arch and continue over the busy N-111 to explore the main street *c/Mayor*. Additional bars and restaurants are located along the tree-lined square that flanks the N-111 (see town plan).

•**Albergue ❶** Jakue *Priv.*[40÷2]+* ☏ 948 341 017 the reception pavilion is the first building you come to on entering town and part of •**Hotel Jakue***** who have reserved the basement area as a pilgrim hostel. 40 beds €10. (2 main rooms but with bunk beds in cubicles). Unusually for an establishment with a restaurant they provide a kitchen, dining and lounge area with washing machine. The lack of outside window space is compensated by the addition of a sauna

Albergue ❶ *Jakue*

and library and *menú peregrino* for €13 and *desayuno* €4. Adjoining the hotel on the main road we can find a modern pilgrim statue erected to mark the joining of the Navarrese and Aragonés routes.

•**Albergue ❸** *Santiago Apostol Priv.* [100÷5]* José Luis ☏ 948-340 220 a large network hostel* at the far end of town across from the medieval pilgrim bridge. An industrial style building on an elevated site, 1.1 km from albergue [1] including the 400m track up to it, but convenient for leaving the next day. 100 places €8 (60 in large dormitory remainder in 4 rooms of 10 each) mixed reports. No kitchen but bar

Albergue ❸ *Santiago Apostol*

and restaurant serving dinner and breakfast and swimming pool.

The town has all facilities including a convenient post office *correos* on the N-111 close to its junction with the c/Mayor. *Perhaps this is the time to send back home all those extra items that you realise that you no longer need?* A **tourist office** ☏ 948-340 845 is located by the medieval bridge. **Calle Mayor** is the well-preserved main street retaining its age-old atmosphere and site of the impressive ❷ *Iglesia de Santiago* with its 12th century facade and portico and a gilded statue of Santiago Peregrino *Beltxa* adding some colour to the sombre interior. The other church is ❸ *Iglesia San Pedro Apóstol* close to the pilgrim bridge with its image of Nuestra Señora del Puy otherwise known as Our Lady of the Bird *N.S del Chori – a reference to the lovely legend of a bird regularly washing the face of the statue when it was kept in a niche on the bridge.* **Other accommodation:** luxury •**El Peregrino** H**** ☏ 948-340 075 adjoining the Hotel Jakue at the entrance to town on the main road. •**Bidean** Hs ☏ 948-341 156 c/Mayor, 20, offers comfortable rooms in the centre of town also •**El Cerco** H ☏ 948- 34 12 69 on c/Rodrigo Ximenez de Rada, 36 parallel to the c/Mayor. Paseo de los Fueros (N-111) has variety of shops and restaurants..

PUENTE LA REINA (Gares) *Puente de Arga*
renamed Queens Bridge ❹ *Puente la Reina* in
honour of its benefactor Doña Mayor, wife of
Sancho III. She commanded the magnificent
Romanesque bridge to be built to support the
safe movement of the increasing number of
medieval pilgrims who joined the route at this
stage from both the camino francés and camino
aragonés. The bridges' six arches span the Arga
that has now swollen to a powerful river since
we first crossed it back at the Puente de Rabia
in Zubiri. Charlemagne is reputed to have stayed
in this town after his victorious battle against the

Monumento al Peregrino

Moors back in Cizur. With a population of 2,000 it straddles the busy N-111
linking Pamplona with Estella and has a frequent bus service to both.

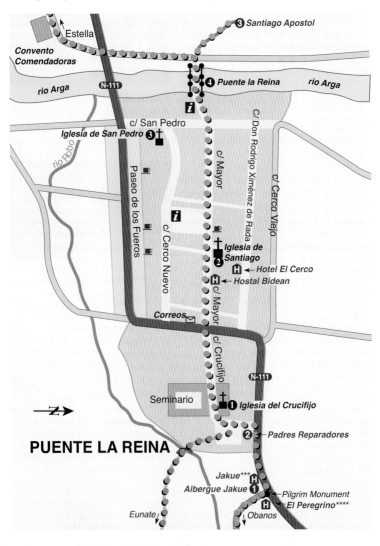

REFLECTIONS:

❏ **Practise random acts of loving kindness and acts of senseless beauty.**

05 **696.7** km (432.9 miles) to Santiago

PUENTE LA REINA – ESTELLA (Navarra)

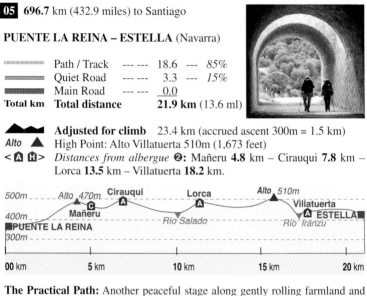

	Path / Track	--- ---	18.6	---	*85%*
	Quiet Road	--- ---	3.3	---	*15%*
	Main Road	--- ---	0.0		
Total km	**Total distance**		**21.9 km** (13.6 ml)		

▲ **Adjusted for climb** 23.4 km (accrued ascent 300m = 1.5 km)
Alto ▲ High Point: Alto Villatuerta 510m (1,673 feet)
< **A** **H** > *Distances from albergue* ❷: Mañeru **4.8** km – Cirauqui **7.8** km – Lorca **13.5** km – Villatuerta **18.2** km.

The Practical Path: Another peaceful stage along gently rolling farmland and vineyards with few trees and little shelter. Some fine examples of Roman roadway between Cirauqui and Lorca and a glorious 85% is on natural tracks. The first section is a steep climb on a heavily eroded path before descending into Estella.

❏ **The Mystical Path:** Will you pause a moment to look upon the ancient stone cross atop the rise and reflect at the speed with which the motorised traveller now whizz past it? Can you see the beauty of the stonemason's craftsmanship that fashioned it, and the deeper meaning behind the symbol? In the rush of modern life we miss so much of true significance. Where else might we take time today to pause and ponder the waymarks Home?

❏ **Personal Reflections:** *"... I started today with the intention to give and receive loving kindness. Here I am less than 2 hours later seething with rage. Someone has stolen items from my rucksack. I note with rising indignation that my new water container has also gone. In this moment of anger I become both judge and jury, condemning my fellow human being to hell and damnation. Where have the loving thoughts I invoked at daybreak gone? Can I bring them back? It is easy to act in a loving manner when the sun is shining and body and kit are together. But can I bring myself to love in adversity? ..."*

0.0 km **Puente La Reina** Leaving albergue ❷ pass under the connecting arch of the Iglesia del Crucifijo and the Padres Reparadores and continue over the N-111 into the narrow and historical c/Mayor. Past the Iglesia de Santiago (right) **[0.4 km]** to cross the famous XIIth century pilgrim bridge **[0.3 km]** (albergue *Santiago Apostol* is up the track straight ahead). Turn <left over the bridge and cross the main road to the Nun's Neighbourhood *Barrio de las Monjas* with its convento Comendadoras del Espíritu Santo [F]. Re-join the Río Arga and pass under new road bridge and along a dirt track before striking off right> uphill along a steep ravine to pass the XIII[th]c site of the Monasterio de Bogota before we crest the top at 470m **[3.9 km]** *(at this point there are fine views back over the Río Arga valley)* then down to the roundabout at Mañeru with [F] **[0.2 km]** to:

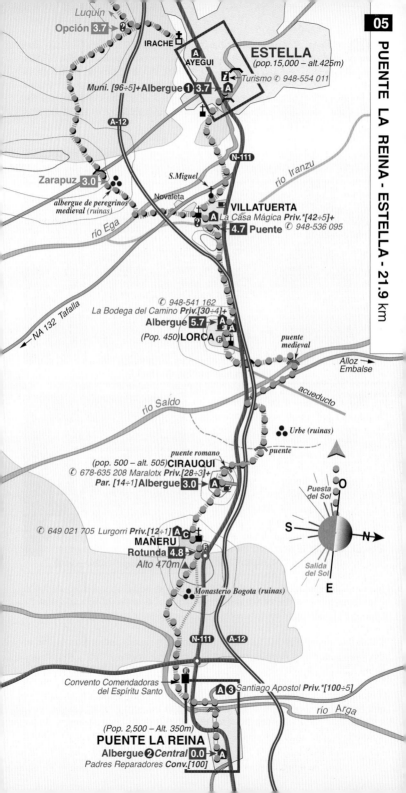

Luquín
Opción 3.7 ?

IRACHE

A
AYEGUI

ESTELLA
(pop.15,000 – alt.425m)

i
Turismo © 948-554 011

A-12

Muni. [96÷5]+Albergue **1** **3.7** **A**

N-111

S.Miguel

Zarapuz 3.0

*albergue de peregrinos
medieval (ruinas)*

río Ega

Novaleta

VILLATUERTA
A *La Casa Mágica Priv.*[42÷5]+*
4.7 **Puente** © 948-536 095

río Iranzu

NA 132 Tafalla

© 948-541 162
La Bodega del Camino Priv.[30÷4]+
Albergue 5.7 **A**
A
*(Pop. 450)***LORCA** **F**

*puente
medieval*

**Alloz →
Embalse**

río Saldo

acueducto

·. *Urbe (ruinas)*

puente romano
*(pop. 500 – alt. 505)***CIRAUQUI**
© 678-635 208 *Maralotx Priv.[28÷3]+*
*Par. [14÷1]***Albergue 3.0** **A**

puente

© 649 021 705 *Lurgorri Priv.[12÷1]* **A** **C**
MAÑERU
Rotunda 4.8 **F**
Alto 470m ▲

Monasterio Bogota (ruinas)

N-111 **A-12**

**Puesta
del Sol**
O

S
N

**Salida
del Sol**

E

*Convento Comendadoras
del Espíritu Santo* **F**

A **3** *Santiago Apostol Priv.*[100÷5]*

río Arga

(Pop. 2,500 – Alt. 350m)
PUENTE LA REINA
Albergue 2*Central* **0.0** **A**
Padres Reparadores Conv.[100]

82

4.8 km Mañeru *Roundabout*. Village linked with the Knights Templar and Order of St. John whose influence in this area was considerable in the Middle Ages. •**Albergue** *Lurgorri Priv.[12÷1]* ☎ 619 265 679 private hostel on c/ Esperanza,5 with 12 beds €10 incl. Church of St. Peter, bar, shop and CR •**Isabel** ☎ 948-340 283. The sleepy meandering streets lead to the cemetery via the street of the 'inevitable' *calle Forzosa* from where a view opens up of the next life… or our next destination, Cirauqui. We now start to pass through vineyards, interspersed with olive trees. The peaceful path winds its way up to:

Pilgrims approaching Cirauqui

3.0 km Cirauqui Plaza (*Zirauki*) a medieval hilltop village, beautifully preserved with narrow winding streets and houses bearing armorial crests and ornate balconies and fine village square. Church (restored) of *San Román* with multi-lobed doorway and Church of St. Catherine *Santa Catalina* both dating from the 13th century. •**Albergue ❶** *Par.[14÷1]* Basic parish hostel with 14 beds *donativo* in one room and small kitchen-dining area. The ancient building is accessed on the right just before entering the square off this traditional street with *supermercado* 50m

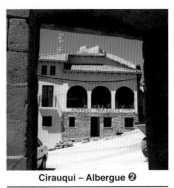

Cirauqui – Albergue ❷

(right) •**Albergue ❷** *Maralotx Priv.[28÷3]*+ private hostal opposite the church in Plaza San Roman at the very top of this tranquil village ☎ 678-635 208 with 28 beds €10 (+ individual rooms) with all facilities, dinner and breakfast available.

Leave the village through an arch from the main square and out on to one of the best examples of **Roman road** on the camino continuing over a single span Roman bridge to cross over the N-111 and A-12 (Will *they* last 2,000 years?) onto a dirt track. The path now takes us gently downhill through open farmland running parallel to the new autopista (left) which we pass under onto the N-111 and back again under the A-12 to take a quiet country road to pass modern aqueduct turning <left over the famous medieval stone bridge (now restored) that crosses the Salt river *río Salado*. Aymeric Picaud, in his epic journal written in the 12th century warns pilgrims not to drink from its deadly waters. It was here that he encountered Basques preparing to skin any pilgrim's horse that might

drink from the river and die – his own horse falling victim to the Basques! Veer <left through an underpass (thoughtfully finished with attractive local stone) and up into the village of:

5.7 km **Lorca** 12th century St. Saviours Church *San Salvador*. This quaint village is the site of a former pilgrim hospice with connections to the monastery at Roncesvalles and now boasting 2 private hostels •**Albergue** ❶ *La Bodega del Camino Priv.[30÷4]*+ Miguel © 948-541 162 private hostel on c/Placeta with 30 bunk beds €8 in 4 dorms + private rooms and restaurant in this restored

Lorca – Albergue ❶

stone building at the far end of the village (open all year). •**Albergue** ❷ *Lorca Priv.[12÷2]*+ c/Mayor, 40 José Ramón © 948-541 190 with 12 places €7 in 2 rooms +. The route from here follows a track alongside the main road through farmland passing the site of an ancient pilgrim hostel *Hospital de peregrinos de Arandigoyen* founded in 1066, before taking a tunnel under the town bypass into the modern suburbs of Villatuerta (café right) to cross the medieval bridge.

4.7 km **Villatuerta Puente** Network* hostel in a medieval building 80m beyond the bridge (signposted). •**Albergue** *La Casa Mágica Priv.*[42÷5]*+ Simone & Miguel © 948-536 095 with 42 places €10, well equipped kitchen, covered yard for relaxing and massage and healing available. Bar / restaurant *Lara* on the main road (400m off route). Just over the

bridge is the 14th century Church of the Assumption [F] with raised flagstone surround and views back over the route from Lorca and towards Monte Jurra to the south. Note: Alternative (original) Route via Zaraputz begins at the church.

Before Estella was founded in 1090, early pilgrims travelled directly to the monastery at Irache via Novaleta, Echavarra and Zaraputz to the south. This route still exists and is marked as part of the GR 65 that also serves as an alternative route to Los Arcos via Luquín (see next stage). The route is now well waymarked and makes a delightful alternative route. Consider this option if you have walked the camino francés before or if are travelling with

ESTELLA-LIZARRA

Zaraputz

Zaraputz <left arrow

a companion and want to experience walking alone and the joy of meeting up again at the end of the day to share your individual insights. This short section may provide the confidence to take other optional routes later on. This alternative route is still virtually unused in comparison to the constant stream of pilgrims on the main camino.

Turn left around the side of the church and s/o at T-Junction onto track and first waymark **[0.1 km]**. The path now drops down at side of factory and under access road to the village of Noveleta **[1.6 km]** and under A-6 motorway **[0.4 km]** over river **[0.5 km]** where the track now climbs steeply for **[0.4 km]** to:

3.0 km **Zaraputz** ruins of the 15th century pilgrim hostel occupying a lovely elevated site (440m). Continue over a pedestrian bridge [**0.7** km] climbing again to ridge (515m) where the first views of Estella open up ahead. The path curves around a valley and up again to cemetery [**1.4** km] turn <left off asphalt road [**0.4** km] and turn right> just before farmyard and cross over old road [**0.4** km] into Holm oak woods. The path now drops down through woodland for [**0.8** km] to route signpost:

Medieval pilgrim hostel – Zaraputz

3.7 km Option signpost with choice of routes: [a] continue by remote path direct to Luquín / Los Arcos (described in next stage) or [b] take the route to Estella / Monjardín by continuing under the A-6 to next option sign [**0.4** km] (left for Monjardín or right for Irache [**0.5** km]. The albergue at Ayegui is [**1.2** km] or the main albergue in Estella an additional [**1.5** km] (see map).

The main waymarked route now bypasses the ruins of the ancient hermitage of St. Michael *ermita de San Miguel arcangel* (all that remains of an extensive pilgrim hospital here, its artefacts dating from the XI[th]C are now in the Navarra museum). Continue along track, down steps beside the main road to rest area [F] and onto path that winds down to a pedestrian bridge over the rio Ega past *Camping Lizarra* and on down to riverside park and the 14[th]C Gothic Iglesia del Santo Sepulchro (left) with the Convento Santo Domingo behind it. Continue through the underpass (N-111) into the c/la Rua and:

3.7 km Estella •Albergue ❶ *Hospital de Peregrinos Asoc.[96÷5]* c/La Rúa, 50 ℂ 948-550 200 conveniently located at the entrance to the town at the beginning of the c/de la Rúa (the noisy N-111 is to the rear) with 96 beds €6 spread tightly over 3 floors and large overflow dormitory next door (open all year). Modern kitchen with extensive dining area, breakfast is available and a small patio to rear provides some open space. Several new hostels now relieve the pressure on bed spaces at this previous bottleneck. La Aljama also on c/Rua has a pilgrim menu. ❏ *Other Albergues de Peregrinos:*

Albergue ❶ Municipal

❷ San Miguel *Par.[32÷2]* ℂ 615 451 909 c/Mercado Viejo, 18 - parish hostel on ground floor of modern residential building with 30 beds €-*donativo* and all facilities. ❸ *ANFAS Mun.[34÷1]* c/Cordeleros, 7 Bajo (ANFAS society for the support of mentally handicapped ℂ 639 011 688 with 34 beds €7. For either hostel cross the bridge opposite albergue [1] and head s/o along c/Asteria and at 2nd crossroads (250m) – for albergue [2] turn up left into c/Mercado Viejo and the hostel is on the right after 100m (opposite Decora Hogar). For albergue [3] continue s/o uphill along c/Asteria and veer right to modern buildings 150m. The other 2 hostels are the opposite end of town on the way out in Ayegui. ❹ •**Albergue Juvenil** *Oncineda Mun.[150÷20]* 300m *off* the route (right) at first roundabout in c/Monasterio de Irache ℂ 948-555 022 with 150 places (€9–13) in mod. building with meals available (open all year) and set in quiet wooded site.

❺ *San Cipriano de Ayegui* **Mun.[80÷2]** c/ Polideportivo, Ayegui. ℂ 948-554 311 left of the camino beyond the 2nd roundabout at the far end of town (1.6 km from albergue [1]) part of the Ayegui sports hall *Polideportivo*. 80 beds €6 (open all year). Pilgrim menú and breakfast available from the canteen.

Albergue ❺ *Polideportivo* - Ayegui

❏ **Other Accommodation:** *Turismo* c/ San Nicolas, 1 ℂ 948-556 301. *Hoteles:* •**San Andrés** P* plaza de Santiago ℂ 948-554 158 popular with pilgrims (as is nearby first floor restaurant *Casa Nova* on C.Fray Wenceslao) •**Cristina Hs** c/Baja Navarra, 1 ℂ 948-550 772 (between the main square and c/Mayor). •**Fonda Izarra** c/Caldería ℂ 948-550 678 often booked out by migrant workers and better known for its pilgrim menu. •**Apartamentos Gebala** plaza Fueros, 31 ℂ 606-980 675 have a special pilgrim price (ideal for small groups). In the modern industrial area near Ayegui are •**El Volante** c/Merkatondoa, 2 ℂ 948-553 957 •**Hostal Area-99** c/Merkatondoa, 32 ℂ 948-553 370. •**Yerri** H** Av. Yerri, 35 ℂ 948-546 034 out past the bullring on the western outskirts. In the upper price bracket directly on the camino on the outskirts of Estella (3.7 km from albergue [1]) is the modern hotel •**Irache** H*** Irache ℂ 948-551 150 ❏ *Restaurantes:* •*Aljama* c/de la Rua. •*Casa Nova* c/Fray Wenceslao.

ESTELLA *LIZARRA: (pop. 15,000 – alt. 425m)* a vibrant town with lots to do and see. Estella is big enough to provide reasonable facilities and yet sufficiently compact to easily explore its wonderful historic buildings, museums, interesting churches and its varied restaurants and bars (perhaps a good place to take a day's rest). Opposite albergue [1] is the restored medieval bridge ❶ Puente de Carcel and 200m past the albergue along c/ la Rua we find ❷ Plaza San Martín with its graceful fountain and the adjoining ❸ XIIthC Palace of the Kings of Navarre *Palacio de los Reyes de Navarra* now a museum and art gallery. Opposite are the impressive flight of steps to ❹ Church of San Pedro de la Rúa with its beautiful

XIIthC cloister, two sides of which are missing, evidence of its troubled past. It was here that the Kings of Navarre took their oaths and is worth a visit despite the noise of traffic on the busy N-111 immediately to the rear. Open before evening mass and guided tours are also available – check with the adjacent tourist office. On the other side of the river Ega we find the parish church of ❺ Iglesia San Miguel and the bustling main square *Plaza de los Fueros* filled with cafés and the austere church ❻ San Juan Bautista taking up the eastern side. A further 200m along the c/Mayor you come to the more intimate Plaza de Santiago with its ancient fountain. A variety of inexpensive restaurants, bars and hotels are located in

Steps to Iglesia San Pedro

the surrounding streets. The area to the north of the river was called Lizarra (Basque for ash tree) and was the original village built on the slopes of the hill of San Millán where today we find the modern Basilica of the Virgin of le Puy. Quick to realise the enormous potential of the pilgrim road to Santiago Sancho Ramírez created a separate Borough in 1090 for French pilgrim settlers on the other side of the river and referred to it as L'Izarra (Basque for star) which became *Estella* (Spanish for star) with all its connections with the Milky

Way *Via Lactea* otherwise known as the 'Way of the Stars' to Compostela. This marks the beginning of stage IV of the Codex Calixtinus.

As in other areas along the Way, artisans were encouraged to return and bring their skills with them. It was this inflow of stonemasons and artists that created the beautiful buildings, monuments and bridges, hospitals and cathedrals that we still admire and use today. However, the ever-present human characteristics of jealousy and greed also created disharmony, open warfare and mindless massacres. The unification of the different boroughs into one town in 1266 did not end the hostilities. The flowering Jewish colony was expelled in the 14th century and the destruction of the castle adjoining San Pedro also destroyed two sides of its exquisite Romanesque cloister. Even up to the last century, Estella was one of the strongholds of the Carlists in the conflict over the successor to King Ferdinand, no doubt contributing to the town's royalist reputation. Today, the fiery Navarrese blood is cooled in the Court of Justice *Juzgado*, which now occupies the original town hall immediately to the left of the steps to the church of San Pedro in Plaza San Martín.

REFLECTIONS:

❏ **To attain knowledge, add things every day.**
  To attain wisdom, remove things every day. *Lao-tzu*

06 674.8 km (419.3 miles) to Santiago

ESTELLA – LOS ARCOS (Navarra)

⸻	Path / Track	--- ---	18.1	--- 86%
═══	Quiet Road	--- ---	2.7	--- 13%
⸻	Main Road	--- ---	0.3	--- 1%
Total km	**Total distance**		**21.1 km**	(13.1 ml)

▲▲ **Adjusted for climb** 22.9 km (accrued ascent 370m = 1.8 km)
Alto ▲ High Point: Albergue Monjardín 650m (2,132 feet)
< Ⓐ Ⓗ > *Distances from albergue* ❶ *in Estella:* Ayegui 1.5 km – Hotel Irache **5.0** km – Monjardín **9.6** km.

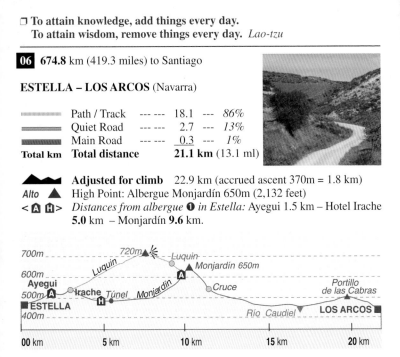

The Practical Path: As in yesterday's stage, the majority of this scenic route (86%) is on delightful natural paths. The first section is through native Holm oak and pine trees as we wend our way up to Monjardín. There are magnificent views southwards over the alternative route, which passes above Luquín. The two routes join for the last stretch into Los Arcos taking us through remote vineyards and open country but with little shade and few water fonts. Take food and water for the isolated day ahead, particularly for the alternative route.

❏ **The Mystical Path:** Will you find the fish that circle the stone fountain, symbol of the hidden Christian life swimming in its waters? The fish are located at the centre of these ancient cloisters. How long will they remain? How long will we? This monastic community was founded here as early as 958 and it became one of the first monasteries to receive pilgrims on their way to venerate the recently discovered tomb of San Tiago. It later earned the status of the first university in Navarre. For over a millennium it was a respected seat of learning and hospitality. Today it is uninhabited, abandoned by the monks that gave it life for over a thousand years. Perhaps the ferns that gave these majestic buildings their name will yet reclaim them.

❏ **Personal Reflections:** *"... Everywhere there are fountains. Some contain refreshing drinking water to hydrate the body; others wine to fortify it. I now find myself being offered a different water to quench a different thirst. In a display of loving kindness, offered without any expectation of anything in return, I am showered with generosity. I leave this oasis of service with the gift of a little booklet entitled* Living Water *and based on the Gospel of Saint John. Tears well up in me as I open the book and find a handwritten message from Anton. "I give this book for you to find Jesus Christ. God help you!" I reflect on my purpose for this journey and smile at the exclamation mark. God help me indeed! ..."*

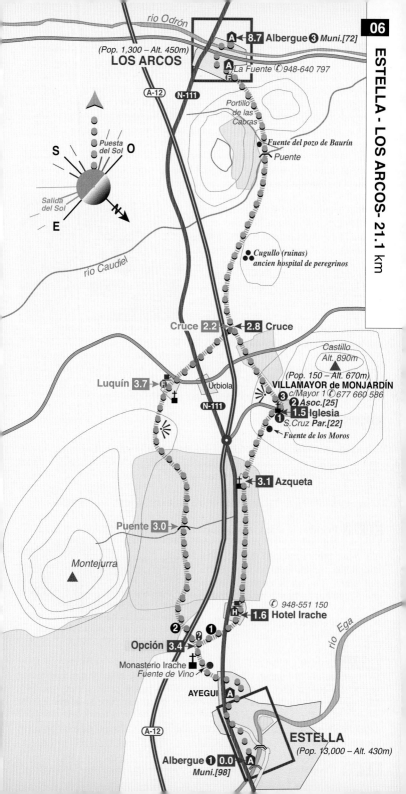

río Odrón

A **8.7** Albergue ❸ *Muni.[72]*

(Pop. 1,300 – Alt. 450m)
LOS ARCOS

A
F *La Fuente* ✆ 948-640 797

A-12 N-111

*Portillo
de las
Cabras*

Fuente del pozo de Baurín
Puente

S
**Puesta
del Sol** O

*Salida
del Sol*

E

río Caudiel

*Cugullo (ruinas)
ancien hospital de peregrinos*

Cruce **2.2** ◀ ▶ **2.8** Cruce

*Castillo
Alt. 890m*

(Pop. 150 – Alt. 670m)
VILLAMAYOR de MONJARDÍN

Luquín **3.7** **F**
Urbiola
c/Mayor 1 ✆ 677 660 586
❸
❷ *Asoc.[25]*
❶ **1.5** Iglesia
S.Cruz Par.[22]

N-111

Fuente de los Moros

3.1 Azqueta

Puente **3.0** ▶

Montejurra

✆ 948-551 150
H **1.6** Hotel Irache

❷
❶
Opción **3.4** ▶
río Ega

Monasterio Irache
Fuente de Vino ▶

AYEGUI
A

ESTELLA
(Pop. 13,000 – Alt. 430m)

Albergue ❶ **0.0** **A**
Muni.[98]

A-12

0.0 km **Estella** from albergue ❶ continue up calle Rúa into Plaza San Martin [F] past the tourist office **[0.2 km]** and out through the medieval city gate *Puerta de Castilla* and cross over the busy junction of the N-111 **[0.3 km]** (albergue [4] right). Veer right> past the Avia petrol station and continue up through the modern suburb of Ayegui passing [F] *el Piojo* **[1.0 km]** (with sports hall and albergue [5] up to the left). Continue s/o up c/Camino de Santiago and c/ Mayor to turn down sharp <left **[0.6 km].** *(For an **alternative** route direct to Hotel Irache continue straight on past children's play area to the Hotel visible straight ahead (1.6 km) where the waymarked route re-joins from the left.)* Turn <left downhill and cross over the N-111 **[0.3 km]** and up the dirt track opposite to rear of the Bodegas Irache with its famous **wine fountain** *Fuente del Vino* **[0.4**

km] where pilgrims can fortify themselves for the journey ahead at the generosity of the Bodegas. Continue to tree-fringed square [F] and the entrance to the ancient Benedictine **Monasterio de Irache [0.1 km]** (left) which has long been connected with Roncesvalles and the camino. A community of monks served pilgrims here since the 10th century but were forced to vacate in 1985 due to a lack of novitiates. Now serving as a somewhat austere museum it can be viewed from 09.30

Irache – Wine Fountain

Wed-Fri and 08.30 Sat & Sun. If it is closed you can still view the impressive Romanesque door to the 12th century Benedictine Church of San Pedro, around to the left. The Bodegas Irache has a **wine museum** opposite. Continue along dirt track for **[0.5 km]** to a fork in the path with wooden signpost.

3.4 km Irache Opción [?]

Alternative scenic route ❷ via LUQUIN (100m shorter). Entire on natural pathways but facilities en route are limited so bring provisions. Veer left under A-12 up through delightful woodland to high pasture and fields of lavender. This route follows the *road less travelled* away from the bustle of the main camino and skirts the lower slopes of the mystical *Monte Jurra* (1045m) to:

3.0 km **Puente** wooden bridge across mountain stream (dry). Shortly afterwards the route breaks through the tree line to reveal the conical peak of Monjardín to the north. The track continues through the ridge ahead where a magnificent view south over Luquin opens up. This is the high point of the route at 720m. We now start the gentle descent into:

Monjardín from Luquin route

3.7 km **Luquin** typical hill village with winding streets radiating out from the Basilica and the parish Church of San Martin. The latter has an interesting and finely carved portico and adjoins the main square with seating and **[F]**. Community café/bar San Isidro (often closed). Wind your way down through the village and out onto an open path crossing over the N-111 (close to the village of Urbiola where the Knights of St. John maintained a medieval pilgrim hospice) continue under the A-12 to:

2.2 km **Cruce** Here we re-join the main waymarked route from Monjardín.

For **recommended route ❶** via Monjardín veer right> at option point (wooden signpost) down and over the N-111 to:

1.6 km **Hotel Irache.** Take the road between the hotel and camping complex under the new bypass and out onto a pathway through peaceful Holm oak and pine forest to:

3.1 km **Azqueta** quiet village now bypassed by the new N-111 with the parish Church of San Pedro. At the far end of the village veer off right> down past farm buildings and then steeply up towards Villamayor. Just before entering the village we pass the 13th century Fountain of the Moors *Fuente de Los Moros* with its splendid double arch of distinctly Mozarabic influence, to:

Fuente de los Moros

1.5 km **Villamayor de Monjardín** with splendid views of the surrounding countryside and dominated by the tower of the XIIthC San Andrés Church. The conical peak of Monjardín with the ruins of St. Stephen's Castle *Castillo de San Esteban* forms a distinctive backdrop to the village. Opposite the church is the parish hostel •**Albergue ❶** *Santa Cruz Par.[25÷2]* renovated parish house with 28 spaces in bunk beds and mattresses. Shared meal (no kitchen). Further up at the top end of the village is the original •**Albergue ❷** *Hogar Monjardín Asoc.[25÷5]* © 948-537 136 run by a Dutch ecumenical group. Prominently situated overlooking the main square with 25 beds €5 in 5 rooms and good facilities in this refurbished village house (no kitchen but shared meals with grace are offered at basic cost). Village Bar with pilgrim menu. Leaving the village (top) casa rural •*Montedeio* © 948 55 15 21 on c/ Mayor, 17 rooms €35-55 shared bathrooms. *[Next Albergue: Los Arcos – 11.5 km].* The route now follows the access road down past the Monjardín Bodega to turn off right> onto a lovely pathway down through vineyards and woodland where the alternative route joins via the A-12 underpass.

Albergue ❶ *(above)*

Albergue ❷ *Castillo (background)*

2.8 km **Cruce** at this point we join pilgrims coming from Luquin and continue along remote farm tracks for a glorious 8.7 km of uninhabited countryside of mixed farmland and vineyards interspersed with olive trees, but with little shade. We pass the site of the ancient pilgrim hospital *Cugullo* and Fountain of the Well *Fuente del pozo de Baurín* (not drinkable) by the adjoining río Caudiel (dry) but with pleasant shade from the pine trees. Finally we take a gentle climb up through the Pass of the Goats *Portillo de las Cabras* before our descent into:

8.7 km **Los Arcos** we enter the town on its sleepy northern side and make our way down c/Mayor passing: •**Albergue ❶** *la Fuente de Austria Priv.[54÷7]*+

Travesia del Estanco corner c/Mayor Ⓒ María Ruiz 948-640 797 with 54 places from €8 in several dorms' +priv' rooms (all year excl. Jan) good facilities and small patio. Continue down the main street to Plaza de la Fruta and •**Albergue** ❷ *Casa de la Abuela Priv.[30÷3]*+ Ⓒ 948-640 250 with 30 beds €8 excellent facilities also has individual rooms. Close by is the splendid Church of St. Mary of the Arches ❶ *Iglesia de Santa María de los Arcos XII*[th]*C*. The church was embellished in 16th, 17th and 18th centuries and in addition to the original Romanesque has Gothic, Baroque and Classical elements without affecting the overall harmony. The bell-tower and peaceful cloisters are particularly noteworthy and the sumptuous interior has a fine statue of Santiago Peregrino. The balcony choir stalls also have a relief of both St. James *Maior* and *Menor*. Pilgrim mass each evening.

Santiago Maior *(left)* **and Menor** *(right)*

Leaving the church to the left, continue out through ❷ *Portal de Castilla* and cross the road *and* river to turn right> by the pilgrim fountain *Fuente de Peregrinos* •**Albergue** ❸ *Isaac Santiago Muni.[72÷8]*Ⓒ 948-441 091 the original municipal hostel administered by a Flemish confraternity and accessed off c/Río Odrón (behind the modern civic centre and library) with 72 beds €6 in a main dormitory + smaller rooms and all facilities including an outside patio.

Close by in c/El Hortal is •**Albergue** ❹ *Casa Alberdi Priv.[24÷3]* María Concepción Alberdi Ⓒ 948-640 764 entered via converted garage which also serves as a lounge area. 24 beds €10 in 3 rooms (open all year). **Alternatives:** Pensión •**Mavi** Ⓒ 948-640 081 on c/ del Medio 7 (separate to bar/ restaurant Mavi at the central crossroads opposite Hotel and bar •**Mónaco** H[**] Ⓒ 948-640 000 on Plaza del Coso. •**Hostal Suetxe** Ⓒ 948-441 175 in a refurbished building on c/Karramendabia (opposite side of N-111) and further out on c/La Serna (on the road to Zarragoza) •**Ezequiel** Hs Ⓒ 948-640 296. There are several shops and bars including the popular basement restaurant below the •*Gargantúa* bar opposite the church and useful grocery *alimentación* adjoining (see town plan).

LOS ARCOS a crossroads town (population 1,300) straddling the N-111 and connecting Estella with Logroño with regular bus service to both. It was and remains a classical pilgrim halt and has Roman origins. The eastern gate (no longer visible) into the old walled city was called Gate of the Shells *Portal de la Concha* which also provided access to the Jewish quarter in the town. A *Turismo* sometimes opens in either the town hall ❸ *Ayuntamiento XVI*[th]*C* or Casa Cultura. Wander around the narrow streets and soak up the tranquillity.

Los Arcos – Santa María

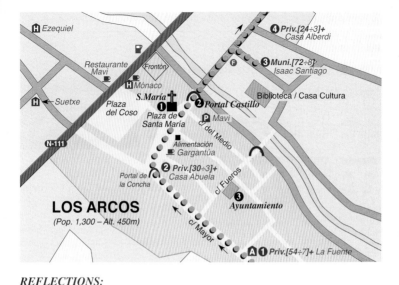

LOS ARCOS
(Pop. 1,300 – Alt. 450m)

REFLECTIONS:

❏ **Your daily life is your temple and your religion.** *Kahlil Gibran*

07 **653.7** km (406.2 miles) to Santiago

LOS ARCOS (Navarra) – LOGROÑO (La Rioja)

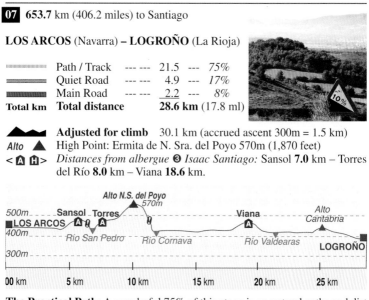

⸻	Path / Track	--- ---	21.5	---	75%
⸻	Quiet Road	--- ---	4.9	---	17%
⸻	Main Road	--- ---	<u>2.2</u>	---	8%
Total km	**Total distance**		**28.6 km**	(17.8 ml)	

Adjusted for climb 30.1 km (accrued ascent 300m = 1.5 km)

Alto ▲ High Point: Ermita de N. Sra. del Poyo 570m (1,870 feet)

< 🄰 🄷 > *Distances from albergue* ❸ *Isaac Santiago:* Sansol **7.0** km – Torres del Río **8.0** km – Viana **18.6** km.

The Practical Path: A wonderful 75% of this stage is on natural paths and dirt tracks through open arable farmland. Shade is limited to a few isolated pockets of pine and drinking fonts are few, so fill up the water bottle and wear your hat. This is a long stage and there are some short but very steep sections into the rio Linares (Torres del Río) and Cornava river valleys so be particularly mindful when negotiating these steep paths. Just before entering Logroño we pass into the great wine-producing region of La Rioja. *Note: If you don't want to stay in a busy city hostel or want more time to visit Logroño, consider staying in Viana where there are now 2 albergues (see details). This would allow a longer stopover at Logroño the following day (9.5 km from Viana centre) to spend more time exploring this interesting city (it may be possible to leave your backpack in the hostel although it doesn't officially open till after noon) or visit the city briefly on your way through to the next intermediate hostel at Navarette (12.4 km) for a total of 21.2 km for this alternative day.*

❏ **The Mystical Path:** Will you visit this holy temple reputedly built by the same Order of Knights that created the magnificent church at Eunate? Will you sense the similarity of form and look up and see the eight-sided star that forms this simple structure, symbol of the sacred and full of grace and mystery? The beautiful 13th century figure of Christ crucified hangs above the altar. If our life is a reflection of our temple, to whom have we dedicated it and what have we placed upon its altar?

❏ **Personal Reflections:** *"... The deepening lines on her aging face cannot hide her welcoming smile. Her name means happiness and she has welcomed pilgrims for decades giving her blessing and stamping credenciales. Some see her unofficial presence an intrusion, preferring to hurry by to avoid interaction. I sit beside her and observe myself judging them as they are judging her. A whole Order was condemned to die by those fearing a loss of control and wanting an exclusive right to bless. We crucified God's Son for the same crime. I realise in this moment that no one needs permission to offer love. We all have the right to bestow blessings – perhaps it is our primary duty..."*

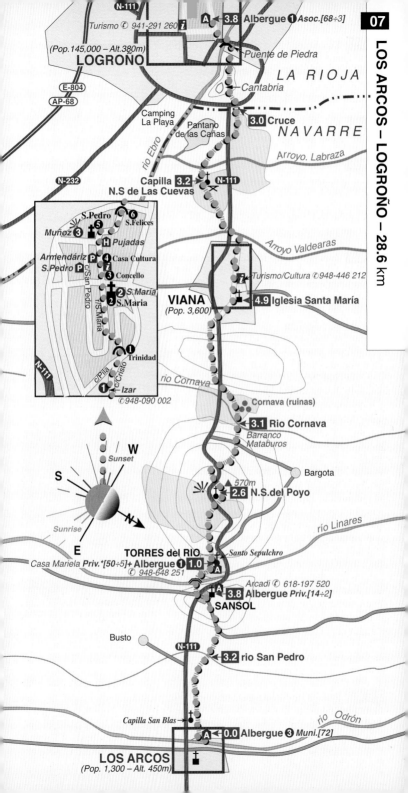

N-111

A ◄ 3.8 Albergue ❶ Asoc.[68÷3]

Turismo ☎ 941-291 260 ℹ

Puente de Piedra

(Pop. 145,000 – Alt.380m)

LOGROÑO

LA RIOJA

E-804
AP-68

Cantabria

3.0 Cruce

Camping
La Playa

NAVARRE

*Pantano
de las Cañas*

Arroyo. Labraza

rio Ebro

N-232

Capilla 3.2
N.S de Las Cuevas

✝ N-111
✗

Arroyo Valdearas

ℹ Turismo/Cultura ☎948-446 212

VIANA
(Pop. 3,600)

4.9 Iglesia Santa María

Inset map (Viana):

S.Pedro

S.Felices

Muñoz ❸

S.Pedro ❺

❻

H Pujadas

Armendáriz P ❹ Casa Cultura
S.Pedro P
c/San Pedro

❸ Concello

✝ ❷ S.Maria
❷ S.Maria
t/S.Maria

❶ Trinidad

N-111

c/P/la
c/Cristo

❶ Izar

☎948-090 002

W
Sunset

S

Sunrise

E

rio Cornava

Cornava (ruinas)

3.1 Rio Cornava

*Barranco
Mataburos*

▲ 570m

Bargota

2.6 N.S.del Poyo

rio Linares

TORRES del RIO

Santo Sepulchro

Casa Mariela **Priv.***[50÷5]+ Albergue ❶ 1.0
☎ 948-648 251

A

Arcadi ☎ 618-197 520

✝A 3.8 Albergue Priv.[14÷2]

SANSOL

Busto

N-111

3.2 rio San Pedro

Capilla San Blas ➤ ✝

A ◄ 0.0 Albergue ❸ Muni.[72]

LOS ARCOS
(Pop. 1,300 – Alt. 450m)

✝

rio Odrón

`0.0 km` **Los Arcos** From albergue ❸ turn up past the cemetery (the inscription over its portal translates; *'you are what I once was, and will be what I am now'*). Flexing our physical and spiritual muscles we stride out along a wide earth track leaving the 13th century Capilla de San Blas and the main N-111 (left). We continue along a delightful track through arable farmland to:

`3.2 km` **Rio de San Pedro** cross this small stream with Sansol directly ahead on the horizon and join the quiet country road into:

`3.8 km` **Sansol** •*café* at entrance. To visit the church or pilgrim hostel turn up right> Iglesia de San Zoilo *(a Christian martyr who gives his name to this sleepy little village and also to the monastery in Carrión de los Condes).* •**Albergue** *Arcadi y Nines* **Priv.[14÷2]** ✆ 618-197 520 with 14 beds €5. From here the way crosses the N-111 down a ravine [!] to a stone bridge over the Río Linares [F] (left) and up steeply, passing the café / restaurant *Casa Lili* (left) up into:

`1.0 km` **Torres del Río Plaza** •**Albergue** ❶ *Casa Mariela* **Priv.*[50÷5]** ✆ 948-648 251 network* hostel with 50 places €7 and all facilities (no kitchen but restaurant and grocery adjacent) •**Albergue** ❷ *la Pata & Oca Priv. [32÷3]*+ ✆ 948-378 457 formerly the popular *Via Láctea* with 32 beds €10 (no kitchen but bar and restaurant). Tucked away behind the church at the top of town in c/Casas Nuevas is •**Albergue** ❸ *Casa Mari* **Priv.*[26÷5]** ✆ 948-648 409 network* hostel with 26 places €7 in 4 rooms and all facilities including patio with terrace overlooking the countryside (all hostels open all year). **TORRES DEL RÍO:** Quintessential pilgrim village best known for its exquisite 12th century church *Iglesia de Santo Sepulcro* linked with the Knights Templar and based on the octagonal church of the Holy Sepulchre in Jerusalem. The lofty cupola, with its cross-ribbed vault forming an 8 sided star, is particularly notable and emblematic of the Knights. The simple interior has a 13th century crucifix and, like the church in Eunate, fine acoustics if you feel inclined to offer a song of prayer. If the church is closed ask for the custodian *guardián* who lives adjacent (usually open mornings and evenings depending on season.)

Albergue ❶ Casa Mariela

Torres del Río – Santo Sepulchro

Continue up through the village past the cemetery and out on a dirt track that undulates across the open countryside avoiding the N-111, which snakes its way around hairpin bends to your right. Join the main road briefly to pass:

`2.6 km` **Ermita de Nuestra Señora del Poyo** Precariously situated on the road at its high point (*poyo* means raised platform or podium) from here we have a good view west over the flat plains with Viana and Logroño in the distance. We now cross the N-111 over a secondary road that leads to the village of Bargota (right). From here the path drops steeply down into a steep ravine [!] to cross the river Cornava (often dry).

3.1 km Rio Cornava (site of an ancient settlement) and up to the N-111 onto a path straight to Viana now clearly visible ahead. Cross the N-111 [!] into the suburbs passing •**Albergue ❶** *Izu Priv.[18÷1]*+ ✆ 948-090 002 (opened 2012) €8-12 all facilities and climb steeply up into the medieval heart of Viana town:

4.9 km Viana Iglesia de Santa María XIII[th]c with fine recessed doorway in front of which is the tomb of the notorious Cesare Borgia who was killed nearby *(initially buried in the church but when his mausoleum was vandalised he was re-interred outside.)* The interior has an early statue of St. James. The parish has recently converted an adjoining building to a pilgrim hostel •**Albergue ❷** *Santa Maria Par.[15÷4]* ✆ 948-645 037 with basic facilities and 15 places *€-donativo* and a shared meal with grace. Access is from the main square *Plaza de los Fueros* with its central fountain and collection of cafes and bars. The town hall has a fine carved façade with colonnades and houses the *Turismo* ✆ 948-446 302. Continue down the main street past the 15th pilgrim hospital at N°18 (now casa de Cultura) to the far end and turn sharp <left by the impressive ruins of San Pedro to the main hostel (400m from Santa María):

Portico Santa María

Albergue ❷ Paroquial

•**Albergue ❸** *Andrés Muñoz Mun.[54÷4]* municipal hostel ✆ 948-645 530 on c/San Pedro located in a quiet part of the old town with wonderful garden terrace to the rear overlooking Logroño in the distance. 54 beds €6 in several open sections in tiers of three! – all facilities including a magnificent lounge-dining hall and a fine terrace overlooking the route to Logroño. Originally a monastery, it was acquired and transformed into a pilgrim hostel by one of the great *amigos* of the way, *Andrés Muñoz.* (open all year).

Albergue ❸ Municipal

Other accommodation •Casa Armendáriz P[**] ✆ 948-645 078 in c/Navarro Villoslada, 19. •San Pedro P[**] ✆ 948-446 221 or, at the top end of the market (and the town – opposite the ruins of San Pedro) is the beautifully restored palace •**Palacio de Pujadas** H[***] ✆ 948-646 464 which also runs the popular cafetaria Portillo (directly on the camino). Beds also available at •Casa Rueda N°46 just off the camino as you leave town ✆ 948-645 149. There is a wide selection of shops bars and restaurants. *[Next accommodation: Logroño – 9.5 km]*

Palacio de Pujadas & Café

VIANA is a lively town with a resident population of 3,500. The camino passes through its historical centre, which is little changed since medieval pilgrims plodded through its ancient streets – its architectural heritage still largely intact. Back in the 15th century Viana was a major pilgrim halt with no less than 4 *hospitales de peregrinos* and it was during this period that Cesare Borgia became linked to the town. *[Illegitimate son of Rodrigo Borgia, who was elected Pope Alexander VI in the pivotal year of 1492, Cesare was appointed commander of the Papal armies and patronised both Leonardo de Vinci, who acted as his military architect, and Machiavelli who, no doubt, helped form some of his political ideology. When Pope Alexander VI died, his successor promptly banished Cesare to Spain where he was killed defending Viana in the siege of 1507. Colourful to the end, it has been suggested that Borgia's strong countenance may have been used by artists of the period, such as Leonardo, to model the popular image of Christ Jesus.]* Owing to its border location the town has always been something of a hot spot and its defensive walls are well preserved on its western side (as you leave).

To stay or not to stay, that is a question – whatever you decide, stay long enough to reflect on the ruins of the Church of St. Peter *San Pedro* and to soak up the atmosphere of this abandoned church and the terraced gardens that lead from it. Leave the town through the medieval stone arch *Portal San Felices* and drop down to the suburbs below following the path around the back of houses and over waste ground and abandoned factory buildings to cross over the N-111 onto a quiet road to:

3.2 km **Ermita de la Trinidad de Cuevas** [F] peaceful picnic spot with grove of trees and a small tributary of the Ebro, site of an earlier pilgrim hospice of the Trinitarian Order of nuns. Continue to fork in the track where a new variant (recommended) continues s/o <left to make a wide curve towards the lakes (original road route right). The extensive lakes *Lagunas de Las Cañas* are now visible ahead with the Cantabrian Hills behind. *The low-lying meadows in this area where notorious for the witches' covens that gathered here in the 16th century.* Bird observatory (left). Watch carefully for the camino waymarks (other local walks around the lakes are also marked) and make your way back to cross the busy N-111 [!] by paper factory over stream to pass from Navarra into the famous wine-growing region of La Rioja:

3.0 km **Cruce / La Rioja** Here the autonomous region of La Rioja begins at the new city bypass adjoining an industrial complex and *Papelaria Ebro*. Make your way under the new ring road towards the Cantabrian hill *Cerro de Cantabria,* its flat outline clearly visible ahead. We follow a new earth-coloured asphalt track, a 'gift' from the local government and climb gently up the northern flank of the hill and past the site of the prehistoric city of Cantabria – excavations of its Roman (and earlier) ruins are still in progress. Just where we begin to drop down again prepare to part with a few cents for good luck and in memory of Felisa, another legendary gatekeeper of the camino whose niece, also called Felisa, is now in charge of this welcoming border post where you can get your credencial stamped while you have some refreshments. Continue to the stone bridge ❶ *Puente de Piedra* across the wide waters of the Ebro into the city of Logroño. The bridge, rebuilt in 1880, replaces the earlier medieval pilgrim bridge attributed to St. John Of the Nettles *San Juan de Ortega*. Once over the bridge turn right> across junction [!] into the cobbled c/Ruavieja (the original 'old' road) passing (right) ❷ *Ermita San Gregorio y Casa de la Danza* opposite ❸ *Iglesia y claustro Santa Maria del Palacio XIIthC* with its graceful octagonal tower (known locally as the needle) which is situated next to:

3.8 km Logroño Albergue ❶ *Asoc.[68÷3]*
c/Ruaviejo in the old quarter. Municipal
hostel ✆941-248 686 with 68 spaces
€7 on 3 floors (in cubicles of 4 in large
dormitories) all facilities and outside patio
(open all year). ❷ *Santiago Par.[15÷4]* c/
Barricocepo, 8. Parish hostel (Jun-Sept) adj.
Iglesia de Santiago. Basic facilities *donativo*
with communal dinner. ❸ *Entresueños Priv.
[14÷1]*+ c/ Portales, 12 adj. the cathedral
✆ 941 271 334 with 14 beds in one dorm
from €16 ❹ *Check In Rioja Priv.[30÷1]*

Logrono –Albergue ❶

c/Los Baños, 2. ✆ 941 272 329 with 30 rooms €11. ❺ *Puerta del Revellín
Priv.*[40÷1]* ✆ 941-700 832 modern building in Plaza Martínez Flamarique, 4
(adj. cafe El Albero) 700m east of Puente Piedra. 40 beds €10 in 1 room.

❏ *Turismo: La Rioja:* Paseo de Espolón ✆ 941-291 260. *Turismo Logroño:*
Portales, 50 Bajo ✆ 941-273 353 ❏ *Hoteles:* •F&G ✆ 941-008 900 av. de
Viana / Marqués de San Nicolás (Puente Piedra) •**La Numantina** Hs ✆ 941-251
411 Sagasta, 4. •**Niza** Hs ✆ 941-206 044 c/Capitan Gallarga, 13. •**La Bilbaina**
P ✆ 941-254 226 c/Capitan Gallarga, 10. •**Marqués de Vallejo** H*** ✆ 941-248
333 c/Marqués de Vallejo, 8. •**Portales** H*** ✆ 941-502 794 c/ Portales, 85.
•**Murrieta** H*** ✆ 941-224 150 Marqués de Murrieta, 1. •**Modesto** P ✆ 941-226
019 Marqués de Murrieta, 44, 2°. •**Conde de Haro** H*** ✆ 941-208 500.

LOGROÑO: Lively University City with a population of 130,000 capital of La
Rioja and a pleasant blend of medieval and modern. At the heart of the old town
is the Gothic ❺ *Catedral de Santa María de la Redonda XIV[th]C* (built on an
earlier round Romanesque structure). Its impressive twin towers *Las Gemelas*
(the twins) were a later addition and it adjoins the Plaza del Mercado lined with
shops and cafés. The city is also capital of the famous wine-growing region of
La Rioja and the festival of San Mateo heralds in the harvest in a weeklong
frenzy of celebration at the end of September. There are a multitude of bars,
restaurants and shops centred around
the pedestrian main street c/ de Portales
– try the delightful Café Moderno on c/
Matínez Zaporta which opens (relatively)
early for pilgrims trying to get back to
the hostel before it closes its doors. Off
the west end of c/de Portales is the neo-
colonial edifice of the main Post Office
Correos de Telégraphos adjoining the 18th
century Palacio del Espartero (museum)
off which is c/Laurel, famous for its tapas

Logrono – Café Moderno

bars. At the east end of c/de Portales close to the junction with the busy c/Muro
de Cervantes is Plaza Amós Salvador and ❹ *Iglesia San Bartolomé* with its
exquisitely carved 13th century porch. For other monuments along the Ruaviejo,
see *leaving the albergue (next stage)*.

Detour: Clavijo is only 16 km south of Logroño. The sombre ruins of its castle
stand sentinel over the fields where legend has it Santiago first appeared on his
white charger to turn the tide of this historic battle in favour of the Spaniards
over the occupying Moors in 844. It is, however, approached through a rather
disappointing and untidy village landscape. Check with the helpful Turismo (La
Rioja) located in the main square on the side of the c/del General Vara de Rey.

LA RIOJA One of the smallest and yet more diverse of the autonomous regions of Spain and justifiably renowned for its superlative wines. However, it is not only its grapes that will tempt you, for here you will meet a friendly people who have been welcoming pilgrims since medieval times. Indeed, kings and noblemen were promoting the camino through La Rioja as early as the 11th century as a means of exporting its famous wine and wares throughout Europe (and a way of attracting artists and stonemasons to build the great cathedrals, monasteries and monuments along the route). Sandwiched between the mountains of Navarra and the flat plains of the Meseta of Castilla y León, La Rioja is geographically split between High Rioja *Rioja Alta* to the northwest (the main wine growing region) and the lower *Rioja Baja* where market gardening is more prominent. The famous battle of Clavijo marks a turning point in the turbulent history of the provinces. With the defeat of the Moors came a great boost to Christianity and by extension, the Camino de Santiago. Logroño has good road and rail connections to all parts of Spain.

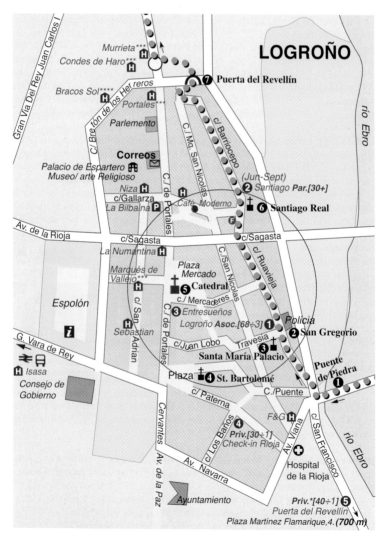

REFLECTIONS:

_____
_____
_____
_____
_____
_____
_____
_____
_____
_____
_____
_____
_____
_____
_____
_____
_____
_____
_____
_____
_____
_____
_____
_____
_____
_____
_____
_____
_____
_____
_____

❑ **We are speeding up our lives and working harder,
in a futile attempt to slow down and enjoy it.** *Paul Hawken*

08 **625.1** km (388.4 miles) to Santiago

LOGROÑO – NÁJERA (La Rioja)

	Path / Track	--- ---	23.0	---	*76%*
	Quiet Road	--- ---	4.8	---	*16%*
	Main Road	--- ---	2.3	---	*8%*
Total km	**Total distance**		**30.1 km** (18.7 miles)		

Adjusted for climb 31.6 km (accrued ascent 300m = 1.5 km)
Alto ▲ High Point: Path at Poyo Roldán 600m (1,968 feet)
< ▲ ⒣ > *from albergue* ❶: **12.7** km and Ventosa **20.4** (+ 0.7 km).

The Practical Path: One third of this stage is alongside the busy main roads that lead out of Logroño and into Navarette and Nájera. With constant road improvements, waymarking may be disturbed, so stay fully focused or you might lose your way – or your body. If nerves become frayed, you can always take refuge in the beautifully renovated intermediate albergues in Navarette or Ventosa. The natural pathways now turn to the rich red clay soil of La Rioja – beautiful in the sun and a nightmare in the wet as it clings to footwear like a leech!

❑ **The Mystical Path:** Hundreds of pilgrims have taken time to make a cross and place it in this godforsaken place. The cross is a symbol of that greater mystery that lies beyond the suffering of this world – are you inclined to add yours? Will you stop awhile to admire the beautiful stone portal, gateway to another journey that awaits us? Will you ponder the adjoining monument to a modern pilgrim who goes this way? Will you notice the roar of traffic and heed its urgency or will you 'get the hurry off you' and take a more leisurely pace? Will you take the direct route or venture to Ventosa? The choice, as always, is yours.

❑ **Personal Reflections:** *"… I found him hanging up some pilgrim's washing. His smile said welcome; his refuge was a veritable haven of peace. He suggested I stop and stay the night – we could share part of our journey over a meal together. Kas had urged me to meet him but I declined his invitation and now hurried onward anxious to reach the destination I had set myself. However, the next hostel was full and the hotel had no vacancy. I hurried on. It was getting late and I was already tired. The next village was two hours away …"*

0.0 km **Logroño** From the albergue ❶ follow the brass scallop shells inlaid into the sympathetically restored c/Rúaviejo which becomes the c/Barriocepo by the time it reaches the handsome pilgrim fountain *Fuente de los Peregrinos* decorated with Jacobean motifs. It adjoins a modernised square with mosaics representing the pilgrimage in a board game *Juego del Oca* and up ahead is the

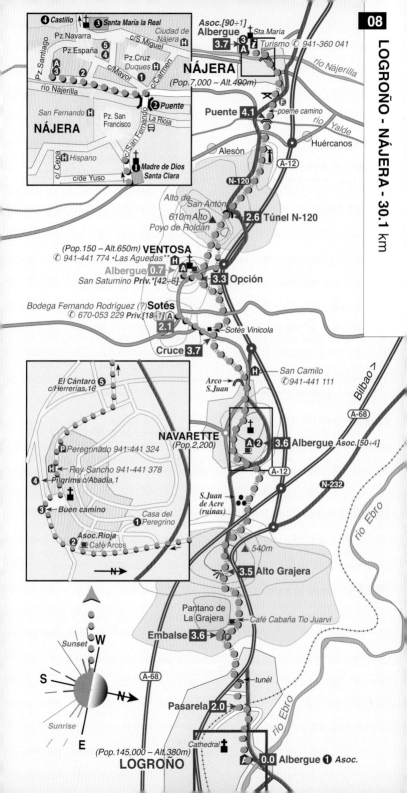

NÁJERA

④ Castillo ③ Santa María la Real
Pz.Navarra c/S.Miguel Ciudad de Nájera
Pz.España ⑤ Pz.Cruz Duques
Pz.Santiago ④ c/Mayor ① c/Carmen
Ⓐ③ ②
río Nájerilla

San Fernando Ⓗ Pz. San Francisco ② Puente
NÁJERA La Rioja

Ⓒ Cepa Ⓗ Hispano
c/ c/de Yuso ① Madre de Dios Santa Clara

Asoc.[90÷1]
Albergue Sta.María
NÁJERA ③⑦ Turismo Ⓒ 941-360 041 3.7 Ⓐ
(Pop.7,000 – Alt.490m)

río Nájerilla

Puente 4.1 poeme camino río Yalde
Huércanos
Alesón A-12

Alto de San Antón
610m Alto 2.6 **Túnel N-120**
Poyo de Roldán N-120

(Pop.150 – Alt.650m) **VENTOSA**
Ⓒ 941-441 774 •Las Aguedas** Ⓗ
Albergue 0.7 Ⓐ
San Saturnino **Priv.***[42÷6] 3.3 **Opción**

Bodega Fernando Rodríguez (?)**Sotés**
Ⓒ 670-053 229 **Priv.**[18÷1] Ⓐ
2.1 Sotés Vinícola
Cruce 3.7

El Cántaro ⑤ Ⓗ³ San Camilo
c/Herrerías,16 Ⓒ941-441 111

Ⓟ Peregrinado 941-441 324 Arco→ S.Juan
Ⓗ Rey Sancho 941-441 378 **NAVARETTE**
④ Pilgrims c/Abadia,1 (Pop.2,200) Ⓐ② 3.6 **Albergue** Asoc.[50÷4]
③ Buen camino A-12
Casa del Peregrino
② Asoc.Rioja S.Juan de Acre (ruinas)
Café Arcos N-232
→N→

▲ 540m río Ebro

3.5 **Alto Grajera**
Pantano de La Grajera ← Café Cabaña Tio Juarvi
Embalse 3.6 → Ⓕ

A-68

Sunset W
S ← →N
Sunrise
E

← tunél
Pasarela 2.0

Cathedral † río Ebro
(Pop.145,000 – Alt.380m) Ⓐ 0.0 **Albergue** ① Asoc.
LOGROÑO

impressive façade of ❺ *Iglesia Santiago Real XVI*th*C* (right) with a statue of Santiago Matamoros high up above the south door (see photo). The present building occupies the site of an earlier 9th century church erected to celebrate the defeat of the Moors at Clavijo. The interior also has several images of St. James. Adjoining the church is the parish pilgrim hostel. Continuing on through the narrow cobbled streets of the Old Town *Casco Antiguo* until it opens up

Logroño – Iglesia de Santiago

into the paved Parliament Square *Plaza del Parlamento* with the impressive facade of the Parlamento de la Rioja whose building has been used for activities as diverse as a Carmelite convent and a tobacco factory!

We now leave the medieval quarter through the original pilgrim's gate ❼ *Puerta del Camino* **[0.5 km]** alternatively called Muralla del Revellín or Puerta Carlos V, the latter being a reference to the splendid armorial shields that adorn it. [!] Take a moment to collect your bearings – the next few kilometres are through the frenzied suburbs of Logroño. Yellow arrows will accompany you but they have to compete with the distracting symbols of commercialism, and are less obvious. With awareness, you will make it to the peaceful lakeshore café of La Grajera with relative ease – but stay focused! The main route out is straight down the busy Marqués de Murrieta (signposted Burgos N-120). *The old route continued s/o over the railway line but for the new waymarked route through parkland* turn <left into c/ de los Duques de Nájera **[1.1** km] and turn off right> into park [F] and over railway line via footbridge *pasarela* **[0.4** km]:

2.0 km Pasarela rail *ferrocarril* through the linear park *Parque de San Miguel* emerging into roadway to take the tunnel under the A-12 motorway **[1.4 km].** The next section is through open parkland along a newly paved track with concrete benches, somewhat hard underfoot (and buttocks) but now thankfully separated from the motorway bypass. This leads to a grove of pine trees visible ahead and after **[2.2 km]** we reach Logroño's reservoir *pantano*:

3.6 km Pantano de la Grajera [F] turn right> along the reservoir wall, through pine forest and over a footbridge past the panoramic •*Café Cabaña del Tio Juarvi* and picnic area with wonderful views of the lake. The route leads around the lake along gravel pathways passing Marcelino's *ermita del peregrino pasante* onto an asphalt track up towards the woodland on the horizon to:

3.5 km Alto de la Grajera providing a good view back over the route and Logroño. Now at the top of the rise the track runs alongside the highway where hundreds of crosses have been made out of strips of bark from the adjoining sawmill and placed on the wire fence that separates us from the busy city bypass: a timely reminder, perhaps, of the sacred nature of our journey and the tenuous boundary that separates us from a secular perspective. Along this stage we are told *there is no way to happiness – Happyness is the Way!* We now join the hard shoulder of the N-120 [!] towards Navarrete before crossing over [!] onto an earth track through fields and vineyards crossing over the autopista A-68 where, on the far side, we come to the ruins of the medieval monastery of the Order of San Juan de Acre founded in the 12th century to look after pilgrims. The splendidly carved entrance porch has been re-sited as the gate to the cemetery that we will pass on the far side of town. Continue up the steep stone steps into Navarrete:

3.6 km Navarrete •Albergue ❶ *Asoc.*
[50÷4] ✆ 941 440 722 located in the old
town c/San Juan with 50 beds from €7 in 3
rooms + attic (hot in summer). All facilities
including clothes-dryer *secadora* which
makes up for the lack of outside drying area.
Popular •*café Los Arcos* adjoins. ❷ *Casa*
del Peregrino Priv.[18÷1]+ ✆ 630-982 928
with 18 bunk beds €8 + ind. from €25. ❸
Buen Camino Priv.[6÷1]+ ✆ 941-440 318

Navarrete – Albergue ❶

€9 *El Cántaro Priv.[12÷1]+* ✆ 941-441 180
modern house in c/Herrerías,16 with 12 bunks €10 + ind. rooms from €20.
(*[Next albergue: Ventosa – 7.6 km]*. Other accommodation: *Central* •**Villa de**
Navarette Hs ✆ 941-440 318 c/La Cruz. •**Rey Sancho** H*** ✆ 941-441 378 c/
Mayor Alta and •**Peregrinando** P ✆ 941-441 324. Near the main roads •**La**
Carioca Hs ✆ 941-440 805/006 c/Prudencio Muñoz, 1 and the modern •**San**
Camilo H** ✆ 941-441 111.

NAVARETTE Another historic camino town where effort has been made to
maintain the original period houses with handsomely carved family crests
and armorial shields. The imposing 16th century Church of the Assumption
occupies a commanding position overlooking the top square [F] and below it is
a Turismo ✆ 941-440 005 (summer only) and tapas bar •*Deportivo* with tables
on the square. At the lower end of the town, on the main road, is another busy
square with a number of cafés and restaurants. Leaving albergue [1] pass along
the arcaded cobbled street up to the church square into the c/de Santiago with
pilgrim information office and c/San Roque down to join the main road. Cross
over the rio de la Fuente and pass the town *cementerio* with its splendidly carved
13th century entrance gateway (relocated here from the ruins of the hospice of
San Juan de Acre on the eastern outskirts). One of the capitals depicts the battle
between Roldán and Ferragut (see *Poyo Roldán* which we pass later). Continue
past the cemetery onto a track of bright red Riojan earth through vineyards to:

3.7 km Cruce *Opción* cross road to Sotés. *[Note: sign to •Albergue Sotés 1,3*
km – is in fact 2.1 km up a steep asphalt road and is often closed – ✆ 670 053
229]. Pass the wine cooperative *Vitivinicola de Sotes* where the route veers back
towards the motorway. An alt. route continues along the A-12 or climb back up
again towards the village of Ventosa atop the rise ahead.

3.3 km Cruce *Opción Ventosa* Waymarks offer the option to bypass the
village. To enter Ventosa turn up into the quiet village main street to: •**Albergue**
San Saturnino Priv.[42÷6]* ✆ 941-441 899 c/Mayor. A sensitively restored
and well-maintained hostel 700m off route
with 42 beds €8 in 6 rooms good facilities
incl. rear patio. *[Next Albergue: Nájera*
9.4 km]. Also H**Las Águedas* ✆ 941-
441 774 Plaza S. Coloma, opened in 2012
rooms from €45. Re-join the waymarked
path passing •*Café Juanka* (free internet)
and take the track that winds its way up
through an isolated pass between two small
hills where you will find little stone 'altars'
erected by individuals pausing to soak up
the mystery of this mythical place. On our

Albergue – San Saturnino

left is *Alto de San Antón* site of an early pilgrim hospital established by the Antonine Order *Ruinas de Convento de San Antón* (no longer discernible) while on the right is Roldan's Hill *Poyo de Roldán. (Here we are led to believe Roldán slew the Muslim giant Ferragut with a well-aimed rock. Roland liberated the town (where Ferragut ruled) and freed the captive Christian knights of Charlemagne's army. This legend, reminiscent of David and Goliath, retains its powerful impact along the camino].* Continue through the narrow pass (the high point of this stage at 610m) and head down towards Nájera passing under the N-120 through pilgrim tunnel:

2.6 km **Túnel** continue along a wide farm track through vineyards passing beehive hut (left) across minor road around the side of the gravel works to:

4.1 km **Puente** pilgrim footbridge over the river Yalde with rest area beyond. We now pass the graffiti poem that asks: *Pilgrim Who Calls You?* And while contemplating the question we pass a canal to La Fuente de Paulino [F]. Cross N-120 [!] to the outskirts of Nájera passing the sports centre *polideportivo* over main roundabout and follow the road as it narrows and descends towards the Río Nájerilla passing ❶ *iglesias Santa Clara* and **Madre de Dios**. Cross over bridge ❷ (it replaced the medieval bridge erected by San Juan de Ortega). For the most direct route to the pilgrim hostel turn <left along the riverside to:

3.7 km **Nájera** **Albergue** ❸*Municipal Asoc.[90÷1]* mod. single-storey building adj. river with 90 beds €-*donativo*. All facilities but somewhat cramped (open all year). ❶*Calle Mayor Priv.[10÷1]*+ © 941-360 407 C/Dicarán,5. 10 bunks + private rooms just off the c/Mayor. ❷*Puerta de Nájera Priv.[32÷6]* c/Carmen,4 near river © 941 362 317. ❹*Alberone Priv.[32÷3]*+ © 674-246 826 with 32 beds + ind. rooms in

Nájera – Albergue ❶

mod. building on c/San Marcial,8. ❺*Sancho III La Judería Priv.[10÷2]* c/San Marcial, 6 © 941-361 138 above restaurant *La Judería on.*

Other accommodation in the old town is limited to •**Fonda el Moro** c/Martires, 21 © 941-360 052. •**Ciudad de Nájera** Hs** © 941-360 660 calleja San Miguel, 14 (backing on to the cliffs) or the up-market •**Duques de Nájera** H*** © 941-410 421 c/ Carmen, 7. On the other side of the river: •**Hispano II** P © 941-363 616 c/La Cepa or •**San Fernando** H** © 941-363 700.

NÁJERA: Another historic town, capital of the Kingdom of Navarre in the 11th and 12th centuries, with strong connections with the Camino de Santiago, marking the beginning of stage V of the Codex Calixtinus. Pride of place is ❸ **Monasterio Santa María de la Real** with its magnificent Royal Pantheon housing the burial place of many of the illustrious kings, Queens and knights of Navarre. Of singular beauty is the tomb of Doña Blanca de Castile y Navarre (1156). The Pantheon is part of this fine church, as is the cave, which gave rise to it. *[The church was built at this spot following the legend that the son of Sancho the Great, Don García, followed his hunting falcon into this cave and came upon a statue of the Virgin Mary - photo opposite].* The church also has interesting choir stalls bearing pilgrim motifs carved into the seat rests. The splendid Knights Cloister is

accessed through the Museum. *Museo Najerillense* (Roman artifacts) opposite. Nájera has a population of 7,000 and we enter through the modern eastern quarter with the old town sandwiched between the river Najerila and high rock face that acts as a dramatic backdrop with its ancient ❹ *Castillo*. The narrow c/ Mayor has a wide selection of shops, bars and cafés and leads to myriad side streets including Plaza San Miguel where we find the ***Turismo*** Ⓒ 941-360 041. At the far end of town (close to the albergue) are the Plazas de España and Navarra with a variety of bars and restaurants serving pilgrim menus.

Detour: ● ● ● ● ● **San Millán de la Cogolla and the monasteries of Suso and Yuso.** This World heritage site represents one of the earliest known monastic communities in Europe dating back to the 6th century and is also credited with being the birthplace of the Spanish language. *(See next section under Azofra for full description of this and the Cistercian abbey at Cañas)*. It can be walked (a very full day) from Nájera to San Millán (18 km on LR 205) and back via Cañas to Azofra (14 km on LR 206) but is more realistically visited as part of a tour or shared taxi from Nájera or Azofra and by staying overnight at San Millán but accommodation is limited so book beforehand (see next section for details or enquire at the tourist office).

REFLECTIONS:

_____

_____

_____

_____

_____

_____

❒ **Yesterday is history, tomorrow a mystery and today a gift – that is why it is called the present.**

09 595.0 km (369.7 miles) to Santiago

NÁJERA – SANTO DOMINGO de la CALZADA

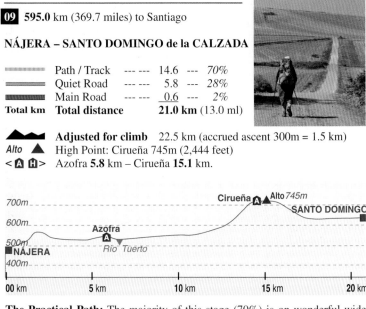

	Path / Track	--- ---	14.6	---	70%
	Quiet Road	--- ---	5.8	---	28%
	Main Road	--- ---	0.6	---	2%
Total km	**Total distance**		**21.0 km** (13.0 ml)		

Adjusted for climb 22.5 km (accrued ascent 300m = 1.5 km)
Alto ▲ High Point: Cirueña 745m (2,444 feet)
< Ⓐ Ⓗ > Azofra **5.8** km – Cirueña **15.1** km.

The Practical Path: The majority of this stage (70%) is on wonderful wide country tracks passing through remote and gently undulating farmland with only the last stretch into Santo Domingo alongside the main road. Beyond Azofra the camino crosses a secondary road (to Alesanco) where the new A-12 has been built – be careful not to follow old waymarks back onto the busy N-120 (right). There is little shade and few drinking fonts on this stage so put on the hat and fill up the bottle as you pass Azofra and Cirueña (both have *fuentes*).

❒ **The Mystical Path:** Will you pause to admire the medieval stone column that marks an ancient border? What does it mark and symbolise to you? Where is the border between your ancient Homeland and the world you now inhabit? Will you rest awhile in the leafy shade of the cool glade beyond to ponder such mysteries? How many pilgrims in the past has this venerable grove sheltered from the noonday sun and how many will it shelter in the future? Will you accept its sombre gift in the passing moment, a present from the acorn past?

❒ **Personal Reflections:** *"... I entered the cool interior and realised I was the only person present. I had the urge to leave but at that moment the bells stopped ringing and the nuns began to file in. I knelt in silence and then lifted my head at the sound of approaching footsteps. I looked up into eyes that beamed such love and acceptance that I momentarily lost any sense of ego-self as I followed her to the choir stall. Tears began to stream down my face as the nuns started their heavenly chanting... The unconditional love with which I was embraced overwhelmed me as my head began to spin and I collapsed onto the pew. The nun in front turned and quietly laid her hand on mine. She produced a tissue from the sleeve of her habit and bent down and whispered gently, 'breathe.' I write these notes in the quiet of the convent, and am struck by the realisation that she could not have known where I was from and yet spoke the only word in English that was needed. In that moment she, or rather that which she represented, quite literally in-spired me. I am utterly unable to convey the gratitude I feel ..."*

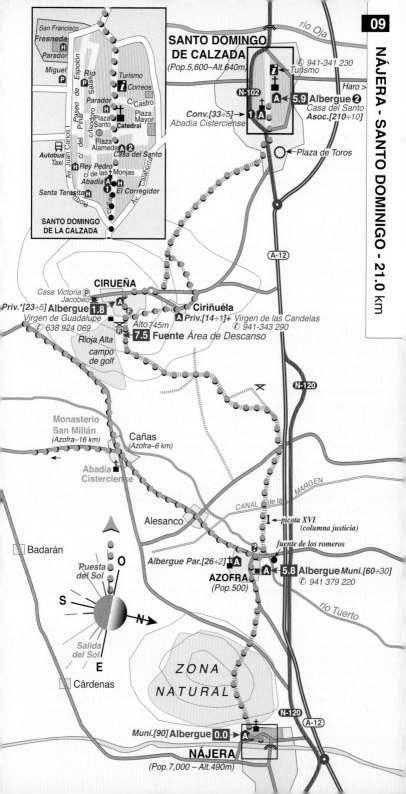

río Oja

SANTO DOMINGO DE CALZADA
(Pop.5,600–Alt.640m)

San Francisco
Fresneda
Parador
Miguel **P**
Río **H** Salas
Paseo de Espolón Turismo **i**
i Correos
Parador **H** C/Castro
H Plaza Santo Plaza Mayor
c/Isidoro Catedral
c/ del Pino Plaza Alameda
Autobus **H** **A 2**
Taxi Casa del Santo
Rey Pedro **H** c/ de las Monjas
H Abadía **A** **H**
Santa Teresita **H** **1** El Corregidor

SANTO DOMINGO DE LA CALZADA

© 941-341 230
i Turismo
Haro >
N-102 **A** **5.9** Albergue **2**
Casa del Santo
1 A Asoc.[210÷10]
Conv.[33÷5]→
Abadía Cisterciense

○ *Plaza de Toros*

(A-12)

CIRUEÑA
Casa Victoria **P**
Jacobeo
Priv.[23÷5] Albergue **1.8** **A**
Virgen de Guadalupe **F**
© 638 924 069 **Ciriñuéla**
A *Priv.*[14÷1]+ *Virgen de las Candelas*
© 941-343 290
Alto 745m **F**
Rioja Alta **X** **7.5** Fuente *Área de Descanso*
campo de golf

(N-120)

Monasterio San Millán
(Azofra–16 km) Cañas
(Azofra–6 km)
Abadía Cisterciense ✝

CANAL de la MARGEN

Alesanco

Badarán **I** ← *picota XVI*
(columna justicia)
Puesta del Sol **O**
fuente de los romeros
S ✽ **N** **?**
Albergue Par.[26÷2] **A**
Salida del Sol **AZOFRA** **A** **5.8** Albergue Muni.[60÷30]
(Pop.500) © 941 379 220
E
Cárdenas río Tuerto

ZONA NATURAL

(N-120) (A-12)

Muni.[90] Albergue **0.0** **A** ✝
NÁJERA
(Pop.7,000 – Alt.490m)

`0.0 km` **Nájera Leaving the albergue** make your way through the Plaza de Navarre past the Church of Santa María Real and continue up the street passing the pelota court (left) and enter the delightful *zona natural* climbing steeply up between pine trees on a wide red earth track to the high point **[1.0 km]** (460m). The track continues down over road **[0.8 km]** by farm buildings to join quiet roads and tracks all the way into Azofra for the remaining **[4.0 km]**.

`5.8 km` **Azofra Centro** •*Cafe Sevilla* •**Albergue ❶** *Muni.[60÷30!]* purpose built hostel ✆ 941 379 220 in c/Las Parras, 200m (right) from the central fountain. 60 places €7 in cubicles with just 2 beds. The extensive facilities include a patio/ cafe area (open all year). •**Albergue ❷** *Par.[26÷2]* ✆ 607 383 811 parish hostel adj. the Church of Our Lady of the Angels *Nuestra Señora de los Ángeles* (statue of Santiago Peregrino and mass at 19:00)

Azofra – Albergue ❶ Municipal

situated at the top end of town. 26 beds and small patio by the entrance that gets the last of the evening sun. The lean-to structure was renovated by a German Confraternity (Herbert Simón) now operated by the council. The cool, atmospheric surroundings compensates for the basic facilities (opens when main hostel is full). **Other accommodation:** Exclusive hotel. •**Real Casona de las Amas** ✆ 941 416 103 on c/Mayor, 5 rooms from €130. Former hostel *La Fuente* remains closed (for sale). *(Next albergue: Cirueña – 9.3 km).*

AZOFRA A tranquil village with a population of barely 500 that owes its continuing existence to the camino. As you leave the village a small park [F] (left) is dedicated to the patroness of La Rioja *Virgen de Valvanera* and on the other side of the road (50m off route) the ruins of the medieval pilgrim's fountain *Fuente de los Romeros* adjoining a lay-by with a modern monument. There are 2 inconspicuous shops (adjacent to the albergues) and several bars that compete to provide the pilgrim with sustenance. There were several pilgrim *hospitales* here in medieval times. Azofra is also the nearest place to start a detour of the 'monasteries route' *ruta de los monasterios* and the birthplace of the Spanish language *la cuna del Castellano* in Yuso.

Detour [1] Cañas ●●●●● 6 km south along a quiet country road. The village is home to the splendid Cistercian abbey of Santa María *Abadía Cisterciense de Cañas* founded in 1170 for the order of nuns that still occupy it (closed Mondays). It is unusual among religious buildings for the natural light *luz* that pours into it through the original alabaster windows that reach up to the vaulted roof. Off the adjoining garden courtyard is a small museum housing the early 13th century sarcophagus of Doña Urraca López de Haro founder of the abbey

and, reputedly, one of the finest sarcophagi in Spain. The abbey is also celebrated for the visit of Saint Francis of Assisi who allegedly stayed here while journeying to Santiago. Cañás is the birthplace of Santo Domingo de Silos (not to be confused with Santo Domingo de Calzada) who restored the famous monastery that now bears his name and the home of Gregorian chant in Spain (see Burgos detours). •**La Casona** ✆ 941-379 150 rooms from €25. Options: from here you can either: (a) return back to Azofra and continue along the camino or (b) take the country road out of Cañas to Cirueña and re-join the camino there or (c) continue to:

Detour [2] San Millán Yuso and Suso Monasteries 10 km south of Cañas (16 from Azofra). Declared a world heritage site by UNESCO in 1997 as testimony to its unique contribution to Christian monasticism from the 6th century and as birthplace of the Spanish language, one of the most widely spoken in the world today. It was here in the 10th century that the native Spanish language, Castilian *Castellano*, was first written down by an anonymous monk. Two centuries later it was further embellished in the verse of the poet monk Gonzalo Berceo. Suso (the smaller and higher of the two monasteries) is set on the hillside in this gloriously peaceful valley located just beyond the village of Berceo. It has Visigothic, Mozárabe and Romanesque characteristics while Yuso, built from 11th century onwards, is mainly Baroque and houses some fine artefacts including the famous library. Realistically you will really need an extra day to explore this area. Part of the monastery at Yuso is now a luxury hotel •**Hospedería de San Millán** H**** © 941-373 277 single from €90. Former pilgrim accommodation in the monastery is no longer available but casa rural •**La Parra** © 606 648 885 has room from €30. •**Hostal La Calera** Hs © 941-373 268 and several other possibilities in Badarán 5 km •**Pensión Alaska** © 941-367 005 is at the cheaper end. Return via Cañas (see options).

From Azofra continue over the junction by the village park [F] by rio Tuerto and bear off <left onto a delightful track that winds its way all the way up to Cirueña passing the medieval marker *la picota* [**1.5 km**] and shortly afterwards a raised canal *Canal de la Margen* and then over road [**1.8 km**] and turn <left and then right> passing river (usually dry) and then up towards the new golf complex on the rise in front *Rioja Alta Golf Club* to:

7.5 km Cirueña *Área de Descanso* [F] continue to new suburbs with maze of empty apartment blocks giving rise to the sad sobriquet *Sevende* (for sale!). **Option**: Mutliple arrows compete for the limited business. Turn right for **Ciriñuela** and •**Albergue** *Virgen de las Candelas Priv.[14÷1]*+ © 941-343 290 mod. building with 14 beds €8 +priv. rooms in c/Real.
or continue s/o on (left) for the main route passing another *Área de Descanso* [F] [**1.2 km**] up to a third rest area [F] [**0.6 km**] and option:

1.8 km Cirueña •**Albergue** *Virgen de Guadalupe Priv.*[23÷5] (100m left c/ Barrio Alto) © 638 924 069 with 23 rooms €10. Also short detour (250m) to •*Café/bar Jacobeo* and pension •**Casa Victoria** © 941 426 105 bed from €20. To continue pass the roundabout *[option for Ciriñuela visible ahead (right) a detour of ½ km]*. Continue down the road and turn <left onto farm track that undulates over the surrounding fields until you reach the outskirts of St. Dominic of the roadway *Santo Domingo de la Calzada*. Here we pass behind industrial buildings before reaching the busy N-120 [**4.7 km**] which we follow until crossing over into the old town. If you lose the waymarks in the busy streets ahead follow the signpost for the *Parador* up the c/Mayor [**1.1 km**] to:

5.9 km Santo Domingo de la Calzada •**Albergue** ❶ *Casa del Santo Asoc.[162÷9]* operated by the Spanish Confraternity © 941-343 390 who also publish the pilgrim magazine *El Peregrino* from here. Centrally situated in the old quarter on c/Mayor, 38 open all year with 162 beds €-*donativo* with an additional 50 in the original (adj.) hostel. All facilities including shaded

garden with chicken coop where the cocks and hens are kept for their pivotal part in the cathedral myth (See below). •**Albergue ❷** *Abadía Cisterciense Conv. [33÷5]* tranquil hostel run by Cistercian nuns © 941 340 700 on c/Mayor, 29 (left) as you enter the old quarter (opposite rear entrance of hotel El Corregidor). 33 beds €5 with good facilities incl. a peaceful shaded terrace and garden to the rear. All pilgrims (both genders) are welcome dinner menú also available. Vespers *Vísperas* at 18.30.

Other accommodation: *Turismo* © 941-341 230 is just past the cathedral at c/ Mayor, 70. •**Hospedería Santa Teresita** Hs** © 941-340 700 modern hostel also run by the Cistercian nuns in c/Pinar, 2 (rear of albergue [2]). •**Rey Pedro** Hs © 941-341 160 on C/S.Roque, 9 (main thoroughfare). •**Río** P © 941-340 277 c/ Etchegoyen, 2. •**Miguel** P © 941-343 252 c/Juan Carlos I, 23 (Main thoroughfare). •**El Peregrino** P © 941-342 128 Av. de Calahorra. •**Albert** P © 941-340 827 c/ Beato Hermosilla, 20.. In the higher price bracket are: •**El Corregidor** H***© 941-340 827 c/Mayor, 14 or for 4 star luxury in the original pilgrim hospital on Plaza del Santo (opposite the cathedral) •**Parador** H****© 941-340 300 or try the latest edition to the Parador chain •**Parador de Santo Domingo Bernardo de Fresneda** H*** © 941-341 150 located at the far end of town beside the pilgrim monument in the recently refurbished 16th century Convento de San Francisco.

SANTO DOMINGO de la CALZADA:

The winding streets of this ancient town evoke a sense of history that is intimately linked with the camino. It owes its inspiration to *Saint Dominic of the Road*, so called because he effectively dedicated his life to improving the physical route for pilgrims and was responsible for building many of the roads and bridges that we pass along. This was in the 11th century, so they have been rebuilt several times since then but his spirit is as alive today as are the cock and hen in the cathedral coop. A giant among men Domingo García was born in 1019 in

Santo Domingo

humble surroundings in Viloria (see next stage). His effort to heed God's call to become a monk was thwarted by the monastery at San Millán but the loss to the intelligentsia has been the gain of pilgrims for the past millennia. He built a pilgrim hospital, now the Parador and a church which has evolved into the Cathedral both are situated in the historic town square *Plaza del Santo* and, like many other religious structures, renovated over many centuries and therefore combining different architectural styles. The original church was consecrated in the 12th century, although the independent tower was not added until the 18th century. The dark interior houses the tomb of Santo Domingo, the chapel of La Magdalena and a fine altarpiece. One of the more unlikely exhibits is a chicken coop at the rear of the church containing 2 live fowl (see panel next page).

A museum is attached to the cathedral and on the opposite side of the square is the original pilgrim hospital dating from 14th century is now a luxury Parador that still retains its medieval splendour (view the main *sala* / bar). The town has a wide variety of restaurants, bars and shops along both the c/Mayor and the busy Paseo and the narrow interconnecting streets all serving the inflow of tourists, pilgrims and the local population of 6,000. The town and its network of medieval streets has been declared a site of historic interest and its main fiesta, in honour of the saint, takes place during the first 2 weeks in May.

The chicken coop relates to the story of the Miracle of the Cock. Embellished over the years it has become one of the more endearing legends along the Way of St. James. Legend has it that a pilgrim couple and their son stopped at an inn here on their way to Santiago. The pretty innkeeper's daughter had her eye on the handsome lad, but the devout young fellow thwarted her advances. Incensed by his refusal she hid a silver goblet in his backpack and reported him for stealing it. The innocent lad was caught and condemned to hang. Some accounts suggest the parents continued on their way, oblivious of the fate of their son and on their return from Santiago they found him still hanging on the gallows but miraculously still alive thanks to the intervention of Santo Domingo. They rushed to the sheriff's house and found him just about to tuck into dinner. Upon hearing the news, he retorted that their son was no more alive than the cock he was about to eat, whereupon the fowl stood up on the dish and crowed loudly. The miracle was not lost on the sheriff who rushed back to the gallows and cut down the poor lad, who was given a full pardon. We are left to speculate on the fate of the foxy maiden. Indeed so many miracles were ascribed to the intervention of Santo Domingo that the town that came to carry his name was also referred to as the Compostela of Rioja.

REFLECTIONS:

❐ **When you meet anyone, remember it is a holy encounter.**
And as you see them you will see yourself. *A Course In Miracles*

10 574.0 km (356.7 miles) to Santiago

SANTO DOMINGO de la CALZADA – BELORADO
(La Rioja)   (Castilla y León)

▦ Path / Track	--- ---	17.3	---	75%
▬ Quiet Road	--- ---	5.2	---	23%
▨ Main Road	--- ---	0.4	---	2%
Total km **Total distance**		**22.9 km** (14.2 miles)		

▲ **Adjusted for climb**   24.4 km (accrued ascent 300m = 1.5 km)
Alto ▲   High Point: above Vilamayor del Río 810m (2,657 feet)
< 🄰 🄷 >   Grañón **7.2** km   Carrasquedo **8.1** km (1.2 km *off* route) – Redecilla
11.1 km – Castildelgado **12.8** km – Viloria de la Rioja **15.0** km –
Villamayor del Río **18.7** km (300m *off* route).

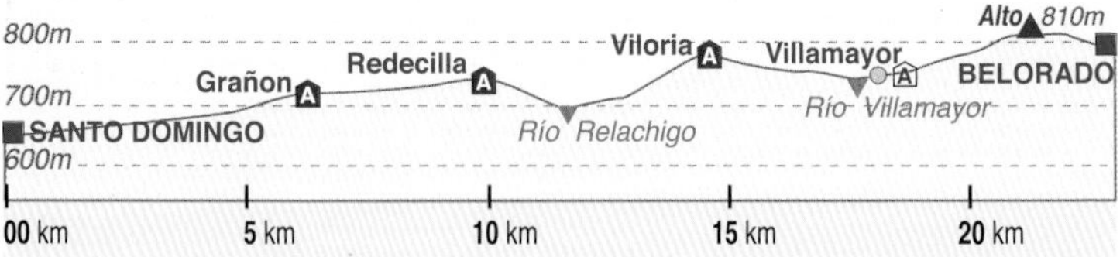

The Practical Path: It is a strange tribute to the Saint who did so much to assist the pilgrim that today we are forced by new roads to travel closer to the dangerous N-120 more than at any other stage of our journey so far. Waymarking may also be confusing with on-going road works and if you are not careful you might end up walking on the main road all the way to Belorado! Be prepared for half today's walk to be parallel to the busy main road with little shelter and water, apart from the villages you pass through.

❐ **The Mystical Path:** There is much to reflect on as you walk the road of the Saint. Denied access to the seat of knowledge, yet endowed with wisdom. Which do you seek? Which will provide you with real meaning? The burial place is on all the maps but will you discover the place of birth? Will you stay awhile and soak up the light of this peaceful place and drink the cool water from the same well that perhaps nurtured the infant child? – not as obvious as the tap in the square, but more refreshing. The only monument to this extraordinary Saint is a ruined house protecting the peace of this place from the tour buses. This is truly an elevated place providing refreshment for the soul and space to contemplate our own renewal.

❐ **Personal Reflections:** *"… I resisted his advances and resented his intrusion. He could see I was limping badly and persisted in his offer to help. My resistance finally crumpled and he removed my boot and sock with tenderness. My foot was an awful mess – it had gone way beyond what any reasonable person would have asked of it. He fetched a basin of warm water and gently washed away the blood. The broken skin was easily dressed and the remaining blisters drained. Afterwards he took my torn boot to the nearby cobbler to have it stitched. He had healed my foot and mended my boot but the real healing was happening inside of me. How many times had I adversely judged my fellow travellers when each one is a Christ in disguise …"*

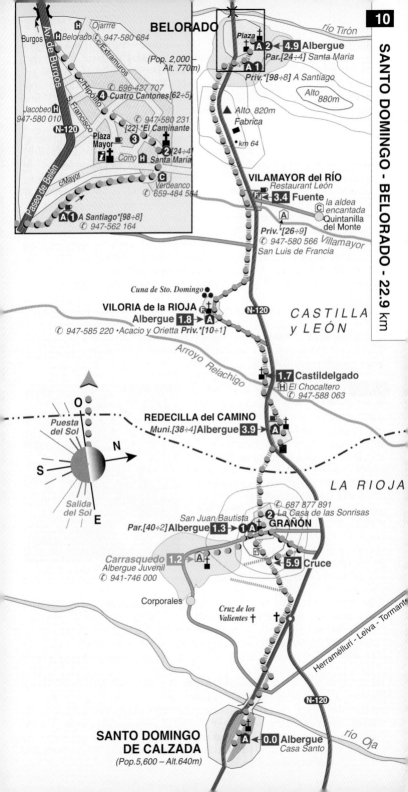

BELORADO

H Ojarrre

Burgos **H** Belorado © 947-580 684

c/Extramuros

(Pop. 2,000 – Alt. 770m)

© 696-427 707
4 Cuatro Cantones [62÷5]

Jacobeo **H**
947-580 010

c/Hipolito

© 947-580 231
S.Francisco [22] *El Caminante*

N-120

Plaza
Mayor **3**
2 [24÷4]
i Corro **H** Santa Maria

c/Mayor **C**
Verdeanco
© 659-484 584

Paseo de Belen

A 1 A Santiago*[98÷8]
© 947-562 164

Plaza **A 2** → **4.9** Albergue
Par.[24÷4] Santa Maria

A 1 Priv.*[98÷8] A Santiago

Alto 880m

▲ Alto 820m
Fabrica

• km 64

VILAMAYOR del RÍO
Restaurant León

F → **3.4** Fuente *la aldea
encantada*
C Quintanilla
del Monte

A
Priv.[26÷9] Villamayor
© 947-580 566
San Luis de Francia

**CASTILLA
y LEÓN**

Cuna de Sto. Domingo

VILORIA de la RIOJA
Albergue **1.8** → **A**
© 947-585 220 •Acacio y Orietta **Priv.*[10÷1]**

N-120

Arroyo Relachigo

1.7 Castildelgado
H El Chocaltero
© 947-588 063

O

*Puesta
del Sol* N

S

E

REDECILLA del CAMINO
Muni.[38÷4] **Albergue** **3.9** → **A**

*Salida
del Sol*

LA RIOJA

© 687 877 891
2 La Casa de las Sonrisas

San Juan Bautista **GRAÑÓN**
Par.[40÷2] **Albergue** **1.3** → **A 1 A**

Carrasquedo **1.2** **A**
Albergue Juvenil
© 941-746 000

5.9 Cruce

Corporales

*Cruz de los
Valientes* †

Herramélluri - Leiva - Tormante

N-120

**SANTO DOMINGO
DE CALZADA**
(Pop.5,600 – Alt.640m)

A ← **0.0** Albergue
Casa Santo

río Oja

0.0 km Santo Domingo From albergue ❶ we pass the cathedral and head out along c/Mayor and pick up the main road (signposted Burgos) to the small *ermita* on the bridge over the río Oja **[0.9 km]**. *[Before the arrival of bridge-building Dominic, medieval pilgrims had to veer off right here along the river towards Leiva to follow the Río Tirón into Belorado via Herraméluri, Leiva (Peregrina) and Tormantos to the North, 3 km longer now all by road].*

Cross the Saint's Bridge *Puente del Santo* along track (right) before crossing over the main road **[1.1 km]** and continuing along a gravel path on the far side. *[A remote cross in this area La Cruz de los Valientes so called because of the combat between two locals, one from Santo Domingo and the other from Grañon, over disputed ownership of some nearby land. In medieval times, it was sometimes the custom to submit such matters to the Divine Judge on the basis that He would protect the innocent party – the guy from Grañón was favoured in this instance. A modern steel replacement appears to have been erected directly on route!]* Road works in this area have disturbed waymarks but continue s/o alongside the road up the new embankment and down the far side and turn off <left onto track **[2.6 km]** and then right> along over river (dry) and up towards Grañón visible on the horizon to track crossroad **[1.3 km]**:

5.9 km Cruce *Opción* new waymarks inexplicably direct you down right and then steeply back up into the village. To save yourself 200m and the climb back up continue s/o at crossroads past cemetery **[0.4 km]** and right on road **[0.5 km]**. Passing the ruins of *Ermita de los Judiós XIV*ᵗʰ*C* and over crossroads by bus stop to the church ahead **[0.4 km]**.

1.3 km Grañón Albergue ❶ *Par.[40÷2]* ✆ 941 420 818 parish hostel located in the upper floors of the annex to the adjoining Church of Saint John the Baptist. Open all year with 40 mattresses €-*donativo* on the attic floor reserved for pilgrims who have travelled from further back than Santo Domingo. The atmospheric lounge dovetails as a dining area with small kitchenette from which a shared meal is prepared. Basic hostel much treasured by pilgrims for the hospitality offered, the cool interior and tranquil setting, accessed directly off the village plaza with its shaded garden. •*Bar* and shop in the village square at the front.

Granón – Parish Albergue

GRAÑÓN VILLAGE: This walled town was inspired by the camino and had 2 monasteries and a pilgrim hospice. Today, we find a quiet village that remains typically Jacobean. Iglesia de San Juan Bautista has a fine high altarpiece, recently restored and a pilgrim mass is offered by the welcoming priest. If the albergue is full or you want to extend your stay in this peaceful oasis you can:

Detour ● ● ● ● ● **1.2 km Carrasquedo** (2.4 km round trip) to the pretty Basilica of Nuestra Señora de Carrasquedo, the patroness of Grañón village, situated amidst a grove of trees on the outskirts of the town (1.3 km) on the road to Corporales along a delightful tree-lined pathway. You can stay in the youth hostel, a venerable period building adjoining the basilica •**Albergue** *de Carrasquedo [40]+* ✆ 941-746 000 no kitchen but dinner (21:00) and breakfast (09:00) available (phone in advance to check availability).

...or at c/Mayor N° 16 **Albergue ❷** *La Casa de las Sonrisas Priv.* ✆ 687 877 891 and casa rural **Cerro de Mirabel** at N° 40 ✆ 941 420 798. Continue out onto tracks that wind around this hilltop village to cross stream **[0.7 km]** and then <left up to a monstrous modern signboard heralding the fact that you have left modest La Rioja behind and stepped into the autonomous region of Castilla y León (province of Burgos) a fact they are keen to demonstrate **[1.3 km]**.

CASTILLA Y LEÓN The largest autonomous region in Spain with an area of 95,000 km² (11 times the size of the region of Madrid) but a population of only 2.5 million (less than half that of Madrid). You will spend over 50% of your time travelling through 3 of its 9 separate provinces BURGOS, PALENCIA and LEÓN. It contains the incomparable *Meseta* the predominately flat table or plateau region that makes up a third of the Iberian peninsular and lies between 1,000 and 3,000 metres above sea level and follows the line of the Duero river basin. Cereal crops *cerales* hold sway here, mainly wheat but with oats on the poorer land and some sheep and goats grazing on the hillier parts. It is a sparsely populated arid region, primarily flat but with gently rolling hills. However, the seemingly endless horizons are broken up with delightful villages seemingly unaffected by the speed of modern life.

We start off through the Montes de Oca with the Sierra de la Demanda to our left (south) and the Cordillera Cantábrica to our right (north) with the occasional view of the snow covered Picos de Europa behind them – the highest peak is Peña Vieja 2,613m (8,500 feet). We then pass through the Montes de León which supports one of the enduring symbols of the *camino francés* the Iron Cross *Cruz de Ferro* at the high point of our route 1,505m (4,937 feet). Beyond this is the western arm of the Cordillera Cantábrica, which forms the boundary between Castilla y León and Galicia, which we enter through the Puerto de Pedrifita do Cebreiro at 1,110m (3,640 feet) but that is over 400 km away!

You will find many pamphlets and books along the way (some in English) that will detail the rich history of this vast region. Suffice to say that the ancient kingdom of Castile is well named for its many castles, which sought to protect and promote the kingdom. This promotion was nowhere more conspicuous than along the *Camino de Santiago*. It is well to recall that, up until the time the Saint's tomb was discovered, Spain was largely under the influence of the Moors. Fernando I established Castile in 1035 and the 1090's saw the legendary figure of El Cid turning the tide against the Moors from his base in Burgos. 200 years after its foundation Castile was united with León under Fernando III *El Santo*. It was an uneasy union and even today you will see many defaced signboards that bear the joint arms of the former separate jurisdictions, a separation that some would clearly like to see re-imposed. The general and medical emergency *emergencias* number for the area is 112.

Cross the N-120 into Redecilla del Camino with rest area [F] and *Turismo* ✆ 947-588 080 (summer only). Proceed into the main street to the church dedicated to Our Lady of the Street *Nuestra Señora de la Calle* which has a beautiful 12th century baptismal font and is located directly opposite the pilgrim hostel and bar **[1.9 km]**.

3.9 km Redecilla del Camino *(Pop. 150)* •Albergue *San Lázaro Mun.[38÷4]* municipal hostel ✆ 947-580 283 c/Mayor built on the site of the medieval hospital of San Lázaro, now a busy bar. 40 beds €-*donativo* in 4 rooms with all facilities. Passing between the church and the albergue continue up the c/Mayor before crossing the N-120 onto track which runs parallel to the road into:

1.7 km Castildelgado *(Pop. 80)* the delightful Romanesque *Iglesia San Pedro XIIthC* adjoins the ruins of the house of the Counts of Berberana and the pilgrim hospice founded by Alfonso VII that the village once supported. Hospitality is now limited to •**El Chocalatero** Hs ✆ 947-588 063 on the main road (+200m). The camino goes through the back of the village to pick up the track again parallel to main road over stream before turning off <left **[0.8** km] onto country road for **[1.0 km]** into:

1.8 km Viloria de la Rioja *(Pop. 70)* •**Albergue** *Priv.*[10÷1]* network* hostel c/ Nueva, 6. Acacio & Orietta ✆ 947-585 220 (m: 679-941 123) just below the church on a tranquil square in the centre of this delightful village with 10 beds €5 and outside terrace with all facilities including shared dinner *donativo*. Acacio is a key figure in the Asociacion Jacobea *paso a paso* and instigated the network association *red de albergues* that has done so much to improve pilgrim facilities along

Viloria de la Rioja – Albergue

the camino. Paulo Coelho is 'spiritual' godfather *padrino* to this hostel, which is funded solely from pilgrim donations. This peaceful village was the birthplace *cuna* of Saint Dominic, but the Romanesque baptismal font that witnessed his Christening has been removed and, inconceivably, the adjacent house where he was born was demolished – a blessing perhaps, as tourist coaches (and some pilgrims) bypass this historic idyll. Perhaps you will pause awhile by the shaded rest area [F] (there is a fresh spring just behind the church) and give thanks for the famous illiterate son of this quaint village who did so much to help pilgrims along the Way. Proceed out of the village by quiet country road to re-join a track alongside the N-120 **[1.3** km] over stream into the village square **[2.1 km]:**

3.4 km Villamayor del Río *(Pop. 50)* [F] *Kiosco* and rest area *área de descanso*. On the far side of the main road is *Restaurante León* with outside terrace and shop selling quality products from the region including quality wines, air-dried sausages *embutidos*, blood sausage *morcillas* and *chorizo*. Also on the far side of the road we find: •**Albergue** *San Luis de Francia Priv.*[26÷9]* ✆ 947-580 566 *off* route 300m (sign visible from the main road). Mixed reports with 26 beds €5, dinner €8 and breakfast also available. At the end of road, in Quintanilla del Monte, is casa rural •**La Encantada** where Ana de la Cruz offers a warm pilgrim welcome and free transport ✆ 947-580 484.

The camino continues parallel to N-120 all the way into Belorado. Just before entering the town cross over [!] **[4.0** km] by picnic area and follow wide track into Belorado passing: •**Albergue ❶** *A Santiago Priv.*[98÷8]* ✆ 947-562 164 with 98 beds €5–10 (open all year). Facilities include café/restaurant & small swimming pool but pilgrims generally prefer the welcome found in the town centre. Continue along the back road to the original parish hostel **[0.7 km]:**

4.9 km Belorado *(Pop. 2,100)* •**Albergue ❷** *Santa María Par.[24÷4]* the original parish hostel ✆ 947-580 085 adjoining the church of Santa María y San Pedro in a quiet oasis 500m north of the main square. Open all year (hospitaleros in summer) with 24 places €-*donativo* in a refurbished building adjoining the church. The welcoming ambience and tranquil setting softens the minimalist furnishings. Behind the albergue are cliffs with ancient (and modern) cave dwellings and a path up to the castle ruins.

•**Albergue ❸** *El Caminante Priv.**[22÷1]*+* Ⓒ 947-580 231 opposite the church with 22 bunk beds €5 +priv. rooms and meals available. At the other end of town we find the popular •**Albergue ❹** *Cuatro Cantones Priv.[62÷5]* Ⓒ 696-427 707 in renovated building just off the main square in c/Hipólito Lopez Bernal, 10 with 62 places €6 in several dormitories and excellent facilities with outside patio area and small swimming pool in summer (open all year). *[Next albergue – Tosantos 5.0 km].* **Other accommodation** several casa rurales. •**Casa Verdeancho** Ⓒ 659-484 584 c/El Corro with bar, near the church. •**Casa Waslala** Ⓒ 947-580 726 c/Mayor, 57. Pensions include •**Ojarre** P Ⓒ 947-580 223 c/Santiago, 16 and •**Toni** P Ⓒ 947-580 525 c/Redecilla del Campo, 7 (by the *Correos*). •**Hotel Jacobeo** Ⓒ 947-580 010 on the main road near the centre and further out •**Belorado** H˚ Ⓒ 947-580 684. •**El Corro** Ⓒ 670 691 173 corner of c/Mayor and El Corro.

BELORADO: has a delightful 'down at heal' ambience where the population of 2,100 conduct their affairs at a leisurely pace. *Turismo* Ⓒ 947-580 226 located in the town hall on the spacious plaza Mayor that has an interesting medieval arcade and is lined with shops, bars and restaurants. Belorado is another historic town along the Way created in the steep valley of the río Tirón. The 16th century Church of Santa María has a fine altarpiece with images of *Santiago Matamoros y Peregrino* and is built up against the limestone cliffs. The ancient cave dwellings, once home to hermits, are still visible behind the Church (as well as an interesting modern conversion!). San Capraiso was one of the hermits that sought refuge here, but inspired by the fearlessness of a young martyr, he gave himself to also be martyred for his faith and subsequently became patron saint of the pilgrim route to Rome *Via Francigena*. The castle ruins also point to the town's defensive past straddling the old border of Castile and it has Roman origins. The hermitage of Our Lady of Bethlehem *Nuestra Señora de Belén* is on the eastern outskirts and is all that remains of the pilgrim hospital that used to adjoin it and as we leave town on the western side we pass the Convento de Santa Clara. The two other churches, in the centre of the town, are dedicated to San Nicolás and San Pedro.

REFLECTIONS:

❏ **Man cannot stand a meaningless life.** *Carl Jung*

11 **551.1** km (342.4 miles) to Santiago

BELORADO – SAN JUAN de ORTEGA

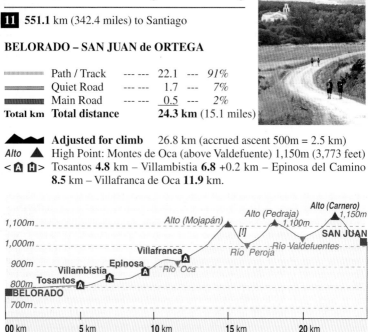

⁝⁝⁝⁝⁝⁝⁝	Path / Track	--- ---	22.1 ---	*91%*
══════	Quiet Road	--- ---	1.7 ---	*7%*
▬▬▬	Main Road	--- ---	0.5 ---	*2%*
Total km	**Total distance**		**24.3 km** (15.1 miles)	

▲▲▲ **Adjusted for climb**   26.8 km (accrued ascent 500m = 2.5 km)

Alto ▲ High Point: Montes de Oca (above Valdefuente) 1,150m (3,773 feet)

< Ⓐ Ⓗ > Tosantos **4.8** km – Villambistia **6.8** +0.2 km – Epinosa del Camino
8.5 km – Villafranca de Oca **11.9** km.

The Practical Path: Today is one of much variation in terrain and unlike
yesterday a glorious 91% on paths and earthen tracks. From the suburbs of
Belorado the path continues parallel to the N-120 along level open countryside
but with some shade provided by hedgerow and woodland. Half way along this
stage, at *Villafranca Montes de Oca*, the path climbs through these 'mountains'
(high point at just over 1,000m) with its cover of oak and then pine before
dropping down to the remote pilgrim village of St. John of the Nettle *San
Juan de Ortega* a disciple of Santo Domingo. Here, far from the distractions
and speed of the modern world we find a slower pace and time, perhaps, to
contemplate the inner journey.

❏ **The Mystical Path:** Here at the start of the 21ˢᵗ century our path takes us past
the ruins of this ancient monastery whose roots extend back to the 9ᵗʰ. The rough
masonry is softened by the horseshoe entrance, a symbol of its Mozarabic past.
Where were we when the first stone was laid in this ancient memorial to God?
Where will we be when the last stone falls to the ground and is lost to physical
sight and memory? Will we have served our purpose for this incarnation? 'It
takes so many thousand years to wake, but will we wake for pity's sake.'

❏ **Personal Reflections:** *"... Finally, I was able to pay my dues. The last time
I stayed here I had been indignant at its shabby interior and as retribution I
had left without offering a contribution towards its upkeep. I never considered
why the mop had been left there. I presumed it was for someone* else *to do the
cleaning. How many times have I passed a mop and bucket with the expectation
that someone else would clean up after me? Is this the pilgrim way? Before
enlightenment: chop wood, carry water, clean floor. After enlightenment: chop
wood, carry water, clean floor. In the trivia of life one finds the meaning of Life.
That I will awaken is not in doubt, but when, oh when? ..."*

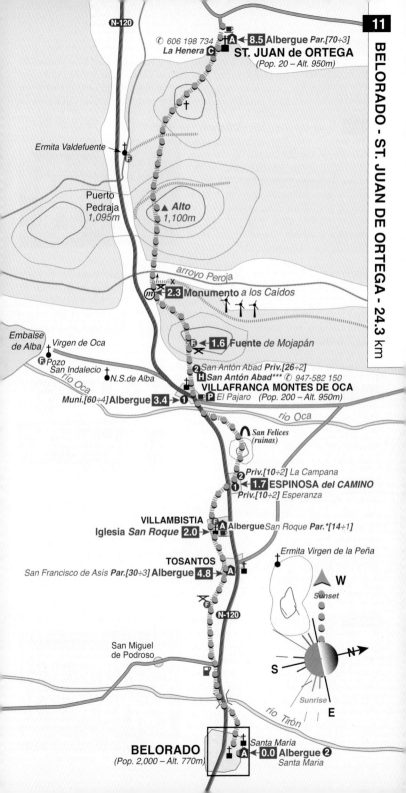

N-120

© 606 198 734
La Henera C

⊣ **A** ◄ **8.5** Albergue *Par.[70÷3]*
ST. JUAN de ORTEGA
(Pop. 20 – Alt. 950m)

✝

Ermita Valdefuente ✝ F

Puerto
Pedraja
1,095m

▲ *Alto*
1,100m

arroyo Peroja

m ✕ **2.3** Monumento *a los Caídos*
✕

F ✕ **1.6** Fuente *de Mojapán*

Embalse
de Alba ✝ *Virgen de Oca*
F *Pozo*
San Indalecio ✝
río Oca ✝ *N.S. de Alba*

❷ *San Antón Abad Priv.[26÷2]*
H *San Antón Abad**** © 947-582 150
VILLAFRANCA MONTES DE OCA
P P *El Pajaro* *(Pop. 200 – Alt. 950m)*

Muni.[60÷4] **Albergue 3.4** ➤ ❶

río Oca

╭ *San Felices*
(ruinas)

❷ *Priv.[10÷2] La Campana*
❶ ◄ **1.7** **ESPINOSA** *del CAMINO*
Priv.[10÷2] Esperanza

VILLAMBISTIA
Iglesia *San Roque* **2.0** ➤ F
✝ **A** Albergue *San Roque Par.*[14÷1]*

Ermita Virgen de la Peña ✝

TOSANTOS
San Francisco de Asís Par.[30÷3] **Albergue 4.8** ➤ **A** ✝

▲ **W**

Sunset

F
N-120

*San Miguel
de Podroso*

P

S ━ **N**

Sunrise

E

río Tirón

✝ *Santa María*
BELORADO ✝ **A** ◄ **0.0** Albergue ❷
(Pop. 2,000 – Alt. 770m) *Santa Maria*

0.0 km **Belorado** From albergue ❷ turn right and then left into the narrow c/ Hipolito Lopez Bernal past albergue Cuarto Cantones (right) and Hotel Belorado (left) to cross the N-12 **[1.2 km]** and over the rio Tirón via footbridge (the road bridge replaces one originally built by Santo Domingo) and onto gravel track parallel to the main road passing picnic site **[3.0 km]** into Tosantos **[0.6 km]**

4.8 km **Tosantos** *(Pop. 80)* •**Albergue** *San Francisco de Asís Par.[30÷3]*
© 947 580 371 parish hostel in a renovated building opposite the church on the main road with 30 places on mattresses on the floor in 3 rooms €-*donativo*. The basic facilities are enhanced by the warm welcome and there is a garden area in front. A shared meal with prayers is sometimes available. Bar *El Castaño* is located on the main road.

Detour: ●●●●●● **0.9 km** (1.8 km round trip) on the opposite side of the main road is the unusual hermitage of Our Lady of the Rock *Ermita de la Virgen de la Peña (la Chiesa)* built into the side of the cliffs with a 12th century image of the Christ Child. It is usually locked and so the mystery of what lies within remains hidden. You can, however, see its white facade from the camino as you leave Tosantos.

Continue to the back of Tosantos along a farm track to:

2.0 km **Villambistia** *Iglesia San Roque* rest area by river [F] •**Albergue** *San Roque Priv.[14÷1]*+ © 680 501 887 private albergue 200m off route (see photo) with 14 beds €6 good facilities and popular bar (menú) in the centre of this small hamlet.

1.7 km **Espinosa del Camino** *Bar* [F] •**Albergue** *La Campana Priv.[10÷2]* © José Mir 678-479 361 with 10 places in 2 rooms. Limited facilities (no kitchen) but meals available. Pass along the short main street of this sleepy hamlet onto an earth track up a short rise at the top of which Villafranca becomes visible. Continue down the other side passing the 9th century ruins of **Monasterio de San Félix de Oca** with its distinctive Mozarabic horseshoe arch *[Count Diego Porcelos, founder of Burgos, was buried here – we pass his statue on the way into the city]*. The track now takes a wide sweep away from the main road before joining it again onto a narrow path over the river Oca and into:

3.4 km **Villafranca de Montes de Oca** *(Pop. 200)* •**Albergue** ❶ *Mun.[60÷4]*
© 947-582 124 municipal hostel (see photo) on the busy N-120 adjoining the farmacia and part of the community health centre and school building with 60 beds €6 in 4 dormitories (rear rooms quieter) with basic facilities and large courtyard to the rear (open all year). •**Albergue** ❷ *San Antón Abad Priv*.[26÷2]*+ © 947-582 150 to the rear of the exclusive hotel (of which it is part). The owner has travelled the camino and this hostel fulfils his wish

Villafranca – Albergue ❶

to 'give something back' a truly win/win situation. 26 beds €8 with all modern facilities. **Other accommodation**: Hotel •**San Antón Abad** ℂ 947-582 151. Casa rural •**La Alpargateria** ℂ 686 040 884 adjoins hostal •**El Pajaro** ℂ 947-582 029 situated above the bar on the noisy main road, popular with both truckers and pilgrims (opens early for breakfast).

VILLAFRANCA de MONTES de OCA: The untidy approach, with its truck stop for vehicles using the Puerto de la Pedraja, belies the historic roots of this town that welcomed pilgrims as early as the 9th century. This is one of several *Villafrancas* along the way that became home to Franks arriving as pilgrims and returning as artisans thus giving these towns their familiar appellation. The Spanish translation for goose is *oca* giving a romantic notion of wild geese whereas the name may actually derive from an earlier settlement *Auca*. The village is located at the foot of the *Montes de Oca*, formerly a wild unpopulated area and notorious for the bandits that roamed its slopes preying on pilgrims. The bandits in turn would doubtless pray for protection from the Saint himself in the safety of the Church of Santiago (rebuilt several times and housing an unusual shell baptismal font and several images of the Saint) or perhaps find shelter and succour from the pilgrim Hospice of Saint Anthony the Abbot *Hospital de San Antonio Abad* which has recently been restored. This handsome building was sometimes referred to as the Queen's Hospice, as witnessed by the royal coat of arms that adorn the entrance gate. Today, the town straddles the noisy N-120 which cuts its way through the Pedraja pass and runs broadly parallel to the camino until the latter strikes off to the remote village of San Juan de Ortega.

Detour: Pozo de San Indalecio ● ● ● ● ● **2.3 km** (4.6 km round trip) at the far end of the village (south of the N-120) we pass *ermita N.S[ra] de Alba (Santa María)* **[1.4 km]** and continue s/o to the remote *ermita Virgen de Oca.* **[0.6 km]** A local pilgrimage *romería* is made here on 11th June each year, the feast day of San Indalecio, to commemorate his martyrdom and to the rear of the chapel we cross the medieval bridge *puente viejo* to the beautiful fountain named in his memory *Pozo de San Indalecio* **[0.3 km]**. If you are feeling adventurous a further 600m up the rocky gorge ahead will bring you to the stunning reservoir *Embalse de Alba* at the head of the rio Oca. Allow 2 hours for this detour, which is not recommended unless you plan to stay in Villafranca.

Opposite albergue [1] turn up passing the Church of Santiago *XVIII[th]C* (left) **[F]** and Hospital de San Antonio Abad *XIV[th]C* (right) and climb steeply up into beautiful oak woods to refresh yourself at:

1.6 km **Fuente de Mojapán** *Moisten Bread Fountain* (one assumes the early pilgrims did just that) and covered rest area with viewing platform. From here until we reach San Juan de Ortega we have the shade of ancient oak woods and pine forest. Continue climbing to monument and picnic area above the road.

2.3 km **Monumento de los Caídos** (1,020m) stark monument to the fallen *caídos* during the Spanish Civil War with picnic tables in the shelter of the trees and a backdrop of wind turbines on the rise behind. From here we descend steeply to a footbridge over the Peroja stream *arroyo Peroja* before climbing up the other side to the high point today at 1,150m where the track widens out and we continue s/o through track crossroads at **[2.4 km]** (*ermita de la Valdefuentes off route left by the main road*) and again s/o at **[1.3 km]** passing wayside cross **[1.2 km]**. The route now begins its gentle descent towards the isolated hamlet of St Juan **[3.6 km]**.

8.5 km San Juan de Ortega *(Pop. 30)* •Albergue *Par.[70÷3]* historic parish hostel ℂ 947-560 438 and one of the classic pilgrim halts for the medieval and modern *peregrino* alike. 70 places €5 in 3 spacious (draughty) rooms and basic facilities with access to fine 16th century courtyard patio. Another traditional gateway on the camino and its peaceful setting and ancient buildings provide a monastic atmosphere and soften the lack of services and spartan maintenance.

San Juan – Bar, Albergue & Chruch

The traditional bread and garlic soup *sopa de ajo* instigated by the former parish priest José María (he died in 2008) continues to be offered to all pilgrims after the pilgrim mass each evening. *[Next albergue: Agés – 3.6 km].* The adjoining •*Bar Marcela* is popular with pilgrims and offers dinner. The owners also operate the only other accommodation in the hamlet •La Henera ℂ 947-409 935 / 606 198 734 a new casa rural opposite the church. Opposite the bar is an information kiosk with internet access (coin operated).

SAN JUAN was a disciple of Santo Domingo and like his mentor became known for his great works to serve the pilgrim to Santiago. He built bridges, hospitals, churches and hostels throughout this region. Here, in this wild and isolated place *(Ortiga* is Spanish for nettle) fraught with danger and difficulty for the medieval pilgrim, he founded an Augustinian monastery in 1150. The chapel is dedicated to **San Nicolás de Barri**, who allegedly saved San Juan from drowning on his way back from pilgrimage to the Holy Land and is constructed in such a way that at each equinox the rays of the setting sun strike the Virgin Mary in the scene of the annunciation *(this amazing phenomenon was only re-discovered in 1974).* A representation of this biennial miracle of celestial light, which is linked to San Juan's miraculous powers in restoring fertility, is portrayed in the adjoining photograph.

The barren Queen Isabel of Castile *la Católica* came here in 1477 and later conceived a child and in consequence greatly embellished the church. In the crypt there is a beautiful Romanesque sepulchre with fine tracery stonework bearing an effigy of the Saint. San Juan, however, is buried in the monastery church in a simpler stone sarcophagus depicting scenes from his life; a more down to earth resting place for this most practical of saints.

Scene of the Annunciation

REFLECTIONS:

_____
_____
_____
_____
_____
_____
_____
_____
_____
_____
_____
_____
_____
_____
_____
_____
_____
_____
_____
_____
_____
_____

❐ **I don't know what your destiny will be, but one thing I do know; the only ones among you who will be truly happy are those who have sought and found how to serve.** *Albert Schweitzer*

12 526.8 km (327.3 miles) to Santiago

SAN JUAN de ORTEGA – BURGOS

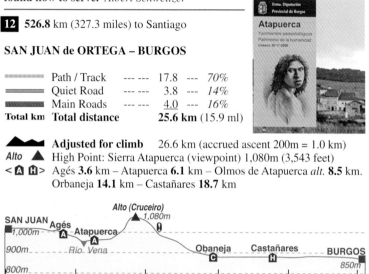

	Path / Track	--- ---	17.8	---	70%
	Quiet Road	--- ---	3.8	---	14%
	Main Roads	--- ---	4.0	---	16%
Total km	**Total distance**		**25.6 km** (15.9 ml)		

▲ **Adjusted for climb** 26.6 km (accrued ascent 200m = 1.0 km)
Alto ▲ High Point: Sierra Atapuerca (viewpoint) 1,080m (3,543 feet)
<🅰 🅗> Agés **3.6** km – Atapuerca **6.1** km – Olmos de Atapuerca *alt.* **8.5** km. Orbaneja **14.1** km – Castañares **18.7** km

The Practical Path: This stage starts along a quiet path through oak and pine-wood that drop down to the valley of the río Vena before ascending the lonely Sierra Atapuerca. From here we descend to the busyness of Burgos. Familiarise yourself with the various options available (see map opposite) and prepare for the hard slog into the city itself – after the relative tranquillity of the camino city life can come as something of a shock. The situation has improved since the long awaited new pilgrim hostel opened its doors next to the cathedral in the city centre and the possibility of taking the riverside path through parkland alongside the rio Arlanzón. The recommended route ❶ follows the more scenic path minimising asphalt. Watch carefully for the more discreet waymarks especially on the section of farm tracks that avoids the road through Cardeñuela.

You might consider staying for an extra day in Burgos to go on one of the several excursions to places of interest in the area (see under detours).

❐ **The Mystical Path:** On each side of the Montes de Oca we find two ancient monasteries each one the final resting place of a noble personage from this area. One inherited his title the other earned it through service to God. Why is one in ruins while the other remains intact to offer shelter? Why does the spirit of *St John of the Nettles* live on to feed the souls of the hungry? How hungry are you and has your soul found nourishment here?

❐ **Personal Reflections:** *"... I met them in the Park. Their welcome was ecstatic even though Ramón was in much pain and was making arrangements to go home. The hospital had diagnosed a stress fracture. He had simply gone too far too fast. His disappointment and sense of failure was palpable. Above all he didn't want to leave the friends he had made along the way. We all have to leave the camino at some stage, but our friendships don't have to end. He looked reassured as I took my leave. I can still see his tears and his hand waving as I passed out of sight – but not out of mind Ramón; not out of mind ..."*

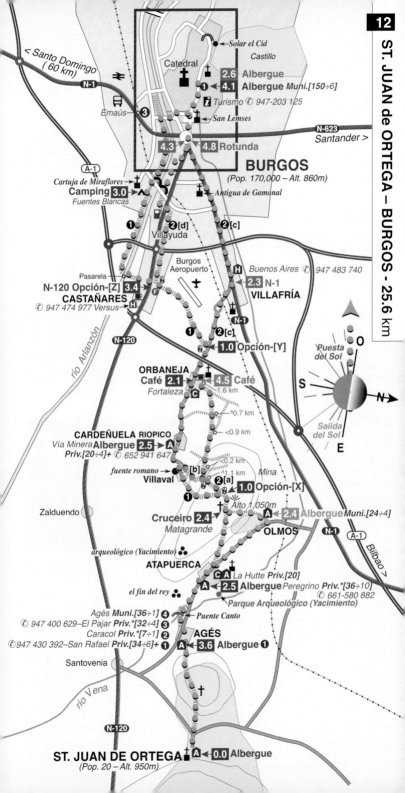

< *Santo Domingo*
(60 km)

N-1

Solar el Cid
Castillo

Catedral

2.6 Albergue
4.1 Albergue *Muni.[150÷6]*

ℹ️ *Turismo* ©️ *947-203 125*

Emaús

San Lemses

N-623
Santander >

4.3 **4.8** Rotunda

BURGOS
(Pop. 170,000 – Alt. 860m)

A-1

Cartuja de Miraflores
Camping 3.0
Fuentes Blancas

Antigua de Gamonal

❶ ❷[d] ❷[c]
Villayuda

Pasarela
N-120 Opción-[Z] 3.4
CASTAÑARES
©️ *947 474 977 Versus*

Burgos
Aeropuerto

H *Buenos Aires* ©️ *947 483 740*
2.3 N-1
VILLAFRÍA

F
H

N-120

río Arlanzón

❶ ❷[c]
1.0 Opción-[Y]

ORBANEJA
Café **2.1** **4.5** Café
Fortaleza 1.6 km
C

^0.7 km
<0.9 km

CARDEÑUELA RIOPICO
Vía Minera **Albergue 2.5** → Ⓐ
Priv.[20÷4]+ ©️ *652 941 647*

<0.2 km
^1.1 km *Mina*

fuente romano →
Villaval
[b] ❷[a]
1.0 Opción-[X]
❶

†☀ *Alto 1,050m*
Ⓐ **2.4** Albergue *Muni.[24÷4]*

Zalduendo

Cruceiro **2.4**
Matagrande

OLMOS
N-1 A-1

Bilbao >

Puesta
del Sol

O
S
N
E

Salida
del Sol

arqueológico (Yacimiento) ⚫⚫

ATAPUERCA

C Ⓐ *La Hutte Priv.[20]*
Ⓐ **2.5** Albergue *Peregrino Priv.*[36÷10]*
©️ *661-580 882*
Parque Arqueológico (Yacimiento)

el fin del rey ⚫⚫

Agés Muni.[36÷1] ❹
©️ *947 400 629–El Pajar Priv.*[32÷4]* ❸
Caracol Priv.[7÷1]* ❷
©️*947 430 392–San Rafael Priv.[34÷6]+* ❶

Puente Canto

AGÉS ❶
Ⓐ ← **3.6** Albergue ❶

Santovenia

río Vena

N-120

ST. JUAN DE ORTEGA † Ⓐ ← **0.0** Albergue
(Pop. 20 – Alt. 950m)

The recommended route into Burgos along the rio Arlanzón now effectively replaces the arduous hike through the industrial suburbs. From option point **X** all routes are a similar distance (c.16 km) however, if you take any of the alternative access road routes into the city centre (via the N-120 from Castañares or the N-1 route via Vilafría) prepare for the noise of traffic and the hard city pavements underfoot. Pilgrims who are not prepared for this entry often have a hard time or end up resorting to public transport. Due to the insatiable demands of a modern economy the bulldozer has obliterated many of the original paths into the city. We can usefully take this time to reflect on areas of our own life where we have allowed these materialistic forces to bulldoze our own inner pathway out of *seeming* existence. Burgos is a good reflection of our 'developed' world. It is easy to blame the faceless developers but they only build to feed our desire for a more convenient lifestyle. How many cars are parked at our home and are we prepared to give them up or look to car sharing? Are we ready to embrace a life of voluntary simplicity, not because we have to but because we want to? We might usefully reflect on the wisdom attributed to the First Nation Cree:

"Only when the last tree has died and the last river been poisoned and the last fish has been caught will we realise that we cannot eat money."

0.0 km **San Juan de Ortega** from the albergue continue over the road (left brings you to Santovenia and the N-120) onto a path that climbs through pine and scrubland levelling out onto open hill pasture. The occasional wooden cross provides some comfort that we're headed in the direction (it's likely to be dark or misty in the early morning mist that is frequently experienced at this altitude of 1,000m). The camino here is little changed from what the medieval pilgrim experienced as we enter the tiny village of:

3.6 km Agés *(Pop. 60)* •Albergue ❶ *San Rafael* **Priv.[34÷6]+** Ⓒ 947 430 392 at village entrance 10 beds €10 +priv. bar/ restaurant (open all year). [F] *Cafe El Alquimista* and *La Taberna.* •Albergue ❷ *Casa Caracol* **Priv.[7÷1]** Ⓒ 947-430 413 c/ la Iglesia 7 spaces on mattresses. •Albergue ❸ *El Pajar (the hay loft)* **Priv.*[32÷4]** Ⓒ 947 400 629 with 32 beds €8 also *La Casa Roja* with 22 beds €5. •**Albergue Agés** ❹ **Muni.[36÷1]** 32 beds €8 and bar (open all year). *[Next albergue: Atapuerca – 2.6 km].*

Albergues ❸ *(left)* **and ❹** *(right)*

[The humble parish church of Santa Eulalia XVI[th]C rose to fame when the mortal remains of the Navarrese King Don García were interred here after he was slain by his brother, Fernando I of Castile, in the battle of Atapuerca in 1054. A stark stone memorial marks the lonely spot between here and Atapuerca (to the left, off the road – not the replica on the main road). Don García's final resting place, you may recall, is back in the Royal Pantheon in the church of Santa María de Real in Nájera but his entrails remain here!]. Beyond the village is the simple medieval stone bridge built by San Juan de Ortega over the río Vena that flows into the majestic río Arlanzón in Burgos. Picnic site and [F]. The peaceful surroundings of *Puente Canto* are a far cry from those in the Plaza San Lesmes in Burgos. Listen to the sound of the trickling brook here and listen again to the self-same waters as they flow under the bridge in front of St. John's Arch. What sounds do you hear and which nourishes you more? The stretch of asphalt ahead is relieved by standing stones placed to commemorate the famous battle here.

2.5 km **Atapuerca** *(Pop. 200)* •**Albergue** *El Peregrino Priv.*[36÷10]+* network* hostel ⊘ 661-580 882 *centro turístico* at the village entrance. 36 Beds €8 +priv.good facilities including garden terrace. •**Albergue** *La Hutte Priv.[18÷1]* ⊘ 947-430 320 private hostel 300m *off* route (right) located just below the parish church of San Martin *XVthC* clearly visible on the rise above. 18 beds €5 in one room but if you want more space and luxury try the adjoining casa rural •**Papasol** managed by the owners with private rooms from €55. Also in this area are: •**El Pesebre** ⊘ 610 564 147 and •**Elizalde** ⊘ 635 743 306. A variety of bars and restaurants serve not

Albergue *El Pergrino*

only pilgrims but tourists who come to view the archeological sites.

Homo Antecessor: It's official – this is where our ancestors came from! The prehistoric caves of Atapuerca were declared a UNESCO World Heritage site in 2000 on account of their source as the earliest human remains ever discovered in Europe dating back over 900,000 years and providing an exceptional record of the way of life of the first human communities. The site is 3 km off route (left) and was discovered while cutting a rail link to the nearby mines. The archaeological dig is on-going and the latest, unconfirmed analysis, is of human activity going back over 900,000 years ago and, yes, it is also confirmed that our ancestors were cannibals. A more accessible information centre has been built just outside the village 500m (right). This includes a mock-up of an early settlement, which feels disappointingly artificial. Continue down the main street past *bar cantina* [F] (right) where we have an option:

Detour: ● ● ● ● ● Alternative route to **Olmos de Atapuerca** with municipal hostel •**Albergue** *Priv.[24÷2]* ⊘ 633 586 876 located in this traditional village house opposite the parish church in c/ La Iglesia. 24 beds €7 with additional mattresses. Basic facilities provided with garden to rear. This is a pleasant 2.4 km detour along a quiet country road with a direct route out of Olmos to the Alto Cruceiro (2.6 km). To re-join the camino turn up through the village onto track that winds its way up the sierra Atapuerca, through holm oak and scrubland – round trip 5.0 km.

For **main route** turn up <left by games field into the Sierra Atapuerca. Shaded picnic site (right) alongside military site (left). The gradual climb becomes a steeper rocky path towards the summit and is rewarded with splendid views.

2.4 km **Cruceiro / Punto de Vista**. This is the high point at 1,070m (3,510 ft). To the west is our first sight of the city of Burgos (unless it is shrouded in the early morning mist that frequents this high sierra). Down below us to the left are the villages we will pass through to reach Burgos. Along the stony ridge to the right (north) are the ugly scars of an open cast mine and radio masts. Pass viewpoint and descend until we reach a fork in the path (the first of 3 options):

1.0 km **Opción [X] [?] [!]** Stop! Focus! Choose! ❖ Turn down <left ❶ *or*:

● ● ● ● ● For peaceful alternative route ❷ **[a]** *(entirely by earthen tracks but waymarks are not so obvious and it bypasses the albergue in Cardeñuela. If visibility is poor take the main route)*. Continue s/o to a **2nd option [1.1 km]**. *[For* ❷*[b] turn off left down steeply towards* **Villalval** *just before entering the village turn right onto track and join the main route on asphalt road [0.2 km]*

Otherwise continue s/o (up right) and turn <left [**0.2** km] and veer <left again after [**0.9** km] *off* main track *(waymarks here also point s/o)* and follow the contour above the slope. Continue s/o at next cross tracks [**0.7** km] down into Orbaneja now visible ahead to road and cafe where main route joins [**1.6** km].

4.5 km Orbaneja *Café* •*Café / Cantina*.

❖ For the main route ❶ turn down left to the village of **Villalval [1.3** km] (no facilities). A remote village at the top of a valley road where the inhabitants seem reluctant to join the world beyond. Pass the dilapidated parish church (right) and the Roman well at the far end of the village *(none the worse after 2 millennia)* that adjoins a picnic area and [F] (left). Continue s/o to bend in road where route ❷**[b]** joins from our right. The route now continues on an asphalt road passing drinks *kiosco* into **Cardeñuela Riopico [1.2** km]

2.5 km **Cardeñuela Riopico Albergue** *Vía Minera* **Priv.[20÷4]+** c/ La Iglesia ℰ 634 407 091 beds €7. •*Bar La Parada* (often closed) and CR •**La Cardeñuela** ℰ 947-210 479. Proceed out of the village passing road (left) to Quintanilla and into **Orbaneja** to the far end near parish church of San Millán Abad and popular •*Café / Cantina* [**2.1** km].

2.1 km Orbaneja *(Pop. 140)* •*Café / Cantina*. Note: this is the last opportunity to obtain a snack and fill your water flasks before heading into the suburbs of Burgos. Casa rural •**Fortaleza** ℰ 678 116 570 c/Principal, 31 single from €35. Proceed over A-1 and just beyond the bridge by new residential development:

1.0 km Opción [Y] [?] [!] Stop! Focus! Choose again!

For **alternative road route ❷[c]** proceed s/o along road, turn right at roundabout over rail [**1.8** km] *(over to right is the bell tower of the parish church presiding over what remains of the old town of Villafría that was granted to the monastery of San Pedro de Cardeña in the 10th century).* Continue down to N-1 [**0.5** km]:

2.3 km **Villafría** with several hotels (from €25) and restaurants •**Iruñako** HsR ℰ 947-484 126. •**Buenos Aires** HR** ℰ 947-483 770. •**Las Vegas** HR** ℰ 947-484 453. Villafría is a modern industrial suburb of Burgos with a bus service into the centre of Burgos. Continue along the N-1 past the industrial complexes of Gamonal over the A-1 [**1.5** km] into c/Vitoria where the city high-rise starts. You pass the impressive 13th century church dedicated to N.S. La Real y Antigua de Gamonal (left) [**2.4** km] (with stone cross and image of Santiago Peregrino) and join the recommended route at the Telefonica roundabout [**0.9** km].

4.8 km **Rotonda** *de Logroño* (Av. de la Constitución Española).

The recommended route ❶ skirts Burgos airport and Gamonal industrial zone on earthen tracks. At option point [**Y**] turn down sharp <left *off* the road (not well signposted) by housing estate onto track around the airport security fence [**1.2** km] and continue over stream [**1.6** km] and up to main road [**0.6** km].

3.4 km **Castañares Opción** [**Z**] [?] [F]. Sleepy city suburb straddling the N-120. Opp. the fountain (on far side of main road) is a small square with chapel and café/restaurante •*El Descanso* also hotel **Versus** ℰ 947-474 977 single from €60 but pilgrim discount available. A regular bus service to the city centre leaves from this point. To avoid the traffic take the recommended path alongside the río Arlanzón or take the road option (see next panel).

Alternative road route ❷[d] turn right on track by the N-120, cross over airport access road and under the A-1 **[1.0** km] over the rio Pico into the Polígono Industrial Gamonal still on gravel track to next junction *c/del Alcade Martín Cobos* and cross over by Repsol garage **[0.9** km] turning right into c/Mayor through **Villayuda** back onto track under railway **[1.4** km] s/o and turn right up to the N-120 (Av. de la Constitución) and then <left to roundabout **[1.0** km]

4.3 km **Rotonda** *de Logroño* (alternative route ❷[c] via Villafría joins here). Guardia Civil HQ and Militar Academia (opp. Telefonica building). *[An alternative here is to go s/o along c/Vitoria into the Paseo Espolón and the Arco Santa María leading to the cathedral and albergue (right) – see city plan].*

For the historic camino route cross over to the *Museo Militar* (right) into c/San Roque crossing over <left just before the new shopping centre *Via de la Plata* **[0.4** km] and veering right> through playground **[F]** **[0.5** km] under red/yellow buildings over the busy Av. Cantabria [!] into c/de las Calzadas which brings us directly into Plaza San Lesmes **[0.9** km] (the recommended route joins here). Continue via c/Avellanos, c/San Gil, c/Fernán Gonzalez to Albergue **[0.8** km].

2.6 km **Albergue** see recommended route for details.

Recommended route ❶ cross N-120 through the modern suburbs *Lugar del Barrio Castañares* past the factory and over footbridge *pasarela* **[0.5** km] turn right> along path through parkland under A-1 **[0.7** km] to camp site **[1.8** km]:

3.0 km **Camping** *Fuentes Blancas* with bungalows for 2 from €39. *(Note: Cartuja de Miraflores is close by and easily visited at this point - see details p.132)* continue around lake under **bridge [0.6** km] under city **by-pass [1.6** km] *(Albergue Emaus c/San Pedro de Cardeña, 31 off route <left).* At **Puente Gasset [0.7** km] cross river turn left and then right (Hotel Gran Teatro) cross c/Vitoria into c/San Lesmes to rejoin all routes in **Plaza San Lesmes [0.4** km].

Formerly plaza San Juan with the lovely ruins of Antiguo Monasterio de San Juan (part of the Museo Marceliano) and Iglesia de San Lesmes. San Lesmes is patron saint of Burgos. Formerly a French abbot called Adelhelm who was persuaded to stay in Burgos by the wife of Afonso VI. In the centre of the square looking up towards the cathedral from atop his steed is a statue of the founder of the city in 884, Diego Porcelos, whose burial site we passed at the Monasterio de San Félix de Oca. We

now cross over the río Vena (whose calm waters we heard back in Agés) over the well-trodden medieval bridge and under the 13thc Arco de San Juan into the medieval city itself. Continue into c/San Juan *[detour left into c/Santander to visit Casa del Cordón, 150m left with its outstanding 15thc facade, Columbus was royally received here on his return from the Americas]* or continue s/o past the hotel •Norte y Londres opp. Plaza Alonso Martínez with main tourist office (right). Continue into c/Avellanos and c/San Gil veering <left into c/Fernán Gonzalez up the cobblestones to no. 28 **[0.8** km].

4.1 km **Burgos** *Centro* **Albergue** ❶ *La Casa del Cubo 'Lerma' Asoc.[150÷6]* c/ Rua Viejo, 32 municipal hostel © 947-460 922 modern building behind 16thc facade adj. to the cathedral (see photo). Open all year with 150 beds €5 spread over 6 dormitories on 4 floors with lift and all facilities. Close by in c/Laín Calvo, 10 •**Albergue ❷** *Divina Pastora Asoc.[16÷1]* ⓒ 947-207 952 central location above the chapel which offers respite from the bustle of the city. 16 beds €-*donativo* in this popopular hostel which fills early (pilgrim mass at 20:00). Further out are: •**Albergue ❸** *Casa de Peregrinos Emaús Par.[20÷4]* C/ de San

Albergue ❶ *La Casa del Cubo*

Pedro de Cardeña, 31 (behind the church of San José Obrero and Jesuit college). 20 beds €-*donativo* with shared meal following the tradition of Emmaus with Christian prayer and blessing. Other possibilities in the busy summer period are: •**Burgos Youth Hostel** *albergue juvenil Gil de Siloé* ⓒ 947-220 277 on Av. de Cantabria with 110 beds and •**Monasterio Benedictinas de San José** ⓒ 947-205 373 who maintain a hostel for religious groups on c/Emperador and may also accommodate individual pilgrims. It is also possible that the old albergue •**El Parral** and the adjacent sports halls may be pressed into service during busy periods – check at the new albergue.

ⓒ **Other accommodation:** *Turismo* Plaza Alonso,7 ⓒ 947-203 125 also several tourist kiosks around the city. Burgos is always busy so find accommodation *before* setting out to explore. The following are on the town plan *sequentially* ■ from the entrance: *€25–€50:* •**Puerta de Burgos** H**** ⓒ947-241 000 c/Vitoria, 69. •**Carrales** HsR** ⓒ 947-205 916 Puente Gasset, 4. •**Acacia** HsR** ⓒ 947-205 134 c/Bernabé Pérez Ortiz, 1. •**Lar** Hs** ⓒ 947-209 655 c/Cardenal Benlloch, 1. •**Manjón** HsR** ⓒ 947-208 689 c/Gran Teatro. •**García** HsR* ⓒ 947-205 553 c/Santander, 1. •**Hidalgo** HsR* ⓒ 947-203 481 c/Almirante Bonifaz, 14. ■ Central (on the camino): •**El Jacobeo** Hr* ⓒ 947-260 102 c/San Juan, 24. •**Joma** Hs ⓒ 947-203 350 c/San Juan, 26. •**Norte y Londres** Hr ⓒ 947-264 125 Plaza Alonso, 10. ■ Central *€200+:* •**Palacio de los Blasones** H****ⓒ 947-257 680 Fernán Gonzaléz, 10. •**Mesón del Cid II** H****ⓒ 947-208 715 Fernán Gonzaléz, 62 €230+. •**Abba Burgos** H****ⓒ 947-001 100 Fernán Gonzaléz, 72-76 (antiguo Seminario). ■ Across river: •**Conde de Miranda** HR** ⓒ 947-265 267 c/Miranda, 4 (adj. estación de autobuses). •**Temiño** HsR ⓒ 947-208 035 c/Concepción, 14. •**NH Palacio de la Merced** H****ⓒ 947-479 900 c/Merced.

❏ **Monumentos históricos:** ❶ *Iglesia de San Lesmes XIV[th]C y Antiguo Monasterio de San Juan* (mueso Marceliano) ❷ *Arco San Juan XIII[th]C* ❸ *Casa del Cordón XV[th]C* ❹ *Catedral de Santa María XIII[th]C* ❺ *Arco y Puente de Santa María XIV[th]C* ❻ *Iglesia San Nicolas XV[th]C* ❼ *Solar del Cid* ❽ *Arco San Martin XIII[th]C* ❾ *Hospital del Rey XII[th]C* (antiguo hospital del peregrino). ❿ *Santa María la Real de Las Huelgas XII[th]C* (museo). ● *Cartuja de Miraflores XV[th]C (4 km south/east)* mausoleum of King John II and Isabella of Portugal.

Burgos cathedral – 13th century Catedral de Santa María among the most beautiful of Spain's many cathedrals and one of its largest (after the Giralda at Sevilla). Essentially Gothic, it nevertheless combines many different styles, having been embellished by the great master builders and architects down through the centuries. Soak in its magnificent edifice and inspirational spires and the bustle of the medieval streets that surround the cathedral – designated a World Heritage Site. Whatever condition you are in, it is worthy of a visit to the interior. You are unlikely to find much peace in its crowded aisles but you will

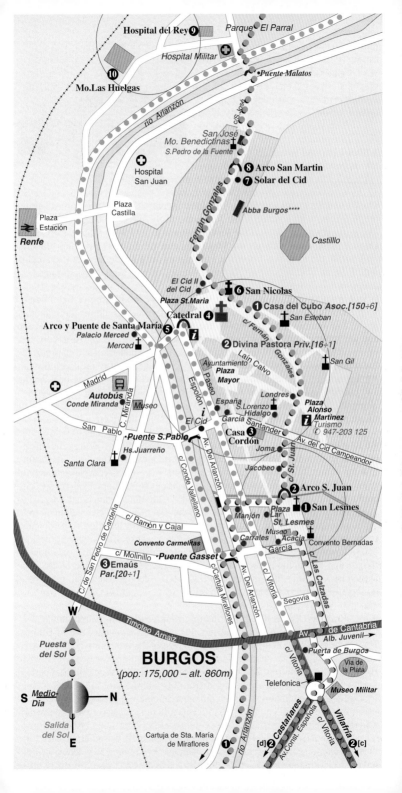

Hospital del Rey 9

Parque El Parral

Hospital Militar

•*Puente Malatos*

Mo. Las Huelgas

10

río Arlanzón

c/S. José

San José
Mo. Benedictinas
S. Pedro de la Fuente

Hospital
San Juan

8 Arco San Martin
7 Solar del Cid

Fernán Gonzales

*Abba Burgos*****

Plaza
Estación

Castilllo

Renfe

El Cid II
del Cid

6 San Nicolas

Plaza St. Maria

1 Casa del Cubo *Asoc.*[150÷6]
•*San Esteban*

Catedral 4

Arco y Puente de Santa María
Palacio Merced
Merced

5

i

2 Divina Pastora *Priv.*[16÷1]

Lain Calvo
Ayuntamiento

•*San Gil*

c/ Fernán Gonzales

Fernán Gonzales

Madrid

Autobús
Conde Miranda
Museo

Plaza
Mayor

Paseo
Espolón

Londres

Plaza
Alonso
Martinez

i
Turismo
© *947-203 125*

San Pablo

España
El Cid

S. Lorenzo
Hidalgo
Garcia

Santander

Puente S. Pablo

Hs. Juarreño

Casa 3
Cordón

Av. del Cid Campeandor

Santa Clara

Av. Del Arlanzón

Joma

Jacobeo

c/ St. Juan

c/ Conde Valleliano

2 Arco S. Juan

1 San Lesmes

Plaza
Lar

c/ Ramón y Cajal

Manjón

St. Lesmes

Museo
Acacia

Convento Bernadas

Convento Carmelitas

Carrales

Garcia

c/ Molinillo •**Puente Gasset**

3 Emaús
Par.[20÷1]

c/ Cartuja Miraflores

Av. Del Arlanzón

c/ Vitoria

c/ Las Calzadas

c/ Segovia

Timoteo Arnaiz

W

Puesta
del Sol

BURGOS
(pop: 175,000 – alt. 860m)

Av. de Cantabria

Alb. Juvenil →

Puerta de Burgos

S **Medio·**
Dia

N

Vía de
la Plata

Salida
del Sol

E

Telefonica

Museo Militar

Cartuja de Sta. María
de Miraflores

río Arlanzón

1

Castañares

[d] **2**

Av. Consti. Española

c/ Vitoria

2 [c]

Villafría

find a wealth of art treasures and artefacts to satisfy the most jaded of palates. The west door, off Santa María square, is the most striking but we enter by the equally evocative south door. Admission (office below south door) is by ticket only which seems to have eliminated the notorious pseudo 'guides' and includes a floor plan and pamphlet (in English) and access to the left luggage lockers

consigna. Open throughout the day in high season (otherwise closed for lunch 13.30 – 16.00). Amongst the many outstanding chapels (there are 21) are St. Thecla and St. James (off Plaza Santa María) and St. John & St. James behind the high altar with a statue of St. James the Moor-slayer *Santiago Matamoros*. The north door (closed) has the lovely Renaissance Golden Staircase *Escalera Dorada* designed by Diego de Siloe, while at the transept crossing, directly underneath the huge star lantern at the heart of the cathedral, lie El Cid and his wife Jimena. The 14th century Gothic cloisters have an array of sculptures.

If you want to find somewhere cool and quiet try the Church of San Nicolás with its magnificent altarpiece, situated directly on the camino immediately above the cathedral (at the top of the steps). Its austere 15th century façade and the steep climb up from the cathedral square *plaza Santa María* acts as a deterrent to the crowds of tourists milling around the cathedral and so preserves the relative peace to be found here. Alternatively head out to the river through the impressive Arco de Santa María the medieval entrance dating back to the 14th century to the Puente de Santa María, which joins the linear park that runs along the banks of the río Arlazón. Rest awhile under the shade of the trees or take a well-earned drink in one of the cafés that line the riverbank.

BURGOS CITY: *(pop: 175,000 – alt. 860m).* While warning of the vagaries of city life (stories abound of theft and overcharging) we must also emphasise the beauty of many of the city's buildings and their artefacts. Burgos is a veritable architectural jewel and full of monuments worthy of exploration and appreciation. The city marks the beginning of stage VI of the Codex Calixtinus. Sometimes referred to as the Gothic capital of Spain, it was also the seat of Franco's Government until 1938, an indication of its nationalist and establishment leanings. A burgeoning population approaching 200,000 seems unable to shake off its austere religious and political image. It is, after all, named after its heavy defensive town towers *burgos* and was home to the warlord El Cid. The week either side of 29th June is the city's main festival of San Pedro y Pablo. Accommodation at this time is doubly difficult to secure at twice the price.

Count Rodrigo Díaz de Vivar the champion *campeador* was better known as *El Cid* a Muslim title of respect, and remains the great legendary son of Burgos. He was born here in 1040 and the camino passes the site of his house by Arco de San Martín. On the death of Ferdinand I the kingdom was divided between the monarchs 5 children. The eldest son, Sancho, felt he should have inherited the lot and so set about recovering it from his siblings and the Moors – enter El Cid who was appointed his commander-in-chief of the armed forces. All was going well for El Cid until Sancho was killed trying to recover the town of Zamora from his sister Urraca. Now enters Sancho's surviving brother Alfonso VI who both despised and feared El Cid and alternately exiled him (twice) and in between married him off to his niece Jimena. El Cid died in Valencia in 1099 having recovered the city from the Moors. His body, and that of his trusty horse

Babieca, were eventually re-interred in the monastery of San Pedro de Cardena and then El Cid and his wife were re-re-interred in the cathedral!

On your way out the following day, suitably refreshed, you might be more inclined to explore the fascinating monastery ***Monasterio de Las Huelgas Reales*** and the adjacent ***Hospital del Rey*** (now part of the university) both of which are within a few minutes walk off the camino near Parque El Parral in the westerly suburbs and well worth a visit. Las Huelgas was founded in 1187 by Alfonso VIII who, along with several other royal personages, was crowned and subsequently buried there. Founded as a Cistercian convent, primarily for aristocratic novitiates, it has a lovely cloister and is now a museum. Amongst its many fine treasures is the statue of St. James with a moving arm that was used by the Order of the Knights of Santiago to bestow knighthoods. Hospital del Rey was one of the largest and best-endowed pilgrim hospitals along the camino. The Pilgrim's Gate *Puerta de Romeros* is a Plasteresque jewel and now forms one of the entrances to the university. Other more distant detours might be considered (check with tourist office): **Detour [1]** Cartuja de Miraflores 4 km. **[2]** Beyond [1] Monasterio San Pedro de Cardeña (9 km from Burgos). **[3]** Santo Domingo de Silos (62 km south) site of the world-renowned Gregorian chanting monks.

REFLECTIONS:

❐ **Foxes have holes and the birds of the air have nests,**
But the Son of Man has no place to lay his head. *Matthew 8.24*

13 **501.2** km (311.4 miles) to Santiago

BURGOS – HORNILLOS del CAMINO

	Path / Track	--- ---	14.5	---	69%
	Quiet Road	--- ---	5.9	---	28%
	Main Road	--- ---	0.6	---	3%
Total km	**Total distance**		**21.0 km** (13.0 miles)		

Adjusted for climb 21.7 km (accrued ascent 150m = 0.7 km)
Alto ▲ High Point: Meseta above Fuente de Praotorre at 950m (3,117 feet)
<𝗔 𝗛> *from central albergue* ❶ *in Burgos:* N-120 on outskirts of Burgos **2.2** km – Tarjados **11.0** km – Rabé de las Calzadas **13.3** km.

[Elevation profile:]
Alto *(Meseta)*
950m ▲
900m
BURGOS
800m
Tarjados **Rabé** ▲ HORNILLOS
🅰 🅰 825m
Río Arlanzón
00 km   5 km   10 km   15 km   20 km

The Practical Path: Today we leave behind the built environment and enter the relative wilderness of the sublime *Meseta*. Over half this stage is by way of earth track (69%) across the peace and quiet of the endless crop fields; wheat on the better ground and barley and oats on the higher and poorer soil. We might come across a shepherd and his flock or the occasional fox, otherwise you will have the birds to keep you company. There is little or no shade on the Meseta, so protect yourself from the sun. Hornillos has limited facilities but these are already improving in response to the closure of the intermediate hostel in the *parque El Parral* following the opening of the new hostel in the centre of Burgos. Hornillos provides a welcome respite from the conspicuous consumerism of the city.

Options: If you plan to stay at Hornillos; this stage is now only 21 kilometres which provides an opportunity to visit the monastery at Las Huelgas and the ancient pilgrim hospital *hospital de Rey* on the way out... and time to recover from the busy-ness of Burgos in the peaceful surroundings of one of the few medieval pilgrim villages still surviving. Many pilgrims continue straight to the popular pilgrim village of Hontanas (+10.8 km – 31.8 km in total). In this latter case you need to leave Burgos early but you can get to Castrojeriz early the following day and take some time there to relax and enjoy the interesting historical sites, cafes and restaurants it has to offer.

❐ **The Mystical Path:** The forces of materialism are nowhere more evident than in city life. A wealthy professional, a man of the law, informed Jesus he would follow him wherever he went – prompting Christ's quotation (above) recorded in Matthew's gospel. Another man then came to Jesus and said he would follow him wherever he went but first he must go and bury his father. Christ's response, 'Follow me and let the dead bury their dead.' As we leave Burgos we pass a former pilgrim hospital converted at great expense to house a law school and the opulent monastery of Las Huelgas built to shelter the elite daughters of the aristocracy and as a royal pantheon to house the dead monarchs of Castilla. Who will we follow today, God or Mammon? Christ or Ahriman?

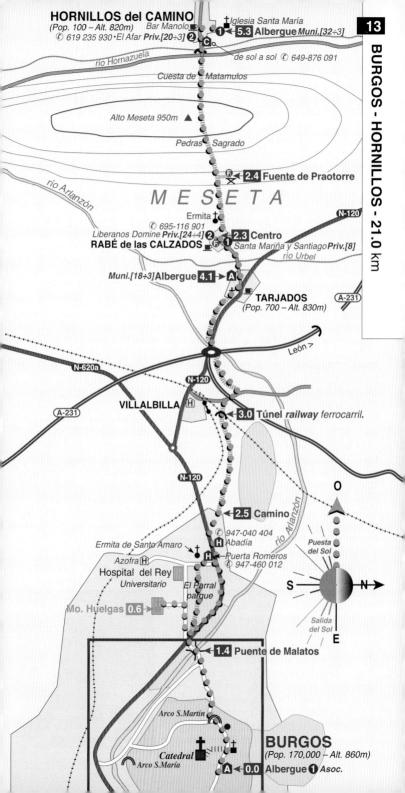

HORNILLOS del CAMINO
(Pop. 100 – Alt. 820m) *Bar Manolo*
© 619 235 930 • El Afar **Priv.[20÷3]** ②

†*Iglesia Santa María*
5.3 Albergue *Muni.[32÷3]*

de sol a sol *© 649-876 091*

Cuesta de Matamulos

Alto Meseta 950m ▲

Pedras Sagrado

2.4 Fuente de Praotorre

M E S E T A

río Arlanzón

Ermita †
© 695-116 901
Liberanos Domine **Priv.[24÷4]** ②
RABÉ de las CALZADOS

2.3 Centro
Santa Mariña y Santiago **Priv.[8]**
río Urbel

Muni.[18÷3] **Albergue 4.1** **A**

TARJADOS
(Pop. 700 – Alt. 830m)

León >

VILLALBILLA Ⓗ

3.0 Túnel *railway* ferrocarril.

2.5 Camino

© 947-040 404
Ⓗ *Abadía*

Ermita de Santo Amaro →†
Azofra Ⓗ
Hospital del Rey
Universitario
El Parral parque

Ⓗ *Puerta Romeros*
© 947-460 012

río Arlanzón

Mo. Huelgas 0.6

1.4 Puente de Malatos

Arco S.Martin

Catedral
Arco S.María

BURGOS
(Pop. 170,000 – Alt. 860m)
A ◄ 0.0 Albergue ❶ *Asoc.*

O

Puesta del Sol

S ——————— N

Salida del Sol

E

❐ **Personal Reflections:** *"… The Aries full moon slowly breaks the eastern horizon, an enormous orb of reflected silver light. It is awesome against the pale blue of the early evening sky. I am alone lost in the deep peace of the empty Meseta. But I don't feel lost or lonely. I take out the small phial I have been carrying since leaving Findhorn. A gift of love from the sacred mountain of Kailash offered to the world and poured into the deep rich soil of the camino. The words of the Great Invocation linger in the cooling air before rippling out into the universe. Two deer break cover in the stillness. I was not alone after all …"*

0.0 km **Burgos** From albergue ❶ *La Casa del Cubo* continue along the cobbled c/Fernán González past the cathedral and church of San Nicolás (right) and luxury Hotel Abba Burgos to the twin obelisks of the *Solar el Cid* **[0.7 km]** which provides a simple monument to this notorious soldier of fortune and pugnacious son of Burgos who lived in a house on this spot. Just beyond we leave the medieval city through what remains of its fortified walls and the *Arco de San Martín*. We now head across the road and down into *c/Emperador* to the Jacobean church of *San Pedro de la Fuente* **[0.2 km]** (left) and *Hostal Monasterio de San José*. Turn <left into *c/Benedictinas de San José* and *c/Villalon* to cross the *río Arlanzón* over the 'Bridge of Maladies' **[0.5 km]**.

1.4 km **Puente de Malatos / Opción:** The waymarked route continues through the parkland *El Parral* ahead. As this is a relatively short stage this is a good opportunity to visit the Royal Monastery *Monasterio de las Huelgas Reales*.

Detour: Monasterio de las Huelgas Reales 600 metres. Take the road alongside the park Paseo de los Comendadores and turn <left [400m] into c/ de Bernardino Obregón to the monastery straight ahead [200m]. Allow at least an hour to look around its copious buildings. The Chapel of St. James *Capilla de Santiago* contains the unusual statue of the saint with a moving arm. The *Sala Capitular* contains the royal standard *pendón* used in the battle of Las Navas de Tolosa (you may have seen the heavy chains, another trophy from this battle, back in Roncesvalles). Soak up the atmosphere in the spacious Romanesque cloisters with their elegant twin columns, reminiscent of the cloisters at San Pedro de la Rúa in Estella (coincidentally this suburb of Burgos was also called San Pedro). There is also the museum of medieval fabrics *Museo de Telas Medievales*.

For the waymarked route continue through *parque El Parral* (former pilgrim refuge left) and out the gate at the far end to the tiny chapel opposite **[0.9 km]** dedicated to the humble pilgrim saint from France *San Amaro de peregrino* who, on his return from Santiago, settled here and dedicated his life to the welfare of other pilgrims leaving a legacy of healing miracles. From here we can also admire another piece of pilgrim history – the beautiful Kings Gate *Puerta del Rey* (60m left) on Pilgrim street *calle de los Romeros*. The magnificent 12th century King's Hospital *Hospital del Rey* was formerly a pilgrims hospice and is now the law faculty of Burgos university. From San Amaro turn right> and join the N-620 and N-120 (to Palencia and Carrión respectively) by •**Hotel Puerta Romeros** H** © 947-460 012 on the corner and turn <left along the main road with handsome pilgrim statue (see photo) and the modern university campus and continue

Pilgrim monument

past the •**Hotel Abadía** ℂ 947-040 404 and •**Hostal Lactea** and leave the main road by car park **[0.8 km]** opposite •**Bellavista** Restaurant and also has rooms available. Follow the minor road past *Iglesia y Residencial N.S del Pilar* where the city effectively ends and the camino begins by the municipal nursery *vivero forestal* **[0.8 km]**.

2.5 km **Camino N.S del Pilar** continue along track with the watch towers of the state prison on the far side of a poplar plantation (right) up to road over the río Arlanzón back to track and through tunnel under the railway line.

3.0 km **Túnel** the track continues to a bridge over the new autopista. *[At this point there is an option to detour (left) to* **Villalbilla** *a suburb of Burgos sandwiched between the rail line and the N-120 with several hotels located on main road]*. Turn right> over bridge and the track wends its way under the A-231 and over the N-120 and río Arlanzón (for the last time) via *puente del Arzobispo*. We now join a track alongside the N-120 past a handsome marker *Rollo* (left) into the village of **Tardajos** with noisy bar •*Ruiz* ℂ 947-451 125 on the main road but with tranquil restaurant to the side also has rooms. Keep s/o into c/Mediodía and past the town square to:

4.1 km **Tardajos** *(Pop. 700)* •**Albergue Muni.** *[18÷3]* ℂ 947-451 189 in modern semi-detached building. 18 beds €-*donativo* No kitchen or lounge but there is a small garden and •*Bar El Camino* opposite. Continue on quiet asphalt road over río Urbel (formerly a marshy area, hence the suffix of the next town Rabé *causeway*) up into the village clearly visible ahead:

2.3 km **Rabé de las Calzadas** *(Pop. 190)* Pass road (right) to *Casa Museo* and •**Hotel Deobrigula** in c/Alta (it is!) 400m at the top of the village with 13 'studios' and •bar/ restaurant. •**Albergue** *Hospital de Peregrinos Santa Marina y Santiago Priv.[8]* ℂ Michèle y Félix 607-971 919 centrally located on Plaza Francisco Ribera (see photo) 8 beds €8 also dinner. Opposite:•**Albergue** *Libéranos Dómine Priv.[24÷4]*+ private hostel with 24 beds

€8 also offer dinner €8 (no kitchen - open all year) run by José Mª & Tinín ℂ 695 116 901 the family owns •*Bar La Peña* at the lower end of town. Fill up your water flask at the drinking fountain [F] (scallop shell motif) in the centre of this ancient camino village with its 13th century Iglesia de Santa Mariña. Continue out the village by the diminutive Ermita de Nuestra Señora de Monasterio before heading up onto the incomparable *Meseta* passing:

2.4 km **Fuente de Praotorre** isolated picnic spot whose fountain may be dry and the young trees still struggling to provide shade. The camino continues up through the peaceful landscape temple with its sacred stones *piedras santos* and cereal fields stretching to the horizon to the high point on the Meseta before descending steeply down the aptly named Mule-Killer Slope *Cuesta Matamulas!* Cross a quiet road that runs alongside the río Hormazuela into:

5.3 km Hornillos del Camino *(Pop. 70)* ❶Albergue *Muni.[32÷3]* ⓒ 947 411 050 centrally located opp. Bar Manolo's adj. the Gothic Church of San Román in the Plaza de la Iglesia in attractive renovated building. Open all year (except Feb) with 32 beds €5 with good facilities incl. kitchen and patio area. Additional 14 beds in the adjacent town hall and overflow space

also available on mattresses *colchones* in the large sports hall to the rear).
❷El Alfar *Priv.[20÷3]* ⓒ 638 964 649 between the shop and bar Manolo on c/ Cantarranas nª8. Opened in 2013 with 20 bunk beds €9. communal dinner available at 19.30 €7.50 breakfast €3.

Other Accommodation: Casa rural at the entrance to the village •**Hostal de sol a sol** ⓒ Samuel Palacín Alcalde 649-876 091 with 7 rooms opposite the village •*Shop*. When full they can arrange for pilgrims to be transported to casa rural •**El Molino** ⓒ 947-560 302 in the adjoining village. Also with free transport *transporte gratis* (there and back) •**Las Postas de Argaño** ⓒ 947-450 156 in Villanueva de Argaño 6 km away close to the A-231. The municipal albergue is managed from the popular Bar / Restaurant on the main street c/ Real •*Casa Manolo* ⓒ 947-411 050.

The church occupies the dominant position in this delightful medieval village and adjoins the picturesque Hen Fountain *Fuente del Gallo*. Hornillos del Camino is a classic pilgrim village and important medieval halt on the way to Santiago, little changed over the past centuries and a good place in which to soak up some of the ancient atmosphere of the way. The name Hornillos possibly derives from kiln or oven *horno* with the diminutive *illos* suggesting a small stove. All along the Meseta we find this suffix – *illos* appended to place names. It has been suggested that this might have arisen due to a sense of the relative impermanence of man when experienced against the seemingly endless horizon under the vast vault of the Meseta sky. We can likewise use this idea to contemplate the relative insignificance of the physical body when compared with the eternal nature of our spiritual identity. Apart from such musings there is little to occupy the pilgrim here other than the priceless peace that pervades this village. A small shop and bar further up the main street offers the possibility of a meal. Chill out and try doing nothing *nada* – and experience being-ness. Note: the closure of the intermediary albergue at El Parral in Burgos is likely to stretch the village resources so expect changes and some increased activity.

REFLECTIONS:

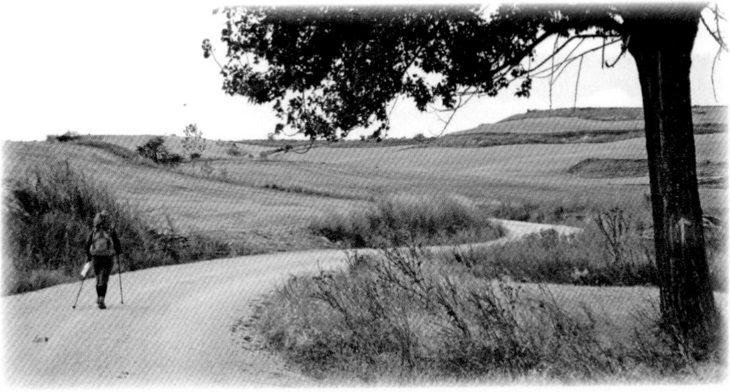

❏ **The holiest of all the spots on earth is where an ancient hatred has become a present love**... *A Course In Miracles*

14   **480.2** km (298.4 miles) to Santiago

HORNILLOS DEL CAMINO – CASTROJERIZ

⸽⸽⸽⸽⸽⸽⸽⸽⸽	Path / Track	--- ---	14.8 ---	73%
▬▬▬▬	Quiet Road	--- ---	5.4 ---	27%
▬▬▬▬	Main Road	--- ---	0.0	
Total km	**Total distance**		**20.2 km** (12.6 ml)	

Adjusted for climb   21.4 km (accrued ascent 250m = 1.2 km)
Alto ▲   High Point: The Meseta above Hontanas at 950m (3,117 feet)
< 🄰 🏠 >   Sanbol **5.8** km – Hontanas **10.8** km – San Antón **16.3** km.

900m Alto Meseta **San Bol** *Alto (Meseta)* 940m
HORNILLOS 🄰 *Río Sanbol* 🄰 **Hontanas** **Arco** **CASTROJERIZ**
800m **San Antón** 800m
700m 🄰
00 km   5 km   10 km   15 km   20

The Practical Path: Today we again travel the lonely Meseta with the sounds of nature the only likely intrusion on the peace that pervades it. There is little or no shade and so again we need to take care with the sun and carry plenty of water.

❏ **The Mystical Path:** ... *Forget not that a shadow held between your brother and yourself obscures the face of Christ and the memory of God. Around you angels hover lovingly, to keep away all darkened thoughts, and keep the light where it has entered in. Your footprints lighten up the world, for where you walk forgiveness gladly goes with you.* Will we walk today with a forgiving heart or hold on to old hurts that keep us feeling separated from our fellow pilgrims, destroying our sense of peace? Will you find the sacred symbol of healing used by knights and monks, ancient and modern? Will you place your hand in the niche that offered bread to passing strangers and will you break bread with a stranger today? Will we compound the problem or become part of the solution?

❏ **Personal Reflections:** "... *She asked me if she could stitch my torn shirt and began to sew. I had not met her before and yet she seemed familiar. Santiago and his jovial friend showed me how to make a real Spanish tortilla. We ate together with great merriment despite our fatigue and difficulty with language. Such deep respect and joy amongst strangers who were not strangers. Our laughter sent great vortexes of loving energy out into the world. If only we would live our lives with this open heartedness – what changes might we bring about to our war-torn world ...*"

0.0 km **Hornillos de Camino** From the albergue / Bar Casa Manolo follow the main street *c/Real* which is part of the original camino and veer right at the far end past the stand of poplars and start the gentle climb back up onto the Meseta. The track levels out and continues in a westerly direction until we begin the gentle descent to the arroyo San Bol where the isolated refuge is clearly visible (left).

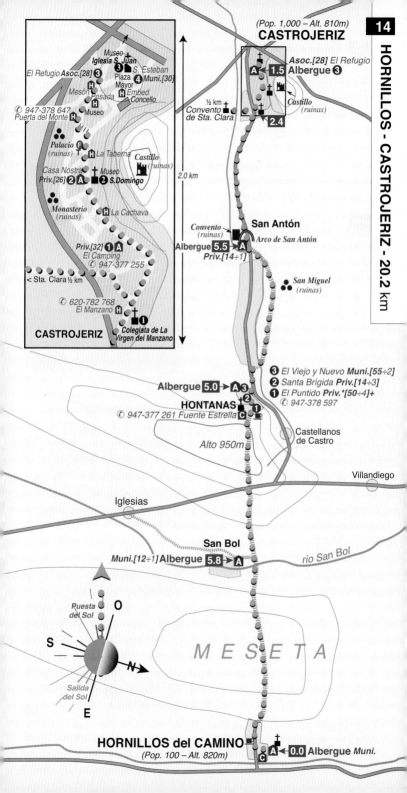

5.8 km **Arroyo San Bol** Cross over the stream and continue s/o *or* turn left to visit San Bol 200m •**Albergue** *Muni.[12÷1]* © 628 927 317 basic hostel (new shower and w.c.!) No kitchen but communal meal offered. 12 beds €5 in one room. Delightful location by grove of poplar trees offering shade by the river. The waters from the well are said to have healing properties and to cure aching feet – the peace of this isolated spot can heal more than feet. The nearest village *Iglesias* lies 4 km further off the camino along a dirt road. At one time a monastery dedicated to San Boal (or San Baudito) of the Antonine order served this area and gave it its name - now managed by Santa Brigida hostel in Hontanas. Climb up again out of the narrow Sanbol valley back onto the Meseta. Pass over a minor road (linking Iglesias and Olmillos de Sasamón) and spectacularly the Meseta suddenly falls away to reveal:

5.0 km **Hontanas** *(Pop. 80)* another classic pilgrim village tucked down in a fold in the Meseta. Situated off a minor road into Castrojeriz and largely undiscovered except by pilgrims. The solid parish church of the Conception *XIV*th*C* (see photo) dominates the tiny village square and contributes to an air of quiet reverence that pervades this little Jacobean haven of the fountains *Fontanas* from which the name derives and a fine example [F] spills out its refreshingly cool waters in the shade of the church.

•**Albergue** ❶ *El Puntido Priv.*[50÷4]+* network* hostel © 947-378 597 centrally located opposite the church. Recently renovated with 50 beds €5 +priv. rooms. Good facilities, no kitchen but popular bar and mesón menú €9. Further down the main street •**Albergue** ❷ *Santa Brígida Priv.*[14÷3]* © 628 927 317 with 14 beds €6 also provides meals. Opposite is the municipal hostel well maintained by a team of ladies from the village. •**Albergue** ❸ *San Juan El Nuevo Muni.[55÷2]* © 947 377 436 with 55 beds €5 in 2 dormitories.

Albergue ❶ *Puntido*

Albergue ❸ *St Juan*

Oen all year with good facilities but no outside patio although pilgrims spill out along the road. The lounge is built over the original medieval foundations (visible through the glazed floor) and the hostel won an architectural award for its imaginative reconstruction. When this hostel is full the other municipal albergues are opened as follows: •**Albergue** ❹ *La Escuela* 21 beds in one dormitory in the old schoolhouse with showers and toilets and use of kitchen in [3] above and •**Albergue** ❺ *El Viejo*

located in the Town Hall with 14 beds in 2 rooms with showers and toilets and use of kitchen in [1] above. Alternative accommodation includes: Opposite El Puntido with up-market rooms •**Fuente Estrella** Hs* © 947-377 261 and just below is casa rural •**El Descanso**. [*The infamous* Vitorino *experience at the end* *of town is no longer available. Vitorino is one of the many colourful characters along the camino and can drink a litre of wine from a porrón (jug with spout) without drawing breath, and frequently does, so the menu was wonderfully erratic. Vitorino is (re)tired from serving pilgrims but not the porrón!]*

Continue through the village past the municipal swimming pool with bar-café (open high summer only) and cross over the minor road shaded with trees (an alternative is to walk the quiet country road and avail of the shade). The waymarked path continues roughly parallel to the road passing the ruins of an old mill and the long abandoned village of San Miguel to re-join the road just before:

5.5 km **San Antón** •Albergue *Priv.[14÷1]* private hostel sited amongst the splendid ruins of the ancient *convento de San Antón XIV*[th]*C.* Open May-Sept. only with 14 beds €-*donativo* and all basic facilities (no electricity) where a shared meal may be available. Pass under St. Anthony's archway *Arco de San Antón* with recessed alcoves where bread was left for pilgrims of old (the tradition continues with pilgrims leaving messages here instead). This was the ancient monastery and hospice of the

San Antón – Albergue *(left)*

Antonine Order founded in France in the 11th century and connected to the work of the hermit Saint Anthony of Egypt *San Antón Abad* patron saint of animals and usually depicted with a pig at his feet. The Order's sacred symbol was the 'T' shaped cross known as the Tau – nineteenth letter of the Greek alphabet and symbolising divine protection against evil and sickness. Increasingly referred to and worn as the Pilgrim Cross *Cruz del Peregrino.* The Order was known for its ability to cure the medieval scourge known as St Anthony's fire (a fungal skin disease often turning gangrenous leading to death) essentially by using the power of the Tau (Love) in its healing practise.

As we leave these magnificent ruins behind Castrojeriz the Convento de Santa Clara *Clarisas* opens up to our left (½ km) founded in the 14th century where you can buy one of the wooden Tau crosses made by the nuns (open most days, closed through lunch, mass 17:15) – or buy one in Castrojeriz which now opens to view in front of us. The prominent castle (also in ruins) stands sentinel over the town and surrounding countryside. We enter the town at:

2.4 km **Castrojeriz** *Iglesia Santa María* ex collegiate Church of Our Lady of the Apple ❶ *N.S Manzano XIV*[th]*C.* Its spacious interior is cool after the road and the delightful rose window sheds light on some interesting treasures, including a statue of St. James in pilgrim regalia festooned with scallop shells and a fine statue of Our Lady. The church has recently been renovated as a museum of sacred art. Opposite the church is bar and hostal El Manzano.

The town is laid out in one long straggling line between the road and the hill and is 2 km from start to finish. Next we arrive at •Albergue ❶ *Camino de Santiago Priv.[32÷1]+* **[0.3 km]** © 947-377 255 part of the camping site with 40 beds €6 in 1 dormitory +priv. rooms & bungalows. The extensive facilities (no kitchen) include large terrace area with a backdrop of trees, a shop, bar and restaurant. Continue along the upper street into c/Real Oriente with a selection of 'up market' casa rurales and rural hotels (see list below) and we arrive at ❷ *Casa Nostra Priv.[26÷3]* **[0.6 km]** *©* 947-377 493 Traditional town house on c/Real Oriente Nº54 with 26 beds €6, cool interior and patio and good facilities. Opposite is the parish church of St. Dominic ❸ *Iglesia de Santo Domingo,* which combines Gothic, Baroque and Plasteresque styles but it lies 'hidden' in narrow streetscape and barely

Albergue ❷ *Casa Nostra*

noticeable. Continue on up to a small square with the option to continue straight on to the Plaza Mayor and directly to municipal albergue [4] (400 metres) or <left *down* the steps and immediately right> for the main route to the next small square beside the Mesón de Castrojeriz and into c/Cordon with several bars and cafés and the original albergue in the centre of town **[0.6** km]:

1.5 km Castrojeriz *Centro* ❸ *El Refugio Asoc.[28÷2]* traditional (original) pilgrim hostel *©* 947-377 400 centrally located on c/ Cordón – part of the camino. An atmospheric local association hostel run by hospitalero *Resti* one of the caminos enduring characters. 28 beds *€-donativo* in 2 dormitories no kitchen but spacious garden. From here you can take a right hand turn (not waymarked) up into the Plaza Mayor (200 metres) to ❹ *San Esteban Muni.[30÷1]* *©* 947-377 001 in a commanding position overlooking Plaza

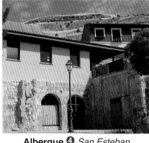

Albergue ❹ *San Esteban*

Mayor at the top end of town. Municipal hostel open all year on upper floor of restored civic building (also the *Casa Cultura)* with 30 beds *€-donativo* (+ mattresses) in one large open dormitory. Good showers and toilets but no other facilities. Pilgrims not staying in this albergue usually bypass the Plaza Mayor (see town map) a delightful square with several cafés and shops. Both routes join at the ❸ *Iglesia de San Juan XVI*[th]*C* largely Gothic but with a Renaissance baptismal font attributed to the 15th century master sculptor and architect Diego de Siloé whose outstanding work we have already come across in Burgos, his city of birth. There is also a fine cloister and the entire has recently been renovated and now acts as a museum and art gallery.

Other accommodation *(sequentially from the entrance):* •**El Manzano** Hs *©* 947-378 618. c/Real de Oriente •**La Cachava** H** *©* 947-378 547 (Nº83) •**La Taberna** P *©* 620-782 768 (Nº43). •**Casa de los Holandeses** CR *©* 947-377 608 (Nº58). •**Puerta del Monte** Hs** *©* 947-378 647 on paseo del Monte •**La Posada** H*** *©* 947-378 610 c/Landelino Tardajos, 3. •**Mesón Castrojeriz** Hs** *©* 947-378 610 c/Cordón, 1. •**Embed Posada** H *©* 639 750 202 Plaza Mayor 5. *[Next albergue: Puente Itero – 9.1 km].*

CASTROJERIZ: Delightfully sleepy town with a resident population of only 600 who seem to be permanently occupied with siesta except during the garlic festival *fiesta del Ajo* in July which adds a bit of seasoning to life. It had a more active past evident in its ruined castles and monasteries. An historic fortified town *castrum* with Roman and Visigothic remains, and scene of much fighting.

Castrojeriz rose to prominence during the *reconquista* and as a major stopping place on the medieval camino with no less than 8 pilgrim hospitals. If you have the energy, a walk to the hilltop castle *castillo* (established in the 9th century) will be rewarded with fine views over the town and countryside – otherwise a short walk to the sites already referred to will give you a flavour of this historic town. Alternatively, just hang out with a cool beer in one of the bars of this typically pilgrim town – or join the locals and take a siesta.

REFLECTIONS:

❏ **If you follow your bliss, you put yourself on a track, that has been there all the while, waiting for you, and the life you ought to be living is the one you are living.** *Joseph Campbell*

15 **460.0** km (285.8 miles) to Santiago

CASTROJERIZ (Burgos) – FRÓMISTA
                                                          (Palencia)

‖‖‖‖‖‖	Path / Track	--- ---	21.8 ---	87%
▬▬▬	Quiet Road	--- ---	3.4 ---	13%
▨▨▨	Main Road	--- ---	0.0 ---	
Total km	**Total distance**		**25.2 km** (15.7 ml)	

◣◤ **Adjusted for climb**   26.4 km (accrued ascent 250m = 1.2 km)

Alto ▲   High Point: Alto de Mostelares at 900m (2,952 feet)

<**🅰 🏠**>   Puente de Itero **9.0** km – *Itero del Castillo* **9.0** *+1.5 km off route.* – Itero de la Vega **11.0** km – Boadilla **19.2** km.

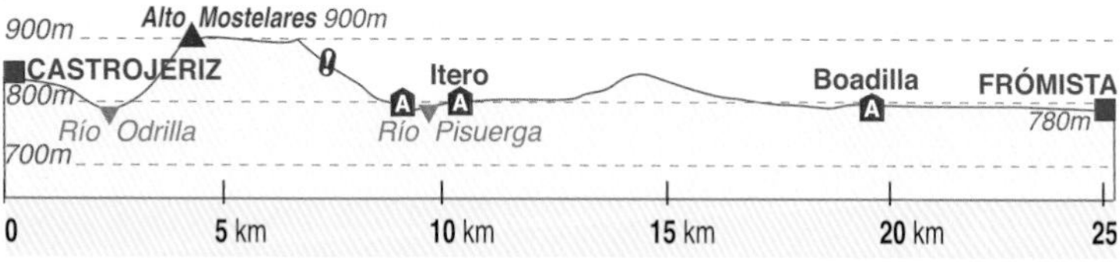

The Practical Path: A glance at the map of today's stage might give you a false impression. Look carefully and you will see that while the camino appears in a web of asphalt roads it seldom connects with them. A glorious 21.8 km (87%) is on earthen tracks. Be prepared for the strenuous climb out of Castrojeriz onto the Meseta. The view back over the valley floor, coupled with the knowledge that what goes up must come down should be enough to revive any flagging spirit. Apart from the trees that line the río Pisuerga and the Canal de Castilla there is little shade and few water fonts, so take precautions.

❏ **The Mystical Path:** The track we start off on today was laid two thousand years ago. Tomorrow's track is the first stretch of the soulless modern *senda* with its ugly concrete bollards that flies over the Frómista bypass and was built only a few years back. How many pilgrims have walked the old Roman road and how many will walk the modern senda? How many followed their bliss? How many have paid equal respect to the inner and outer path? Which path are we on? Is our life in tune with our purpose? What is our purpose? Life without an inner direction is fruitless and only leads down a cul-de-sac called despair with only disillusionment and death at the end. Bliss is found another way – along the inner pathways of soul.

❏ **Personal Reflections:** *"… I have seldom witnessed such dedication to a path of service – the whole family's unwavering hospitality to pilgrims on their way to Santiago. Every action is performed with such care and precision and made to feel right, not just look right. I am reminded how much my own life has been squandered in posturing. The pretence that comes from making something look right on the surface, while ignoring the underlying lack of integrity and the feeling of discontent that follows. Tamed man addicted to the approval of family and friends masking the wild man desperate for the freedom that comes with authentic living while painting a larger canvas. Eduardo's mother is an artist in more ways than one …"*

↑ Carrión

A-67

N-611

< Palencia

S.Martín XII

❶ † **A 2** ◄ **6.0** Albergue *Muni.***[56÷6]*

H

S.Pedro XV

2

© 979-810 193

Estación *Priv.[40÷1]* **❶ A**

© 979-810 053

H A 3 Estrella *Priv.[34÷3]+*

FRÓMISTA
(Pop. 800 - Alt. 790m)

3

† H

(Leyenda del Camino)
S.Maria del Castillo

Santa María XV
columna justicia XV
En El Camino © 979-810 284
Priv.**[48]+*Albergue **8.2** **3 A** † **BOADILLA del CAMINO**

Escuela Muni.[12] **2 A**

F

Putzu Priv.[16] **❶ A**

Canal de Castilla

T I E R R A *de* C A M P O S

Canal Pisuerga

Bodegas

2.0 Albergue *Muni.[12÷1]*

† **3 A**

ITERO de la VEGA **2** La Mochila

P A L E N C I A

† **❶** Fitero

Muni.[7÷1]

Puente Itero

A ◄ **1.5** Albergue

río Pisuerga

A

Albergue **1.5** ◄

St. Nicolás *Asoc. [12÷1]*

Itero del Castillo

B U R G O S

⚔ F ◄ **4.1** Fuente del Piojo

▲ Alto 900m

⚔ **3.4** Alto Mostelares

Puesta
del Sol

O

río Odrilla

S

N

Salida
del Sol

E

(Pop. 600 – Alt. 810m)
CASTROJERIZ **A** ◄ **0.0** Albergue **3** *Central*

† St.Juan

0.0 km Castrojeriz *Centro* From albergue ❸ in the centre of Castrojeriz pass by the church of San Juan, and cross over the main road to join a track that runs alongside the Roman causeway to a bridge over the río Odrilla (tributary of the río Pisuerga which we cross later). The slopes of Mostelares lie ahead as we start the steep climb to:

3.4 km Alto de Mostelares A masterful covered rest area with local flora information has been created to help us get our breath back but the real masterpiece is the landscape temple that surrounds us. Continue along the high Meseta dropping down again track (right) **[1.8 km]** (alternative route to Itero del Castillo see below) and thence to the only shade on this section **[2.3 km]** at:

4.1 km Fuente del Piojo [F] a modern picnic area with some shade and cool spring water. We now join the minor road to:

1.5 km Ermita de San Nicolás •Albergue *Asoc.[12]* directly on the camino just before the bridge. This popular hostel (June-Sept only) no electricity, phone or other mod-cons (excepting a shower and toilet in an extension to the rear) but a shared dinner and breakfast €-*donativo*. The 13th century buildings were restored by an Italian

Confraternity who retain candlelight as the source of illumination which adds to the healing atmosphere of this veritable haven. Space is limited to 12 so count your blessings if a bed or mattress is available. The original pilgrim hospice was founded in the 12th century and later a Cistercian monastery was added.

Detour: *Itero del Castillo* **1.5 km** along the road to the right (before crossing the river). You can just make out the tower of the church on the horizon. Its name refers to its strategic position on this historic border point on the banks of the río Pisuerga. •Albergue *Mun.[7÷1]* basic municipal hostel © 608 977 477 located in the town hall on Plaza Ayuntamiento. Open all year with 7 beds €5. Limited facilities (no kitchen). Return via the asphalt road.

Puente de Itero whose eleven arches carry us over the río Pisuerga and into the Provincia de Palencia. The river provided the natural historical boundary between the kingdoms of Castilla and León. *[Several place names around here start with Itero a derivation of Hito meaning landmark or boundary stone].*

Provincia de PALENCIA Land of Fields *Tierra de Campos* an extensive agricultural area well served with rivers and canals that irrigate its rich soils. Here we also see the cultivation mainly of wheat with some vegetable and wine production. It is a flat region lying between the rivers Pisuerga and Cea at Sahagún. There are few trees to offer shade from the relentless sun that dries the deep red earthen walls of many of the adobe villages we pass through. The absence of wood and stone made earth the natural building material – initially air-dried bricks and eventually kilns speeding up the process and stability but still lacking long-term durability. There is also increasing evidence of wine cellars *bodegas* whose Hobbit-like structures, built into the sides of hillocks, appear all over the countryside to store the local wine in the relative cool of their subterranean stores.

A shaded track follows the river past the *Ermita de la Piedad XIII^thC* with picnic area [F] and Jacobean motifs at the entrance of this sleepy village:

2.0 km Itero de la Vega *(Pop.190)* •Albergue ❶ *Puente Fitero* **Priv.[20]** © 979-151 822 as you enter with private rooms and popular bar and restaurant (the family run the Hostal Santiago in Carrion). •Albergue ❷ *La Mochila* **Priv.[20÷4]** © 979-151 781 on c/Santa Ana 20 beds from €6. No kitchen but meals available (open all year). •Albergue ❸ *Muni.[12÷1]* © 605-034 347. By the parish church *San Pedro XVI^thC* in Plaza Iglesia. 12

Albergue ❸ Municipal

beds €5. Limited facilities, no kitchen but rear patio. *[Next albergue: Boadilla – 8.0 km]*. The camino veers left into c/Santa Ana past albergue La Mochila and the adjoining *Bar Tachu [to visit the Plaza Mayor with its attractive fountain of prancing ponies watched over by a handsome Gothic rollo veer right]*.

Leave town by the asphalt road and continue s/o T-junction onto a wide farm track. The village of Bodegas (left) with a wind farm on the ridge beyond. We next cross the ***Canal Pisuerga* [2.2 km]** *[This whole area has been opened up to intensive farming as the result of the building of a series of canals in the late 18th century]*. The farm track continues all the way up a gentle incline and then down to a shaded river stretch with unusual wheel pump in the woodland glade [F] (left) **[5.6 km]** on the outskirts of Boadilla. •Albergue ❶ *Putzu* **Priv.[16]** Basic refugio €7 with snack bar adjoining the water wheel. The village centre is 400m further on. Cross the river to pass •Albergue ❷ *Escuela Muni.[12÷1]* © 979 810 390 municipal hostel in the former school building on c/Escuelas. Open all year with 12 beds €3 in 1 room, basic facilities (no kitchen). The run-down children's playground provides space for relaxation. We next arrive in the central square ***Plaza Mayor* [0.4 km]**

8.2 km Boadilla del Camino *(Pop.140)* and •Albergue ❸ *En El Camino* **Priv.*[48÷2]+** © 979-810 284 popular network* hostal centrally located by the church and historic cross *Rollo* with Jacobean motifs. 48 beds €6 in 2 dorms in converted barn +priv. rooms in the main house *Casa Rural*. Excellent facilities including extensive landscaped grounds with small swimming pool. Typical

Albergue ❸ En El Camino

Castilian menu prepared by artist Begoña whose paintings adorn the walls and the whole family work tirelessly to offer the pilgrim a welcome. *[Next albergue: Frómista – 6.4 km]*.

Boadilla del Camino: The original population of over 2,000 that once served the several pilgrim hospitals here has now fallen to less than 200 – a characteristic of many rural communities along the way. But the re-awakening of the camino is beginning to turn the tide. The school has been turned into a pilgrim hostel and the schoolmaster returns at weekends to help his family run the albergue and casa rural in the village centre! The 16th century parish Church of Santa María contains an exceptional 14th century stone baptismal font and there is an equally fine medieval jurisdictional column *Rollo* in the square complete with scallop shell motifs. *Bar Dory* has patio-seating area out the back and shop to the rear, neither of which is evident from the outside.

Continue out the village onto another farm track through the *Tierra de Campos* to the **Canal de Castilla** [2.0 km] that flows all the way into Frómista along a peaceful tree-lined path. While the modern Canal Pisuerga was designed exclusively for irrigation purposes, this 18th century canal provided transportation of the cultivated crops as well as power to turn the corn mills. With the advent of motorways its use is now restricted to irrigation and leisure. There is a plan to restore the canal system with all its original 50 locks. We now have a delightfully shaded canal side walk to the lock gates *esclusa* [3.2 km] which we cross on the uppermost of a flight of locks (disused), that stretch out below us, and continue down to the main road to pass under the rail line up

Frómista – *Esclusa*

to the main crossroads **Turismo** ✆ 979-810 180 (summer only) in Paseo Central which we cross over veering right and then left into the Plaza de San Martín [0.8 km]:

6.0 km Frómista *(Pop. 800)* •Albergue ❶ *Canal de Castilla Priv.[40÷1]* private hostel ✆ 979-810 193 converted railway building at the station €7. No kitchen but adjoining restaurant *Mesón Bodega*. •Albergue ❷ *Muni.*[56÷6] ✆ 979-811 089 municipal hostel adjoining the hotel. 56 beds €7 in 6 rooms. Modern facilities (lacking a kitchen) and open patio. •**Albergue** ❸ *Estrella del Camino Priv.[34÷3]+* ✆ 979-810 053 private hostel with sheltered garden terrace 34 beds €7. **Other accommodation:** Adjacent to albergue [1] •**San Martín** HR° ✆ 979-810 000 and •**Marisa** P ✆ 979-810 023. Behind albergue [3] (same family) •**Camino de Santiago** Hs ✆ 979-810 053. Several

Frómista – Albergue ❷

casas rurales: •**Antonio y Marcelino** CR y •**Serviarias** CR ✆ 626 959 079. •**El Milagro** CR ✆ 979-810 944 and •**San Telmo** CR ✆ 979-811 028. *[Next albergue: Población – 3.8 km].* There are a variety of bars and cafes but for an authentic Castillian meal in an historic pilgrim *hospital* try Hostería Los Palmeros, opposite the Church of San Pedro on Plaza San Telmo. The square is presided over by San Telmo, patron saint of sailors, who was born here in the 12th century and who died along the *camino Portugués* and is buried in Tui.

FRÓMISTA is best known (and visited) for the beautiful 11th century Iglesia de San Martín (consecrated in 1066) and reputedly one of the finest examples of pure Romanesque in Spain. The church has exquisite proportions and is built with a lovely mellow stone with over 300 external corbels each carved with a different human, animal or mystical motif. It was de-consecrated, painstakingly restored and declared a national monument all in the same breath. Endless coach parties have turned it into a must-see tourist site and it appears to have lost something vital in the process. At the other end of town is the 15th century Gothic Church of San Pedro that has a more prayerful atmosphere and a small museum of religious artwork and a statue of St. James. Sta. Mª del Castillo houses the Vestigia multimedia presentation *Leyenda del Camino*.

Iglesia de San Martín

The importance of Frómista to the camino is evident in the fact that there were several pilgrim hospitals here in medieval times such as the Hostería Los Palmeros. *Palmeros* is a reference to pilgrims to the Holy Land whose symbol was a palm leaf as distinct from the scallop shell representing the pilgrim to Santiago. Frómista is derived from the Latin word for cereal *frumentum* this area having provided copious supplies of wheat to the burgeoning Roman Empire and is also perhaps the reason why we find the unusual reference to pilgrims heading east to Jerusalem via Rome rather than west to Santiago. This marks the beginning of stage VII of the Codex Calixtinus.

REFLECTIONS:

❐ So I began to have an idea of my life… as the gradual discovery and growth of a purpose that I did not know. *Joanna Field*

---

16 **434.8** km (270.2 miles) to Santiago

FRÓMISTA – CARRIÓN DE LOS CONDES

	Path / Senda*	--- ---	15.2	---	74%
	Quiet Road	--- ---	5.3	---	26%
	Main Road	--- ---	0.0		
Total km	**Total distance**		**20.5 km** (12.7 ml)		

Adjusted for climb   20.7 km (accrued ascent 50m = 0.2 km)

Alto ▲   High Point: Carrión 830m (2,725 feet)

< 🅰 🅗 >   Población de Campos **3.5** km – *[Alt. Vilarmentero 9.3 km]* – Villalcázar de Sirga **14.9** km.

```
                              Villalcázar          CARRIÓN
800m    Población    Villarmentero       🅰                    
  ■FRÓMISTA     🅰           🅰                              850m
700m        Río ⩔Ucieza            Río ⩔Ucieza
      |            |            |            |            |
00 km        5 km        10 km        15 km         20
```

The Practical Path: Yesterday over 80% of our journey was on natural paths. Today we have our first taste of the soulless *senda** sometimes referred to as *pilgrim autopistas* that run alongside the main roads. We have entered Palencia, which along with its neighbouring province of León, has engaged in a modernisation programme built, perhaps, on the back of too much wealth and too little forethought. In today's stage we can increase the natural paths by leaving out the senda from Poblacíon to Villalcázar de Sirga and taking the scenic path via Villovieco. This recommended follows a tree lined riverside path, which offers both shade and peace. Try and find time to visit the monumental Templar church in Villalcázar.

❐ **The Mystical Path:** Each step takes us nearer our destination, but where are we headed for? Today we will walk around 21 km approximating to 21,000 steps and we can choose to make each step a prayer for peace as we walk through the 21st century. Humanity is coming of age and we hold the key to a new era. The choice is ours as to which way we turn it, but we have only two real choices. We can add to the problems humanity currently faces or become part of the solution. Know that the choice we make will imbue the next millennia with either love or fear. May each step we take be blessed as we awaken to the purpose of life.

❐ **Personal Reflections:** *"… I sit on the balcony and look out to the soft evening colours changing from delicate blue to pink and now turning to a deepening red. It is strange how we universally experience the sun sinking whereas in reality the light is fixed and the earth and I are merely turning away from it into the shadow. The Inquisition offered Galileo the opportunity to recant on his challenge to the orthodox view or face a painful death. The possibility that the earth was not the centre of the universe was simply too threatening to the established authority. As I, too, begin to challenge the consensus reality around me, I ask for the courage to stay open to truth as it is revealed in each changing moment and not to seek the protection afforded by the popularly held perspective. My purpose becomes clearer with each passing day …"*

Real Monasterio H*
© 979-880 050
San Zoilo ❹

**CARRIÓN
DE LOS
CONDES**

Río Carrión

San Zoilo Ⓗ (N-120) (A-231)

S.Maria Par.[52÷2]
Ⓗ Ⓐ **5.6** Albergue ❷
← Santa María

*(Pop. 2,400
– Alt. 840m)*

Sta. Clara ✝Ⓐ ❶

Albe. Ⓗ
Pz. Generalísimo
Pz.Santillana ✝ ❸ *Santiago*
Ⓗ *Santiago*
← *El Resbalon*
Espíritu Santo Pz.
Ⓐ ❸ S.María.
979-880 138 ✝ Ⓐ ❷ *S. María*
La Corte Ⓗ ❷ *S. María*
La Abuela *i*

centro salud

Museo ❶
Santa Clara ❶ Ⓐ

VILLALCÁZAR DE SIRGA
Ⓐ *Casa Aurea Priv.[26]* © 979-888 163
✝ *Santa María la Blanca XIII*
Alb. **4.3** → Ⓐ **2.1** Albergue
Muni.[20÷2]

río Ucieza

✝ *Virgen del río*
✝ **4.8** Puente

Arconada

VILLARMENTERO DE CAMPOS
© 979-065 978 *Casona Doña Petra* Ⓒ +Tipis
Priv. [10÷1]
S.Martín de Tours → *Amanecer*
Albergue 2.1 Ⓐ

✝ **VILLOVIECO**
4.1 Puente

REVENGA DE CAMPOS
Centro 3.3 ⓕ

W
Sunset
S
Sunrise E

❷ ❶
Opción 0.4 *Amanecer* © 979-811 099
 Ⓒ Ⓐ **3.5** Albergue *Muni.[18÷1]*
Ermita de San Miguel → ✝
POBLACIÓN de CAMPOS

río Ucieza

(A-67)

(N-620)

0.0 Albergue
✝ *S.Martín* Ⓐ ❷
← Palencia ✝ *S.Pedro* Ⓐ
Estrella
del Camino
FRÓMISTA

156

`0.0 km` **Frómista** From albergue ❷ return to the crossroads and bar *Garigolo* and head out along the P-980 signposted Carrión de Los Condes over the Frómista bypass N-611 and the new A-67 roundabout onto the pilgrim gravel track *senda*. On the outskirts of Población (left) is the Romanesque Ermita St. Miguel *XIII[th]C* in a shaded glade on the opposite side of road [F]. Turn right> down the concrete path *Paseo del Cementerio* to:

`3.5 km` **Población de Campos** *(Pop. 150)* •Albergue *Muni.[18÷1]* basic hostel converted from a former school building as you enter the village with tranquil playground. 18 beds €4. Keys held at adjacent hotel/CR •Amanecer *(dawn)* ℂ 979-811 099 with private rooms from €40 and pilgrim menú €9. Also •Paso Camino Santiago CR ℂ 979-882 012 on c/Francesas.

Municipal Albergue

The parish church *XVI[th]C* is dedicated to Mary Magdalene. Continue past the diminutive *Ermita de la Virgen del Socorro XIII[th]C* (left) to the stone bridge over the río Ucieza.

`0.4 km` **Puente / Opción [?]**

For **alternative route** ❷ via *senda* ● ● ● ● ● continue over the bridge into:

`3.3 km` **Revenga de Campos** small village with church of San Lorenzo. Pick up the *senda* again as you exit with picnic halt and [F] right s/o into:

`2.1 km` **Villarmentero de Campos** •Albergue *Amanecer Priv.[20÷2]* ℂ 662 279 102 private hostel with 20 beds €6 + tipis or hammock €3! All facilities incl. snack bar and communal meal. Church of San Martín de Tours on opposite side of road, adjacent to casa rural •Casona de Doña Petra CR ℂ 979-065 978 which also offers dinner. Continue through the town – shaded picnic tables [F] (right) at far end and back onto the *senda* straight into:

`4.3 km` **Villalcázar de Sirga** where the riverside route joins from the right .

For the recommended riverside path ❶ do *not* cross the bridge but turn right> (signposted Ermita del Socorro) along road and then track and turn off <left [0.3 km] parallel to the tree-lined río Ucieza (left) to Villovieco bridge [3.8 km].

`4.1 km` **Villovieco** *(Pop. 100)* parish Church of St. Mary with Santiago artefacts. Leave the village by the bridge *Parque* with •*Bar* [F] and turn immediately right> along the rio Ucieza for a delightful 4.8 kilometre of shade to join the quiet country road from Arconada into:

`4.8 km` **Puente** *Ermita de la Virgen del Río* Hermitage of Our Lady of the River housing an image of Santiago. Turn <left, continue along road into:

`2.1 km` **Villalcázar de Sirga** *(Pop. 200)* [F] turn right into the main square and •Albergue *Muni.[20÷2]* basic municipal hostel ℂ 979-888 041 with access off the Plaza del Peregrino (see photo) with 20 beds €-*donativo* in 2 rooms. Limited facilities in this traditional pilgrim hostel overlooking the main square and church of Santa María la Blanca. Other

accommodation: •**Albergue** *Tasca Don Camino* **Priv.[26÷4]** © 979-888 053 also has individual rooms and restaurant. •**Infanta Doña Leonor** HsR* © 927-888 015 as you enter which also operates •**Las Cántigas** Casa Vidal CR © 927-888 013 on c/Cantarranas [*Next albergue: Carrión de los Condes – 5.8 km*].

VILLALCÁZAR DE SIRGA (VILLASIRGA – town of the canal towpath) is well known for its hospitality having welcomed pilgrims here since the 12th century when it became a commandery of the Knights Templar. There is a popular •*Café-Bar* opposite the church and fine fare at the traditional •*Mesón Villalcázar* also on the main square in a well-preserved medieval inn. The town is home to the magnificent Templar church of **Santa María la Virgen Blanca** *XIIIthC* housing the tombs of nobles and royalty and now declared a national monument. The porch with its sculptured south door is particularly noteworthy

as is the rose window. If visiting churches along the way is not your 'thing' make an exception for this one: open 10:00–13:00 and 16:00–20:00 and have a look in the side aisle (opposite the entrance) and light up the retablo (coin operated) which has a splendid panel depicting the life of St. James; his meeting with Jesus, his subsequent ministry, martyrdom and transference to Galicia. In a side chapel is the statue of Santa María La Blanca, to whom is ascribed many miracles. The tombs of Infante Don Felipe (son of Fernando III and brother of Alfonso X the wise *el Sabio*) and Felipe's wife Doña Leonor are also located here.

We leave town and make our way back to the main road and pick up the gravel *senda* that runs parallel to it all the way to the outskirts of Carrión de los Condes where we cross over to •**Albergue** ❶ *Santa Clara* **Conv.[30÷6]+** © 979-880 837 prominently located (left) at the entrance to the town. Convent hostel run by the *Madres Clarisas* with 30 beds €5 also single rooms €22 (double rooms €44) and all facilities off a delightful courtyard that also provides access to ❶ **Real Monasterio y Ermita de La Piedad** *XIIIthC*. St. Francis of Assisi allegedly stayed in these 13th century buildings.

The town centre and parish hostel are now only 300m further on – continue up to the main road and cross over by **Turismo** © 979-880 932 (summer only) site of the *Puerta de Santa María* that provided the entrance to the old walled city and the 12th century Romanesque church of St. Mary of the Way *Santa María del Camino*. Unusual buttresses form the main entrance which depicts the miracle wrought by the Church's namesake, when the notorious annual 'tribute of the 100 maidens, *doncellas*' imposed by the Moors on the Christian population was finally broken. Turn right> immediately after the church into square (market every Thursday) and:

5.6 km **Carrión de los Condes** •**Albergue** ❷ *Santa María* **Par.[52÷2]** © 979 880 500 centrally located parish hostel behind the church in c/Clérigo Pastor off plaza Santa María. 52 beds €5. No kitchen but facilities include *lavadora* and *secadora*. •**Albergue ❸** *spíritu Santo Conv.[90÷7]* run by the brothers *Hijas de San Vicente de Paul* Ⓒ 979-880 052 Plaza San Juan near the health centre (behind *Pescaderia Amaya* on main road). Open all year with 90 beds €5. Basic facilities (no kitchen). *[Next albergue: Calzadilla de la Cueza – 17.5 km]*

Other Accommodation: •**La Corte** Hs* Ⓒ 979-880 138 c/Santa María, 34 (opposite the church) popular restaurant rooms also off a rear courtyard. •**Santiago** HsR* Ⓒ 979-881 052 Plaza de los Regentes (central). •**La Abuela** Me CR adjoining café Yadira on main road (Plaza Conde Garay). •**El Resbalon** P* Ⓒ 979-880 433 c/Fernan Gomez, 19 above the restaurant of the same name. •**Alba** HsR* Ⓒ 979-880 874 Esteban Colantes,2. On the other side of the river the luxurious •**Real Monasterio San Zoilo** H*** Ⓒ 979-880 050. The town has a wide selection of shops, bars and restaurants.

Albergue ❷ Santa María *(above)*
Albergue ❸ Espíritu Santo *(below)*

CARRIÓN DE LOS CONDES occupied a strategic position in this volatile border area and at the height of its influence had a population in excess of 10,000; now reduced to some 2,300. This interesting town retains a medieval atmosphere within its meandering side streets and was home to no less than 14 pilgrim *hospitals*. It was effectively the capital of much of the *tierra de campos* area and ruled by the Leónese Beni-Gómez family, the Counts of Carrión, several of whom met a premature death at the hands of the equally pugnacious El Cid, after they reputedly, and very unwisely, mistreated his daughters. Mistreatment was endemic here further attested to by the frieze in the ❷ *Iglesia de Santa María del Camino XIIthC* which depicts the frightful annual 'tribute' of 100 maidens demanded by the conquering Moors. These intrigues and disputes were not limited to this medieval period. The Church of Santiago ❸ *Iglesia de Santa XIIthC* was destroyed during the War of Independence (1809) but thankfully leaving the magnificent facade and frieze intact (Christ in majesty) as a national monument and the church itself has been adapted as museum where image of *Santiago Matamoros* continues the theme of death and retribution.

SAN ZOILO Real Monasterio de San Zoilo XIth–XVIthC connected with Order of Cluny and dating from 11th century with Romanesque elements but largely influenced by the Renaissance period including the splendid Plateresque cloisters. We pass San Zoilo on the way out of town. It is now a national monument and has been restored as a private hotel similar to a Parador. Here you can rest your weary limbs and stroll at leisure around the cloisters and 'meet' the Counts of Carrión whose murdered remains are laid to rest more permanently in its hallowed halls.

"If we could read the secret history of our enemies, we should find in each person's life – sorrow and suffering enough to disarm all hostility." Longfellow

REFLECTIONS:

_____

_____

_____

_____

_____

_____

_____

_____

_____

_____

_____

_____

_____

_____

_____

_____

_____

_____

_____

_____

_____

_____

_____

❏ **An eye for an eye only ends up leaving the whole world blind.**

Mahatma Gandhi

17 **414.3** km (257.4 miles) to Santiago

CARRIÓN de los CONDES – TERRADILLOS de los TEMPLARIOS

▦	Path / Track --- ---	18.7	---	70%
▬	Quiet Road --- ---	8.1	---	30%
▰	Main Road --- ---	0.0	---	
Total km	**Total distance**	**26.8 km** (16.7 ml)		

Adjusted for climb 27.3 km (accrued ascent 100m = 0.5 km)

Alto ▲ High Point: Picnic area above Ledigos 900m (2,950 feet)

⌁ Calzadilla de la Cueza **17.1** km – Ledigos **23.5** km.

```
900m    Calzada                        Calzadilla   910m  TERRADILLOS
■CARRIÓN Romana                              Ⓐ         Ledigos
800m                                          Río Cueza   Ⓐ    880m
Río Carrión
00 km      5 km      10 km      15 km      20 km      25 km
```

The Practical Path: We pass through a flat and somewhat featureless landscape with little or no shade. 70% is on natural paths, most of which forms the old paved Roman road known as the *Via Aquitana* that connected with Astorga. The few drinking fonts between the villages are often dry so make sure your water flasks are full and you either have breakfast before you leave or bring something to eat with you as there are no facilities on the first stretch to Calzadilla, a distance of 17.1 km.

❏ **The Mystical Path:** Today we leave a fortified town that has witnessed countless battles, conquests, re-conquests, shameful violations, betrayals and revenge killings. We pass the murdered relics of the Counts of Carrión and the martyred San Zoilo. But what of our own sense of justified retribution and how often have we wished someone ill? When did we last send healing thoughts of love and peace to our supposéd enemy? Mahatma means Great Soul and it takes one to incarnate in a Hindu body to re-interpret the Christian scriptural teaching (above) to remind us of the futility of revenge. Will we find the courage today to open our hearts and offer love instead of fear whenever we feel attacked?

❏ **Personal reflections:** *"… I only saw him after I had collapsed onto the rickety metal chair. He just sat there looking at me with those intense black eyes framed by jet-black curls of hair that fell down over his shoulders. Spread across his face was a half smile that disappeared into the thick beard. I think he had intended to scare me. He reminded me of a picture I once saw of Rasputin … I returned from the village, thankful that he was nowhere to be seen. My sense of relief quickly faded when I opened the door to the bunk room. Behind it stood his evil looking staff, festooned with black feathers and other symbols of his craft. It was strange how I felt him before I actually saw him …"*

0.0 km **Carrión** from the centre *albergue* ❷ continue through the old town down c/Santa María turning right> past the main square with Church of Santiago (right) into the narrow c/Esteban Collantes turn <left into c/Pina Blanco and over the main bridge to the poplar-lined path and causeway to:

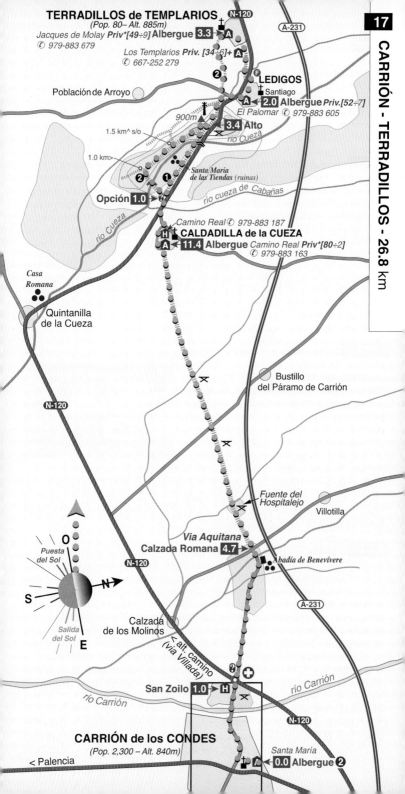

TERRADILLOS de TEMPLARIOS N-120 A-231
(Pop. 80– Alt. 885m)
Jacques de Molay Priv*[49÷9] Albergue 3.3 ▸ A
℡ 979-883 679

Los Templarios Priv. [34÷6]+ A
℡ 667-252 279
2

Población de Arroyo ◯ **LEDIGOS**
† Santiago
A Albergue *Priv.[52÷7]*
El Palomar ℡ 979-883 605
900m
3.4 Alto
1.5 km^ s/o *río Cueza*
1.0 km▸
2 **1** *Santa María de las Tiendas (ruinas)*
Opción 1.0 *río cueza de Cabañas*

río Cueza

Camino Real℡ 979-883 187
H † **CALDADILLA de la CUEZA**
A **11.4** Albergue *Camino Real Priv*[80÷2]*
℡ 979-883 163

Casa Romana
◯ **Quintanilla de la Cueza**

◯ **Bustillo del Páramo de Carrión**

Fuente del Hospitalejo
◯ Villotilla

Vía Aquitana
Calzada Romana **4.7** ▸
■ *Abadía de Benevívere*
N-120 A-231

◯ **Calzada de los Molinos**
◂ *alt. camino (vía Villada)*

? ✚
San Zoilo 1.0 ▸ H
río Carrión
CARRIÓN de los CONDES
(Pop. 2,300 – Alt. 840m) N-120
Santa María **0.0** Albergue **2**
◂ Palencia

O *Puesta del Sol*
S N
E *Salida del Sol*

1.0 km San Zoilo the former monastery is now a luxury hotel. Just beyond San Zoilo we cross the Carrión by-pass [!] *[Note: an alternative route Antiguo camino francés along the N-120 to Sahagún via Villada (Albergue © 979 844 005) turns left here]*. We head s/o along a quiet country road passing the *Cruz Rioja* building and just before crossing the second of 2 streams we find the ruins of the once illustrious 12th century Franciscan Abbey *Abadía Santa María de Benevívere* known for its 'good living' *bene vivere* (right). Shortly afterwards we cross the river and at a T-Junction we head s/o onto the roman road.

4.7 km Calzada Romana *Via Aquitana*. *[We now join a stretch of the original Roman road still intact after 2,000 years of use – save for a new gravel covering! What is more remarkable is the fact that this section goes through an area of bogland devoid of any stone for its construction. It is estimated that 100,000 tons of rock was needed just for the substrata to raise the surface above the winter flood levels and every ton had to be transported from elsewhere. No wonder Roman villas and other remains have been found in the area – most notably at Quintanilla de la Cueza 5 km South of Calzadilla on the N-120].* We next pass *Fuente del Hospitalejo* **[1.8** km] in a small poplar grove (right) and cross an ancient drove road *cañada [linking this area to the south of the Iberian peninsular via the camino de Madrid]*. We cross several small streams *arroyos* an asphalt road **[2.6** km] and another rest area and then straight into Calzadilla **[7.0** km]:

11.4 km Calzadilla de la Cueza •Albergue *Camino Real Priv.*[80÷2]* © 979-883 187. Network* hostel with 80 Beds €7 on 2 floors in a modern building at the village entrance. No kitchen but outside patio area and pilgrim Menú €10 in •Hostal Camino Real © 979-883 187 waymarks point to the popular bar and restaurant behind the albergue (the owner César Acero, a seasoned

pilgrim, owns both). CALZADILLA *(Pop. 60)* is a typical camino village with a central street that forms the way itself. The parish Church of San Martín has an altarpiece installed when the nearby *monasterio de Santa María de las Tiendas* was de-consecrated. We leave the village by rest area and [F] and continue over the bridge and the N-120 to option:

1.0 km Opción [?] Here a map carved into a stone block shows 4 optional routes. Essentially you have 2 choices: continue s/o via roadside senda or turn <left for quiet woodland path (300m longer more remote and few waymarks).

● ● ● ● ● Option ❶ Turn left over bridge onto woodland path that climbs gently and veer right **[1.0** km] to continue along the top of an escarpment (radio mast visible ahead). Continue s/o at junction **[1.5** km] (track to the left provides an alternative 'loop' but no waymarks). We now begin a gentle descent to re-join the main route **[1.2** km]. Both routes continue down to the main road.
● ● ● ● ● Option ❷ Continue s/o along farmtracks. It again provides a quieter alternative but bypasses the facilites in Ledigos and albergue [1] in Terradillos.

The main route takes the gravel track alongside main road past *monasterio de Santa María de las Tiendas* (left) *[the ruins a distant memory of its illustrious past as the Hospice of the Great Knight, a reference to its 12th century existence as a grand hospice administered by the Knights of St. James]*. The path crosses the rio Cueza up to the top of the rise where the other route joins from the left.

`3.4 km` **Alto** High point of this stage (910m) where both routes join down to main road. Option ❷ continues s/o. To access Ledigos cross main road [!].

`2.0 km` **Ledigos** •**Albergue** *El Palomar Priv.*[52÷7]* ©️ 979-883 605 private hostel (adj. to the main road). 52 beds from €6. Basic facilities incl. swimming pool! around a central courtyard. There is a small shop and bar in the village and the XIII[th]C Parish church of Santiago has images of the saint.

Continue past rest area [F] and cross the N-120 [!] [0.7 km] onto gravel senda and just before entering Terradillos we pass [2.1 km] •**Albergue** *Los Templarios Priv.[34÷6]+* ©️ 667 252 279 new private hostel with 34 beds €7-9 + priv. rooms €28-€36 excellent modern facilities including laundry room. No kitchen but provides pilgrim menu in the dining room. Continue along senda and turn <left into the village to the original albergue [0.5 km].

`3.3 km` **Terradillos de los Templarios** •**Albergue****Priv.[49÷9]* *Jacques de Molay* ©️ 979-883 679 original network* hostel in the centre of this small village. Open all year with 49 beds €8-10 depending on Nº beds in each room. No kitchen but the resident family follow in the traditions of the Templars by offering wholesome home cooking (dinner and breakfast) there is a small private garden with public picnic area opposite. *[Next albergue: Moratinos– 3.2 km].*

TERRADILLOS DE LOS TEMPLARIOS *(Pop. 80)* After the relative luxury of Carrión here in we experience the simplicity of this humble village, thankfully bypassed by the N-120 and the modern world. Formerly a stronghold of the Knights Templar nothing, on a physical level, remains of this noble Order but its spirit lives on in the place name and that of the stream *arroyo de Templarios* that separates it from the next village that, like Villalcázar de Sirga, also had historical links with the Templars. Jacques de Molay was the last Grand master of the Order. The simple red brick parish church is dedicated to San Pedro and houses an unusual 13th century crucifix. Terradillos de los Templarios is the halfway point between St. Jean de Pied de Port and Santiago de Compostela.

❐ Something opens our wings. Something makes boredom and hurt disappear.
Someone fills the cup in front of us. We taste only sacredness. *Rumi*

18 387.5 km (240.8 miles) to Santiago de Compostela

TERRADILLOS de los TEMPLARIOS *(Palencia)* via SAHAGÚN *(León)*
to: [1] HERMANILLOS de la CALZADA – [2] El BURGO RANERO

▦	Path / Track	--- ---	22.3	--- 83%
▬	Quiet Road	--- ---	4.4	--- 16%
▨	Main Road	--- ---	0.2	--- 01%
Total km	**Total distance**		**26.9 km**	(16.7 ml)

▰▲ **Adjusted for climb**   26.9 km (effectively a level walk)

Alto ▲   High Point: Terradillos de los Templarios 880m (2,890 feet)

< 🅰 🅷 >   Moratinos **3.2** km – San Nicolás **6.0** km – Sahagún **13.0** km – Calzada
del Coto **18.2** km *in addition for route [2] Bercianos 23.1 km.*

```
TERRADILLOS 880m                                                    CALZADILLA
900m Moratinos   San Nicolás ----SAHAGÚN ---- Calzada de Coto
  ■   🅰    🅰                      🅰               🅰                      ■
800m -------------------- Río Sequillo --- Río Cea ----------------------------
   |            |              |             |              |             |
00 km        5 km          10 km         15 km          20 km         25 km
```

The Practical Path: Many pilgrims stopover in Sahagún, a town full of ancient
monuments. If you stay the night the next logical step is to El Burgo Ranero
(a further 17.8 km) – both towns have a wide choice of accommodation. The
alternative is to visit Sahagún and possibly stop for lunch on your way to
Hermanillos de Calzada. The first section is parallel to the N-120. Option ❶ *Via
Romana 26.9 km* almost the entire is by rough earth tracks across remote bush
country so take water, especially for the section from Calzada de Coto. The
path is level but with little shade and only one water font just before Calzadilla.
Option ❷ *Real Camino Frances 30.7 km* the most popular route by gravel path
senda with shade alongside quiet road parallel to the autopista.

❐ **The Mystical Path:** Yesterday we sought to forgive another and to see past
any apparent attack – to the cry for help that it disguised. Perhaps when we look
past error we will witness our own innocence. Will you look for the mundane
or the divine in your fellow traveller? What will fill your cup today? Will you
drink the pure waters that flow from the scallop shell at the pilgrim fountain and
taste only sacredness?

❐ **Personal Reflections:** *"… The evening light was painting the countryside
pure pink. I stopped to rest awhile and to absorb the warmth of the colours. It
was not until I slaked my thirst from the pilgrim fountain that I noticed him. He
stood 100 metres from me and yet I could see every facet of his wrinkled face.
He wore a smile of such unconditional love that I became enraptured by the
embrace. Surrounded by his flock of quietly grazing sheep, this shepherd held
the focal point of a biblical picture of such sublime proportions and colours, that
I was momentarily transported to an overwhelming sense of pure bliss… While
leaning on his crook, he raised his hand slowly to greet and bless me. Tears
rolled down my cheeks in a flood of joy. No words passed between us and none
are able to convey the sense of total love and acceptance I felt from this stranger
who yet seemed so familiar. My heart began to ache with the unfamiliar intensity
of this greeting. My hands spontaneously went to my longing heart. Namasté, I
whispered, 'When the God in me greets the God in you, in that, we are One'…"*

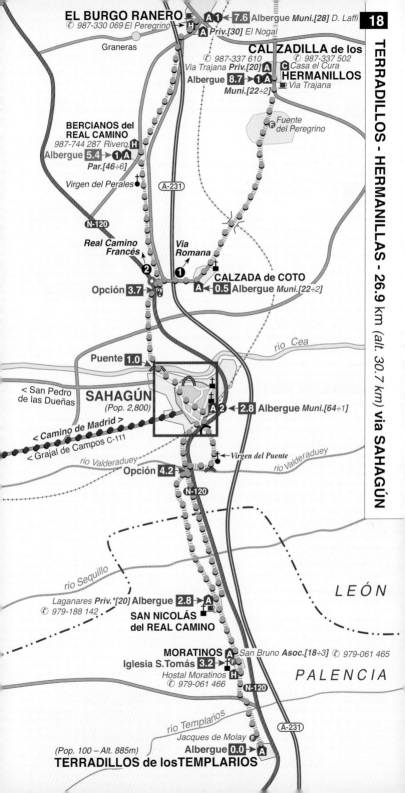

TERRADILLOS - HERMANILLAS - 26.9 km (alt. 30.7 km) vía SAHAGÚN

18

EL BURGO RANERO
© 987-330 069 El Peregrino
Graneras

A **1** ◄ **7.6** Albergue *Muni.[28]* D. Laffi
A *Priv.[30]* El Nogal

CALZADILLA de los
© 987-337 610   © 987-337 502
Via Trajana *Priv.[20]* **A** **C** *Casa el Cura*
Albergue **8.7** ► **1 A** **HERMANILLOS**
Muni.[22÷2] ■ Via Trajana

**BERCIANOS del
REAL CAMINO**
987-744 287 Rivero **H**
Albergue **5.4** ► **1 A**
Par.[46÷6]
Virgen del Perales ●

F Fuente
del Peregrino

(A-231)

N-120

*Real Camino
Francés*

*Via
Romana*

2

1   **CALZADA de COTO**
Opción 3.7   **A** ◄ **0.5** Albergue *Muni.[22÷2]*

Puente **1.0**

río Cea

< San Pedro
de las Dueñas

SAHAGÚN
(Pop. 2,800)
A **2** ◄ **2.8** Albergue *Muni.[64÷1]*

< Camino de Madrid >
< Grajal de Campos C-111
río Valderaduey

Opción **4.2**

† ◄ Virgen del Puente

río Valderaduey

N-120

río Sequillo

LEÓN

Laganares *Priv.*[20]* Albergue **2.8** ► **A**
© 979-188 142
**SAN NICOLÁS
del REAL CAMINO**

MORATINOS A San Bruno *Asoc.[18÷3]* © 979-061 465
Iglesia S.Tomás **3.2** ► ■ †
Hostal Moratinos **H**
© 979-061 466

N-120

PALENCIA

río Templarios

(A-231)

Jacques de Molay **F**
Albergue 0.0 ► **A**

(Pop. 100 – Alt. 885m)
TERRADILLOS de los TEMPLARIOS

0.0 km **Terradillos** from albergue ❷ proceed out of the village onto earth track and continue over the arroyo Templarios and a country road (to Villada) onto track again with a line of poplar trees passing shaded rest area (site of the medieval village of Villaoreja) past cemetery into:

3.2 km **Moratinos** *(Pop. 30)* •**Hostal Moratinos** ℂ 979-061 466 c/ Real 12 at entrance to the village. Continue down the main street past the parish church dedicated to St. Thomas with large shaded porch [F]. and •**Albergue** *San Bruno Asoc.[18÷3]* ℂ 979-061 465 c/ Ontanón with 18 beds €8 large garden and menú. Continue out onto gravel track all the way into.

2.8 km **San Nicolás del Real Camino** •**Albergue** *Laganares Priv.*[20÷4]+ ℂ Marisa* 979-188 142 network* hostel adjoining the church in the village square. 20 beds €8. Good facilities (except kitchen) in this delightful hostel, which has a friendly bar and restaurant. Refurbished using the traditional local mud and straw method. This is another peaceful village

linked to the Templar Order. The parish church *Iglesia de San Nicolás Obispo* is built of the familiar clay brick of the area. Its humble exterior serves as a pelota court and disguises a fine Baroque altarpiece. At the far end of the village is a shaded picnic spot and water font [F]. Leave the village (the last in Palencia) and take the track to the left to Alto del Carrasco. **Option** s/o along main road.

PROVINCIA DE LEÓN: The largest, wealthiest and most populous province we pass through (population 2.5 million) offering the pilgrim the most varied terrain on the camino. We start off with a continuation of the now familiar *Tierra de Campos* with its flat and well-irrigated agricultural land. The adobe walls of the villages, bright red in the intense Leónese sun, rise up to greet us out of the flat plains. Then we enter the busy and sophisticated style of the capital of León itself. Artisans, museums, restaurants, hotels and shops all compete for your attention. León is famous for its pork products – cured hams, chorizos and morcilla or try the local cheese and quince jelly *queso con membrillo*.

Later on we enter the *Maragatería* and the *Montes de León* (between Astorga and Molinaseca) where we experience the remnants of Maragato culture in the distinctive dress and cuisine of this mountainous region. The pastries *mantecadas* are worth sampling and the hills provide game with trout from the streams. The obscure origins of the Maragatos may date back to the 7th century when King Mauregato and his followers became isolated in this remote area during the Arab invasions. Today the isolationism continues in the abandoned villages of the mountains, such as Foncebadón. Beyond Ponferrada we enter the magic of the Bierzo with its gently rolling hills and vineyards. In the spring, you can see the white of the cherry blossom, in the autumn the bright red of its fruit and, in between, every shade of green. Eat of its sun ripened fruits and drink of its wines and the friendliness of its people. Windswept Galicia lies beyond.

4.2 km **Rio Valderaduey** [?] Another option to continue along the main road by senda ● ● ● ● ● directly into Sahagún. For the recommended route turn right> along the river to the tranquil (except on April 25th when a local pilgrimage *romería* takes

place here) hermitage of Our Lady of the Bridge *Ermita Virgen del Puente*, an unpretentious sanctuary with XII[th]C. Romanesque foundations but the original pilgrim hospice has long gone. The tiny Mudéjar-style chapel occupies a cool and shady poplar grove adjoining the river. Continue along track up towards Sahagún under the N-120 bypass towards the grain silos past the modern hotel *Puerto de Sahagún* and bullring up to the railway bridge. 200m off route (right) is: •**Albergue ❶** *Viatoris Priv.*[50]*+ Ⓒ 987-780 975 Travesía del Arco network* hostel 50 beds €7 in one main dormitory +private rooms). Excellent facilities and breakfast is available in reception area. Continue towards the town centre over the railway bridge (station left) and turn right> to:

Albergue ❶ *Viatoris*

`2.8 km` Sahagún *Centro* •**Albergue ❷** *Cluny Muni.[64÷1]* Ⓒ 987-782 117 central hostel with 64 bunks €4 in cubicles of 6 on the upper floor of the *iglesia de la Trinidad* with tourist office and exhibition space on the ground floor - pilgrim statue at the church entrance. (Winter hostel 16 beds c/ Antonio Nicolás, 55). At the other end of town (on the way out) •**Albergue ❸** *Monasterio de Santa Cruz (Madres Benedictinas) Conv. [16÷4]*+ Ⓒ 987 781 139 c/ Nicolas, 40 part of the convento de Santa Cruz (single rooms €20). Immaculate rooms maintained by the voluntary hospitaleras from the Madrid association 16 beds €5. Limited facilities include a small kitchenette and use of a delightful courtyard and an air of tranquillity. Just beyond at the crossroads is Sahagún's latest hostel •**Albergue ❹** *El Labriego Priv. [10÷1]* Ⓒ 616 478 417 with restaurant. *[Next albergue: Calzada del Coto – 5.2 km].* ❏ **Other accommodation:** *Turismo:* Iglesia de la Trinidad C/ del Arco, 87 Ⓒ 987-782 117. *Hoteles:* •**La Asturiana** P Ⓒ 987-780 073 Plaza de Lemses Franco, 2. •**Don Pacho** Hs* Ⓒ 987-780 775 Av, Constitución, 86. •**El Ruedo** Hs* Ⓒ 987-780 075 Plaza Mayor, 1. •**Escarcha** Hs* Ⓒ 987-781 856 c/Regina Franco, 12. •**La Cordoniz** Hs* Ⓒ 987-780 276 c/ Arco opposite albergue [2]. •**Alfonso VI** Hs** Ⓒ 987-781 144 c/Nicolás. •**Puerta de Sahagún** H*** Ⓒ 987-781 880 by albergue *Viatoris* on the way into town.

Albergue ❷ *Cluny*

Albergue ❸ *Benedictinas*

SAHAGÚN: *(pop: 2,800 – alt. 860m)* seat of great ecclesiastical power, largely courtesy of the influence of Alfonso VI who, along with his various wives, is buried in the Benedictine convento de Santa Cruz. Owing to the lack of stone for building purposes many of the grand edifices were constructed with brick and, accordingly, many have disappeared. Little remains of the famous abbey of San Benito that was founded in the 10th century and rose to become one of the most important Benedictine monasteries in Spain. Charlemagne was also linked with the town, which from these earliest times has given shelter to the pilgrims on their way to Santiago de Compostela, so we follow illustrious footsteps. Monasteries, churches and pilgrim hospices abounded. The foundations of the town however extend much further back to its Roman past. It was here that Saint Facundo was martyred which gave rise to a monastery bearing his name as early as the 9th century. Despite Arab invasions and counter attacks that destroyed the monastery on several occasions, it was ultimately the loss of interest in things religious that finally reduced it to the rubble that now lies to the west of the town. However, the martyr lives on in the name Sahagún itself, a derivation of Sanctum Facundum, whose remains lie buried in the church of St. John along with fellow martyr Primitivo. Despite decaying edifices you will not be at the loss of religious buildings and art to admire. If you follow the *blue* detour route shown on the town map you will pass the following: ❶ *Iglesia de la Trinidad XIII–XVIIthC* (municipal albergue [2] and Turismo). ❷ *Iglesia San Juan XVIIthC* (tombs of San Facundo y Primitivo) Baroque Church just past albergue [2] with a sculpture of the town's patron saint *San Facundo*. Continuing down c/del Arco into Plaza San Lorenzo and its outstanding ❸ *Iglesia San Lorenzo XIIthC* a fine example of the brick Mudejar style and whose prominent tower is a good landmark. From here it is a short walk to the Plaza Mayor where you can refresh yourself in its array of cafés and bars and admire its handsome Town Hall *Ayuntamiento*.

Exit via c/Flora Florez (the narrow street behind the bandstand) and turn sharp right> down c/San Benito into Plaza Lesmes Franco and turn <left to Plaza de San Tirso where the distinctive tower of Iglesia de San Tirso leads to the first church, built in the 12th century, to use brick and credited with starting the craze for the Mudejar style in the area ❹ *Iglesia San Tirso (Mudejar – ruins)*. Adjoining is Parque San Benito and the ruins of the monastery of that name which became one of the most powerful in Spain leading, inevitably, to its downfall. We now have an opportunity to walk under its impressive ❺ *Arco San Benito* adjoining and *Monasterio y Museo de Santa Cruz* (Madres Benedictinas) with tomb

of Alphonso VI and *museo* which houses the beautiful statue of the Virgin dressed as a pilgrim which originally adorned the church of the *Monasterio de la Peregrina* whose crumbling brick walls and Moorish arches are situated on the outskirts of town ❻ *Iglesia Señora La Peregrina XVthC* formerly a Franciscan convent (past the Escolar Fray Bernardino c/San Francisco on the rise ahead).

Arco San Benito / Sta. Clara

Note [1]: If you want to view the interior of *all* the above sites you will need to stay the night. Otherwise, allow extra time to walk around them but don't leave Sahagún at such a late hour that you end up, unintentionally, short of your planned destination. **[2]:** If you are continuing on the **recommended route** (less travelled but little shade) to Calzadilla de los Hermanillos it might be advisable to have a midday meal in Sahagún or to buy supplies for the journey ahead. **[3]:** Not particularly recommended (unless you have specific interest) are 2 detours on the camino from Madrid that joins here in Sahagún. **Detour [a]** (5 km south of Sahagún on the LE-941) is a gem of a national monument, the Romanesque monastery of *San Pedro de las Dueñas* where the Benedictine Mothers operate another hospedería adjacent to the 12th century church with its impressive crucifix. **Detour [b]** 8 km south on the C-611 are the sweeping walls of the monumental castle and palace at *Grajal de Campos* birthplace of legendary knights and scene of epic battles.

For the waymarked route through town head into c/Antonio Nicolas at crossroads by •*Café Asturcon* down into the unimpressive Plaza de Santiago to the next crossroads by •*El Labriego* and down to:

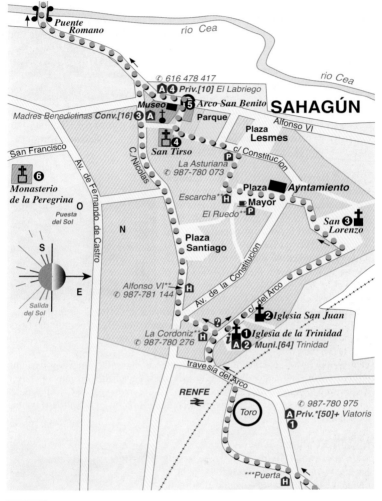

SAHAGÚN

© 616 478 417
Ⓐ④ Priv.[10] El Labriego
Museo ⑤ Arco San Benito
Madres Benedictinas Conv.[16] ③ Ⓐ Parque
San Francisco
C./Nicolas
San Tirso ④
Plaza Lesmes
Alfonso VI
P
La Asturiana © 987-780 073
c/ Constitucion
Monasterio de la Peregrina ⑥
Plaza Mayor
Ayntamiento
Escarcha* Ⓗ
El Ruedo** P
Puesta del Sol
San Lorenzo ③
N
Plaza Santiago
Av. de la Constitucion
Alfonso VI** Ⓗ © 987-781 144
c/ del Arco
Iglesia San Juan ②
La Cordoniz* Ⓗ © 987-780 276
Ⓗ
i Iglesia de la Trinidad ①
Ⓐ② Muni.[64] Trinidad
travesia del Arco
RENFE
Toro
© 987-780 975
Ⓐ Priv.*[50]+ Viatoris ①
***Puerta Ⓗ

1.0 km **Puente Canto** (1 kilometre from albergue ❷ turismo) to this historic stone bridge (originally Roman but reconstructed in the 11th and 16th centuries) its five strong arches have stood the test of time and the powerful waters of the river Cea. Continue along the side of the main road (the N-120 is now realigned as part of the new town

bypass). This stretch offers some shade from the poplar grove otherwise known as *The copse of Charlemagne's lances* where legend has it that the lances of his troops turned into saplings after they had been planted in the earth here; an ominous sign to the forthcoming battle with the Moors which was to litter the area with corpses. Continue out past the *Camping Pedro Ponce* and municipal sports grounds to:

3.7 km **Option [?]** junction with N-120 and N-601. **For recommended route** ❶ The original Roman road *Via Trajana* proceed right> over the motorway into Calzada de Coto.

For alternative route ❷ the Royal French Way *Real Camino Francés* (via Bercianos to El Burgo Ranero) stay on this (left) side of the bridge. Note the alternative route is by modern *senda* ● ● ● ● ● alongside a quiet country road now with good shade parallel to the autopista. Under new motorway extension

[2.8 km] pass the simple brick hermitage of Our Lady of the Pears *Ermita de Nuestra de Perales XI[th]C* **[1.2 km]** which formed part of the Hospital of O Cebreiro and is scene of an annual pilgrimage on 8th September. The *senda* continues past [F] into Bercianos crossroads **[1.4 km]**.

5.4 km **Bercianos del Real Camino** *Centro (Pop. 200)* the name derives from the settlement of the town with citizens from the Bierzo in 955. •**Rivero** HsR* ✆ 987-744 287 on c/Mayor with popular bar and restaurant. The parish hostel is 700m off route (waymarked) to the left on entering. ❶ **Albergue** *Par.[46÷6]* ✆ 987-784 008 on c/ Santa Rita with 46 beds €-*donativo*. Dining room where a communal meal is served.

Tranquil meditation room where evening prayers are offered. ❷ *Santa Clara Priv.[26÷6]* c/ Iglesia, 3 ✆ 605 839 993 extended in 2013 from 8 to 26 beds €-*donativo*. An inconspicuous shop is available 100m.

Pick up the *senda* again on the western edge of the village passing wetland reserve (right) and under autopista to pick up the asphalt road into El Burgo Raneros. *[The road to the right leads to the Via Roman – 3.1 km]*. Veer right to albergues (head for the water-tower) or continue s/o down c/Real to the centre and church:

7.6 km **El Burgo Raneros** *Centro (Pop. 250) Iglesia San Pedro.* If you are staying the night or need refreshment turn right to the main hub of activity on the north side of the town: •**Albergue** ❶ *Domenico Laffi Muni.[28÷4]* ✆ 987-330 023 municipal hostel dedicated to the 17[th]c. Italian pilgrim and located at the edge of the town on c/Fray Pedro. Open all year with 28 beds €-*donativo*. Excellent facilities and attractive hostel in the idiom of the area using mud and straw in its

Albergue ❶ *Domenico Laffi*

construction. Close by on the other side of the street is •**Albergue** ❷ *El Nogal Asoc.[30÷8]* ✆ 627 229 331 Association hostel with 30 beds €7-10 in various rooms with all basic facilities. Also in this area are a number of restaurants, cafés and other accommodation as follows: •**Hostal el Peregrino** ✆ 987-330 069 with popular restaurant and the adjacent •**Piedras Blancas** ✆ 987-330 094. Further out is •**Albergue** ❸ *La Laguna Priv.[20÷2]+* ✆ 987-330 094 c/ La Laguna private hostel part of *Piedras Blancas*. 20 beds €8 and all facilities + private rooms. Opposite the railway station is the latest addition •**Albergue** ❹ *Ebalo Tamaú Priv.[16÷4]* ✆ 679 490 521 c/Estación by the rail station 1 km out of town 16 beds €10. *[Next albergue: Reliegos – 13.0 km. or 19.1 km to the albergue in Mansilla de las Mulas – See next stage for details.]*

Recommended route ❶ For the original Roman road *Via Romana* part of the *calzada Trajana*. Cross over the bridge (A-231) into:

0.5 km Calzada del Coto •Albergue

San Roque Muni.[24÷2] ✆ 987-781 233 prominently located at the entrance to the town beside the pelota court and children's play area. Open all year with 24 beds €-*donativo* basic facilities (no kitchen) - key at bar Xanadú. The town has few facilities with small shop, bar and restaurant. A new albergue is planned.

Continue through the town via c/Mayor, past the parish church of San Esteban and out onto the *Via Romana* on the western outskirts of the town [0.5 km] where you pick up the earth track. Waymarks are few but you head straight out for the railway bridge on the horizon and cross over [1.8 km]. Continue on the earth track that winds its way though scrubland in the area of the remote farm *Dehesa de Valdelocajos*. Here there is nothing to disturb the wilderness except the occasional shepherd grazing his flock and a few sporadic metal camino signposts with their inane cartoon character. Even the game hunters appear to have taken offence at these signs, as evidenced by the lead shot that has been fired at them. We pass a remote country lodge (right) to arrive at a shallow valley with the village of Hermanillos in the distance and [F] pilgrim fountain *fuente del peregrino* [4.5 km] in a shaded rest area in a poplar grove by an old riverbed. Continue for the final leg [1.9 km] into:

8.7 km Calzada de los Hermanillos •*Via Trajana* pilgrim restaurant (right as you enter) and just beyond (left) is •**Albergue**

❶ *Muni.[22÷2]* ✆ 987-330 023 in former school building (part of the El Burgo Ranero municipality). Open all year with 22 beds in cubicles of 4 bunks €-*donativo*. ❷ *Via Trajana Priv.[20÷5]*+ ✆ 987-337 610 C/Mayor, 57. 20 Beds €15 +priv. rooms €35 meals available. Other accommodation: •**Casa El Cura** CR ✆ 987-337 502 on c/La Carratera on the northern outskirts. Casa rural with 18 places in variety of rooms with dinner, bed & breakfast package for pilgrims – helpful

Albergue

owner. *[Next albergue:* Reliegos 17.4 km (1.0 km *off* route) or albergues at El Burgo Raneros on opposite side of rail tracks on alternative route [2] 6.5 km (3.1 km off route).

In days long gone by the monks *Little Brothers of the Road* welcomed pilgrims here but the hospitality is still felt here especially in *Comedor Via Trajana* and *El Cura* adjacent to the albergue that cater for hungry pilgrims. A small inconspicuous shop (behind the Pelota court and only open late afternoon for a short period) and 2 smoky bars make up the other facilities. The parish church is dedicated to St. Bartholomew where there is an impressive statue of him overpowering the devil.

Casa El Cura

❐ **Silence is golden.**

---

19 **360.6** km (224.1 miles) to Santiago de Compostela

HERMANILLOS DE LA CALZADA – MANSILLA DE LAS MULAS

▦ Path / Track	--- ---	19.5 ---	80%
▬ Quiet Road	--- ---	4.5 ---	18%
▬ Main Road	--- ---	0.5 ---	2%
Total km **Total distance**		**24.5 km** (15.2 ml)	

◣◣ **Adjusted for climb** 24.7 km (accrued ascent 50m = 0.2 km)
Alto ▲ (Effectively a level walk along the *Via Romana*).
< Ⓐ Ⓗ > Reliegos **18.9** km (1.0 km *off* route).

CALZADILLA 870m
900m
800m   *Río Valdelcasa*   **Reliegos** Ⓐ   **MANSILLA**
         Río Madriz Cava
00 km   5 km   10 km   15 km   20 km

The Practical Path: On the Calzada Romana we will encounter no asphalt roads, no sendas, no town, no village, no farmyard no house but also no water fonts and little shade apart from the few rivers that crisscross this tranquil landscape. Classified as the most perfect extant stretch of Roman road left in Spain today, we follow in the footsteps of Emperor Augustus himself but he will have travelled with a retinue of servants not available to a humble pilgrim – so make sure your flask is full and that you bring some food to fortify you along this ancient way. Enjoy the silence and 80% of traffic free walking.

❐ **The Mystical Path:** Only the weeds and wild flowers have changed in the two millennia since this path was laid. While Roman artefacts lie behind glass cages in dislocated museums in the cities, here you walk on the original Roman road itself. The muted silence of the museums, broken by the giggles of tour parties, are nothing to match the original stone in its original setting and the golden silence of the wide prairie. Here the call of the occasional bird of prey only seems to emphasise the silence and adds to the tranquillity. The hum of the bee busily extracting pollen from the wild flowers brings a sense of unhurried calm that pervades this place. The bee transforms the pollen to golden nectar. Will the alchemist in you extract the purest gold from this day?

❐ **Personal Reflections:** *"… In my exhaustion I missed the hostel on the way into the village. Seemingly out of nowhere a group of children appeared and started to dance around me shouting and waving. They evidently did not know of my need for quiet at the end of a long day. What an unreasonable expectation of mine. A few minutes later I saw their enthusiasm in a different light, as a means to gain access to the albergue in order to empty out the donation box, which they did with alacrity. Why did I assume it would go straight into their pockets and not straight to the hospitalero or parish priest? I am still so quick to judge and condemn others. Perhaps it is a reflection of my own dishonesty. But it takes only an instant to change an unloving thought to a loving one – What, then, is this process? Is it just intention? Can it be that I simply see what I choose to see? What did the shepherd see in me? What did Christ see in the thief crucified alongside him? …"*

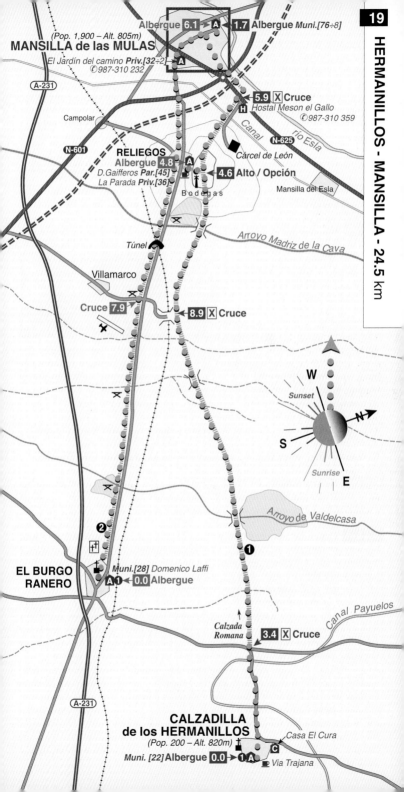

Albergue **6.1** Ⓐ ◄ **1.7** Albergue *Muni.[76÷8]*

(Pop. 1,900 – Alt. 805m)
MANSILLA de las MULAS
El Jardín del camino **Priv.[32÷2]** → Ⓐ
ⓒ *987-310 232*

5.9 ☒ **Cruce**
Ⓗ *Hostal Meson el Gallo*
ⓒ *987-310 359*

A-231

Campolar

Canal

N-625

río Esla

Cárcel de León

N-601

RELIEGOS
Albergue **4.8** Ⓐ
D.Gaifferos **Par.[45]**
La Parada **Priv.[36]**

4.6 **Alto / Opción**

Bodegas

Mansilla del Esla

Arroyo Madriz de la Cava

Túnel

Villamarco

Cruce **7.9**

8.9 ☒ **Cruce**

W

Sunset

N

S

E

Sunrise

Arroyo de Valdelcasa

❷

✝

**EL BURGO
RANERO**

Ⓐ❶ ◄ **0.0** Albergue
Muni.[28] Domenico Laffi

❶

*Calzada
Romana*

3.4 ☒ **Cruce**

Canal Payuelos

A-231

**CALZADILLA
de los HERMANILLOS**
(Pop. 200 – Alt. 820m)
Casa El Cura

Muni. [22] **Albergue** **0.0** → ❶ Ⓐ
Ⓒ
Via Trajana

Alternative route ❷ El Burgo Ranero – Mansilla de las Mulas *via Reliegos*
18.8 km (11.7 miles). The entire section is by modern senda running alongside an asphalt road parallel to the motorway. The monotony somewhat relieved by several small streams, mostly dry in summer and the maturing shelter belt of trees that line the path. From El Burgo Ranero continue down the main street and onto the ***senda*** passing the town cemetery and the first of several picnic sites amongst trees by the river **[2.3 km]** pass aerodrome **[4.1 km]** and over road with picnic site **[1.5 km]** at crossroads:

7.9 km **Cruce** *[Villarmarco (left) and railway halt (Calzada Romana (right)]* continue along senda under railway tunnel **[2.6 km]** over river with picnic site (right) and up to the high point of this stage **[1.6 km]** before descending past a series of *bodegas* built into the surrounding hillocks into Reliegos **[0.6 km]**:

4.8 km **Reliegos** *(Pop. 200)* •*Bar Gil II* on main road and the trendy •*Bar La Torre* with its equally colourful proprietor *Sinín* 100m off route in village centre
[F]. ❶**Albergue** *La Parada Priv.[36÷5]*+ ©
987 317 880 with 36 beds €7 +priv. rooms.
100m further in c/Escuela ❷**Albergue**
D.Gaiferos Muni.[45÷2] © 987-317 801
hostel in former school building 45 bunk
beds €5 +20 *colchonetas* and all facilities but
no outside space. Shortly after leaving the
village pick up the *senda* again and take the bridge over the N-601 and over the canal up to the main crossroads and albergue [1] (details on other route) Enter the town through the medieval gate *Puerta Castillo* (only the walls remain) up c/Santa María and into *Plaza del Pozo* where the recommended route (from Hermanillos) joins from the right. Continue s/o into c/del Puente to:

6.1 km **Mansilla de las Mulas** •**Albergue** (see recommended route for details).

Recommended route ❶: Original Roman road *Via Romana (Via Trajana).*

0.0 km **Hermanillos** From the albergue proceed down the main street and out onto a vast flat plateau of wheat and other cereal crops to cross over irrigation canal **[1.2 km]** and continue for **[2.2 km]** to:

3.4 km **Cruce** T-junction (El Burgo Ranero left on the alternative route 3.1 km) but we now leave the asphalt and continue straight onto the *Calzada Romana* for a glorious 19.4 km of uninterrupted (but uneven) track although the last section has recently been covered with gravel suggesting future 'improvements'.
[This stretch of Roman road is largely intact despite the intervening 20 centuries. It is part of the east/west highway built to link the gold mines of Gallaecia to Rome via Astorga Asturica Augusta and used by Ceasar Augustus in his campaigns against the Cantabrians. It was subsequently used by the armies of Islam and Christianity including Charlemagne in their battles for supremacy over the Iberian peninsular. After the re-conquest it became known as the Pilgrim Road Calzada de los Peregrinos and countless millions of pilgrims have walked this self-same path that is known and loved today as the Camino de Santiago. Of course this is not the only stretch left for us to walk but it is the most complete and spectacular section. It is also referred to as the Via Trajana this latter being the spur that connected the route to Bordeaux]. On our right (northern) horizon are the Cordillera Cantábrica (an extension of the Pyrenees) and just visible beyond (on a clear day) are the Picos de Europa with the highest peak at 2,648m (8,687 feet).

The track leads to a bridge [**3.2 km**] over the meandering *arroyo Solana* with a small plantation of pine struggling to establish itself in the bleak landscape. We now takes a wide curve towards the railway line and remote halt [**5.7 km**]:

8.9 km Cruce *Paso de Villarmarco* level crossing to the village of Villarmarco just visible on the horizon. Stay this side of the tracks and continue over several shallow riverbeds and we encounter a more pronounced river valley with a grove of poplars (left) offering shade if a rest or picnic is needed. A new concrete bridge [**2.8 km**] over the *arroyo Madriz d la Cava (Valle de Santa María)* has removed the need for pilgrims to ford this river and the path now climbs gently through scrubland to the high point of this day's stage [**1.8 km**]:

4.6 km Cruce *Opción* (Alto 920m): We now have the option to [1] continue straight past the radio mast and join the alternative route in Reliegos which is now only 1 kilometre and which has several bars and an albergue (see alternative route for details) or [2] turn right> and start the long descent into the río Esla valley towards Mansilla de las Mulas just visible on the horizon. Continue down the wide gravel track passing road (right) [**4.3 km**] to prison compound *Cárcel de León*) and continue along track to (left) side of road to junction with N-625 [**1.7 km**]:

5.9 km Cruce *N-625* cross over and continue on rough path on far side past football ground and modern bordello Bahillo [**0.6 km**] down under the bypass into Paseo del Esla past the water tower and town cemetery through the only remaining medieval city gate still in existence **Arco de Santa María** [**0.7 km**] s/o up c/de la Concepción passing the •Alberguería del Camino (left) and parish church of Santa Maria (with pilgrim statue) to turn right> into Plaza del Pozo with town hall and into c/del Puente and on our (left) [**0.4 km**]:

1.7 km Mansilla de las Mulas *Centro* •Albergue ❶ *Muni.[76÷8]* ✆ 661 977 305 municipal hostel c/del Puente, 5 where *Laura* and a team of volunteers has been welcoming pilgrims for many years. 76 beds €5 spread over 8 dormitory rooms and all facilities. The hostel is actually several buildings that stretch back to the main street and grouped around a central patio. A new hostel has been opened up at the eastern entrance by the *Puerta Castillo* (alternative route). •Albergue ❷ *El Jardín del Camino Priv.[32÷2]* ✆ 987-310 232 with 32 beds €8-10. All facilities (no kitchen) but cafe and pilgrim menú.

Albergue ❶ *Centro*

Albergue ❷ *El Jardín*

❏ **Alternative accommodation:** *Turismo* ✆ 987-310 012 in the Ayuntamiento on Plaza del Pozo (summer only) and Pilgrim association in the San Martin cultural centre. *Hoteles:* •Las Delicias Hs* ✆ 987-310 075 c/Mesones, 22 adjacent to albergue [1] with popular bar and restaurant. •**Alberguería del Camino** Hs** ✆ 987-311 193 c/ Concepción, 12. •San Martín Hs* ✆ 987–310 094 Av. Picos de Europa, 32 further out on the eastern side of town •El Gallo Hs** ✆ 987-310 359 c/Carret Cistierna, 17. *Bahillo on N-626 is not recommended.* The town has a range of shops and a variety of bars and restaurants (most offering a pilgrim menu).

MANSILLA DE LAS MULAS: *(pop: 1,900 – alt. 805 m)*. An important pilgrim halt today, no less than in its illustrious medieval past, which sheltered pilgrims in 3 separate pilgrim *hospitales* (long disappeared). This was and remains the meeting place for the two converging routes, the *Real Camino Francés* which enters the old quarter via the east gate *Puerta de Castillo* (only the wall remains) and the *Calzada Romana* that enters via the north gate *Arco de Santa María*. The name of this interesting old town is derived from *Mano en Silla* (hand on the saddle) that also defines the town's coat of arms. The addition of *de las mulas* (of the mules) most likely refers to the town's earlier prominence as a livestock market. Whatever about its agricultural roots, the medieval wall (12th century) still protects the town from the encroachment of modernity. The best preserves section is by the bridge (left). Take time to wander the meandering streets and admire the architectural layout and buildings around Plazas del Grano and Leña or just watch the trout jumping for the evening fly as the sun sets over the río Esla... or join them and take a swim from the sandy shore accessed by a footbridge towards *el camping* (see town plan).

Several detours are available from here (only advised if you have special interest) as follows: **Detour [1]** Over the bridge (first turning left 1.1 km) takes you through Mansilla Mayor and on to Vilaverde de Sandoval and the Romanesque **Monastery of Santa María de Sandoval** *XIIthC*, an important Cistercian monastery in its day but now de-consecrated – 8 km round trip (or continue on to León). **Detour [2]** Over

San Miguel de Escalada

the bridge (first turning right 1.4 km) takes you via Vilafalé to **Monastery of San Miguel de Escalada** *XIIthC* designated a national monument on account of its exceptional Mozarabic architecture – 25 km round trip (share a taxi?).

Forward planning for León: While it is only 18.6 km into León we have been on remote paths over the past few days so prepare for the slog into the city centre along the busy N-601. There is the possibility to avoid the busy (and dangerous) main road into (and out of) León by taking the bus from Mansilla direct to the city centre. Both the route into León alongside the N-601 and out along N-120 can be wearisome. The bus depot is ½ km on the outskirts of Mansilla on the Valladolid road. Several bus companies vie for this lucrative route and leave every half hour or so from about 07:00. This way you could explore the city at leisure, stay overnight and bus it to La Virgen del Camino early again the following morning. Refreshed from your break you could pick up the recommended route via Villar de Mazarife and make it to Hospital de Órbigo (29.1 km) a pleasant town with 3 good albergues and several restaurants.

The majority of pilgrims will have committed to travel the whole route by foot, which is highly commendable but others have different time constraints. If the idea of taking public transport seems like heresy it might be useful to ask yourself – why not? You could more than make up the distance by walking to Finisterre! The ego and its obsessive behavioural patterns can be just as limiting as a *laissez faire* attitude and indifference. What is your motivation for this journey, the intention you set out with? How does your decision to walk rather than take the bus serve that purpose? Do you judge other pilgrims who take the bus as inadequate in some way? Can we know all the circumstances surrounding individual decisions to be able to judge the actions and motivations of others? Let us walk today with love in our hearts and an open mind – making every step a prayer for peace and acceptance

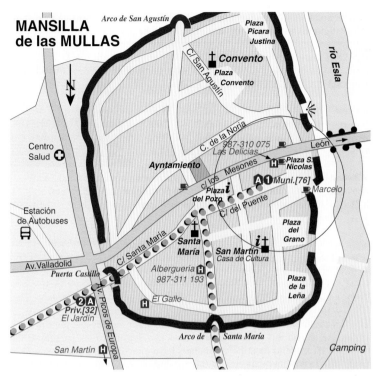

MANSILLA de las MULLAS

Arco de San Agustín

Plaza Picara Justina

río Esla

Cl San Agustín

✝ *Convento*

Plaza Convento

C. de la Noria

987-310 075 Las Delicias

León →

Centro Salud ✚

Ayuntamiento

cl los Mesones

H Plaza S. Nicolas

A 1 Muni.[76]

Marcelo

Plaza i del Pozo

Cl del Puente

Estación de Autobuses

Santa María

Plaza del Grano

i ✝

Albergueria H 987-311 193

San Martín Casa de Cultura

Av. Valladolid

Cl Santa María

Puerta Castillo

Plaza de la Leña

H El Gallo

2 A Priv.[32] El Jardín

Av. Picos de Europa

Arco de Santa María

Camping

San Martín H

REFLECTIONS: *When we judge others – we condemn ourselves.*

❑ **Here inside of me is a force that makes its own weather, winning through thickest clouds to the shining sun.** '*J.B.' His Life and Works*

20 **336.1** km (208.9 miles) to Santiago

MANSILLA DE LAS MULAS – LEÓN

▥▥▥▥	Path / Track	--- ---	10.2 ---	55%
▬▬▬	Quiet Road	--- ---	3.7 ---	20%
▮▮▮▮	Main Road	--- ---	<u>4.7</u> ---	25%
Total km	**Total distance**		**18.6 km** (11.6 ml)	

◤◣ Adjusted for climb   19.1 km (accrued ascent 100m = 0.5 km)
Alto ▲   High Point: Arcahueja (Alto del Portillo) 890m (2,920 feet)
< ⒶⒽ >   Villarente **5.6** km – Arcahueja **10.4** km.

900m
MANSILLA   Vilarente   Arcahueja   Valdelafuente   Alto del Portillo   LEÓN
■ 800m   Ⓐ   Ⓐ   ●   ▲   820m
     Río Porma
00 km   5 km   10 km   15 km

The Practical Path: Apart from a brief respite along a dedicated pilgrim track around Arcahueja this stage is mostly road or *senda* that runs parallel to the busy N-601. It seems as if the city fathers have more pressing matters on their hands than to consider the needs of the walking pilgrim. Tourism and industrial activity, with their requirement for rapid transport, are decidedly *número uno*. A walking pilgrim requires nothing more than a simple path and respect for the ancient camino and both are in short supply around León. From this point on you need to stay very focused so as not to miss the waymarks amongst the busy-ness of the city centre.

❑ **The Mystical Path:** What route does your heart follow today? Never mind about the outer path, what awareness is there of the inner journey – is it flat or mountainous? Never mind about the outer weather, are you aware of the inner conditions – is there sunshine or cloud? The outer is fixed, only the inner can be changed at will. "*It is not what life does to you that is important – but what you do with what life does to you that really matters.*"

❑ **Personal Reflections:** "*... The rain was heavy and persistent, drenching my papers every time I tried to take notes. I followed the sign by the consultorio and shortly afterwards realised the only way forward was across a deep trench. Too lazy to return and not realising the depth of the ditch I slithered down the steep bank and found myself waist deep in cold, grey water. I started to curse out loud, the offending expletives borne away on an unusually stiff wind. Old regretting patterns started to emerge and by grace, not will, I came to the sudden realisation that I created my own weather. I started to smile, cleansing my dark thoughts in the ripples of laughter that bubbled up from somewhere deep inside ...*"

0.0 km **Mansilla de las Mulas** from albergue **❶** proceed out over the río Esla and onto the *senda* that runs parallel to the main road passing turn-off for Mansilla Mayor / Sandoval (left) and Vilafalé-San Miguel (right). Next we pass an Agip petrol station behind which is the ancient hill fortress and settlement

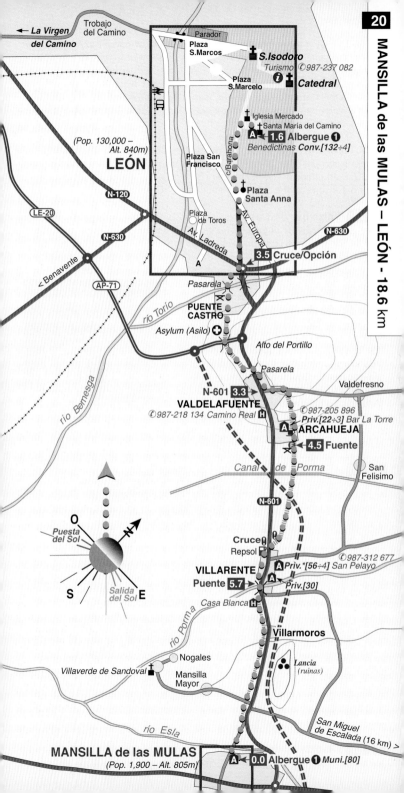

← *La Virgen del Camino*

Trobajo del Camino

Parador

Plaza S.Marcos

✝ *S.Isodoro*

Turismo ©987-237 082

ⓘ ✝ *Catedral*

Plaza S.Marcelo

Iglesia Mercado
✝ Santa María del Camino

Ⓐ ← **1.6** Albergue ❶

Benedictinas Conv.[132÷4]

c/Barahona

(Pop. 130,000 – Alt. 840m)

LEÓN

N-120

Plaza San Francisco

• Plaza Santa Anna

Av. Europa

N-630

N-630

LE-20

Plaza de Toros

Av. Ladreda

Ⓐ

3.5 Cruce/Opción

< Benavente

río Torío

Pasarela

PUENTE CASTRO

AP-71

Asylum (Asilo) ✚

Alto del Portillo

río Bernesga

Pasarela

Valdefresno

N-601 **3.3** →

VALDELAFUENTE

©987-218 134 Camino Real Ⓗ

©987-205 896
Priv.[22÷3] Bar La Torre

Ⓐ **ARCAHUEJA**

☖ ← **4.5** Fuente

San Felismo

Canal de Porma

O

Puesta del Sol

N-601

N

S

E

Salida del Sol

Cruce ☖

Repsol

©987-312 677

Ⓐ *Priv.*[56÷4] San Pelayo*

VILLARENTE

Puente **5.7**

Ⓐ

Priv.[30]

Casa Blanca Ⓗ

río Porma

Villarmoros

Lancia (ruinas)

Nogales

Villaverde de Sandoval ✝

Mansilla Mayor

San Miguel de Escalada (16 km) >

río Esla

MANSILLA de las MULAS

(Pop. 1,900 – Alt. 805m)

Ⓐ ← **0.0** Albergue ❶ *Muni.[80]*

of Lancia *[where the indigenous Asturians, despite their heroic defence of their native lands, met their demise at the hands of the Roman legions. Artefacts have also been recovered here from the Neolithic period and excavations are on-going and compete with excavations for the new motorway that ploughs through this ancient site]*. Continue over the río Moro into **Villarmoros de Mansilla** [**4.1** km] formerly known as *Villamoros del Camino Francés* with its Iglesia de San Esteban. Continue on the pilgrim track passing fonda •**Casa Blanca** © 987-312 164 to the medieval bridge where we have to compete with the road traffic [**!**] to cross over the río Porma on the Giant bridge *Puente Ingente* so called on account of its 20-arch span. Plans for a pedestrian bridge have still not materialised although, ironically, the construction of the new motorway here will relieve some of the traffic. Continue into Villarente [**1.6** km]:

5.7 km Villarente shaded rest area down by the river. *[The first building (left) was a medieval pilgrim hospital which operated a donkey 'ambulance' service for sick pilgrims into León]* while (right) we pass •**Albergue ❶** *El Delfín Verde Priv.[30]* © 987-312 065 private pilgrim hostel set back off the main road but readily visible with 30 places in several rooms with basic facilities. 50 metres further on *off* the main road (right) at the end of c/El Romero beside a grove of trees is the popular •**Albergue ❷** *San Pelayo Priv.*[56÷4]+ © 987-312 677 network* hostel with 56 beds €8 +priv. rooms and excellent facilities, meals also available. Continue through this modern satellite town of León past the health centre *Centro de Salud Consultario* and turn off right> [**1.5** km] onto the dedicated pilgrim track (opposite Repsol garage) and continue for [**3.0** km] over the

Albergue ❷ *San Pelayo*

canal del Porma under new motorway climbing up the gravel path past rest area [**F**] (often dry) to the top of the rise in:

4.5 km Arcahueja [**F**] This is the last chance to take a rest in the relative quiet before we hit the city traffic. 300 metres off route (left) is the welcoming bar and •**Albergue** *La Torre Priv.[22÷3]*+ © 987-205 896 private hostel with 22 beds €7 (dinner + B&B €18) +priv. rooms from €35. No kitchen but meals available in the bar. Continue along track through Valdefresno [**F**] and turn <left at the asphalt road into industrial park and up to the main road at:

3.3 km N-601 Valdelafuente various bars and showrooms spread along this busy section of the N-601, one of the main arterial roads into León, also modern hotel •**Camino Real** © 987-218 134. We skirt up briefly around the side of Alto del Portillo before taking the new pilgrim footbridge *pasarela [1]* over the main road and proceed down the narrow margin at the far side of the dual carriageway to cross another high level pedestrian bridge *pasarela [2]* over the motorway ring road passing the mental asylum Hospital Santa Isabel and veering <left off the main street in Puente Castro into c/ de Victoriano Martinez [**2.4** km]. *[The modern buildings here disguise the fact that this was an influential Jewish district in the 12th century and site of a former Roman settlement]*. Continue via the footbridge *pasarela [3]* over the río Torio with pilgrim information kiosk *Turismo* (summer only). We now make our way up to the wide main road to busy roundabout *glorieta* [**1.1** km]:

3.5 km Glorieta information board at this major roundabout. *Note*: The old municipal hostel in c/Campos Góticos has now closed but there are several new alternative hostels in León offering cheap accommodation. For the **recommended route** along the historic camino into the old city and the *central* albergue❶ proceed over the roundabout (pedestrian crossing) into Av. Miguel Castaño that merges with Av. Del Europa which we also cross to bring us into St. Anne's Square *Plaza de Santa Ana* where a fountain and small shaded park provides an opportunity to calm any frayed nerves and take stock; we're nearly there but "many a slip t'wixt…" Take the street to the left of Iglesia de Santa Ana (painted a warm ochre) into c/Barahona and through Money Gate *Puerta Moneda* one of the original gateways to the medieval city (note the vast city walls as you pass) and just *before* reaching Iglesia N. S. del Mercado (with its lions guarding the entrance) turn right> into c/Escurial to:

1.6 km Centro •Albergue ❶ *Santa María de Carbajal Conv.[132÷4]* ℭ 987-252 866 Benedictine monastery situated in the old city on the tranquil *Plaza de Santa María del Camino y Grano*. 132 beds €5 incl. in 4 dormitories with good basic facilities. Run by the Benedictine nuns who issue *credenciales* and have created a haven of peace and serenity (excepting when the adjacent school is open) in this otherwise busy city area. Few pilgrims attend the sung Vespers (19:00) or the pilgrim

Albergue ❶ *Santa María*

benediction (21:30) in the convent chapel which can provide a powerful sense of the sacred and reminder of the true nature of all our journeying. *[Next albergue: La Virgen de Camino – 8.7 km].*

Before turning in for the night you might visit the adjacent and atmospheric *Barrio Húmedo* (wet quarter, as in drink – on account of the variety of bars that abound here!) which is centred around the beautiful and intimate squares of Plaza Martín that leads into Plaza Mayor with the original 17th century Baroque Town hall (only 500 metres from the albergue) or simply lose yourself in the maze of narrow streets that connect them. Or simply hang out in the lovely *Plaza Santa María del Camino* watched over by the cherubs who play in the central neoclassical fountain symbolising the two rivers that embrace this magical city. Also in this square we find the 10th century Church of Our Lady of the Market *Iglesia Nuestra Señora del Mercado* (with the lions). Here you can see a statue of the Virgin, Patroness of León (some say of the camino itself). Indeed the church was formerly called Iglesia Virgen del Camino until that honour was bestowed on the sanctuary on the western suburbs, which, along with the route through the city and the main sites, are described in the next stage.

Following the closure of the municipal hostel, 2 additional hostels are now available   as follows: ❷ *Residencia Fundación Ademar 'San Francisco de Asís' Priv.[54÷10]* on Av. Alcalde Miguel Castaños, 4 ℭ 637 439 848 a drab building owned by the Capuchin Brothers with 54 beds (130 in summer) from €10. Directions: at Plaza Santa Ana continue s/o down Av.Europa and the hostel is on the left close to the gardens *Jardin San Franciso.*

❸ *Unamuno Mun.[53÷15]* C/ San Pelayo, 15 ℭ 987 233 010 residence of *Universitaria Unamuno* and available to pilgrims in the busy summer season (July to August only). 53 beds in small dormitories €10 double rooms €18 per person.

❏ **Accommodation:** *Turismo:* Plaza Regla (Catedral Square) ✆ 987-237 082

❏ *Hotels Central* (in the old quarter include): •**París** H*** ✆ 987-238 600 c/ Ancha, 18. •**La Posada Regia** Hr*** ✆ 987-213 173 c/Regidores, 9. •**Guzmán el Bueno** HsR* ✆ 987-236 412 c/López Castrillón, 6. •**Hospedería Fernando I** Hr*** ✆ 987-213 173 •**San Martín** HsR* ✆ 987-875 187 plaza Torres de Omaña, 1. •**Boccalino** Hs** ✆ 987-223 060 plaza S. Isodoro, 9. ✆ *Other* (options in the modern quarter between Plaza Francisco and Plaza San Marcos include: •**Reina** Hr* ✆ 987-205 212 c/Puerta de la Reina, 2. •**Alvarez** HsR* ✆ 987-072 520 c/ Burgo Nuevo, 3. •**Orejas** H*** ✆ 987-252 909 c/Villafranca, 6 (close to the bus and train stations).•**Padre Isla (1)** HsR* ✆ 987-228 097 Av.Padre Isla, 8 and opposite (with 3 stars and 3 times the price) is•**Alfonso V** H*** ✆ 987-220 900 Av. Padre Isla, 1. Further on (just off the avenue) is •**Padre Isla (2)** HsR* ✆ 987-092 298 c/Joaquín Costa, 2. •**Londres** H* ✆ 987-222 274 Av. Roma, 1. •**Don Suero** HsR** ✆ 987-230 600 Av. Suero de Quiñones, 15. and for incomparable 5 star luxury in the original pilgrim hospital try •**San Marcos** H***** ✆ 987-237 300 Plaza San Marcos (one of the best value 5 stars).

❏ **Historical Monuments:** ❶ *Puerta Moneda* (*muralla romana*) ❷ *Iglesia de Santa María del camino* (o mercado) *XII*th*C* ❸ *Catedral XIII*th*C* museo y claustro ❹ *Basilica de San Isidoro XII*th*C* ❺ *Panteón XI*th*C* ❻ *San Marcos Museo* ❼ *San Marcos Parador y claustro XII*th*C– XVI*th*C*.

LEÓN CITY (*pop: 130,000 – alt. 840 m*): at one time León was a Roman military garrison and base for its VIIth Legion, hence the name – León, derived from *Legion*. Later it became the capital of the old kingdoms of Asturias and León. It was conquered and re-conquered by Visigoth, Moor and finally Christian forces. Ancient and modern now straddle the banks of the río Barnesega and, within the hectic nature of any modern city it is a meeting that seems somehow effortless. The city, like the river, flows naturally along its tributaries, absorbing all in its welcoming embrace. Here every period and style is seamlessly accommodated: from Roman remains which now support the medieval walls to the exquisite Romanesque Royal Basilica of St. Isodoro *Real Basílica de San Isodoro*, the Gothic splendour of León Cathedral *Pulchra Leonina*, the magnificent intricacy of Renaissance *San Marcos* with its Plasteresque façade, the controversial austerity of the neo-Gothic in Gaudi's *Casa de Botines*, to the glass and steel edifices of today's modern architects.

This resident population of 130,000 plays host to many tourists and pilgrims who pour through the city. You could spend days here and not see the half of it especially if you arrive during any one of the festivals that seem to take place throughout the year but particular highlights include: *San Juan and San Pedro* from the 21st – 30th June which sees giant displays and running of the bulls during the day and concerts and fireworks at night. *San Froilán* runs from the 5th – 12th of October with more parades and a local pilgrimage *romería* to the Virgin of the Way *Virgin del Camino*. If you are just passing through – then the camino itself (marked rather too discreetly with tasteful brass scallop shells embedded in the pavement) will bring you around the prime sites in the medieval quarter. These historic sites are described in detail in the next stage.

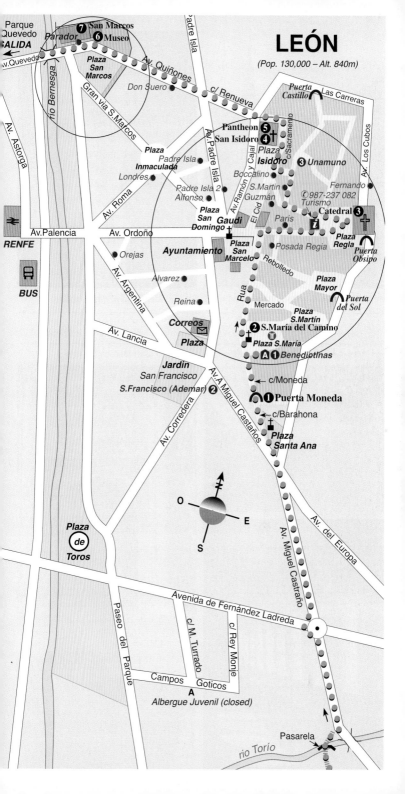

Town Hall *(left)* **& Casa Botines** *(right)*

Cathedral at night *(above)*

Río Bernesga & Snow covered peaks

Santiago over the Parador Entrance

Cloisters – San Marcos Parador

San Marcos Square

REFLECTIONS:

_____

_____

_____

_____

_____

_____

_____

_____

_____

_____

_____

_____

_____

_____

_____

_____

_____

_____

_____

_____

_____

_____

_____

_____

_____

_____

_____

_____

❏ **Solitude shows us what we should be – society shows us what we are.**
Lord Cecil

21 **317.5** km (197.3 miles) to Santiago

LEÓN – VILLAR de MAZARIFE

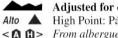

	Path / Track	--- ---	5.5	---	25%
	Quiet Roads	--- ---	8.2	---	37%
	Main Roads	--- ---	<u>8.5</u>	---	38%
Total km	**Total distance**		**22.2 km** (13.8 ml)		

Adjusted for climb 23.4 km (accrued ascent 250m = 1.2 km)
Alto ▲ High Point: Páramo 901m (2,956 feet)
<Ⓐ Ⓗ> *From albergue* ❶: Virgen del Camino **8.5** km. *[Alt. Valverde 11.9*

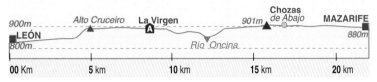

The Practical Path: The route described below follows the waymarked circuit past the cathedral and out of the city via San Marcos but you need to have pencil sharp eyes to see the discreet shells in the pavement that compete with the many distractions in the busy streets. Once you leave Virgen del Camino, on the **recommended route**, there are few facilities along this relatively isolated stretch, so take a break and stock up with fruit or snacks in Virgen del Camino for the latter part of this stage.

❏ **The Mystical Path:** To what small band of pilgrim friends do we owe the gratitude for discovering an alternative way to the intrusive main road? In one stroke it has changed a frenetic experience into another, more peaceful, world, *'Never doubt that a small group of thoughtful people can change the world, indeed it's the only thing that ever has.'* And what of the ultimate peace, that passes all understanding? Where will that be found? What needs to change in us to discover what was never lost, only hidden behind some imagined veil?

❏ **Personal Reflections:** "… The cafe was crowded and our small group comprised six different nationalities all huddled in heated debate into city life versus the countryside. For me, the city has too many distractions, too much sensual and intellectual stimulation. I become isolated from my Self amongst the shops and factories, the museums and churches. The glamour of the sense-perceptible world hides the reality of the super-sensible. It is in the solitude of the camino that I seem to reach some altered state and find a deep peace. It is easier, for me, to see the Christ in the lone shepherd than in the shop assistant. Each mirrors a different aspect of my-self; in one I find peaceful serenity, the other pretentious servility masking bored indifference.

0.0 km **León** from the central albergue ❶ in Plaza de Santa María pick up the brass pavement waymarks in c/de la Rua and turn <left into Plaza de San Marcelo presided over by the splendid *Ayuntamiento* and the 12th century Iglesia San Marcelo. Here we have a good view of Gaudi's architectural masterpiece, the neo-Gothic palace *Casa de Botines*. *[This structure marks an historical and artistic turning point – it is one of the first monumental buildings constructed with private funds as a secular, middle class statement. Heretofore, buildings of this magnitude were funded by religious institutions or the aristocracy. While*

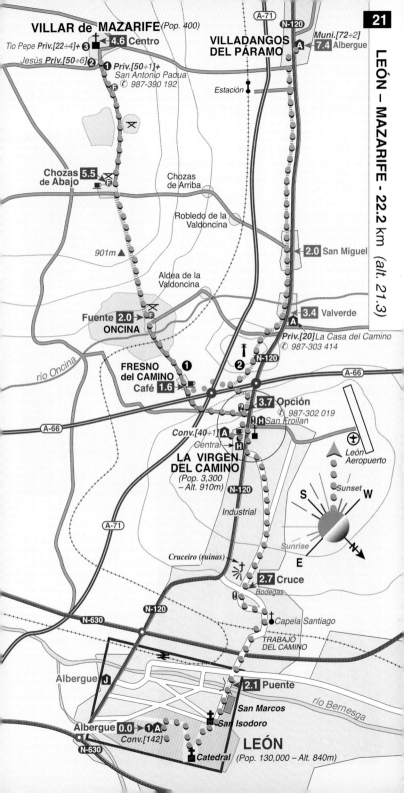

VILLAR de MAZARIFE *(Pop. 400)*

Tio Pepe **Priv.[22÷4]+ ❸**   **4.6** Centro

Jesús **Priv.[50÷6] ❷**

❶ **Priv.[50÷1]+**
San Antonio Padua
Ⓒ 987-390 192

VILLADANGOS DEL PÁRAMO   Ⓐ   *Muni.[72÷2]*
7.4 Albergue

Estación

Chozas de Abajo **5.5**

Chozas de Arriba

Robledo de la Valdoncina

2.0 San Miguel

901m ▲

Aldea de la Valdoncina

Fuente 2.0 ONCINA

3.4 Valverde   Ⓐ

Priv.[20] La Casa del Camino
Ⓒ 987-303 414

FRESNO del CAMINO   ❶

Café 1.6   ❷   N-120

3.7 Opción
Ⓒ 987-302 019
San Froilan

río Oncina

A-66

Conv.[40÷1] Ⓐ
Central ❯ Ⓗ

LA VIRGEN DEL CAMINO
(Pop. 3,300 – Alt. 910m)   N-120

León Aeropuerto

S   *Sunset*   W

Industrial

A-71

Sunrise

E

Cruceiro (ruinas)

2.7 Cruce

Bodegas

✝ *Capela Santiago*

TRABAJO DEL CAMINO

N-630   N-120

Albergue Ⓙ

2.1 Puente

río Bernesga

San Marcos

Albergue 0.0 ❶ Ⓐ   *San Isodoro*
Conv.[142]

N-630

Catedral (Pop. 130,000 – Alt. 840m)

LEÓN

built on the back of a new wave of industrial endeavour Gaudí still follows a medieval expression with the slender towers and the image of St. George slaying the dragon above the main door]. Adjoining it (right) is the equally magnificent 16th century *Palacio de los Guzmanes* now the council offices and worth popping in to have a look at the marvellous inner courtyard. We now pass up the shopping mecca *c/Ancha* to:

Catedral [0.8 km] *Pulchra Leonina* taking up the whole east side of Plaza Regal, opposite the Turismo where you can obtain more detailed information (in English) on the cathedral and other sites. Enter the late 13th century Gothic Cathedral via the west door with the Virgin *Nuestra Señora la Blanca* adorning the central column (photo opposite) and *Santiago Peregrino* to the right – now well worn by the hands of devout pilgrims. The cathedral is renowned for its magnificent 125 stained glass windows set high in the walls that shed such a lightness of touch to the interior. H. V. Morton described it as, *"… a conservatory that instead of keeping out the light, as most Spanish churches do, actually invites it in, showering this mosaic of colour all over it to become the gayest church in Spain."* He goes on to remind us, *"one of the chief functions of the medieval church was to instruct the illiterate and to give them pictures they could understand, to show them the story of the Gospels and the legends of the Saints – the novels of the medieval world. What more glorious picture book could there be than this church, whose illustrations are illuminated by God's own light."*

One consequence of this lightness is that the structural integrity of the building has been compromised and part of the nave caved-in during the 19th century following an earlier collapse in the 17th century! The cloisters off the north side and the cathedral museum *Catedral Museo* are also worth a visit. Next make your way back down the side of the tourist office to the tiny plaza Torres de Omaña where myriad narrow medieval streets branch out in all directions, head down c/Fernandez Regueral (Hostal San Martín left) into Plaza San Isidoro, and:

San Isidoro [0.5 km] the fountain in the square was built to commemorate the VIIth Roman Legion. Here, bedded into the Roman foundations and the medieval city wall, is this wonderful 11th century Basilica Church. The remains of San Isidoro were brought here from Sevilla to be buried in Christian Spain as the south was still under Moorish influence at that time. Admire the Door of Forgiveness *Puerta del Perdón* (right) through which medieval

pilgrims, too ill to travel on to Santiago, could still receive the same indulgences. The exquisite sculptural work is from the hands of Maestro Estaban who also created the justly famous Puerta de las Platerías in Santiago cathedral.

Take time to visit the fascinating *Museo* that provides access to the cloisters *claustros* and the royal burial vaults *Pantheón Real*. The Pantheón is the only part of the original 11th century building remaining and the final resting place of no less than 11 Kings, 12 Queens and 23 Princes. Look at the beautiful frescoes, still vivid 800 years after they were first painted, and because of which it has been called Spain's *Romanesque Sistine Chapel*. If you now need fresh air and refreshment try the cafés opposite the entrance in c/El Cid that also has a delightful small park – or continue into c/Sacramento and turn left at the rear of the basilica and cross directly over the busy Av. de Ramón y Cajal into c/Renueva, crossing Av. del Padre Isla into Av. de Suero de Quinoñes to:

Plaza San Marcos [0.8 km] take time to admire the Renaissance craftsmanship that built and adorned the stunning Plasteresque edifice of this ancient monastery dedicated to St. Mark. Originally a more modest pilgrim hospital built by Doña Sancha in the 12th century it became the headquarters of the Knights of the Order of Santiago which was formed to protect the pilgrim way. Later still it was acquired and further embellished by King Ferdinand. The façade is a storybook in itself with many pilgrim motifs including the sword of Santiago entwined with the lion of San Marcos. A profusion of scallop shells cover the pediment of the church (and museum) entrance. Less evident are the interesting copper medallions all along the front (just behind the dwarf hedge) with scenes from the pilgrim cities and towns we have passed through. You may also notice a modest pilgrim sitting at the base of the stone cross, admiring the stately surroundings while resting his weary feet.

Take a peek inside the magnificent courtyard of the Parador (its cloistered galleries a museum in themselves) or perhaps treat yourself to a night in these sumptuous surroundings. You will find many fellow pilgrims checking out in the morning! Visit the Museo next door and admire the tantalising 11th century ivory crucifix *Cristo de Carrizo* (many of the artefacts are in the process of being moved to another location). All reminders of the influence and the gifts of the Way of St. James on León which, in times past, had no less than 17 such pilgrim *hospitales*. Take your leave of the central city and San Marcos Square, over:

2.1 km **Puente *río Bernesga*** 16th century stone bridge over the river Bernesga. We now make our way through the busy suburbs of León until we reach the open countryside of the páramo. The first 2.7 km are between the N-120 (signposted Astorga) and railway line before branching off uphill through an industrial area to re-join the main road again in La Virgen del Camino.

Continue past the Parque de Quevedo (right) *[named after the great 17th century Spanish poet whose writings so challenged the nobility that he was incarcerated in San Marcos during its spell as a prison!]* until we reach a pilgrim cross and pedestrian bridge (tourist kiosk) **[1.5 km]** where we have a brief respite from the N-120 as we take an elevated walkway over the railway line and re-join the main road again in ***Trobajo del Camino***. This area has many links with the original camino as evidenced by the small chapel dedicated to St. James *Ermita Santiago* (right) and just beyond the waymarked route takes a short detour (left) into *Plaza Sira San Pedro* back up to the main road **[1.2 km]** to:

2.7 km **Cruce** cross main road and turn immediately right> steeply uphill (**3t** sign). **[!]** Many pilgrims, their heads bent low against the incline, miss this turning and keep on along the busy main road. We now pass a collection of *bodegas* to the crest of the hill with stone pedestal (left) base of another former pilgrim cross no doubt pillaged, like the one in San Marcos square, to adorn some more 'important' setting. Its ruined state is a strangely powerful reminder that we are on the historic camino. Hopefully, sufficiently out of sight of the city fathers, it will long remain in its dilapidated state and we will be saved some modern concrete replacement. A good point from which to look back over the sprawling expanse of León below, before proceeding along the *c/Camino de la Cruz* into industrial estate to join the N-120 **[1.8 km]** passing Repsol petrol station and •**Villa Paloma** H*** ℂ 987-300 990 past selection of cafes to the modern church of San Froilán **[1.5 km]**. Iglesia San Froilán **La Virgen del Camino**. Last of the suburban sprawl of León and opportunity to take some refreshment at café •*El Peregrino* adjoining hostal •**San Froilán** Hs ℂ 987-302 019 just off the main road opposite the ultra modern sanctuary of the Virgen built in 1961 *[on the site of the shrine where a shepherd, in the early 16th century, saw a vision of the Virgin who told him to throw s stone and then build a church on the spot where it landed. The place became a pilgrimage in its own right on account of the miracles performed here]*. The huge bronze statues of the 12 Apostles stand above the west door with St. James looking out towards Santiago and the Virgin floating above them all. Cross over **[!]** the N-120 to camino information board showing the alternative routes available. Up to our left is the café and hostal •**Central** Hs ℂ 987-302 041 and behind the latter, in peaceful gardens at the edge of town in c/Camino de Villacedré is •**Albergue** *D.Antonino y Dña.Cinia Priv.[40÷1]* ℂ 615-217 335 previously part of the adjoining seminary. 40 beds from €5 Spotlessly clean with excellent modern facilities including washing and drying machines in each of its separate ladies and gents washrooms. From the pilgrim information board on the N-120 proceed down the parallel side road to the point where the routes diverge [?] marked by unsightly (and unseemly) paint sprawled across the asphalt road as Mazarife competes with Villadangos for your soul and wallet! [**0.4** km]

3.7 km Option Recommended scenic route [1] via Mazarife or alternative road route *senda* [2] to Villadangos. ❖

Alternative route ❷ via Valverde to Villadangos del Páramo – a total distance of 21.3 km (8.5 km from León to this point and a further 12.8 km). The new motorway has actually reduced the traffic along this stretch of the N-120.

At the hand-painted sign (Mazarife left) keep s/o along the road past the cemetery (left) and s/o parallel to the N-120 onto track that winds its way around the maze of roadways ahead through tunnel under the A-71 [**1.6** km] (a track from the left connects with the route to Mazarife) and turn right up past radio mast and water tower and down s/o through industrial area back to the N-120 at Valverde to pick up the parallel track *senda*.

3.4 km **Valverde de la Virgen** •**Albergue** *La Casa del Camino Priv.[20÷1]* ℂ 987-303 414. hostal at the junction of N-120 and c/Camino de Jano. All facilities including meals and small garden and terrace. *(under sale–check)* Continue straight through the town alongside the main road all the way into:

2.0 km **San Miguel del Camino**. The camino continues on a path adjoining the main road all the way into Villadangos passing the hotel •**Avenida III** Hr^2 ℂ 987-390 311 and petrol station for a long stretch before crossing the road to:

7.4 km **Villadangos del Páramo** •**Albergue** *Muni.[72÷2]* hostel ℂ 987-390 003 on main road as you enter the town with 72 beds €4 in 2 main rooms with additional floor space available in this converted former schoolhouse. All facilities+ and set back slightly from the main road by a lawn.

Other accommodation: •**Alto Paramo** Hs** ℂ 987-390 311. •**Libertad** Hs^2 ℂ 987-390 123 several shops, bars and restaurant. Visit the Iglesia de Santiago with its statue of Santiago Matamoros above the main altar that, unusually, shows him leaping out towards us (rather than in profile). This old town of Roman origins sits uneasily astride the main road. In the past it supported a pilgrim hospital and legend has it that in the numerologically significant year of 1111 a battle was waged here between the forces of Doña Urraca of León and those of her former spouse Alfonso of Aragón.

❖ **Recommended route ❶ via Mazarife** here we veer <left away from the N-120 on a gravel track to cross over the A-71 intersection and then under the A-66 over river and into:

1.6 km Fresno del Camino •*Bar* (here a track under the motorway connects with the route into Valverde). Continue s/o into over railway and into:

2.0 km Oncina de la Valdocina *Fuente* peaceful hamlet with parish church of San Bartolomé. Turn right and immediately left to picnic area and [F]. We now head up the track out of the valley onto the glorious open countryside of the *páramo*. The rich red earth provides nourishment for crops and wild flowers in equal proportion. This wonderful natural path continues all the way to:

5.5 km Chozas de Abajo another peaceful village with rest area and [F] (bar and shop in Plaza San Martin 300m off route). Continue s/o along a quiet country road passing rest area and [F] just before entering the next village:

4.6 km Villar de Mazarife *Centro* on the outskirts we pass •Albergue ❶ *San Antonio de Pádua Priv.[50÷1]+* ℭ 987-390 192 private hostel at entrance to the village in modern bungalow with 50 beds €6 + private rooms. All facilities. Pepe Giner who runs this albergue is dedicated to the pilgrim way and a physiotherapist to boot which might come in handy.

Opposite is the colourful •Albergue ❷ *Casa de Jesús Priv.[50÷12]* ℭ 686 053 390 private hostel with 50 beds €5 in variety of rooms (and an open balcony) built around a central courtyard.

In the centre of the village by the church (100m off route) we find •Albergue ❸ *Tio Pepe Priv.[22÷4]+* ℭ 987-390 517 private hostel on c/Teso de la Iglesia with 22 beds €7 + private rooms and all facilities (no kitchen) but popular bar provides meals and has a patio and garden with small *piscina*. [*Next albergue: Hospital del Órbigo – 14.4 km*].

VILLAR DE MAZARIFE is a decidedly pilgrim friendly village where even the grocery store is called *Frutas de Camino de Santiago* and the church is also dedicated to St. James with several images of the saint inside. Several bars and restaurants, a gift shop, museum and art gallery make up some of the facilities of this peaceful hamlet. The local artist *Monseñor* a neo-Romanesque painter *Pintor Románico* specialises in religious works of art.

REFLECTIONS:

❏ To dry one's eyes and laugh at a fall,
And, baffled, get up and begin again. *Robert Browning*

22 **295.3** km (183.5 miles) to Santiago

VILLAR DE MAZARIFE – ASTORGA

	Path / Track	--- ---	21.1	---	68%
	Quiet Road	--- ---	10.1	---	32%
	Main Road	--- ---	0.0		
Total km	**Total distance**		**31.2 km** (19.4 ml)		

▲ **Adjusted for climb** 32.4 km (accrued ascent 250m = 1.2 km)
Alto ▲ High Point: Cruceiro Santo Toribio 905m (2,970 ft).
< Ⓐ Ⓗ > Villavante **10.4** km – Hospital de Órbigo **14.6** km – Villares **17.1** km
Santibáñez **19.6** km – San Justo **27.6** km. *(Alternative route [2] from Villadangos by the N-120 – San Martin 4.7 km).*

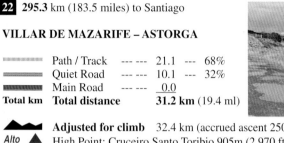

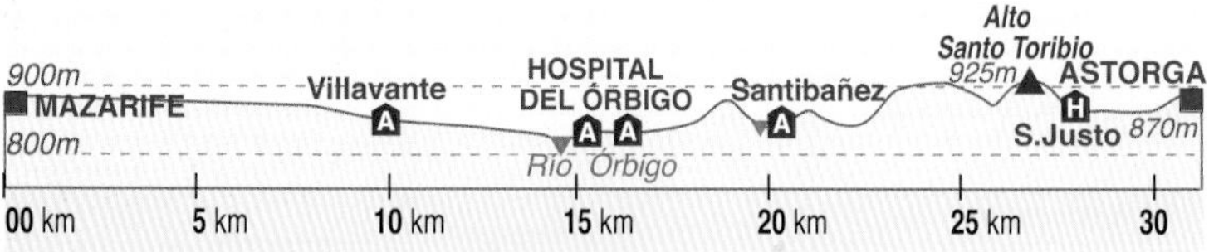

The Practical Path: The majority of this stage is relatively solitary so bring food and water (there are few villages on the way) however there are attractive sections with trees and other shade in which to rest out of the sun. The first part to Hospital de Órbigo (13.6 km) is relatively flat and easily covered. If you are planning to continue to Astorga (16.3 km) the total distance is 29.9 km so leave early and allow some time to savour Órbigo (you could lunch here, it's around halfway). Note that the last section beyond Órbigo has some (gentle) hills.

❏ **The Mystical Path:** What of your own inner battles, the jousting tournaments of the soul? How easily do you fall and how quickly do you get up again? Many knights, even an exiled bishop, fell to the earth on this very spot and rose again, dusted themselves down, and began afresh. True greatness is not in ever falling, but in picking ourselves up every time we do.

❏ **Personal Reflections:** *"… I sit in the shade of a grove of orange trees and sketch a stork patiently waiting by the pond to pluck a fish from its cool waters. I wonder why I don't take more time to observe and draw the beauty of life around me. I am so often caught up in my mental world of worries and responsibilities that I miss the wonder of the present moment. More tears begin to flow as I write this. Are they tears of sadness at lost opportunities or of gratitude at the peace that surrounds and holds me in its tranquil embrace?"*

0.0 km **Villar de Mazarife** from albergue ❶ head down through the town, over the secondary road (linking Villadangos on the alternative route with Santa María del Páramo) over river and canal and out on the quiet country lane through the open *páramo* over *rio de la Mata* **[3.3** km] past *Finca las Matillas (exploración Gandera)* **[1.0** km] canal **[1.0** km] s/o to crossroads **[0.5** km]:

5.8 km **Cruce** *Camino* s/o onto earthen track <left and right> over the canal de la Mata to follow remote track (and power lines) passing **[F]** (natural) and right> into the village.

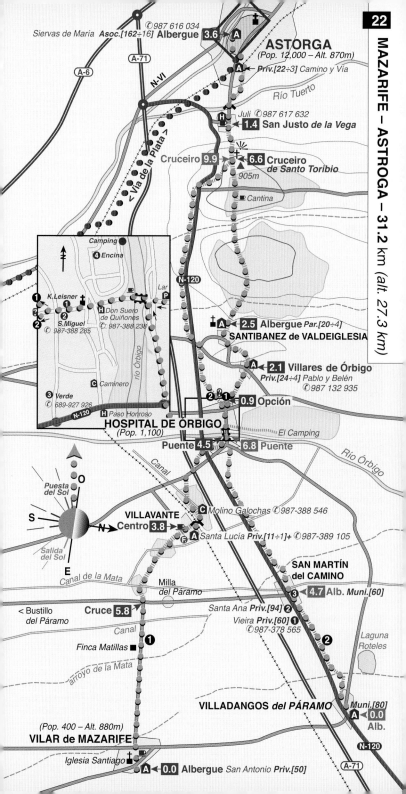

Siervas de María **Asoc.**[162÷16] **Albergue** 3.6 Ⓐ ✆987 616 034

ASTORGA
(Pop. 12,000 – Alt. 870m)

Ⓐ ← **Priv.**[22÷3] Camino y Vía

Río Tuerto

Ⓗ ← 1.4 **San Justo** de la Vega Juli ✆987 617 632

A-71

A-6 N-VI

< Vía de la Plata >

Cruceiro 9.9 6.6 **Cruceiro** de Santo Toribio
905m

▲ Cantina

N-120

Ⓐ ← 2.5 **Albergue** *Par.*[20÷4]
SANTIBANEZ de VALDEIGLESIA

Ⓐ 2.1 **Villares de Órbigo**
Priv.[24÷4] Pablo y Belén
✆987 132 935

② ① 0.9 **Opción**

Camping ●
④ *Encina*

① **K.Leisner** ✝
② **S.Miguel**
✆987-388 285
② Ⓗ **Don Suero de Quiñones** ✆987-388 238
Lar Ⓟ

río Órbigo

Ⓒ *Caminero*

③ *Verde* ✆689-927 926
N-120 Ⓗ **Paso Honroso**

HOSPITAL DE ÓRBIGO
(Pop. 1,100)

Puente 4.5 6.8 **Puente** El Camping

Río Órbigo

Canal

O Puesta del Sol
S N E
Salida del Sol

Ⓒ *Molino Galochas* ✆987-388 546

VILLAVANTE
Centro 3.8 → Ⓐ
Ⓕ *Santa Lucía* **Priv.**[11÷1]+ ✆987-389 105

Canal de la Mata

Milla del Páramo

SAN MARTÍN del CAMINO

③ ← 4.7 **Alb.** *Muni.*[60]
Santa Ana **Priv.**[94] ②
< Bustillo del Páramo **Cruce** 5.8
Vieira **Priv.**[60] ① ✆987-378 565
Canal

Finca Matillas ■ ①

② Laguna Roteles

arroyo de la Mata

(Pop. 400 – Alt. 880m)
VILLADANGOS del PÁRAMO *Muni.*[80]
Ⓐ 0.0 **Alb.**

VILAR de MAZARIFE
Iglesia Santiago ✝ Ⓐ ← 0.0 **Albergue** San Antonio **Priv.**[50]
N-120
A-71

3.8 km **Villavante** pass picnic site to *Iglesia de las Candelas (candles) XVII[th]C.* **Albergue** *Santa Lucía* **Priv.[11÷1]+** © 692 107 693 c/ Doctor Vélez 11 beds €7 + priv. €40 double. Continue out over rail bridge [**0.4** km] turning <left onto a track alongside to casa rural in renovated mill by the river CR **Molino Galochas** © 987 388 546 [**0.5** km]. Turn right> onto asphalt road and then take the track up over the A-71 [**1.9** km] and immediately <left on far side onto track veering right> over canal [**0.8** km] which we follow to cross the N-120 [**!**] onto track where the alternative routes join at an ornate brick water tower and we turn <left and make our way onto a cobbled path for into the village of Puente de Órbigo (on *this* side of the river) with the parish church of Santa María (right). The significance of this village diminished in the 12th century when the Knights Hospitaller of St. John built a hospital on the far side of the river. We now cross the famous bridge puente de Órbigo [**0.9** km].

4.5 km **Puente de Órbigo** one of the longest and best preserved medieval bridges in Spain dating from the 13th century and built over an earlier Roman bridge which formed one of the great historical landmarks on the camino. Its myriad arches carry you across the Río Órbigo via the passage of honour *Paso Honroso* so called because of the famous jousting tournament that took place here in the Holy Year 1434. *A noble knight from León, Don Suero de Quiñones,*

scorned by a beautiful lady, threw down the gauntlet to any knight who dared to pass as he undertook to defend the bridge (and presumably his honour) against all comers. Knights from all over Europe took up the challenge. Don Suero successfully defended the bridge for a month until the required 300 lances had been broken. Together with his trusted comrades he then proceeded to Santiago to offer thanks for his freedom from the bonds of love and for his honour, now restored! Or, in the words of Rupert Brooke:

> Honour has come back, as a king, to earth
> And paid his subjects with a royal wage;
> And Nobleness walks in our ways again;
> And we have come into our heritage.

Apart from its link to such chivalrous acts, which may have been an inspiration for Cervantes *Don Quixote*, it also witnessed the battle in 452 when the Visigoths slaughtered the Swabians and subsequently provided the scene of confrontation between Christian forces under Alfonso III and the Moors. More productively it has facilitated trade since Roman times including the passage of livestock as part of the cattle trail *camino de la cañada* not to mention sweaty pilgrims like you and I! Pass over the bridge to the equally delightful village which, on the far side, becomes Hospital de Órbigo and a Knights Commandery of the ancient Order of St. John *Caballeros Hospitalarios de San Juan* who maintained a pilgrim hospital here.

A short detour north from the bridge is the municipal camping ground ● and woodland park and a new private albergue in a modern house on Avenida de

Suero de Quinoñes. •**Albergue** ❹ *La Encina* **Priv.[16÷4]** ✆ 987-361 087 with 16 bunk beds from €9 and double room €38. Continue past parish church *Iglesia de San Juan Bautista* up the main street *Álvarez Vega* to:

Hospital de Órbigo [0.4 km] •**Albergue** ❶ *Karl Leisner* **Par.[90÷10]** ✆ 987-388 444 parish hostel (photo right) on the main street with 90 beds €5 *in variety of dormitories.* All basic facilities in this historic building renovated by a German Confraternity yet retaining its antiquated charm around its central courtyard providing a convivial place to congregate. •**Albergue** ❷ *San Miguel*  **Asoc.*[40÷2]** ✆ 987-388 285 opposite parish hostel with good facilities in refurbished building that acts as an artists gallery and retains its period features with tranquil atmosphere €7. •**Albergue** ❸ *Verde* **Priv.[26÷2]** ✆ 689-927 926. New hostel close to the N-120 in Av. Fueros de León €9. ***Other acc:*** •**El Caminero** Jesus & Mayka Abad ✆ 987-389 020 popular upmarket B&B on c/ Sierra Pambley 56 just off (left) of the main street. Dinner bed and breakfast rate available in this finely restored 17[th]c town house. •**Don Suero de Quiñones** Hs[**] ✆ 987-388 238 great position on the bridge (you can't miss its gaudy neon sign) but you pay for its position! •**Paso Honroso** H ✆ 987-361 010 on the N-120. •**Lar la Puente** P ✆ 987-361 100 *before* you cross the bridge.

Alternative route via N-120 from Villadangos del Páramo
Leave albergue and turn up right through the old town and onto a tree-lined path that comes out on to the N-120 at a camping site. A track runs parallel to the N-120 for most of the way into:

4.7 km **San Martín del Camino** *Centro* all hostals are directly on the N-120: At the entrance: •**Albergue** ❶ *Vieira* **Priv.[60÷8]** ✆ 987-378 565. Modern hostel 60 beds from €3–5 all amenities including *menú peregrino* + •**Albergue** ❷ *Santa Ana* **Priv.[36÷3]**+ ✆ 987-378 653 another modern hostel (left) with 36 bunk-beds €4 + variety of private rooms. All facilities including garden rest area and diningroom serving meals. At the far end of town (right) under (literally) the water-tower is: •**Albergue** ❸ *San Martín* **Muni.[68÷2]** ✆ 616 354 331. Municipal hostel with 68 beds €5 in converted schoolhouse. All facilities and garden area also on the main road. Continue through the town and immediately past the Canal del Páramo turn off right> onto a shaded path lined with poplars that essentially runs parallel to the main road before turning right towards the distinctive water tower (see photo right) where recommended route [1] joins at the cross-tracks before heading into:

6.8 km **Puente de Órbigo** (see route [1] for details).

From the bridge continue over the canal de la Barbacana s/o past the church of St. John the Baptist and albergues in c/Álvarez Vega **[0.4 km]** s/o over the crossroads into c/ Camino de Jacobeo and up to the next crossroads **[0.5 km]**

0.9 km **Opción [?]** For **recommended route [1]** fork right> at the last house (with artesian well) and continue on a track into:

2.1 km Villares de Órbigo •Albergue *Villares Priv.[24÷4]* © 947-132 935. Private hostel with 24 beds at €6 in renovated house at the entrance to the village which has several bars and parish church dedicated to St. James with an image of *Santiago Matamoros*. We now enter onto a pleasant pathway that climbs gently passing rest area with [F] [0.6 km] to high point to join an asphalt road down across a small stream turning up right [1.9 km] to:

2.5 km Santibañez de Valdeiglesia •Albergue *Par.[20÷4]* © 626 362 159 just beyond •*bar Centro Social*. 20 beds in 4 rooms basic facilities, including orchard to the rear. Generally poorly maintained. The church of the Holy Trinity *Iglesia de la Trinidad* has images of San Roque peregrino and Santiago Matamoros.

Continue *up* out of the village through farmyard onto one of the most serene and naturally beautiful paths of the camino for a glorious 8.0 km. We first pass Cruz del Valle with seating area veering left and left again at cross of 5 tracks as we wind our way through woodland (mostly holm oak) through an isolated wetland area before climbing out of this gentle valley through scrubland into arable fields past a farm building •*Cantina* where shortly afterwards we cross an asphalt road and the alternative route joins from our left as we come to the prominent:

6.6 km Cruceiro Santo Toribio stone cross commemorating the 5th century Bishop Toribio of Astorga who supposedly fell to his knees here in a final farewell having been banished from the town. It is Astorga's *Monte Gozo* where we have a wonderful view over the town. Behind the city stand the Montes de León that we cross in the days ahead through the highest part of the whole journey at 1,515m (4,970 feet). Over to the left (southwest) is El Teleno a mountain sacred to the Roman god Mars at 2,185m (7,170 feet) while due north stands Peña Ubiña at 2,417m (7,930 feet) marking the eastern flank of the Cordilera Cantábrica – and behind (not visible) lie the Picos de Europa and Santo Toribio de Liébana where the good bishop is buried along with a fragment of the True Cross which he brought back from Jerusalem and a place of pilgrimage (not to be confused with Santo Toribio Alfonso Mogrovejo, a 15th century bishop also from this area who was an early missionary to South America). Just below the cross is a viewpoint with orientation map. When you have taken in the scale of the horizon, focus carefully on the ground immediately ahead as the path now drops steeply to pick up the asphalt road into:

1.4 km San Justo de la Vega *(Pop. 2,100)* an expanding residential satellite of Astorga with several bars, restaurants and •Hostal Juli HsR* © 987-617 632 on the main street.

Alternative route ❷ via N-120: at the option point by the last house in Hospital de Órbigo – continue s/o onto track which veers left to the N-120 [**1.5** km] from here a track runs parallel to the main road which undulates up and down the rolling countryside before turning off right> at the top of a rise [**7.4** km] and follow track to cruceiro and viewpoint [**1.0** km]:

9.9 km   **Cruceiro Santo Toribio** recommended route [1] joins from the right.

From San Justo de la Vega we continue out over the bridge and the *río Tuerto* and turn off right> [**0.8** km] to take a pleasant track that runs along the river valley past the side of a large factory crossing the Roman footbridge *Puente de la Moldería* [**1.5** km] up to the main road and over railway *pasarela* into the outer suburbs of Astorga and maze of bypass roads [**0.6** km] •**Albergue** *Camino y Via* **Priv.**[*22÷3*] private hostel located amongst the maze of bypass roads around the town. 22 beds €6. Continue s/o left on the roundabout [!] before climbing up steeply through the *Puerta del Sol* [**0.7** km] into:

3.6 km   **Astorga** *Plaza San Francisco* and •**Albergue ❶** *Siervas de María Asoc.* [*162÷16*]+ ✆ 987-616 034 municipal hostel administered by local pilgrim association on the left side of the square. 162 beds €5 in dormitories + individual rooms all with excellent modern facilities (*this hostel has replaced the previous barracks at the other end of town, now part of the police department.*

The fate of the other municipal hostel diagonally opposite is also uncertain but may provide additional accommodation). •**Albergue ❷** the original municipal hostel on the corner of the square adjoining the town park *Jardín de Sinagoga* with 36 beds and basic facilities. The other main hostel is situated at the other end of town close to the cathedral.
•**Albergue ❸** *St Javier Asoc.**[*95÷5*] ✆ 987-618 532 network* hostel associated with the Via de Plata which joins here in Astorga. Conveniently located close to the cathedral in c/Portería, 6. – 95 beds €8 (4 rooms + attic) and all facilities with extensive dining and lounge areas and small open yard. This is a lovely conversion of one of the historic buildings in the old quarter close to the main

sites in the town including hotel Gaudí with which it is also connected.

❏ *Hoteles Central:* •**La Peseta** Hsr** ✆ 987-617 275 Plaza San Bartolomé (and popular *Maragatería* restaurant). •**Pensión García** ✆ 987-616 046 c/Bajada Postigo. •**Astvr Plaza** H*** ✆ 987-618 900 Plaza Mayor. •**Casa de Tepa** H*** ✆ 987-603 299 Santiago,2. •**Gaudi** Hr*** ✆ 987-615 654 opposite Gaudí palace. ❏ *Outskirts*: •**Gallego** Hsr** ✆ 987-615 450) Av. Ponferrada and •**Coruña** ✆ 987-615 009. ❏ There are a variety of restaurants, bars and cafés – try some of the local cuisine *cocido maragato* which starts with a hearty meat stew, usually pork *and* black pudding with beans and cabbage followed by vegetables and finished off with a bowl of broth!

❑ *Turismo:* ✆ 987-618 222 Glorieta Eduardo Castro, 5 near the cathedral which provides a map showing the pilgrim route *Ruta Peregrino* and Roman route *Ruta Romana*. If you are just passing through the town and want to visit the main sites *or* for the most direct route to albergue [3] take the following 'tour' that takes in the main sites (see town plan) starting where we entered at the southern entrance *Puerta del Sol.*

❶ **Plaza San Francisco** with pilgrim hostels and lovely public gardens (fine views over the mountains), the Church of St. Francis of Assisi *Convento de San Francisco* (St. Francis allegedly came here on his pilgrimage to Santiago in 1212) and the adjoining Roman foundations (under a glass covering).

❷ **Plaza Bartolomé** where we find the *Iglesia San Bartolomé* and the *Ergástula* a Roman construction used down the ages as access tunnel, slave enclave, gaol and now a museum that also provides a short video (in Spanish) of life in Astorga during its Roman period.

❸ **Plaza Mayor** *España* and the graceful 17th century Baroque facade of the *Ayuntamiento* that houses one of the flags from the battle of Clavijo. Take a break in the square so that you can watch its ornate clock strike the hour as two mechanical figures (a man and a woman dressed in Maragato costume) strike the central bell. Before leaving this end of town there are a number of other Roman sites of interest. To the rear of the municipal library *biblioteca municipal*, situated off Synagogue Garden, are substantial remains of the original Roman walls and drains *murallas y cloachas Romanas* and the Roman baths *termas Romanos.*

❹ **Plaza Santocildes** identified by the handsome lion monument *monumento a los Sitios* in memory of the siege of Astorga during the Peninsular War. Continue out the far side of the square and on the left is c/Jose María where we find the *Museo del Chocolate*. Astorga was a main centre for the production of chocolate and the curator is a friend of the way and has been president of the local association.

❺ **Plaza Obispo Alcolea** here we another of the original entrances to the walled city – the King's Gate *Puerta de Rey* no longer visible but to one side of which we can admire the façade of the Casa Granell. We now head towards the jewels in Astorga's crown:

❻ **Plaza Catedral** where the sensational Gaudí building known as the Bishop's Palace *Palacio Episcopal* greets us, its neo-Gothic turrets soaring heavenwards. It houses no bishops but the splendid museum of the Ways *Museo de los Caminos* with historical notes and artefacts on the many Roman roads that converged on this city and provided the main trade, military and pilgrim routes through northern Spain. Don't miss the section on the *Caminos de Santiago* and the original Iron Cross *Cruz de Ferro* that once stood atop Monte Irago. Also in this area is the cell which housed the city's hookers *Celda de las Emparedadas*, the Turismo and the Iglesia de Santa Marta behind which is the splendid 15th century Gothic Cathedral standing majestically over the square, a wonderful blend of Romanesque, Gothic and later styles of architecture and a Renaissance altarpiece with a Romanesque statue of the Virgen de la Majestad after whom the cathedral is dedicated. Behind the cathedral are the Puerta Romana and a well-preserved stretch of the original Roman walls that acts as an open-air museum in its own right.

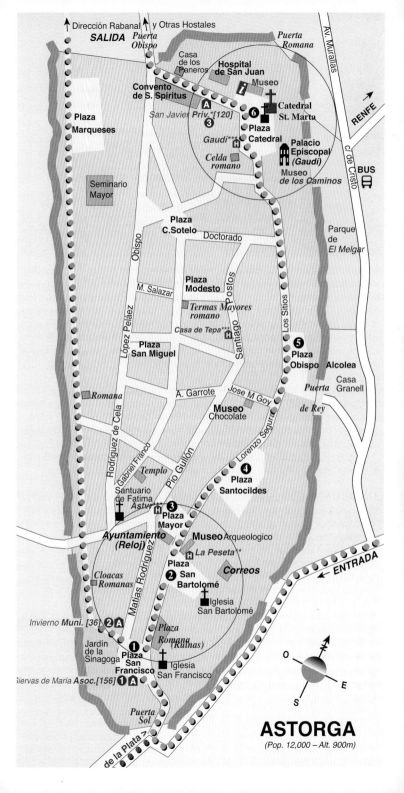

ASTORGA

(Pop. 12,000 – Alt. 900m)

Try and make time to visit the adjoining diocesan museum *Museo de Catedral* (a joint ticket will provide access to this and the Palacio Episcopal). This museum has a magnificent 15th century painting of the burial of St. James entitled 'The bridge of Life and Queen Lupa' *El puente de la Vida y la Reina Lupa* it shows the bulls pulling the sarcophagus of St. James and the bridge caving in by divine intervention, thus preventing the Roman soldiers from seizing the Apostle's disciples and their sacred cargo. There are many other depictions of pilgrimage and sacred art and artefacts sensitively displayed.

Adjoining the cathedral museum is the ancient Hospital de San Juan in which St. Francis reputedly stayed on his way to Santiago and further on the extensive monastery buildings of the Holy Spirit *Convento de Sancti Spiritus*. If you are heading on towards Rabanal turn right> and make your way out through Bishop's Gate *Puerta Obispo* into c/San Pedro and over the busy N-VI Madrid to La Coruña road. Alternatively, if you are staying the night then head towards your preferred hostel or the bars and restaurants around the many lively *plazas*.

ASTORGA *Asturica Augusta (pop: 12,000 – alt. 870 m)*. An attractive city (more akin to a lively market town) set atop a steep ridge with a wide range of shops and general facilities and an interesting array of historic buildings all tightly packed within its medieval walls. Originally a powerful Asturian community it became an equally important Roman city on account of its prominent position at the junction of several major routes. This is where the French Way *Camino Francés* (part of the Via Trajana linking this area with Bordeaux) and the Roman Road *Calzada Romana* (otherwise known as the Via Aquitana) joined the Roman Silver route *Vía de La Plata* (otherwise known as the *Camino Mozarabe*) from Sevilla and the south. This convergence of routes gave rise to over 20 pilgrim hospitals in medieval times. George Borrow, visiting Astorga in 1840, wrote 'Almost the entire commerce of nearly one-half of Spain passes through the hands of The Maragato whose fidelity to their trust is such that no one accustomed to employ them would hesitate to confide to them the transport of a ton of treasure from the sea of Biscay to Madrid'. As if this wasn't enough activity Astorga also acted as a crossroads for the royal drove roads *Cañadas Reales* that herded livestock up and down the Iberian peninsular. This European-wide system of nomadic grazing is known as transhumance and can still be witnessed on various caminos and is celebrated in Astorga (along with many other towns) in the festival *Fiesta de Transhumancia* when sheep are driven through the town.

Next we enter the *Maragatería* and the *montes de León*. Here, between Astorga and Molinaseca, we experience the remnants of Maragato culture in the distinctive dress and cuisine of this mountainous region. The cakes and pastries *mantecadas* are worth sampling and the hills provide game and trout from the streams. The obscure origins of the Maragatos may date back to the 7th century when King Mauregato and the Visigoths became isolated in this remote area during the Arab invasions. Today the isolationism continues in the abandoned villages of the mountains, such as Foncebadón.

Astorga is also sometimes referred to as the 'capital' of the Maragatería but the Maragatos themselves defy classification. Some suggest they are descended from the Berber tribes who came to Spain as part of the Moorish invasion in the 8th century becoming 'misplaced' in this remote mountainous region. Others link them to the Visigoths and their king Mauregato. The name may derive from captive Moors *Mauri captus* forced to work the mines in the area. Most agree they were muleteers and their number has dwindled to 4,000 spread around 40 villages in the area. Martin Martinez, president of the Maragato Cultural Society, in a recent Telegraph interview stated simply, 'We are trying to recuperate some of our traditions before it is too late. By celebrating our traditional games and weddings in our way we hope to keep it alive.' It is the same story we will hear in the Bierzo and Galicia. The mystery of the Maragatos may never be penetrated but we can experience the hospitality found amongst the villages that line the path ahead.

REFLECTIONS:

❐ **Distrust yourself and sleep before you fight.**
T'is not too late tomorrow to be brave. *John Armstrong*

23 264.1 km (164.1 miles) to Santiago

ASTORGA – RABANAL DEL CAMINO

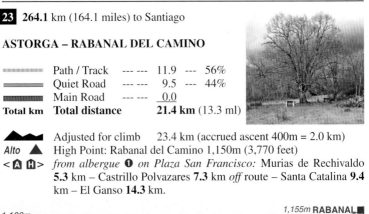

	Path / Track	--- ---	11.9	---	56%
	Quiet Road	--- ---	9.5	---	44%
	Main Road	--- ---	0.0		
Total km	**Total distance**		**21.4 km** (13.3 ml)		

Adjusted for climb   23.4 km (accrued ascent 400m = 2.0 km)
Alto ▲   High Point: Rabanal del Camino 1,150m (3,770 feet)
<❐ ❐> *from albergue* ❶ *on Plaza San Francisco:* Murias de Rechivaldo
5.3 km – Castrillo Polvazares **7.3** km *off* route – Santa Catalina **9.4**
km – El Ganso **14.3** km.

The Practical Path: Today we head towards the mountains and tomorrow we
climb to the highest point of the entire route. Rabanal can feed you, but it won't
clothe you for the mountain weather, which can be unpredictable at the best
of times. Astorga is the last opportunity to kit-out before the ascent. However,
there are several small villages on today's stretch where you can buy food and
refreshments, many bearing the suffix *somoza* from the Latin *sub montia* or
under the mountain. This should be a relatively gentle day and the promise of a
good nights rest in Rabanal to prepare you for the climb the following day.

❐ **The Mystical Path:** Where are the mountains of the soul? How high do you
need to climb to reach the top and what will you find there? How well are you
equipped and what do you need to take and, perhaps more importantly, leave
behind? Rest awhile and pause for reflection before attempting to meet the
guardian of the threshold. Tomorrow is time enough to climb towards another
peak in your journey. What gift will you deposit at the top so that you can
continue on, unburdened by the dross in your life?

❐ **Personal Reflections:** *"... The wind howled against the window as I warmed
myself by the log fire. It was the constant squeaking of the bookcase that eventually
roused me to quieten it and an old and faded document fell out from behind. It
appeared to have been hidden and was entitled* The Third Secret of Fátima – The
Collapse of the Roman Catholic Church. *The more I read, the deeper I became
aware of the awesome impact that this document, true or false, would have on the
future of the Church. Recent press revelations of scandals reaching at the very
heart of the hierarchy made its predictions utterly clear. The irrational fear I felt
was compounded when I read that the person who had professed to having seen
the original letter had died in mysterious circumstances. I hid the document back
where I found it, pondering on both the risk of collapse and the opportunities for
renewal that the fulfilment of such a prophesy would entail..."*

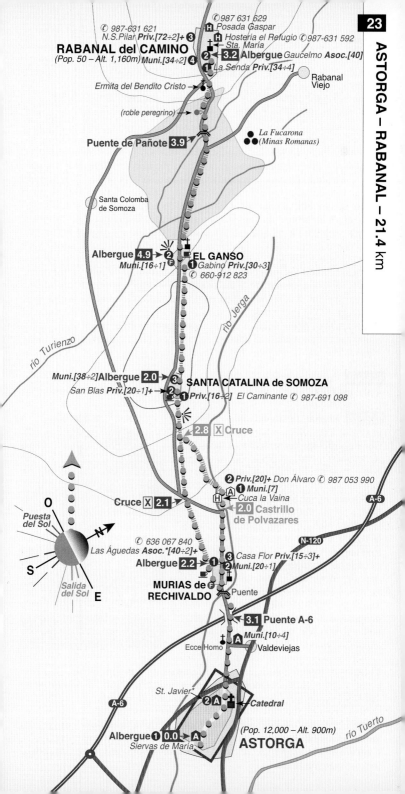

© 987 631 629
Posada Gaspar
Hostería el Refugio © 987-631 592
Sta. María

© 987-631 621
N.S.Pilar **Priv.**[72÷2]+ **3**
RABANAL del CAMINO
(Pop. 50 – Alt. 1,160m) **Muni.**[34÷2] **4**

3.2 **Albergue** Gaucelmo **Asoc.**[40]

1 La Senda **Priv.**[34÷4]

Rabanal
Viejo

Ermita del Bendito Cristo →

(roble peregrino) →

La Fucarona
(Minas Romanas)

Puente de Pañote **3.9**

Santa Colomba
de Somoza

río Turienzo

Albergue **4.9** → **2**
Muni.[16÷1]

EL GANSO
1 Gabino **Priv.**[30÷3]
© 660-912 823

río Jerga

Muni.[38÷2]**Albergue** **2.0** → **3**
San Blas **Priv.**[20÷1]+ → **2**

SANTA CATALINA de SOMOZA
1 **Priv.**[16÷2] El Caminante © 987-691 098

2.8 X Cruce

2 **Priv.**[20]+ Don Álvaro © 987 053 990

Cruce X **2.1**

1 **Muni.**[7]
Cuca la Vaina

2.0 Castrillo
de Polvazares

A-6

N-120

© 636 067 840
Las Águedas **Asoc.***[40÷2]+
Albergue **2.2** → **1**

3 Casa Flor **Priv.**[15÷3]+
2 **Muni.**[20÷1]

O
Puesta
del Sol

N

S

Salida
del Sol E

**MURIAS de
RECHIVALDO**

Puente

3.1 Puente A-6

Ecce Homo

† **A** **Muni.**[10÷4]

Valdeviejas

A-6

St. Javier*

2 **A** †
Catedral

(Pop. 12,000 – Alt. 900m)
ASTORGA

río Tuerto

Albergue **1** **0.0** → **A**
Siervas de María

0.0 km **Astorga** from albergue ❶ in Plaza San Francisco follow the waymarks past the cathedral **[0.8 km]** and turn <left opposite the west door and out through the Puerta Obispo into Barrio de Rectiva thence c/San Pedro and past the modern church of the same name across the N-VI (Madrid – A Coruña) at busy crossroads (shops and cafés) signposted to Santa Colomba de Somoza straight ahead.

Note: Astorga was a major crossroads since Roman times and the connecting point for the route from Sevilla and the south usually referred to as the Silver Route *Via de la Plata* although scholars suggest 'plata' is a corruption of the Arabic word for wide *not* silver. Semantics aside, we travel the next few days over mountain terrain that produced gold, silver and other valuable ores from the mines between here and Ponferrada (Las Médulas). Here also medieval pilgrims would have to choose between the shorter but steeper route through Rabanal and Puerto Irago (1,505m) or the more circuitous but less steep Puerto Manzanal (1,225m) which today is where the N-VI and A-6 autopista and rail line cut through the Montes de León to connect Ponferrada and Astorga. The medieval writer König von Vach stated, "I advise that you avoid Rabanal at all costs." Today we can ignore such advice as Rabanal has since earned the reputation as one of the most authentic and welcoming villages along the entire camino so we can continue confidently but cautiously (several pilgrims have been killed on these very roads in recent years and a cross on our right marks one such spot) for the next **[2.3 km]** to the medieval hermitage *Ecce Homo* remnant of a former pilgrim hospice. Opposite the chapel is the road to Valdeviejas and adjacent is municipal hostel •**Albergue** *Ecce Homo Muni.[10÷4]* © 620-960 060. 10 beds €5. Continue s/o to:

3.1 km **Autopista flyover** we now enter onto a dedicated pilgrim track parallel to the road to cross over the río Jerga and pick up a grass track <left into:

2.2 km **Murias de Rechivaldo** •**Albergue** ❶ *las Águedas Priv.[40÷2]+* © 636 067 840 private hostel the last building on the right as we leave town. 40 beds €8 + priv. rooms from €35. Open all year and all meals available. Centred around a delightful courtyard in this traditional village house.

•**Albergue** ❷ *La Escuela Muni.[20÷1]* © 987-691 150 municipal hostel located on the main road adj. a picnic site. 20 beds €4 and all basic facilities in a former school building. On the opposite of the road is albergue ❸ *Casa Flor Priv.[15÷3]+* © 609-478 323 offering *cocido Maragato* and B&B with 15 beds €10. *Other accommodation:* •**La Valeta** © 616 598 133 on Plaza Mayor in the centre. *[Next albergue: Santa Catalina – 5.7 km].*

Albergue ❶ *Las Águedas (top)*
Albergue ❷ *Municipal (below)*

Murias de Rechivaldo is a typical Maragato village with interesting rustic parish Church of St. Stephen *San Esteban* and several bars, restaurant, shop and [F].

Option [?] Route [1] directly to *Santa Catalina* via earth track (4.3 km) or take the alternative route [2] via the local road to the classic Maragato village of *Castrillo de Polvazares* (declared a national monument) and thence via path to join the main route (5.7 km).

For alternative route [2] pick up the minor road by albergue [2] and turn <left (LE-142 to Santa Columba) straight to the village visible ahead:

2.0 km **Castrillo de Polvazares** traditional Maragato village with cobbled main street lined with stone buildings providing tourist rooms, bars and restaurants. Painstakingly rebuilt by local artisans it lacks the authentic ambience found in the crumbling villages spread along the camino itself. At least the tourist buses are kept at the entrance car park. The village is brought to life by the novelist Concha Espina who depicted life in Castrillo

Castrillo de Polvazares

in her novel The Maragato Sphinx *La Esfinge Maragata*. **Albergue ❶** *Muni. [7]* ✆ 655-803 706. New hostel on c/ del Jardín with 7 beds €3. **Albergue ❷** *Don Álvaro Priv.[20÷2]+* ✆ 987 053 990 with 20 beds €8 + priv. rooms. •**Hostería Cuca La Vaina** ✆ 987-691 034. Proceed the **[0.7 km]** through the village veering left at the central cross to pick up the camino over small stream and start the **[1.9 km]** climb up to re-join the asphalt road above you:

2.8 km **Cruce** to join the recommended route for the remaining **[1.1 km]** into Santa Catalina.

For recommended route [1] via a wide earth track, continue past the pilgrim fountain [F] and café (left) and albergue (right) onto the track that runs in a straight line alongside the overhead power cables to:

2.1 km **Cruce** cross the minor road (Castrillo de Polvazares right) and pick up the pilgrim track that runs parallel to the old asphalt road to enter:

2.0 km **Santa Catalina Albergue ❶** *El Caminante Priv.[16÷2]* ✆ 987-691 098 private hostel open all year with 16 beds €6 + priv. rooms also café/bar and patio. Just beyond is: **Albergue ❷** *Hospedería San Blas Priv.[20÷1]+* ✆ 987-691 411 with 20 beds €5 + ind. rooms. Café/bar serving meals. Further down the main street, just past bar •*Camino Real* through an opening (left) in the stone wall we find **Albergue ❸** *municipal Muni.[38÷2]* ✆ 987-691 819 the original municipal pilgrim hostel on c/ La Escuela with 38 beds and basic facilities (no kitchen) but pleasant building in quiet location, now generally bypassed by the commercial opportunities on c/Real itself. *[Next albergue: El Ganso – 4.6 km].*

Albergue ❸ *Municipal*

Santa Catalina is another village typical of the region in both its layout and population now reduced to a mere 50 persons – in bygone days it supported a pilgrim hospital. The parish church houses a relic of San Blas after whom the church and albergue are named. Continue through the village and back out onto the minor road and a track parallel that escorts us into:

4.9 km **El Ganso** a hauntingly crumbling village, evoking a sense of loss or, perhaps, a reminder of a less hurried time. In the 12th century it boasted a monastery and a pilgrim hospital. El Ganso is the first of several semi-abandoned Maragato villages that we pass through in the relatively solitary mountains.

However, amidst the collapsing thatch cottages are some signs of new life, such as the Cowboy Bar adding to the incongruity of the modern *sendas* by which you arrive and leave this enchanting piece of history. There is a Parish church dedicated to St. James with a statue of Santiago Peregrino and the Capilla de Cristo de los Peregrinos. If the opportunity arises to meet the locals, don't pass it by! (with side entrance to Bar la Barraca) and the latest hostel •**Albergue ❶** *Gabino Priv.[30÷3]* ⓒ 660-912 823 private hostel on c/Real 30 beds €8 incl. with all facilities. 300m *off* route is •**Albergue ❷** *La Escuela Muni.[16÷1]* ⓒ 987-691 088 part of the village health centre and converted from the school and located on the left (southern) outskirts at the end of c/las Eras beside [F]. 16 beds and basic facilities only but clean and what it lacks in creature comforts it makes up for in the splendid view across the wide valley to the peaks of Monte El Teleno, often capped with snow. *[Next albergue: Rabanal – 6.9 km].*

From here all the way to the top at the Cruz de Ferro true 'Friends of the Way' have recently forged tracks either side of the LE-142. This road is heavily undulating with many blind spots so take care and do take every opportunity to use the natural pathways on either side. Here again we find many pilgrims, heads bent to the incline, staying on the narrow asphalt road – several accidents have been reported in recent years so don't let fatigue rob you of focus. Ignore signs to Rabanal Viejo and the Gold route *Ruta de Oro* (unless you want to visit the *site* of the original Roman gold mines 1.5 km up on your right, the *Minas de La Fucarona*. Continue straight on through this tranquil valley to the

3.9 km **Puente de Pañote** a modest bridge carries you over the arroyo Rabanal de Viejo a good place to refresh ourselves in its cool mountain waters before continuing the steeper ascent through mixed native woodland, holm oak e*ncina*, oak *roble* and pine *pino* past the specimen 'pilgrim oak' which now has a bench seat so you can rest in the shade of its branches (the leafy season is very short up at this altitude). Just before entering Rabanal we pass *Ermita del Bendito Cristo de la Vera Cruz XVIII[th]C* (left) and veer right> off the road into c/Real the typical paved main street of Rabanal del Camino and •**Albergue ❶** *La Senda (formerly El Tesin) Priv.[34÷4]* ⓒ 650-952 721 private hostel in converted traditional stone house (left) as we enter. 34 beds from €5+. Café/bar and shop. Continue up the steeply past *Capilla de San José XVIII[th]C* (right) with entrance porch enabling viewing of the ornate retablo with image of Santiago Peregrino and up past small shop into the main village square:

3.2 km **Rabanal del Camino** *Centro* Iglesia de la Santa María *XII[th]C* Romanesque parish church occupying the tiny central square with •**Albergue ❷** *Gaucelmo Asoc.[46÷2]* ⓒ 987-631 647 administered by the London based Confraternity of St. James and the Bierzo association. 46 beds € *donativo* (pilgrims with back-up support not admitted). the extensive facilities include a small library, courtyard and orchard area. Sensitively restored and exceptionally well maintained. Breakfast is

Albergue ❷ *Gaucelmo*

provided. •**Albergue ❸** *N.S del Pilar Priv.[72÷2]*+ ⓒ 987-631 621 located down on the main road in plaza Gerónimo Morán Alonso. 72 beds €5 in 2 large dormitories + ind. rooms from €35. Facilities including lively bar with tables around a central courtyard. Adjacent, also fronting the main road •**Albergue ❹** *Muni.[34÷2]* ⓒ 987-631 687 municipal hostel with 34 beds (incl. mattresses) €4 + picnic BBQ area adjoining the road. *[Next albergue: Manjarín 10.0 km].*

Other accommodation •**Hostal el Refugio** Hs ✆ 987-631 592 centrally located adjoining the church with popular bar and restaurant (pilgrim menu). and rooms from €35 ind. Further up the street is the more exclusive •**La Posada de Gaspar** ✆ 987-631 629 located at the top end of the village in a renovated 17th century former pilgrim hospital.

Rabanal del Camino continues a centuries old tradition of caring for the pilgrims before they take the steep path up and over Monte Irago. This was the IXth stage of Aymeric Picaud's classic itinerary and the Knights Templar are thought to have had a presence here as early as the 12th century ensuring the safe passage of pilgrims over this remote mountain terrain – the parish Church of Santa María was reputedly built by them. Today an order of monks originating from Bavaria have again (following earlier local concerns) taken up residence in a building on the square and the church, now restored, is once again resounding to the sound of Gregorian chant with Vespers at 19:00 and Compline 21:30 and pilgrim blessing offered by the Benedictine missionary monks of the monastery of *San Salvador del Monte Irago* established here in 2001 and affiliated to the Abbey church of St. Ottilien based in Austria. They have an adjoining retreat house for up to 10 pilgrims who wish to stay for a min of 2 nights.

REFLECTIONS:

❏ **On all the peaks lies peace.** *Goethe*

24 **242.7** km (150.8 miles) to Santiago

RABANAL DEL CAMINO – MOLINASECA

	Path / Track	--- ---	13.6	---	51%
	Quiet Road	--- ---	12.5	---	47%
	Main Road	--- ---	0.4	---	2%
Total km	**Total distance**		**26.5 km** (16.4 ml)		

Adjusted for climb   29.5 km (accrued ascent 600m = 3.0 km)

Alto ▲   High Point: La Cruz de Ferro 1,505m (4,940 feet)

< 🅰 🏠 >   Foncebadón **5.8** km – Manjarín **10.0** km – El Acebo **17.0** km – Riego de Ambros **20.8** km.

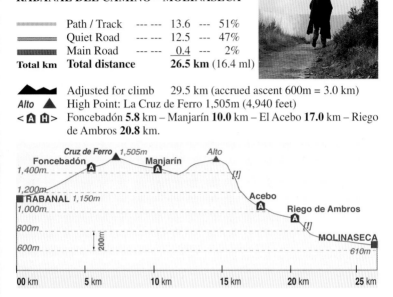

The Practical Path: Today we head up through the pass of Irago to the highest point of our whole journey. While the ascent is steep in places and will require your determination and physical exertion remember that far more injuries (sprains, strains and breaks) are experienced going *down*hill. Many pilgrims stick to the asphalt road which has many blind spots and is therefore dangerous. Use the new track that runs roughly parallel to the road effectively making the majority of this stage a safer natural pathway. When pausing to rest or meditate, remember that body sweat will turn cold quickly at this altitude as soon as physical exertion stops – so find a sheltered spot out of the mountain breeze and dress warmly. There are several drinking fonts **[F]** along the way and the mountain villages are coming to life again supporting pilgrims with hostels and cafés but it is sensible to take some snacks and we need to fill our water bottles before leaving Rabanal.

❏ **The Mystical Path:** For many, today is a peak experience. How allusive to the rational mind is that peace that passes all understanding. What does an altered state mean to you? Words cannot convey the experience of a unified perspective, beyond the duality offered by the physical eyes. How long yet will we allow the sense-perceptible world to limit our perception and keep us imprisoned in our separate state? Will we allow our Self soar to new heights today and sense the super-sensible, beyond space, beyond time?

❏ **Personal Reflections:** *"... How my spirit soars in high places, connecting me to that place within me that touches God. My perspective shifts and I get an expanded sense of Self. This giant chestnut supports my back as I write these notes, shading me from the afternoon sun. I feel peaceful in its giant embrace and welcomed through the connection from previous visits and blessed by its unyielding yet undemanding presence. Strong yet silent but for the gentle rustle the your leaves ..."*

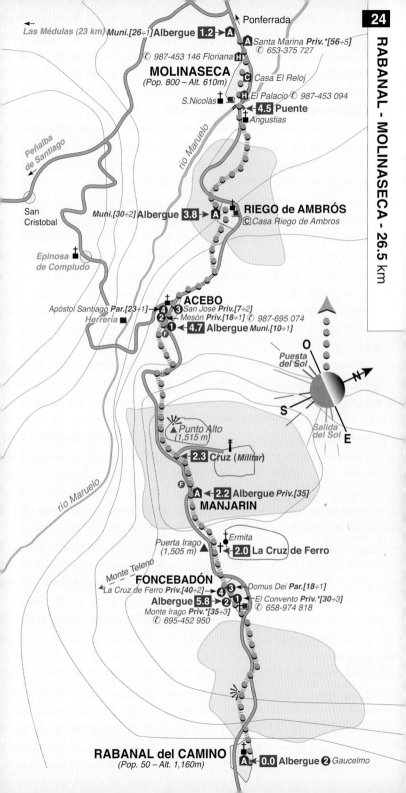

← Las Médulas (23 km) *Muni.[26÷1]* **Albergue** 1.2 → A

↑ Ponferrada

A *Santa Marina* **Priv.***[56÷5]*
© 653-375 727

© 987-453 146 *Floriana* H

MOLINASECA
(Pop. 800 – Alt. 610m)

C *Casa El Reloj*

H *El Palacio* © 987-453 094

S.Nicolás ✝ 4.5 **Puente**

Angustias

río Maruelo

Peñalba de Santiago

San Cristobal

Epinosa de Compludo ✝

Muni.[30÷2] **Albergue** 3.8 → A

✝ **RIEGO de AMBRÓS**
© *Casa Riego de Ambros*

Apóstol Santiago **Par.***[23÷1]* ✝ 4 **ACEBO**
3 *San José* **Priv.***[7÷2]*
2 *Mesón* **Priv.***[18÷1]* © 987-695 074
Herreria ■ 1 4.7 **Albergue** *Muni.[10÷1]*
F

O
Puesta del Sol

N

▲ *Punto Alto*
(1,515 m)

✝ 2.3 **Cruz** *(Militar)*

S

Salida del Sol

E

F
A 2.2 **Albergue** *Priv.[35]*
MANJARIN

río Maruelo

Puerta Irago ▲ ✝ *Ermita*
(1,505 m) 2.0 **La Cruz** de Ferro

Monte Teleno

FONCEBADÓN
← *La Cruz de Ferro* **Priv.***[40÷2]* 3 *Domus Dei* **Par.***[18÷1]*
Albergue 5.8 → 2 1 *El Convento* **Priv.***[30÷3]*
Monte Irago **Priv.***[35÷3]* © 658-974 818
© 695-452 950

RABANAL del CAMINO
(Pop. 50 – Alt. 1,160m) A ← 0.0 **Albergue** ❷ *Gaucelmo*

0.0 km **Rabanal** from albergue ❷ *Gaucelmo* proceed up through the village onto a rough track at the far end that criss-crosses the asphalt road with spectacular views across the río Turienzo valley towards Monte El Teleno all the way up until we reach a camino signboard and turn off <left into:

5.8 km **Foncebadón** •**Albergue** ❶ *Convento de Foncebadón* **Priv.[30÷3]** Ⓒ 658-974 818 with 30 beds €7 and bar with restaurant. •**Albergue*** ❷ *Monte Irago* **Priv.[35÷3]** Ⓒ 695-452 950 network* hostel open all year with 35 beds €6 all facilities incl. vegetarian menu. •**Albergue** ❸ *Domus Dei* **Par.[18÷1]** Basic parish hostel in renovated church in the village centre. 18 mattresses € *Donativo* communal breakfast. •**Albergue** ❹ *La Cruz de Ferro* **Priv.[40÷2]** Ⓒ 665-258 169. Newest hostel (re-opens 2012) with 40 beds €7.

Albergue ❸ *Domus Dei*

This semi-abandoned village is now stirring back to life with the reawakening of the camino. It was home of the 12th century hermit Gaucelmo who built a church and simple pilgrim hospital here. A stark wooden cross adds a haunting beauty to this isolated mountain hamlet. During the last few years several of the abandoned houses have been undergoing renovation together with its 'main' street including •*La Taberna de Gaia* with its adjoining *palloza* adjacent to the hostal Convento on the main road. We continue out the top end of the village onto a muddy track (mountain springs) to re-join the road and make our way up through the mountain gorse and heather to *the doorway through the mountain* and its memorable cross that opens up to guide us, as it has for countless millions of other pilgrims over many centuries.

2.0 km **Puerto Irago / Cruz de Ferro** such a humble monument to mark such a noble gateway. This majestic spot stands 1,504m (4,934) above sea level and a simple iron cross stands atop its weathered pole that has become one of the abiding symbols of the pilgrim way of St. James. Pause awhile to reconnect with the purpose of your journey before adding your stone or other token of love and blessing to the great pile that witnesses to our collective journeying. A modern stone chapel *Ermita de Santiago* built to commemorate an earlier Holy Year, remains locked but a grander chapel surrounds us that will remain forever open and welcoming. A track continues parallel to the road to:

Cruz de Ferro

2.2 km **Manjarín** •**Albergue** **Priv.[35]** private hostel open all year with 35 places (mattresses) € *donativo* and very basic facilities which includes an outside toilet and water from a well on the other side of road. The simple facilities are being organically developed along ecological lines with a solar panel providing (some) hot water while an open fire provides the smoky space heater. A simple communal meal is offered for those staying the night in this mountain sanctuary. *[Next albergue: Acebo – 7.0 km].* This is another 'abandoned' village brought vividly to life by the modern knight *hospitalero Tomás* who now gives the village an official resident population of 1 and has renovated one of the abandoned houses (a pilgrim's hospital existed here as early as the 12th century linking it to the Knights Templar). You may have arrived in time for the Temple ritual of blessing the new day and all pilgrims on the path. Perhaps Gregorian chant (from a well-worn tape out of the Cluny sanctuary of Taizé) will call you to stop or maybe the inviting aroma of coffee is your cue to visit this little mountain refuge. The atmospheric surroundings are enhanced by a virtually constant mountain mist. Continue by road below the communication mast and military base that watches over our every step. A threatening image to some and to others an encouraging sign of habitation and potential support in the lonely mountains.

2.3 km **Cruce Militar** continue past the turn off to this mountain top observation post to another high point on the path at 1,515m. (4,970) *[or you can have a peak experience by taking the wide track straight on (right) to climb to the cairn at 1,535m (5,036 feet!) and soak in the panorama, weather permitting and continue down the*

track to join the waymarked route below]. The sprawling suburbs of Ponferrada are still an insignificant blot on the landscape ahead towards the western horizon. The path now descends sharply [!]. Don't miss the path through a narrow gorge right> (it relieves some of the road work and a hairpin bend) shortly afterwards you cross the road and descend (very sharply) [!] to the *Fuente de la Trucha* [F] before entering:

4.7 km **Acebo** •**Albergue** ❶ *Elisardo Panizo Muni.[10÷1]* basic municipal hostel, first building (right) as we enter the village. 10 beds in one room, shower and toilet make up the limited facilities – key with next albergue. •**Albergue** ❷ *Mesón El Acebo Priv.[18÷1]*+ © 987-695 074 private hostel (left) on main street *c/Real.* 18 beds €5 + priv. rooms. Bar with pilgrim menu and open terrace to the rear. When full they open the former private hostel of José ❸ •*Taberna de José Priv.[7÷2]* at the lower end of the village (right) with 7 beds €5 and basic facilities. •**Albergue** ❹ *Apóstol Santiago Par.[23÷1]* © adjacent to the parish church (left off the main street) in a renovated stone building with 23 beds € *donativo* incl. communal meals and evening prayers. *[Next albergue: Riego de Ambrós– 3.6 km].*

Albergue ❹ *San Miguel*

Acebo is a typical mountain village of the region with one principal street running down the middle and an open surface drain as a token gesture to channel the rain that frequently overflows it. The parish Church of San Miguel has a statue of Santiago Peregrino and is located at the far end (left). *Casa rurales:* just below albergue [1] •**La Posada del Peregrino** © 987-057 875 •**La Rosa del Agua** © 616-849738 •**La Trucha** © 987-695 548 •**La Casa del Monte Irago** © 639-721 242. In plaza Pena by the church is a small shop •*Tienda Casa Josefina* and a good picnic spot. On the way out of the village we pass a modern sculpture of a bicycle outside the village cemetery **[0.5 km]** memorial to another pilgrim killed on the roads here and an opportunity for several detours by quiet country roads (signposted but not waymarked) as follows:

Detour [1] Herrería immediately beyond the cemetery is a turn off for the medieval iron foundry of Herrería **[2.0** km] 'hidden' in the steep valley floor. One of the oldest forges still in use with a millrace providing power to its heavy machinery. A delightful and peaceful tree-lined glade alongside the river brings you to this historic site. Note: The 4 km round trip is equivalent to twice that on account of the very steep descent and ascent – only contemplate it if you plan staying in El Acebo or the next village. **Detour [2] Compludo [3.5** km] (2 km beyond Herrería) is the birthplace of monasticism in this region with the founding of a monastery here in the 7th century by San Fructuoso. This is a strenuous 7 km round trip by quiet road from El Acebo. This was one of the routes followed by pilgrims to the Valley of Silence and was protected by the Knights Templars and the Monastery of Compludo (no longer evident). There are a number of *casa rurales* in Espinoso de Compludo •**Las Cuatro Estaciones** ℂ 987-970 092 from €50 single. The beautiful valley of silence *Valle del Silencio* and Peñalba de Santiago is a further 19 km beyond Compludo *uphill* by asphalt road. You need to be fit and in need of space and silence to contemplate this detour to the hilltop monastic settlement founded by San Genadio in the 10th century on these white crags *peñalba*, which are often covered in snow. Only the church with its Mozarabic double horseshoe arch remains (a national monument) but the lasting legacy is the mountain scenery and silence now under threat by tourist parties coming from Ponferrada 27 km away and the easiest access route by taxi or bus.

Continue along asphalt road veering off <left **[1.8** km] onto a path that winds down for **[1.5** km] into:

3.8 km Riego de Ambros •**Albergue** *Muni.* *[30÷2]* ℂ 987-695 190 municipal hostel just below the chapel of San Sebastián as we enter this pretty village. 30 beds €5 in cubicles of 4 (+mattresses). Good facilities with small patio in this bright and spacious building. This is another attractive mountain village with the traditional overhanging balconies.

Due to the relative proximity of Ponferrada and a distinctly warmer climate at this lower altitude, almost all the previously abandoned houses have been renovated for residential use (including, unfortunately, the former bar in the delightful village centre). However, a friendly bar and restaurant with pilgrim menu can be found on the main road up right from the centre of the village opposite the parish Church of Santa María Magdalena which has a beautiful early 18th century altarpiece. •*Restaurante Ruta de Santiago* ℂ 987-418 151 200m *off* route. Also •**Casa del Horno** ℂ 687 932 699 and back on the main road is pension •**Riego de Ambros** ℂ 987-695 188. Make your way down the main street veering left in the centre (restaurant straight on) and veer off right down a steep rock defile [!] (very slippery when wet) onto a beautiful path past a magical grove of giant sweet chestnut trees *castañas* some of which have recently been torched.

> Up the airy mountain,
> Down the rushy glen,
> We daren't go a hunting,
> For fear of little men.

William Allingham

We now make our way up and over the road to continue down this breathtakingly beautiful valley to re-join the road just above Molinaseca, passing the *Iglesia de las Angustias* built up against the steep cliffs to cross:

4.5 km Molinaseca *Puente de Peregrinos* handsome medieval bridge carries us over the río Meruelo into the delightful and historical village of Molinaseca. The 17th century Church of San Nicolás (with statue of San Roque) stands atop a rise to the left while the original camino continues along c/Real. The house at the junction of c/Torre is reputedly that of Doña Urraca, later Queen of Castilla y León, which provides some idea of the exclusivity attached to this genteel area that today provides a range of bars and restaurants to suit all tastes and pockets. Accommodation in this tranquil quarter includes: •**El Palacio** HsR[**] © 987-453 094 by the bridge and •**La Posada de Muriel** H[**] © 987-453 201 on Plaza del Cristo (Michelin recommended). Several *casa rurales* around c/Real including •**Paquita** © 987-453 037 and •**El Reloj** © 987-453 124 and further out on the main road is the modern •**Floriana** © 987-453 146 with rooms from €50.

1.2 km Molinaseca •**Albergue*** ❶ *Santa Marina* **Priv.[56÷5]** © 987-453 077 private network* hostel with 56 beds €7 in spacious dormitories and good modern facilities (no kitchen) dinner and breakfast available and an outside terrace. •**Albergue** ❷ *San Roque* **Priv.[26÷1]** municipal hostel open all year © 987-453 077 on the main road as you leave town. 26 beds €5 + 40 mattresses in the summer and all facilities with adjoining field

Albergue ❶ *Santa Marina*

for camping. Imaginative conversion of the former chapel of San Roque and while directly on the main road, passing traffic is minimal. *[Next albergue: Ponferrada – 6.9 km].*

REFLECTIONS:

_____

_____

_____

_____

_____

_____

_____

_____

❏ **In hoc signo vinces** *In this sign thou shall conquer.* Knights Templar

---

25 **216.2** km (134.3 miles) to Santiago

MOLINASECA – VILLAFRANCA DEL BIERZO

(via PONFERRADA)

▦▦▦▦	Path / Track	--- ---	12.4	--- 40%
▬▬▬	Quiet Road	--- ---	14.4	--- 47%
▦▦▦	Main Road	--- ---	4.1	--- 13%
Total km	**Total distance**		**30.9 km**	**(19.2 ml)**

◣◣◣ Adjusted for climb   31.9 km (accrued ascent 200m = 1.0 km)
Alto ▲   High Point: Alto Villafranca (albergue) c. 550m (1,805 feet)
<**A** **H**>   Ponferrada **7.5** km – Cacabelos **23.0** – Pieros **24.7** – Valtuille de Arriba **26.6** km.

MOLINASECA   *Alto*
600m   PONFERRADA   605m ▲
           ▲   Camponaraya   Cacabelos   **VILLAFRANCA** ■
500m   Río Boeza   Río Sil   **A** **A** Pieros — 570m
400m   Río Cúa

00 km   5 km   10 km   15 km   20 km   25 km   30 km

The Practical Path: There are several options to avoid the worst of the busy road network around Ponferrada. And while this stage involves some road walking as we pass through the city, there are many cafés and bars to refresh us along the way. Remember also that waymarks through the city and its suburbs have to compete with the consumer culture and its advertising signs so extra vigilance is required. And we also have the beautiful *Bierzo* to look forward to with its sheltered microclimate and vineyards.

In order to make sense of the road layout into and out of Ponferrada, this stage has been shown from Molinaseca to Villafranca. If you decide to stay in Ponferrada there is much to do and see and several interesting detours that you can take from there. Alternatively, you can visit the main sites (all of which are directly along the camino) and still make your way relatively easily to the albergue in Cacabelos (23.8 km) or with greater effort to Villafranca del Bierzo (31.6 km) by evening. But in this latter case, you must leave Molinaseca early in the morning.

❏ **The Mystical Path:** Out of the ruins of the Templar Castle and the fire that consumed its inhabitants, arises the phoenix and the tau, ageless symbols of change and growth that reveals the Divine behind the manifested form. Behind the symbols is the reality of the Love that informs them. Will we allow the flames to burn up our old outworn beliefs and allow the new to reveal itself? Are we ready for a leap of faith, ready to withdraw our investment in the limited consensual reality and bank instead on the Unlimited?

❏ **Personal Reflections:** *"... Somewhere I passed an old man pushing a wheelbarrow. His toothless smile touched me so deeply that I had a momentary impression that he was my father: a representation of The Father. Tears well up again and I am left speechless ... my reality is shifting ... why is it that I cannot recall the last few hours? This altered perception and emotional surge*

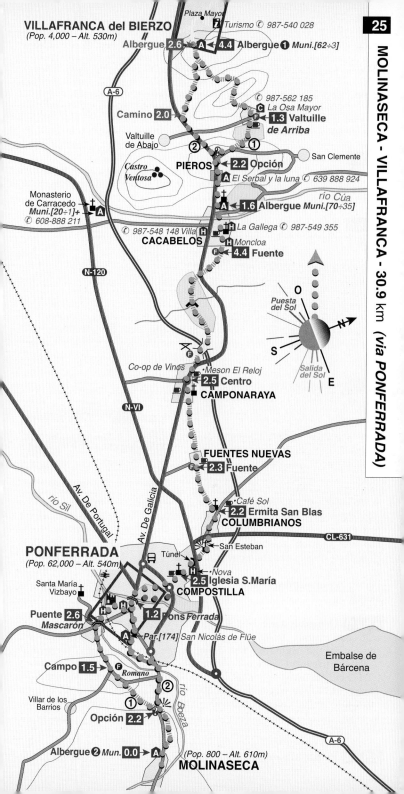

VILLAFRANCA del BIERZO
(Pop. 4,000 – Alt. 530m)

7 *Turismo* © 987-540 028

Plaza Mayor

Albergue **2.6** **A** **4.4** Albergue **1** *Muni.[62÷3]*

© 987-562 185

C *La Osa Mayor*

F **1.3** **Valtuille de Arriba**

Camino 2.0

Valtuille de Abajo

② **2.2 Opción**

① San Clemente

PIEROS

A *El Serbal y la luna* © 639 888 924

Castro Ventosa

A **1.6** Albergue *Muni.[70÷35]*

© 987-548 148 Villa **H** **H** *La Gallega* © 987-549 355

Monasterio de Carracedo **A** *Muni.[20÷1]+*
© 608-888 211

CACABELOS

H *Moncloa*

F **4.4** **Fuente**

río Cúa

N-120

Co-op de Vinos

F

Meson El Reloj

2.5 **Centro**

CAMPONARAYA

N-VI

Puesta del Sol

O

S   N

E

Salida del Sol

FUENTES NUEVAS

F **2.3** **Fuente**

río Sil

Av. De Portugal

Av. De Galicia

Café Sol

2.2 **Ermita San Blas**

COLUMBRIANOS

CL-631

San Esteban

PONFERRADA
(Pop. 62,000 – Alt. 540m)

Túnel

Nova

H **2.5** **Iglesia S.María**

COMPOSTILLA

Santa María Vizbayo

H **H**

Puente 2.6
Mascarón

1.2 **Pons Ferrada**

A *Par.[174]* San Nicolás de Flüe

Campo 1.5 **F** *Romano*

río Boeza

Villar de los Barrios

②

①

Embalse de Bárcena

Opción 2.2

A-6

Albergue **2** *Mun.* **0.0** **A**

(Pop. 800 – Alt. 610m)

MOLINASECA

is overwhelming me. My heart feels so open my chest is aching. I seem to break in and out of conscious awareness, one instant of complete clarity, the next only haziness. I resolve in this moment to continue my pilgrimage in total silence. I don't know for how long; I know only that something is seeking to reveal itself that can only be heard in the quiet. Amidst these uncontrollable tears I write this simple message to hang around my neck. I trust others will understand what I can't articulate and barely comprehend myself. I don't even know if it makes sense in Spanish, 'Saludos. Yo peregrino a pie, caminante en silencio. Paz.'

`0.0 km` **Molinaseca** from albergue ❶ continue down the main road (or just beyond the tennis court turn off right> to pick up a track parallel with the road that winds its way alongside fruit orchards before picking up the road again) to top of a rise with Ponferrada visible ahead:

`2.2 km` **Opción [?]** another *Monte Gozo* with towers of the basilica, occupying the high point in the old town, now visible in the middle distance.

The alternative route ② **into Ponferrada** 0.9 km shorter (3.9 km to the Templar castle – recommended route 4.8 km but more direct if you are staying in the albergue). Veer right and stay on the main road down to Puente río Boeza **[1.5 km]** *[formerly this entry into Ponferrada was known as the Passage of the Boat* Paso de la Barca *as there was no bridge and the deep river could only be crossed with the help of the ferryman].* After **[0.4 km]** veer left off the main road by factories onto a path through waste ground veering up right **[0.8 km]** and right again to cross railway line **[0.4 km]** veering left to albergue **[0.2 km]**:

`3.3 km` •**Albergue** *San Nicolás de Flüe Par.* *[174]* © 987-413 381 situated in the grounds of the convento del Carmen on c/de la Loma (off Av. del Castillo). Open all year with 174 beds € *donativo* and all modern facilities in this purpose-built hostel with patio and garden area. Evening prayers offered. *[Next albergue: Cacabelos – 17.5 km].* To continue to the Templar Castle and the camino turn left

Albergue *San Nicolás de Flüe*

on Av. del Castillo and shortly after veer right at a tourist information board into Av. del Castillo to re-join the recommended route at **Castillo de los Templarios [0.6 km].** Alternatively, go s/o Av. del Castillo into c/Esteban de la Puente and into the main square *Plaza Ayuntamiento* where most of the shops and restaurants are situated and the relocated Tourist office (see town plan).

For the **recommended** route ① veer <left onto wide gravel track down and up steeply into:

`1.5 km` **Campo** historic village with well preserved buildings emblazoned with coats of arms. An interesting Roman water cistern *Fuente Romano* is still functioning and worth the 150m detour (to the right as you enter the village) and the 17th century Church of St. Blase in a grove of olive trees. Continue down c/La Francesa past Meson •*El Rincón d'Alicia* over stream to open ground with football pitch. The waymarked route follows the asphalt road (note: you can take a loop around the parkland on a track above the high banks of the rio Boeza to re-join road 1 km later). We now enter *Los Barríos*, a modern suburb of the city to:

`2.6 km` **Puente Mascarón** *Opción* **[?]** Several options at this point as follows:

[a] If you intend staying the night in Ponferrada at the albergue then keep s/o on over the river bridge (río Boeza) then over the railway (Santiago-León) and up onto the busy Av. del Castillo **[0.4 km]** were the hostel is visible over to the right **[0.3 km]**. **[b] Detour [1]** (see other detours later) *Iglesia de Santa María de Vizbayo* (national asset). Just before the bridge turn up the *camino de Otero* that snakes uphill for 0.7 km [1.4 km round trip] to this delightful 11th century Romanesque church with a fine view back over the city from its wooded site.

Note: the following (waymarked) route [1.2 km] takes us through the medieval city and past the main historic sites (see town plan): Any visit will depend on whether you are continuing to Villafranca today. Veer <left over the medieval bridge up the camino Bajo de San Andres under the railway bridge and turn right> into c/del Hospital past Hospital de la Reina and turn <left at the far end opposite the Baroque Church (town plan) ❶ *Iglesia San Andrés XVIIthC* (with its statue *Cristo del Castillo* linking it to the Templars) to arrive directly at the entrance of ❷ *Castillo de los Templarios*. The magnificent 12th century Templar castle has been declared a national monument and recently reopened after extensive renovations so we are again able to explore its interior and revel in its romantic past. An incongruous modern exhibition centre has been added which currently displays replicas of Templar and other religious texts in the *Templum Libri* accessed by a lift! Ponferrada came under the protectorate of the Templar Order by decree of King Fernando II in 1178. Their official presence here was short lived as the Order was outlawed in 1312 and disbanded by a Church

fearful of their increasing power and esoteric tradition. The modern town is on the other (western) side of the río Sil, visible from the castle entrance. If you don't want to pay the entrance fee there is a delightful walk riverside of the castle. Several cafés in the area serve pilgrim menus (and breakfast if you have come from Molinaseca) and adjoining the castle walls is a tourist office.

From the Templar Castle we can head back towards the pilgrim hostel or continue up the c/Gil y Carrasco (Fitzroy's outdoor clothing and equipment left) into the attractive Plaza Virgen de la Encina with popular café (right) and ❸ *Basílica de la Encina XVIthC. [In bygone days this whole region was covered with evergreen holm oak encina and in one such tree a vision of the Virgen appeared elevating this church to Basilica status and the Virgin to patroness of the Bierzo region].* Take the c/del Reloj and just before the clock tower that gives the street its name (right) is the Royal Prison ❹ *Cárcel Real XVIthC* worth a visit just for the beautifully restored building now the *Museo del Bierzo* displaying artefacts from the Palaeolithic, Roman and modern eras. Continue under the Clock Tower ❺ *La Torre del Reloj XVIthC* into the Plaza Mayor with its impressive town hall *Ayuntamiento*. This covers the main highlights of the old city. If you plan to go on to Villafranca del Bierzo then you won't have time for any further exploring and should proceed <left down the winding steps (beside the modern kiosk) turning <left again into c/Calzada where the waymarked route joins from the left (c/El Randero) to cross the río Sil at:

1.2 km Pons Ferrada *Iron Bridge* ❖ (waymarked route is 1.2 km from our entry into the city at Puente Mascarón).

PONFERRADA: modern metropolis with a population of 62,000 and capital of El Bierzo with its unique micro climate that produces the respected Bierzo wines worth sampling along with the thick pork sausages *botillo* locally marinated and served with boiled potatoes and vegetables *cachelos*. Most of the historic sites are neatly condensed into the old medieval city that occupies the high ground around the castle. The camino winds its way past these sites and so they can be explored on the way through (see previous page) between *Puente Mascarón* (entry) and Iron Bridge *Pons Ferrata* (exit). This latter bridge gives the city its name and is the reason for the sprawling modern suburbs that support a strong industrial base built on the back of the coal and iron reserves that have been mined in this area from medieval times. The original bridge was reinforced with iron as far back as the 11th century. There are a number of earlier Roman and Mozarabic sites in the area that include:

Detour ● ● ● ● ● **[1] Iglesia de Santa María de Vizbayo** (described above from Puente Mascarón). It is one of the oldest churches in the area and has a splendid view over the city from its quiet hillside site. **Detour [2] Iglesia de Santo Tomás de las Ollas** in the northern suburbs (2 km north of the Plaza Mayor, past the Parque del Planto) we find this magnificent Mozarabic 10th century church with its distinctive horseshoe arches. The original pilgrim road into the city used to go by here. It is little visited by pilgrims but well worth the trip if you are staying in Ponferrada for the night. Further afield – by bus or share a taxi are: **Detour [3] Santiago de Peñalba** another 10th century Mozarabic Church located in its magnificent mountain hideaway in the Valley of Silence *Valle del Silencio* 25 km out of Ponferrada (referred to under Acebo detours) and usually visited along with **Detour [4] Las Médulas** – the Roman gold mines on the slopes of the Montes Aquilianos 23 km away off the road to Peñalba.

❏ **Accommodation:** *Turismo:* ✆ 987-424 236 c/ Gil y carrasco, 4. ❏ *Albergue de Peregrinos:* ❶ San Nicolás de Flüe *Mun.[210]* c/ de Loma details see p.218. ❏ *Hoteles Centro:* ❷ El Castillo H*** ✆ 987-456 227 av. Castillo. ❸ La Virgen de la Encina Hr** ✆ 987-409 632 c/Comendador from €40 +pilgrim discount. ❹ Los Templarios H** ✆ 987-411 484 c/Flores Osorío, 3. ❺ Aroi Bierzo Plaza H*** ✆ 987-409 001 on Plaza del Ayuntamiento. *Other side of rio Sil:* ❻ Río Selmo Hs* ✆ 987-411 550 c./Río Selmo. ❼ Madrid H*** ✆ 987-411 550 Av. Puebla,44. ❽ San Miguel II Hs ✆ 987-426 700 c/Juan de Lama,18. ❾ San Miguel Hs ✆ 987-411 047 c/Luciana Fernández,2. ❏ *Restaurantes:* wide selection includes: •*La Fortaleza* c/ Gil y carrasco (by the castle). •*Galeria* plaza Virgen del Encina. •*La Fonda* plaza Mayor (first floor with pilgrim menu).

❖ *Pons Ferrada Iron Bridge* Turn immediately right> into Pasaje de Telefonica c/Río Urdiales where the waymarks direct us diagonally left over the carpark. ❖ (● ● ● ● ● *There is an opportunity here to take a path through* Parque de la Concordia *that runs beside the río Sil to turning left at the next bridge* Puente de Hierro [0.5 km] *into c/del Reino de Léon or, for the really adventurous, to continue under the next bridge [0.6 km]* Av. de América *(earthworks here may require a degree of flexibility) before veering up left on one of the paths by pedestrian bridge to re-join the waymarked route into Av. Segunda [0.3 km]*). ❖ From the carpark the waymarked route turns right along Av de las Huertas del Sacramento s/o at roundabout *La Máquina* [0.8 km] *[monument to the pepper growers* pimientos *and c/del Reino de Léon joins from the right]*. Turn right at next roundabout *Glorieta* [0.4 km] into Av. de la Libertad and s/o left at next major roundabout (Av. de América). Here at the outskirts of the city we continue past the coal slag-heaps and derelict power station turning <left into *Av. Segunda* [0.6 km] and the neatly ordered suburb of Compostilla. The route

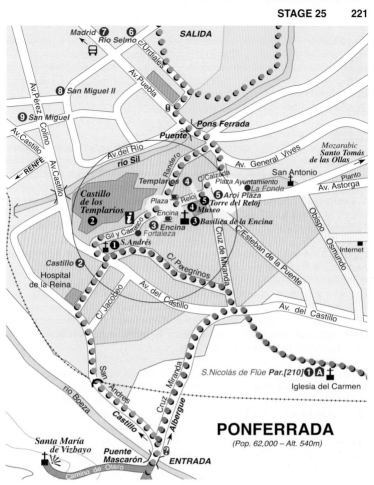

Madrid **7** **6**
Río Selmo c/Urdiales   **SALIDA**

Av. Puebla

San Miguel II **8**

9 San Miguel

Av. Pérez Colino

Av. del Río
río Sil

Pons Ferrada
Puente

Mozarabic
Santo Tomás
de las Ollas

Av. General Vives   San Antonio
Planto
Plaza Ayuntamiento   Av. Astorga
Templarios **4**   c/Calzada   **La Fonda**

Castillo
de los
Templarios
2

Plaza   Reloj   **5** **Aroi Plaza**
Encina   **4**   **5** Torre del Reloj
3 Encina   **Museo**
Fortaleza   **3** Basílica de la Encina

RENFE   Av. Castillo   c/Calzada

† **1** S.Andrés
Gil y Carrasco

C/ Esteban de la Puente

Obispo Osmundo

Internet

Castillo 2
Hospital
de la Reina

C/ Peregrinos

Av. del Castillo   Av. del Castillo

C/ Jacobeo

San Andrés

C/ Miranda

río Boeza   Cruz Miranda

Castillo   Albergue

Santa María
de Vizbayo   **Puente**
Mascarón   **ENTRADA**

Camino de Otero

S.Nicolás de Flüe Par.[210] **1** **A** †
Iglesia del Carmen

PONFERRADA
(Pop. 62,000 – Alt. 540m)

here is well waymarked with concrete bollards past the Red Cross *Cruz Roja* and •*Café-bar Compostilla* through an ***archway*** [**0.6** km] to:

2.5 km Compostilla *Iglesia Santa María* with decorative murals around the covered portico and memorial to Santiago Peregrino. Turn right> down the side of the sports club passing a pilgrim cross and another mural on the gable end of a small chapel onto a track and under pylons to skirt the end of the suburbs at c/Cubo de Finisterre. The camino now heads out through a tunnel under the N-IV *ring road* [**1.1** km] and (back right) pilgrim friendly hotel •**Novo H***** *C* 987-424 441 past vineyards to the *Iglesia San Esteban* [**0.5** km] with delightful views from its arcaded rear porch. Cross main road [**!**] into the village of Columbrianos, a busy suburb of Ponferrada veer <left by ermita [**0.5** km].

2.2 km Columbrianos *Ermita San Blas y San Roque* this small chapel with its colourful pilgrim mural is the site of the original pilgrim hospices. •*Café Sol* on the main road (right). Follow sign to Felix Castro along minor road through market gardens all the way to:

2.3 km FuentesNuevas•*CaféFuenteNuevas*

tiny chapel *ermita del Divino Cristo* with pilgrim fountain [F]. Proceed down the main street of this sleepy village to manic Camponaraya a straggling industrial suburb with the busy N-120 running through it (the waymarks impressed in the pavement slabs) pass a small park with shade and fountain [F] adjoining the modern parish Church of San Ildefonso. Proceed over the río Naraya to roundabout and the 'centre' of town.

2.5 km **Camponaraya** *Centro* •*Meson El Reloj* and •*La Guitarra* offer some respite from the traffic, several alternatives in the immediate area. Continue along the main road to the wine cooperative *Cooperativa Viñas del Bierzo* **[0.8 km]** with shop *tienda* enticing us with an offer of a sample of wine and pincho for €1! or immediately beyond is free *agua* and a rest area *zona de descanso*. Continue over the A-6 pick up a lovely earth track through vineyards over the arroyo Magaz **[1.6 km]** and continue through woodland to cross over the N-120 **[1.2 km]** [!] and continue to pilgrim rest area at the start of cacabelos **[0.8 km]**.

4.4 km **Fuente Cacabelos** [F] opposite modern wine bodega at the entrance to the town. Note that the albergue is the far side of Cacabelos (1.6 km away). **CACABELOS** with a population of 5,000 was an important medieval pilgrim halt with 5 hospices founded for the care of pilgrims on the way. Today you will find a like number of hotels and pensions to care for you. The town has an archaeological museum displaying artefacts found at the nearby Roman settlements and a wine museum celebrating the increasingly popular wine from the area and the history of its production.

We enter the village from the quiet eastern end via c/de los Peregrinos with wine store *Prado del Tope* built on the site of the former 17th century pilgrim hospital in Plaza San Lázaro which also offers us the exclusive hotel •**Moncloa de San Lázro** H[**] © 987-546 101 and adjoining restaurant (*try the magnificent first floor café – part of the original hostel accessed via staircase in the yard*). Continue past a variety of bars and restaurants to the church of **Santa María** XVI[th]C (its original 10th century apse still in place) inside it safeguards a Baroque statue of the Virgin. Detour 100m (left) to the attractive tree-lined *Plaza Mayor* with colonnaded houses and cafés and Turismo © 987-546 011 (summer only) and just beyond, on the main road, the pilgrim friendly •**Villa** H[***] © 987-548 148. **Other accommodation** in the central area directly on the camino in c/ Santa Maria include: •**Santa María** Hs[**] © 987-549 588 N°20. •**El Molino** © 987-546 829 N°10 and •**La Gallega** Hs[*] © 987-549 355 with cyber café.

There are several detours to sites of historical interest in the area: **[1]** 10[th]c **Monasterio de San Salvador de Carrecedo** •**Albergue** *Mun.[20÷1]*+ © 608-888 211. Open all year with 20 beds €10 +ind. rooms from €30. Located 3 kilometres south (left) of the route in a beautiful and very peaceful landscape. Interesting monastic complex with royal palace including the exquisite Queen's balcony and museum on monastic life. **[2] Castro Ventosa**-Bergidum Flavium birthplace of El Bierzo with pre-Roman and Roman settlements. Situated on an elevated site 1 km south (left) of the camino, easily accessed from Pieros.

Continue past the church to join the N-120 to cross the bridge over the río Cua past the ancient olive press and weir to:

1.6 km **Las Angustias** at the far end of Cacabelos on the right •**Albergue** *Mun. [70÷35]* municipal hostel © 987-547 167

on Plaza del Santuario. 70 beds €5 in chalet style rooms with 2 beds in each arranged in a semi circle patio around the church *Capilla de Las Angustia XVIII[th]C* occupies the site of an earlier chapel and pilgrim hospice. *[Next albergue: Villafranca – 7.5 km].*

Continue out along the N-120 on gravel track up past simple wooden cross (left). *[The entire hill behind was the site of the Asturian city of Castrum Bergidum, which was later conquered and occupied by the Romans].* We now enter the small village of **Pieros [1.7 km]** with 11th century parish church and [F] on the main road and in c/El Pozo •**Albergue** *El Serbal y la Luna* **Priv.****[20÷3]* © 639 888 924 network* hostel with 20 beds €5. No kitchen but communal vegetarian meal also library/quiet room. Casa rural •**Castro Ventosa** CR © 670 508 530 San Roque, Pieros. Continue to option point at top of the rise **[0.5 km]**:

2.2 km Opción [?] ❖

For the alternative road route ② keep s/o over rio Valtuilles and mesón Venta del Jubileo. Stay on the N-120 and watch out for the arrows that will take you off the main road to a pleasant track (right) past *Estudio de Escultura*:

2.0 km **Camino** turn right up onto a track that winds its way up through vineyards to rejoin the recommended route [1.4 km] into Villafranca [1.2 km].

2.6 km **Villafranca del Bierzo** •**Albergue [1]** see below for details.

❖ For the **recommended** old road *c/Viejo* ① turn right> onto a short stretch of asphalt and veer off <left **[0.2 km]** onto a wide track that winds its way through vineyards onto a shaded lane down to the delightful sleepy hamlet of:

1.3 km **Valtuille de Arriba** •*Café Escuela* (access lower level) continue along c/Camino de Santiago *[unfazed by the constant flow of pilgrims along the more established routes, the villagers appear to have retained their deep respect for the Way of Santiago and its pilgrims]* to the main square Plaza Miguel Ochoa [F] •**La Osa Mayor** CR © 987-562 185. Continue over the stream at the far end into Plaza del Fondo del Lugar and head up the farm track into the stunning beauty of the El Bierzo landscape. Proceed up (and down) through the rolling hills covered with vineyards (towards a whitewashed house between two pines on the horizon – left) before beginning our final descent past •Burbia down to:

4.4 km **Villafranca del Bierzo** •**Albergue ❶** *Mun.[62÷3]* © 987 542 356 situated below the path (first building right as you enter) overlooking the town. 62 beds €6 in 3 separate rooms incl. attic *buhardilla* (hot in summer) and all modern facilities in this purpose built municipal hostel. Just beyond it we come to the beautiful 12th century Romanesque Church of Santiago with its north entrance Door of Forgiveness *Puerta del Perdón.* Medieval pilgrims unable to continue to Santiago received absolution here the same as they would in Santiago. On this account Villafranca was sometimes referred to as the 'other or little' Santiago. Certainly in these contemporary times an 'alternative' physical and spiritual healing may be available to the modern pilgrim for immediately adjoining the church is the legendary: •**Albergue ❷** *Ave Fenix Priv.[80÷5]* ℭ 987-540 229 former network hostel open all year with 80 beds €5. Facilities include solar heated showers (may run cold later in the day) and no kitchen but bar and dining room offering a communal

Albergue ❷ *Ave Fenix*

pilgrim supper followed, perhaps, by a mystical *Queimada*. There is a pleasant patio area overlooking the town. An additional service offered by the Jato family is transport of backpacks *mochilas* up to O'Cebreiro to await arrival at the albergue. (These services are available whether staying at this hostel or not). The Ave Fenix rises, literally, from the ashes. The previous hostel was destroyed by fire, although many will recall the interim encampment, a veritable haven of hospitality. Recent feedback has not been so favourable and bedbugs reported in 2013 but the pilgrim accepts with equanimity the changing standards he finds along the way. However the truth behind the philosophy of Jesús does not change *"El Camino es tiempo de meditación interior, no itinerario turístico."*

❸ •**Albergue y Restaurante** *Viña Fermita Priv.[50]* ℭ 987-542 490 newly opened hostel (also with private rooms) set in beautiful gardens on c/Calvo Sotelo. No kitchen but popular restaurant. •**Albergue ❹** *de la Piedra Priv.***[28 ÷2]+* ℭ Unai 666-655 052 & Livia 987-540 260. network* hostel on c/Espíritu Santo (one of the last houses as you leave town) 28 beds €8 + priv. rooms. Facilities include healing massage. Villafranca is a

Albergue ❹ *de la Piedra*

popular tourist venue as well as a pilgrim halt, so there is a wide range of **alternative accommodation**. At the top end of the town and price bracket is •**Parador** H*** ℭ 987-540 175 Av. Calvo Sotelo (just beyond the Castillo de Marqueses) also •**La Puerta del Perdón** CR ℭ 987-540 614 Plaz Prim 4. *Central adj. Plaza Mayor*: •**Ultreia** Hs ℭ 616 703 693 corner on Puentecillo. •**San Francisco** H* ℭ 987-540 465. *Lr. end nr. exit*: •**La Llave** CR ℭ 987-542 739 c/del Agua 37. •**Las Doñas del Portazgo** H*** ℭ 987-542 742 corner of c/del Agua and bridge over rio Burbia – luxury boutique hotel with pilgrim discount (formerly toll house). •**Hostel Burbia** Hs** Fuente Cubero, 13 overlooking rio Burbia also •**Casa Mendez** Hs* ℭ 987-542 408 c/Espiritu Santo 1. •**Venecia** P ℭ 987-540 468 on main N-VI. •**El Cruce** Hs* ℭ 987-542 469 c/San Salvador 37. *N.B: wherever you stay make sure you get a good nights sleep to fortify yourself for the strenuous but stupendous hike the next day. Tomorrow brings us up and over the pass into O'Cebreiro and Galicia.*

VILLAFRANCA DEL BIERZO with a population of 5,000 has a full range of restaurants and shops including *La Casita del Espejo* on c/del Agua which offers gifts for the pilgrim including Reiki massage and Tarot with Paula. A helpful Turismo ℭ 987-540 028 on Av. Bernardo Díez Olebar is located beyond the main square and overlooking the park. This delightful town began to develop in this idyllic spot along the *camino francés* in the 11th century. A tour of the main historic sites includes: ❶ **Church of Santiago** *XI[th]C* a Romanesque jewel with its fine *Puerta de Perdón* and handsome statue of St. James in full pilgrim regalia inside. ❷ **Castillo Palacio de los Marqueses** *XV[th]C* (just below albergue 2) with its distinctive turrets, several of which were destroyed during the Peninsular War of 1808 and, further down in town **Plaza Mayor** with Ayuntamiento and

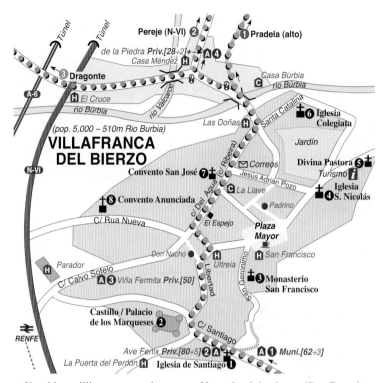

cafés tables spilling out onto the square. Up to the right along c/San Geronimo we come to ❸ **Monasterio de San Francisco** founded at the request of Doña Urraca in the 13th century (some say by Saint Francis himself). *[Note: if you continue past this church a footpath will bring you back to the albergues on the opposite side of the valley.] Beyond* Plaza Mayor we arrive at the austere ❹ **Iglesia San Nicolás** *XVIIthC* further on we pass the ***Turismo*** and adjacent ❺ **Convento Divina Pastora** (formerly one of the 5 pilgrim hospices that attended the large numbers of medieval pilgrims that passed this way). A walk through the public gardens ***Jardin Municipal*** *Alameda* brings us to ❻ **Iglesia Colegiata** formerly the Iglesia Nuestra Señora de Cluniaco (the monks from Cluny were amongst the first arrivals here from France). We can end this circular route by continuing out and up towards O'Cebreiro or return to the albergues via the medieval Water street ***calle Agua*** with its noble houses bearing their armorial shields. The famous Spanish novelist Gil y Carrasco was born here and we also pass ❼ **Convento y Iglesia de San José** founded in the 17th century by the canon of Santiago Cathedral and finally into c/Rua Nueva to ❽ **Convento de la Anunciada** where the Marqueses from the Palacio above are buried.

❒ **This is the way of peace; overcome evil with good, falsehood with truth and hatred with love.** *Peace Pilgrim*

26 185.3 km (115.1 miles) to Santiago

VILLAFRANCA DEL BIERZO – O'CEBREIRO
Recommended route [1] via Pradela.

	Path / Track	--- ---	15.3	---	51%
	Quiet Road	--- ---	12.6	---	42%
	Main Road	--- ---	2.2	---	7%
Total km	**Total distance**		**30.1 km** (18.7 ml)		

Adjusted for climb 36.1 km (accrued ascent 1,200m = 6.0 km)
Alto ▲ High Point: O Cebreiro 1,310m (4,297 feet)

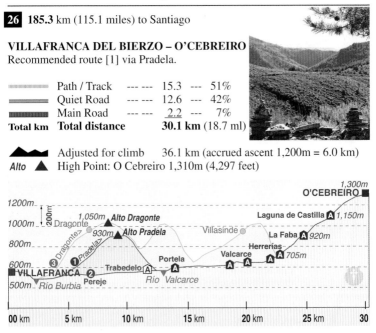

The Practical Path: A strenuous stage, particularly at the end, but wide choice of hostels en route. 3 options on leaving Villafranca; choice will be determined by: **[a]** prevailing weather conditions **[b]** personal level of fitness and **[c]** the kind of experience you want to create. All routes are likely to prove demanding. This stage represents one of the steepest of the whole pilgrimage but the climb is rewarded with stunning views along the Valcarce valley that will keep spirits high. The least taxing option is the noisy N-VI stretch and while the completion of the A-6 motorway has greatly reduced traffic using it, there are several dangerous bends, so stay alert. **Intermediate accommodation:** on recommended route ❶ *distances from albergue* ❶*:* Trabadelo **11.7** km – Portela Valcarce **15.5** km – Ambasmestas **16.9** km – Vega de Valcarce **18.5** km – Ruitelán **20.7** km Herrerías **22.0** km – La Faba **25.0** km – Laguna **27.6** km. *Note*: first hostel on alternative route ❷ is Pereje (5.8 km) and first available hostel on alternative route ❸ is Herrerías (26.1 km). The valley is steep sided (Val carce *Latin; Vallis Carceras =* narrow valley) and heavily wooded with mostly pine and chestnut, so all options provide shade. There are shops, bars, hotels and pilgrim hostels all along the valley floor in the villages we pass through, but make sure you have water and some snacks for the Pradela route before leaving Villafranca and full provisions for the remote and poorly waymarked Dragonte route (seasoned pilgrims only).

❒ **The Mystical Path:** We cannot give peace unless we first create peace in our own hearts and minds. By giving Love we extend Love and thereby reverse the laws of this world for Love increases the more we give it away. How much can we find to give away today? When we are able to respond lovingly to all our interactions we send an expansion of loving energy into our fear-filled world.

❒ **Personal Journal:** *"… Sleeping out under the stars has deepened my experience but today my physical and spiritual muscles ache and my heart feels*

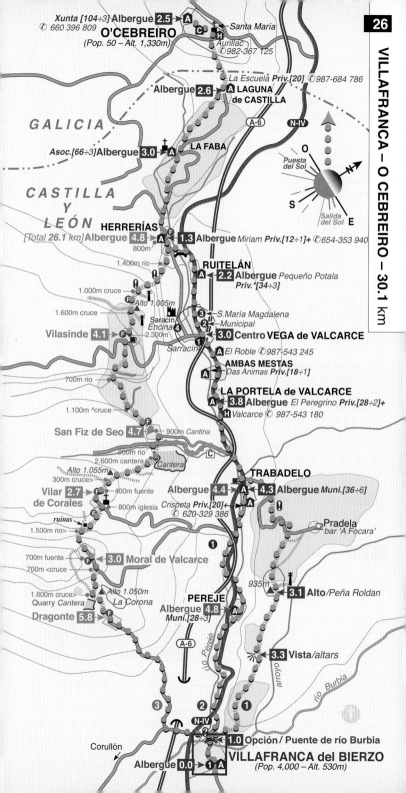

Xunta [104÷3] Albergue **2.5** **A**
© 660 396 809
O'CEBREIRO
(Pop. 50 – Alt. 1,330m)
C
H ┼ ←*Santa María*
Aurillac
© 982-367 125

La Escuela **Priv.[20]** © 987-684 786

Albergue **2.6** **A** **LAGUNA**
de CASTILLA

G A L I C I A

A-6   N-IV

Puesta del Sol
O

Asoc.[66÷3] Albergue **3.0** ┼ **A** **LA FABA**

C A S T I L L A
Y
L E Ó N

S

Salida del Sol   E

HERRERÍAS
[Total 26.1 km] **Albergue** **4.8** **A** **E** **1.3** **Albergue** *Miriam* **Priv.[12÷1]+** © 654-353 940
800m
1.400m *rio*
RUITELÁN
1.000m *cruce*
A **2.2** **Albergue** *Pequeño Potala*
Priv.*[34÷3]
F *Alto 1.005m*
1.600m *cruce*
↑ *Saracin*
Encina   ←*S.María Magdalena*
Vilasinde **4.1** **F**   **3** ←*Municipal*
D   2.300m
2
3.0 **Centro** **VEGA de VALCARCE**
Sarracín   **1**
700m *rio*   **A** *El Roble* © 987-543 245
AMBAS MESTAS
Das Animas **Priv.[18÷1]**
A
1.100m ^*cruce*
LA PORTELA de VALCARCE
F   **A** **3.8** **Albergue** *El Peregrino* **Priv.[28÷2]+**
San Fiz de Seo **4.7** ←900m *Cantina*   **H** *Valcarce* © 987-543 180
900m *rio*
2.600m *cantera*
Alto 1.055m   **C**
300m *cruce*→
F ←400m *fuente*   **TRABADELO**
Vilar **2.7** **F**   **Albergue** **4.4** **A** **4.3** **Albergue** *Muni.[36÷6]*
de Corales
F ←800m *iglesia*   *Crispeta* **Priv.[20]+**   **A**
ruinas   © 620-329 386   **A**
1.500m *rio*>   ☐ *Pradela*
bar 'A Focara'
700m *fuente* **F** **3.0** **Moral de Valcarce**   **1**
700m <*cruce*
935m ┼
1.600m *cruce*→   *Alto 1.050m*   **3.1** **Alto** /*Peña Roldan*
Quarry Cantera   ▲ *La Corona*
Dragonte **5.8** **F**   **PEREJE**
Albergue **4.8** **A**
Muni.[28÷3]
A-6
rio Pereje   **3.3** **Vista**/*altars*
↰
arroyo
rio Burbia
3   **2**   **1**
↰
N-IV   **1.0** **Opción** / **Puente de río Burbia**
Corullón
Albergue **0.0** **1** **A** **VILLAFRANCA del BIERZO**
(Pop. 4,000 – Alt. 530m)

heavy. I don't understand what is happening to me but I will continue to walk in silence and trust that everything will reveal itself in time; 'when the student is ready the Teacher will appear.' The weariness I felt was intensified by a busload of raucous pilgrims. They might have been touring for charity but there was nothing charitable about the way in which they swamped the path and when I finally arrived soaked and exhausted they had completely surrounded the bar. It was an age before I could get the owner to read my note requesting a room and so I chose, unwittingly, to extend anger instead of love. They were my teachers and I failed the lesson that peace starts within myself. If I am dependent on the behaviour of others for my sense of serenity, I will never become free …"

❶ **Ruta Pradela [30.1** km] (adjusted for climb 36.1 km – total ascent 1,200m). This recommended route is very beautiful and makes the most of the early morning sun which doesn't penetrate into the lower Valcarce valley until later in the day. The steep climb up (400m) is rewarded with wonderful views back over Villafranca, but you will need to allow an extra hour or two for this longer route with the extra the ascent *and* steep descent it involves.

❷ **Ruta Carretera [28.6** km] (adjusted for climb 32.6 km – total ascent 800m). The road route is the shortest with several villages providing shops and bars along the way. However, it is dangerous where you have to cross the N-VI so stay focussed and walk inside the crash barriers wherever provided. The new autopista has reduced traffic on the N-VI but it is still unsightly and noisy.

❸ Camino Dragonte **[34.4** km] (adjusted for climb 44.0 km /ascent – 1,950m). *Note: Plan to stay at Herrerias 26.1 km (32.5 adjusted).* To avoid the main road completely you need to take this route, the longest and most arduous and, accordingly, the most beautiful and spectacular. You need to be fit and take food and water with you as the way is remote with only one bar (often closed), although there are several water fonts. Waymarking is poor so you need a good sense of direction and reserve energy to retrace your steps should you get lost. The extensive woodland offers protection from rain or sun but mountain weather is unpredictable at any time of year so stick to the other routes if in any doubt.

0.0 km **Villafranca del Bierzo** from albergue ❶ make your way down the c/ Aqua (c/Ribadeo) and at the far end turn <left (by hotel Las Doñas) up the steps by pilgrim statue and:

1.0 km **Opción** – *Puente río Burbia* cross over the bridge, just above its confluence with the río Valcarce (Hostel Burbia upriver right) to the first option point only 50m [!] *not* well indicated. If you intend to take the recommended Pradela route you *must* leave the asphalt road here up the steep cobbled street right> [!] past the new peluquería Ana.

Alternative road route [2] via the main N-VI is described after Trabadelo. Alternative detour route [3] via Dragonte is described after Herrerías.

For **recommended route ❶ Camino de Pradela** turn up right> into c/Pradela and, if the warning signs for fitness worry you, remember that if you have made it this far you should encounter no undue problems. Indeed, the lower route along the main N-VI may carry greater risk of injury and, depending on the time of day and year, the sun will not penetrate the valley floor in the morning.

It appears that many pilgrims use the road route because they are unaware of a choice or miss the narrow turning up into Pradela. Continue up the steep incline that shortly gives way to an earthen path that skirts smallholdings and vineyards on our left and pine forest above until we reach a rock outcrop – here a large boulder protrudes onto the path and acts as a 1 km marker from the bridge (2 km from the albergue). The path now climbs less steeply and levels out as we make our way along a ridge to:

3.3 km **Vista / *altares*** stunning views have inspired the creation of personal 'altars' to the journey of life. Continue above the tree line to the high point at:

3.1 km **Alto / *Peña Roldan*** (track to radio mast right) we now enter a delightful stretch through chestnut woods *castaño* (sign to bar -*A Focara 500m*- is just over 1 km into Pradela from here). Several woodland paths converge in this area but continue straight ahead to emerge onto an asphalt road (to Pradela) and cross over onto path that winds down steeply [!] on a new pilgrim track (cutting out the gentler but longer road bends) to re-join the main road at:

4.3 km **Trabadelo** [F] with several bars and albergues (see below). Pilgrims who have come via road route [2] (described below) join here. ❖

Alternative road route ❷ via N-VI this snakes its way up alongside the main road and follows the river valley. It has been realigned many times and the traffic is now much reduced on account of the new autopista. It has also been improved with the addition of crash barriers that now separate pilgrims from the traffic but care is still needed when crossing over. At  Puente del río Burbia (option point 1.0 km from albergue [1]) keep straight on (ignoring Pradela waymarks on your right) and continue for 150m to 2nd option point by Casa Mendez *(turn left over 2nd bridge for Dragonte route [3] (see later)* for road route turn right at hotel and continue along the río Valcarce on the old N-VI all the way into:

4.8 km **Pereje** •Albergue *Priv.[28÷3]* © 987-540 138 municipal hostel open all year with 26 beds + mattresses €5 in 2 rooms and all facilities with outside terrace. •**Las Corinas** CR on the main street © 987-540 138. The original main street is called *Camino Santiago* witnessing to its pilgrim focus in earlier times. *[Indeed the administration of Pereje was the cause of a long dispute between the establishments at O'Cebreiro and Villafranca taking both the monarchy and papacy to resolve it in favour of O'Cebreiro who had built a pilgrim hospice there. This seems to mirror the struggle between the culture of the lowlands and the highlands and between León and Galicia. Although we do not officially enter Galicia until just below O'Cebreiro, the atmosphere, topography and weather all seem to change in this valley].* Re-join the N-VI into:

4.4 km **Trabadelo** •Albergue ❶ *Crispeta Priv.[20÷1]+* © 620-329 386 private hostel with 20 beds €6 + ind. rooms from €25. All facilities+ outside terrace. •**Albergue [2]** *Mun.[36÷6]* © 647 635 831 with 36 beds €6 and adjoining bar. Other accommodation: •**Nova Ruta** Hs & restaurant © 987-566 431 (same family run Crispeta). •**Casa Ramón** CR © 665-610 028. •**Pilar Frade** CR and vegetarian restaurant and pension run by Santiago and Elly which is proving popular •**El Puente Peregrino** P © 987-566 500.

From as early as the 9th century the church here was under the possession of the cathedral in Santiago. An uneasy peace existed here with other centres of administration and the castle of Auctares and the hills above Trabadelo were a base for outlaws to exact their own 'tolls' on innocent pilgrims. Out the far side of the village we join the pilgrims who have taken the Pradela route. ❖ The path continues parallel (above) the main N-VI re-joining it briefly several times before reaching the outskirts of Portela •**Valcarce** H ℂ 987-543 180 single from €25 and restaurant on main road (primarily a truckers-stop before braving the mountain doorway into Galicia *Puerto de Pedrafita*). We cross the N-VI into:

3.8 km La Portela de Valcarce •**Albergue** *El Peregrino Priv.[28÷2]*+ ℂ 987-543 197 prominent position with 28 beds €8 also ind. rooms €25+ in modern building. No Kitchen but bar and restaurant with pilgrim menu. Continue through Portela before turning off for Ambasmestas (signposted Vega de

Valcarce). At this point we finally leave the N-VI *[we now have 4 days walking ahead before we have to join the national network again, the N-547 at Palas de Rei.]* Continue into the traditional village of Ambasmestas **[1.4 km]** where the ríos Balboa and Valcarce join to give the village its name *aguas mestas*. A rural idyll somewhat spoilt by the A-6 flyover that serves as the backdrop. For the hostel turn left in the village centre and cross over the river (left hand building) is •**Albergue** *Das Animas Priv.[18÷1]* ℂ 619-048 626 private hostel on c/Campo Bajo. 18 beds €5. All facilities (kitchenette with microwave only) and terrace overlooking the river. •**Ambasmestas** CR ℂ 987-233 768 €35+. Continue along the valley floor for a further **[0.6 km]** to •**Albergue** *El Roble Priv.***[18÷1]* ℂ 987-543 245 (formerly *O Brasil*) modern building set back from the road on the outskirts of Vega de Valcarce. 18 beds €5 in one main dormitory. All facilities and shared meals available. Continue for **[1.0 km]** around the next corner to:

3.0 km Vega de Valcarce *Centro* Albergue ❶ *Sarracin Priv.[20÷2]* ℂ696 982 672 adj. river beds €10. ❷ *Mun.[72÷7]* ℂ 987-543 006 c/Pandelo (below A-6 flyover) 72 beds €5. ❸ *S. María Magdalena Priv.[8÷1]*+ ℂ 646 128 423 €9 + priv. rooms.❹ *Virgen de la Encina Par.[26÷5]* ℂ 649 133 272 € donativo. •**Pandelo** CR ℂ 987-543 033. •**El Recanto** CR ℂ 987-543 202. •**Meson Las Rocas** CR ℂ 987-543 202. Over the bridge in Plaza del Ayuntamiento (near ❹) •**Fernández** P ℂ 987-2543 0278. Pleasant village built around the río Valcarce with shops, bars and restaurants, marred somewhat by the A-6 above. Shortly after leaving the village the menacing outline of the XIV[th]C *Castillo de Sarracín* is visible to our left. The town was founded in the IX[th]c by Count Sarraceno from Astorga (not a Sarracin). Continue by quiet road past the old parish church of St. John the Baptist in a delightfully dilapidated condition and often open (left). The motorway is now thankfully out of sight thus preserving the tranquil setting of this quaint hamlet where San Froilán had a hermitage as we enter:

2.2 km Ruitelán •**Albergue** *Pequeño Potala Priv.[34÷3]* ℂ 987-561 322 private hostel open all year on corner with 34 beds €5. Good facilities (no kitchen but shared dinner and breakfast offered) massage also available. Small shop and bar adjacent. Continue out of the village passing new *posada rural* •**El Paraíso del Bierzo** CR ℂ 987-684 137 to turn off <left (opposite bar and sign for La Faba) cross the Roman bridge over the río Valcarce into the village ahead.

1.3 km Herrerías •**Albergue** *Priv.[12÷1]*+ Miriam ℂ 654-353 940 private hostel located on the left at the start of the village with 12 beds €5 + 2 doubles.

Vegetarian meals in traditional village house (see photo). Popular CR & restaurant •**Casa do Ferreiro** 626 452 237 also •*Café/bar Polin* with shop opposite and local taxi José Lopez Barreiro ✆ 649-647 504. This ancient hamlet stretches lazily along the river, its name derived from the iron foundry whose  furnaces have long since disappeared. This is the point where the Dragonte route (described next) re-joins the recommended route.

Alternative route ❸ via Dragonte. The route described here is was one of the ways that pilgrims used to traverse the Valcarce Valley. It is longer, with 3 deep river valleys to cross, and is poorly waymarked as part of the GR-11 and is variously referred to as *Camino de los Franceses* or *Camino Dragonte* with the more discreet green and white circular walking plaques or the red and white blaise predominating although the yellow arrow pops  up occasionally. There are few facilities along the way and no accommodation until you reach Herrerías although you can take any of the roads down into the main valley and re-join the other routes with their plentiful accommodation.

It is the 'road less travelled' and on this account will appeal to those seeking a more contemplative way and wishing to travel in the 'silence' of nature. It is not suitable for groups but individual pilgrims might sensibly join with another for added security in the mountains. It is very beautiful and, as yet, unspoiled. The distance from the albergue in Villafranca to Herreías, via Dragonte, is 26.1 km with an extra 8.3 km up to O'Cebreiro (total 34.4 km) in addition there is a total height climbed in the day of 1,900m (6,230 feet) so best plan to stay in Herrerías or, if accommodation is not available there then consider staying in Ruitelán or La Faba. *Waymarking is obscure* and the paths beyond Dragonte are frequently overgrown by scrub vegetation, particularly the last stretch down into Herreíras, so only contemplate this route if you are fit, have a good sense of orientation and an instinctive nature when faced with unexpected options. Don't expect to get lost but allow some additional time in case you do! Leave early in the morning and don't tackle it in the winter months when daylight hours are restricted or if the weather is bad or set to deteriorate. *"Ten hours after setting out, we emerged from the woodlands at the base of the slope into the village of Las Herrerias. It had been a very hard day, with almost 1300m of climbing (1100 of descent) and over 30km of walking (including our unintended detours), but the rewards were magnificent mountain scenery and walking a path that few pilgrims tread. In the end, it was the day which gave us the greatest sense of achievement of our camino experience."* Pilgrim couple from Australia.

1.0 km **Option point** at 1st Bridge (rio Burbia) on the outskirts of Villafranca (1.0 km from albergue [1]) veer <left and continue <left over the 2nd bridge (río Valcarce) at Hostel Mendez **[0.2 km]** and head over the old N-VI **[0.4 km]** by the A-6 tunnel (signposted Corullón) and turn up sharp right> **[0.4 km]** signposted Dragonte by a walkers notice board and map. This first section into Dragonte is all by steep asphalt road **[4.8 km]** but rewarded with splendid views back over Villafranca. Head up into and through the village of:

5.8 km Dragonte **[F]** (right) a welcome pilgrim fountain has been installed here. The path continues up (less steeply now) onto wide track keep straight on maintaining the contour as the track veers left in between quarry (left) and hill *La Corona* (right) to a high point on the track of 1,050m (3,445 feet) where, opposite a grove of trees down to the left of the track, we turn off right> [!] at GR-11 sign [**1.6** km] onto narrow path through scrubland following a ditch around to our left and down to an asphalt road [**0.7** km] which we follow for another [**0.7** km] into:

3.0 km **Moral de Valcarce** village [**F**] (no other facilities). Drop down through wooded valley to stream at bottom [**1.5** km] which you have to wade and must turn right> [!] *before* derelict stone building to regain dry path <left in 30m the path now winds its way up (keep to larger of the several indistinct tracks through the woods) to emerge by church [**0.8** km] (formerly monastery and pilgrim hospice of San Fructuoso, viewpoint to rear) pass the access road (right) and up [**0.4** km] into:

2.7 km **Vilar de Corrales** isolated hamlet with [**F**] at far end but no other facilities (make sure water bottles are full before proceeding). Continue up right along the *Camino de los Franceses* and after a sharp left-hand bend in the road veer right (don't continue left) [**0.3** km] [!] and head s/o up track for 100m and then s/o left (several tracks branch off right at this point at the brow of a wide mountain shoulder and our high point (1055m). We now begin the descent into the second of the 3 valleys we have to cross. Turn off left 750m down track which veers right after 150m and follow it past an old quarry where it turns left to descend toward the main open cast stone quarry below. The descent is steep and the narrow paths are confusing as the waymarks here may have been obliterated by the quarrying activity but our destination, the valley floor, is obvious so zigzag down as best you can. St Fiz is visible across the valley (335'/NNW). For general orientation keep to roads on the left of the ridge, which eventually swing right towards the main quarry face. To add spice to an already exhilarating ride note that this is a blasting area *Zona de Voladuras!* Console yourself with the fact that many have passed this way before you and there will be others following! You finally join an access road into the quarry *cantera* [**2.6** km] and

make your way through the quarry itself (watch out for trucks). The dirt road now crosses the river onto the public road [**0.9** km] where there are signs for the GR-1 *Ruta Wolfram* and *Ruta Verde* (*be careful not to confuse the various local walking paths in this area*). Turn right> along the asphalt road and take the next turning <left 400m for the final 500m up steeply to the village above [**0.9** km]:

4.7 km **San Fiz do Seo [F]** Church dedicated to Virgen de los Dolores (right). *Option: at this point it is a long climb up and* down *into Herrerías (allow 3+ hours for 'end of day' pace). An alternative is to take the main road (or parallel high road) to accommodation along N-VI [3.0 km] + Hotel Valcarce [1.4 km].* Turn up left by small cantina (often closed) and make your way up through the village with [**F**] right at exit (make sure you have water for this next section before proceeding). The path now levels out – essentially we maintain the contour around the base of the hill on our right ignoring tracks that turn right up

towards it continuing gently down at fork **[1.1 km]** passing beehives (right) all
the way to the valley floor and over stream **[0.7 km]** before beginning our ascent
up steeply for **[2.3 km]** towards Villasinde ignoring path down to the left Ruta
Verde GR-1 to cross asphalt road into:

4.1 km Villasinde **[F]** and bar (knock on door if closed – Celia will generally
open). Note: from here it is possible to take the minor road down to the albergues
at Vega de Valcarce (4 km all on asphalt) or if you are still feeling adventurous
and there is sufficient light left in the day then head up and out of the village
passing parish church before veering right uphill following GR11 signpost to
pass between the rise *Teso Redondo* (left) and *Vilela* (right) towards the radio
mast ahead visible on the horizon. Pass **[F]** (left) continuing up to crest the
hill and join track to radio mast (right) **[1.6 km]** we turn <left on this track
(Alto 1,002m) and keep this contour as it swings around to the right (ignore
path signposted Ruta S.Julián up to the left). Shortly afterwards pass **[F]** and

another radio mast appears on the peak in front and at broken signpost **[1.0 km]**
turn off <left to start our descent into the valley floor with the A-6 viaduct and
Herrerías now coming into view in the middle distance. Until this point the
paths have been reasonably well maintained and signposted but the path down
to the valley floor is little used and may require effort to break through new
undergrowth. The path at the top is steep and the broom maybe useful to hold
to avoid slipping but be alert for the occasional bramble growing across the
path that can act as a trip wire! If you are on course you will come to a walkers
sign at a muddy section before the path begins to level out and becomes more
obvious through woodland to cross a small stream **[1.4 km]** down to a river
where we turn right> into the village and the pilgrim hostel **[0.8 km]** at:

4.8 km Herrerías to finally join the pilgrims coming up Valcarce for the climb
up into O'Cebreiro – another demanding stage of 8.4 km and an ascent of 620m
(2,035 feet). This will have been a very full day so secure a bed here or Ruitelán
(1.1 km further back) or try one of the several casa rurales in the area.

From **Herrerías Bridge** we wind our way through this quaint village (see p. 231
for facilities) that meanders alongside the river with its simple stone architecture.
The fountain by the river was known as *Fuente de Quinoñes* linking it with the
chivalrous knight who defended the Puente de Órbigo. We pass several bars
and an old forge *A Casa do Ferreiro* and the even more distant English hospice
Hospital Inglés at the far (western) edge of the village, a reference to the
medieval English pilgrims who passed this way (a pilgrim chapel and cemetery
were known to have existed here though the buildings are no longer discernible)
Fill up the water flask and gird your loins for the final assault on the mountain
ahead. Continue along the quiet asphalt road before turning off <left onto **path**
[1.9 km] that drops down briefly to the valley floor where we start our steep
ascent through delightful woodland, mostly chestnut *castaños* on a rocky path
(slippery in wet) for **[1.1 km]** up into the pretty hillside village of:

3.0 km La Faba •Albergue *Asoc.[66÷3]* ☎ 630 836 865 with 66 beds €5 100m up track (right) in parish house renovated by a German Confraternity in shaded parkland setting adjoining the church *Iglesia San André*. This delightful hamlet has a small shop, bar and alternative hostel •**Refugio** *Vegetariano* offering tea and massage (and possibly a bed if you're spaced out after a massage). The path continues up and out of the village along a path lined with Spanish chestnut trees and splendid views back over the Valcarce valley to reach:

2.6 km Laguna de Castilla •Albergue *La Escuela Priv.*[20÷3]* ☎ 987-684 786 with 20 beds €9 and menú in the •*Café/bar*. This tiny hamlet may represent the last outpost in Castille but it houses a wonderful example of a functional Galician *palloza* in the farmyard just behind the fountain [F]. These traditional structures built in the round with straw roofs can be visited in O'Cebreiro. Just above Laguna we pass the first concrete marker post *K.152.5 OS Santos*. These markers will accompany us all the way to Santiago (the route has been changed since they were originally surveyed so distances are no longer accurate but

they provide reassuring waymarks) and we arrive at the Galicia Frontera **[1.1 km]** a substantial marker records the fact that we are finally leaving the autonomous region of Castilla y León (provincia León) to enter Galicia (provincia de Lugo). The path continues through gorse and scrubland to skirt the stone wall that brings us the remaining **[1.2 km]** to:

O'Cebreiro Iglesia one of the earliest surviving buildings on the Camino de Santiago welcomes you to its sheltered interior *Iglesia de Santa Maria Real* dating, in part, from the 9th century and the oldest extant church associated directly with the pilgrim way. O'Cebreiro (Pron: *Oh-thay-bray-**air**-oh*) another significant gateway on the camino has administered to the needs of pilgrims since the twilight of the first millennium. ***Santa María la Real*** is patroness of the area and her 12th century statue is prominently displayed along with the chalice and paten connected with the miracle of O'Cebreiro *Santo Milagro* in which, 'a

haughty celebrant of the mass, dismissive of a devout and humble peasant, saw the bread and wine turn into the body and blood of Christ as he offered them to the supplicant who had risked life and limb to attend mass in a terrible snowstorm – the statue itself was also said to have inclined its head at the miraculous event.'

The church also marks the resting place of ***Don Elias Valiña Sampedro*** (1929–1989) the parish priest who did so much during his life to restore and preserve the integrity of this route – it was his idea to mark the route with the familiar

yellow arrow ➜ and it was largely as a result of his efforts that we walk the route today. His bust presides over the church square and many confraternities have placed their names on the plinth as a mark of their deep respect for his life and efforts on behalf of the modern pilgrim. He was also responsible for the restoration of the adjoining Hostal *San Giraldo de Aurillac*

that is now run by members of the family. These handsome stone buildings originally formed part of the monastic settlement dating back to the 11th century when King Alfonso VI assigned their care to the monks of the Abbé de Saint Giraldo from France. Queen Isabella stayed here in 1486 on her pilgrimage to Santiago. Opposite the church is a museum in a renovated Palloza. It is now only a short walk past the several bars, shops and restaurants **[0.2 km]** to:

2.5 km O'Cebreiro •Albergue *Xunta.* *[104÷3]* © 660-396 809 on the western (far) end of the village on an exposed and elevated site above the main road. Modern purpose built hostel (recently renovated) open all year with 104 beds €5 on 3 levels and all facilities.

Note on Galician Albergues: the regional government *Xunta de Galicia* has constructed modern purpose-built pilgrim hostels or converted former school buildings all along the route from here to Finisterre. This is one of the better examples of a rather uninspiring uniform design. These hostels can generally be identified by the stark white walls and the blue Telefonica kiosk outside. They all have reasonable facilities, such as ample hot showers and toilets, but kitchens are frequently out of commission or lacking in cooking utensils. The more cynical might point to commercial exploitation by local restaurants but forewarned is forearmed and everyone needs to make a living – there is usually a restaurant close by, often run by the hospitalera.

Other accommodation. •**San Giraldo de Aurillac** HsR** © 982-367 125 adjoining the church with popular bar and dining room. You need to book here also for the •**Santuario do Cebreiro** H* © 982-367 125 above the adjacent bar and souvenir shop. •**Casa Carolo** CR © 982-367 168 and •**Venta Celta** CR & Restaurante © 667-553 006 in the centre of the village while below on the main road is •**Mesón Anton** © 952-151 336. O'Cebreiro has become a popular tourist venue as well as pilgrim halt – accordingly demand for beds can outstrip supply in the summer months so find a bed before celebrating.

GALICIA PROFILE: The Valcarce valley and O'Cebreiro provide a wonderful foretaste of the distinctive Galician culture that now awaits you. The mountains of Galicia are the first object in 5,000 km that the westerly winds coming across the Atlantic hit so you can expect an immediate change in weather with frequent rain showers and thunderstorms *lluvia y tormenta* and thick mountain fog *(see photo)* all feeding a maze of mountain streams and deep river beds. The countryside is reminiscent of other Celtic lands with its small, intimate fields and lush pastures grazed by cattle with sheep, pigs, geese and chickens

all foraging amongst the poorer ground. Thick hot soups *caldo gallego* and rich vegetable and meat stews provide inner warmth from the damp. Nearer the coast, fish dishes such as steamed octopus dusted with paprika *pulpo a la galega* and shellfish *mariscos* will dominate. Local red wines with their coarser characters accompany most meals and help to fuel the inner glow. For more delicate whites to accompany scallops *vieiras* try the white Ribeiros or the incomparable Albariño. Round up your meal with local cheese and quince jelly *queso y membrillo* or the famous almond tart *tarta de Santiago.* If you are still feeling cold try the distilled grape skin *orujo* or its marginally more refined cousin *hierbas* mixed with local herbs. Stone granaries *hórreos* are *everywhere* storing the local harvest (primarily maize *maíz)* out of reach of rat and rain.

Galicia shares many historical and physical similarities with other Celtic regions particularly the west of Ireland. Too poor to provide much employment for its large family structures, emigration (particularly of the younger men) has cast it spectre across the region. Here, women drive the tractors or herd the oxen and seem to find time to do the cooking and tend the bars as well. Surprisingly you may find locals that now speak some English on account of having spent time working abroad (or while visiting children working in the UK or USA). If any doubt remains as to its Celtic past then the strident whirl of its bagpipes *gaita* should dispel them. The language *Galega* is still spoken by a substantial minority and understood by the majority while writers and poets such as Rosalia de Castro have helped preserve it more robustly than Irish or Scottish Gaelic. The most visible difference is in the spelling of place names and signposts where, for example, X now replaces J as in Xunta or Igrexa. *Céad míle fáilte!*

Galicia's material poverty has left her with an abundance of spiritual wealth and the region is generally at peace with itself and its traditions largely intact. While a strong Catholic faith overlays its earthy spirituality, its pagan past never totally faded. Deep respect, even veneration of the natural elements remains as evident as the elements themselves. *Finis terra* was, after all, the end of the ancient world – west of Finisterre was the 'Land of Eternal Youth' *Tir-na-nog* where the sun never set. Long before the tomb of St. James was discovered and before Christianity spread to these shores, pilgrims from all over the known world came here to witness the sun sink in the west – and to open to some transcendental reality that emphasised the temporal aspects of earthly life.

The countryside ahead is full of the dolmens and mamoas of these earlier settlers who were deeply reverent in character and who handed down this earthy respect for the natural world. The wayside *cruceiros* add an air of solemnity to the path and are a reminder of the deep spirituality of Galicia that seems to have survived the consumer culture and materialism that has swept over much of the rest of Europe. Santiago de Compostela is the capital of the autonomous region of Galicia that is divided into the 4 provinces of A Coruña, Lugo, Ourense and Pontevedra. See *A Pilgrim's Guide to Finisterre* for a detailed account of the history and legends of this fascinating corner of Galicia – and try and make time to walk the route out to the end of the way and the world.

REFLECTIONS:

❏ **If you want the rainbow, you've gotta put up with the rain.** *Dolly Parton*

27 **155.2** km (96.4 miles) to Santiago

O'CEBREIRO – TRIACASTELA

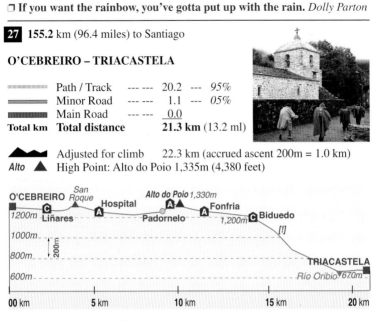

⬜ Path / Track	--- ---	20.2	---	95%
▬ Minor Road	--- ---	1.1	---	05%
▬ Main Road	--- ---	0.0		
Total km **Total distance**		**21.3 km** (13.2 ml)		

▲ Adjusted for climb   22.3 km (accrued ascent 200m = 1.0 km)

Alto ▲ High Point: Alto do Poio 1,335m (4,380 feet)

The Practical Path: While this stage is only 21.3 kilometres and mostly downhill, remember most injuries are sustained going down (not up) so extra care is needed. There are several villages and drinking fonts along the way and splendid views in every direction (weather permitting). Early morning mists can give rise to the most astounding ethereal *floating islands* where hilltops appear above the clouds. These exotic experiences generally give way to clearer skies, as the sun burns the swirling mists away. Whatever time of year, be prepared for *any* weather, as the mountains, and particularly Galicia, can be very unpredictable. **Intermediate accommodation:** Liñares **3.1** km Hospital **5.5** km – Alto do Poio **8.8** km – Fonfría **12.3** km – Biduedo **14.7** km.

❏ **The Mystical Path:** High places help lift us towards Higher Mind. At such heights, a wider perspective opens up to both the physical and the inner eye. What do you see, feel and hear from this elevated space? Do the angels incline their heads to listen to your prayers? Does the silence and peace in your heart allow the inner voice to be heard? Are you open to receiving a miracle and to seeing the inner rainbow – symbol of God's Covenant?

❏ **Personal Reflections:** *"... The deluge continues and not a break to be seen in the clouds in any direction. I ask myself was it serendipity that sent the brief shaft of light through the tiny church window bathing me in its warm rich glow; its light so strong I was momentarily dazed by it. I sense again that altered state, devoid of ego, and all the pain of yesterday has gone. I feel inspired to write a pilgrim guidebook and Don Elias Valiña Sampedro appears to have given me his authority and blessing and so I commit to it right here and now ..."*

0.0 km **O Cebreiro** A forest track starts just above the albergue and winds around the hill before dropping down into Linares, thus avoiding the road.

3.1 km **Liñares** *Iglesia San Esteban* small hamlet that once grew flax *lino (Linares)* for the linen trade. Today •**Casa Jaime** CR ✆ 982-367 166 and bar

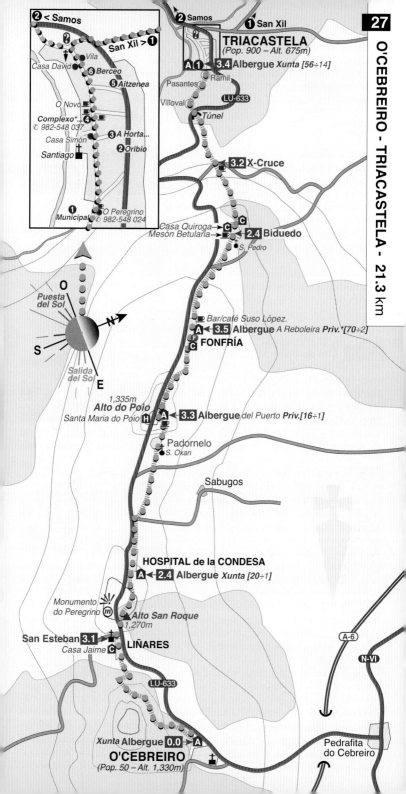

2 < Samos

2 Samos

1 San Xil

TRIACASTELA
(Pop. 900 – Alt. 675m)

San Xil > **1**

Vila

Casa David

6 Berceo

5 Aitzenea

O Novo

Complexo*...**4**
© 982-548 037

Casa Simón

Santiago

3 A Horta...

2 Oribio

1
Municipal
O Peregrino
© 982-548 024

A 1 **3.4** Albergue Xunta [56÷14]

Pasantes
Ramil

Villoval
LU-633

Túnel

3.2 X-Cruce

Casa Quiroga **C** **C**
Mesón Betularia **2.4** Biduedo
S. Pedro

O
Puesta
del Sol

Salida
del Sol

Bar/café Suso López.

A 3.5 Albergue A Reboleira Priv.*[70÷2]

F
C **FONFRÍA**

1,335m
Alto do Poio
Santa Maria do Poio **H** **A** ← **3.3** Albergue del Puerto Priv.[16÷1]

Padornelo
S. Okan

Sabugos

HOSPITAL de la CONDESA
A ← **2.4** Albergue Xunta [20÷1]

Monumento
do Peregrino **m**
Alto San Roque
1,270m

San Esteban **3.1**
Casa Jaime **C** **LIÑARES**

LU-633

A-6

N-VI

Pedrafita
do Cebreiro

Xunta Albergue **0.0** → **A**
O'CEBREIRO
(Pop. 50 – Alt. 1,330m)

provide a suitable replacement. The path takes us past the ancient parish church of San Esteban and shortly afterwards we cross the road onto track up to Alto de San Roque **[0.8 km]** where an imposing statue of a medieval pilgrim looks out over the vast expanse of Galicia and its deep valleys. A path continues parallel to the road for **[1.6 km]** into:

2.4 km Hospital de la Condesa •**Albergue** *Xunta.[20÷1]* © 660 396 810 prominently located above the road (right) as we enter the village. Xunta hostel open all year with 20 beds €5 and all facilities. The village once boasted a pilgrim hospital (hence its name) and was reputed to have been one of the earliest ever built for Christian pilgrims on the way to Santiago. Take time to visit the pre-Romanesque *Iglesia St Juan XI[th]C* (also dedicated to San Roque) with delightful interior and unusual stone roofed belfry and cross of Santiago aloft.

The track continues parallel to the main road turning off right> **[1.2 km]** down a minor road (signposted Sarbugos) for **[0.3 km]** before picking up a path into Padornelo **[1.0 km]** with the recently restored chapel *ermita San Oxan* connecting this area with the Order of St. John. A short but steep climb brings us to the highest spot on the camino in Galicia 1,335m. (4,380 feet) **[0.8 km]**:

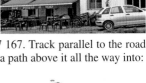

3.3 km Alto do Poio •**Albergue** *del Puerto Priv.[16÷1]* © 982-367 172 private hostel with 18 beds €6. Basic facilities (no kitchen) but Bar Puerto caters for meals and the breakfast trade is livened up with pilgrims from O'Cebreiro. On the opposite side of the road hostal • **Santa María de Poio** © 982-367 167. Track parallel to the road for a short stretch before turning off right onto a path above it all the way into:

3.5 km Fonfría typical Galician village and •**Casa Núñez** CR © 982-161 335 with bar and restaurant. Fill your flask from the cool waters of the *fons fría* [F] after which the hamlet is named. At the far end of the village is •**Albergue** *A Reboleira Priv.*[70÷2]*+ © 982-181 271 mod. building + adj. palloza with 70 beds €8 + priv. rooms (No kitchen) but meals available. *Bar/café Suso López.* Continue on track parallel to main road and turn right> into:

2.4 km Biduedo a rural idyll with its *pequeño capilla de San Pedro* and •*Meson Betularia* and the adjoining •**Casa Quiroga** CR © 982-187 299. The path now begins to descend more steeply with wonderful views over the countryside to the west. Next we arrive at crossroads and rest area. Cross the main road to:

3.2 km Filloval •*Casa Olga* café *Aire do Camino*. New (2012) **Albergue** *Filloval* © 666 826 414 *Priv.[18÷2]*+ from €9. Cross country lane onto path that winds down steeply to cross the main road (muddy underpass) through *As Pasantes* and *Ramil* on the ancient camino worn down with the feet of countless pilgrims and local livestock, a classic stretch of *corredoira* (narrow lane walled-in with granite). Soak up the peace as you meander above the wooded valley of the arroyo Roxino that flows down from Monte Oribio. This primitive way is guarded by a venerable oak and chestnut trees that offer shade all the way to:

`3.4 km` **Triacastela** •*O Peregrino* café-bar-restaurant and adjoining hostel •**García** Pr* ℭ 982-548 024 the first buildings (right) on entering the town opposite which is •**Albergue ❶** *Xunta.[56÷14]* ℭ 982-548 087 situated on a green-field site to the left of the camino at the start of the village overlooking the river. Imaginatively restored from traditional stone buildings with modern extensions. Open all

Albergue ❶ *Municipal*

year with 56 beds €5 in 14 rooms with good facilities (no kitchen) but large lounge and extensive outdoor recreation area. The ramp up at the side of bar O Peregrino ❖ [connects to: •**Albergue ❷** *Oribio Priv.[27÷2]* ℭ 982-548 085 modern building on the main road with 27 beds €9 and all facilities.

❖ [**0.0m**] Continuing down c/del Peregrino we next come to •**Albergue ❷** *A Horta de Abel Priv.[14÷2]*+ [**310m**] ℭ 608-080 556 up short lane (right) adj. main road. 14 beds €9 + priv. rooms. Next •**Casa Simón** pension on corner left [**30m**] with *Igrexa de Santiago* behind. Next [**30m**] we come to •**Albergue ❸** *Complexo Xacbeo Priv*.[36÷3]+ ℭ 982-548 037 network* hostel open all year directly on the camino 36 beds €9 in modern extension to the rear also priv. rooms and adj. •*Bar-restaurant Xacobeo* with which it is connected. This marks the central 'hub' of town and •**O'Novo** Hs ℭ 982-548 105. Further along [**150m**] is a slip road to •**Albergue*** ❹ *Aitzenea Priv.[38÷4]* ℭ 982-548 076 with 38 beds €8. Sympathetic conversion of traditional stone house by a Basque architect *(aitzenea is Basque for stone-house).*

At the end of town we have an option [**150m**] [**0.7 km from Albergue [1]** and: •**Albergue ❺** *Berce do Camiño Priv.[27÷6]* ℭ 982-548 127 private hostel open all year with 27 beds €8 in 6 rooms and all facilities in modernised terraced house adjoining Caixa Galicia and opposite •**Casa David** Pr** ℭ 982-548105 and •**Vilasante** Pr** ℭ 982-548 116. *Note: Santiago city is now only a week away and pilgrim numbers increase exponentially from this point and accommodation is often full.* [*Next albergue: Route [1] Calvor (13.4 km) – Route [2] Lusio (4.5 km).*

TRIACASTELA town of the *three castles* none of which survive and an important stop for medieval pilgrims coming down off the mountain with several hospices and an extensive monastery (XI[th]C stage in the Codex Calixtinus). It is no less an attractive stop today with a wide selection of bars, restaurants and hostels serving the increasing number of pilgrims passing through. The parish church is dedicated to Santiago and has an unusual 18th century tower on which is carved a relief of the three castles. Nearby are the quarries that provided the limestone used in the building of Santiago Cathedral. Medieval pilgrims would carry as much as they were able to the lime kilns in Casteñeda (through which we pass during stage 31) and the pilgrim monument in the lower town square recognises this ancient tradition while acknowledging the rebirth of the camino – paying equal respect to both.

❐ **Happiness is a mystery, like religion, and should never be rationalised.**

G.K. Chesterton

---

28 **133.9** km (83.2 miles) to Santiago

TRIACASTELA – SARRIA (via San Xil)

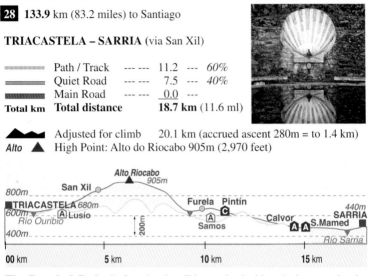

	Path / Track	--- ---	11.2	---	60%
	Quiet Road	--- ---	7.5	---	40%
	Main Road	--- ---	0.0	---	
Total km	**Total distance**		**18.7 km** (11.6 ml)		

Adjusted for climb   20.1 km (accrued ascent 280m = to 1.4 km)

Alto ▲ High Point: Alto do Riocabo 905m (2,970 feet)

The Practical Path: Before leaving Triacastela decide whether to take the northern **recommended route ❶ *via San Xil*** or the southern **alternative route ❷ *via Samos***. Recent improvements to the historic San Xil route (new woodland paths) have increased the natural pathways to 60% while new busy roadworks around Samos have decreased these to 36%. *(The criteria used in this guide is to always favour natural pathways).* The San Xil route is shorter by 6.4 km and has the steep climb up to alto do Riocabo with splendid views. The Benedictine monastery of Samos is one of the oldest and largest in Spain and draws large tourist numbers but the addition of several new albergues and hostels caters for the increased volume of traffic. Both routes are attractive and offer alternative accommodation en route as follows: **Intermediate accommodation:** *distances from albergue ❶ in Triacastela. Route ❶ via San Xil:* Pintín **12.2** km– Calvor **13.6** km – San Mamed **14.8** km where both routes join. *Route ❷ via Samos:* Lusío **4.7** km (+ 0.4) – Samos **10.5** km –San Mamed **21.2** km

---

❐ **The Mystical Path:** Will the winding river reveal her natural weir to you? The man-made example, that diverts water to the village mill, is no match for the beauty of this one. Will you rest awhile in the tiny Hobbit-like shelter whose entrance is shielded by the branches from the adjacent *castaño*? The unadorned beauty of this path remains largely undiscovered by officialdom. How long will it remain in its pristine state uncluttered by the trappings of man?

❐ **Personal Reflections** *"... The deepening silence of my journey coupled with a rare break in the downpour combine with the glorious Landscape Temple to create an overwhelming sense of well being. I am entirely alone and yet I feel more connected to a larger way than at any other time in my life. The outer weather fades into insignificance as I open to an inner reality that seems more alive than anything on the level of form. My body is wet and cold for the umpteenth day in a row and yet I glow with an inner warmth as I sit under a dripping chestnut tree and contemplate the irrationality of it all. I am beginning to turn the conventional world on its head and everything suddenly becomes clearer. I feel at last I am turning towards Home ..."*

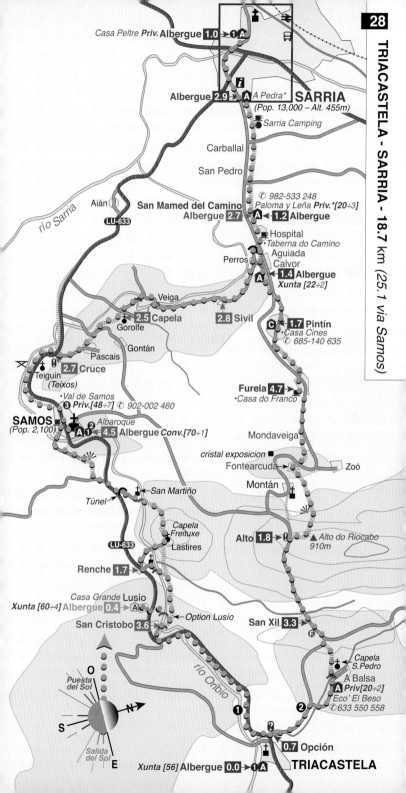

Casa Peltre **Priv. Albergue** `1.0` → `1` `A`

i

Albergue `2.9` → `A` *A Pedra** **SARRIA**
(Pop. 13,000 – Alt. 455m)

Sarria Camping

Carballal

San Pedro

río Sarria

Aián

San Mamed del Camino
Albergue `2.7`

© 982-533 248
Paloma y Leña **Priv.*[20÷3]**
`A` `1.2` **Albergue**

LU-633

Hospital
Taberna do Camino
Aguiada
Calvor

Perros

`A` `1.4` **Albergue**
Xunta [22÷2]

Veiga

`2.5` **Capela**

`2.8` **Sivil**

Gorolfe

Gontán

`C` `1.7` **Pintín**
Casa Cines
© 685-140 635

Pascais

Teiguín
(Teixos)

`2.7` **Cruce**

Val de Samos
`3` **Priv.[48÷7]** © 902-002 460

Furela `4.7`
Casa do Franco

SAMOS
(Pop. 2,100)
`A` `1` *Albaroque*
`4.5` **Albergue** *Conv.[70÷1]*

Mondaveiga

cristal exposicion
Fontearcuda

Zoó

Montán

Túnel † — San Martiño

Capela
Freituxe
Lastires

Alto `1.8` → `Alto do Riocabo`
910m

LU-633

†
Renche `1.7`

Casa Grande **Lusío**
Xunta [60÷4] **Albergue** `0.4` `A`

San Cristobo `3.6`
← *Option Lusío*

San Xil `3.3`

`F`

río Oribio

O

Puesta
del Sol

N

`1`

`2`

Capela
S.Pedro
A Balsa
`A` **Priv[20÷2]**
Eco' El Beso
© 633 550 558

S

E

Salida
del Sol

`?`

`0.7` **Opción**

Xunta [56] **Albergue** `0.0` → `1` `A`   **TRIACASTELA**

0.0 km Triacastela from albergue ❶ proceed down through the town and at the far end we reach the decision point:

0.7 km Opción [?] For **recommended route ❶** via San Xil turn right> down over main road [!] (the road to Samos) onto secondary road and where it veers up left, we turn down right> **[1.0 km]** onto into **A Balsa [0.5 km]** *Albergue Ecologico El Beso Priv.[10÷1]* ©️ 633 550 558 recently restored stone house with 10 beds €8 (plans for 20) & communal dinner available (donation). Continue through the hamlet and over river **[0.5 km]** past the tiny chapel to Our Lady of the Snows *ermita N. S. de las Nieves* (right) and up steeply on woodland path to re-join road at rest area **[0.9 km] [F]** with unusual scallop shell motif and into San Xil **[0.4 km]**:

3.3 km San Xil no facilities beyond a drinks vending machine (left). From here we have a steep climb up by road to our high point today at alto do Riocabo (910m). At this point leave the road onto forest track right> [!].

1.8 km Alto do Riocabo delightful new high level path above Montán through the forest down through the hamlet of Fontearcuda and over the road **[3.3 km]** (there is a ½ km detour to visit the stone artwork and crystals at Mondaviega) we cross over onto path over a stream onto road into Furela **[1.4 km]**:

4.7 km Furela •*Casa do Franco* popular café-bar on slip road. Continue over the main road into the next hamlet:

1.7 km Pintín [F] •**Casa Cines** ©️ 685-140 635 Pensión with 7 rooms and popular pilgrim •*café/bar* – proceed s/o back over the main road to:

1.4 km Calvor •**Albergue** *Xunta.[22÷2]* ©️ 660 396 812 in former school building located on the roadside. Open all year 22 beds €5. We continue over the main road into the straggling hamlets of **Aguiada** and **Hospital** with bar •*Taberna do Camiño* where the **alternative route** from **Samos** joins from the left to:

1.2 km San Mamed del Camino •**Albergue** *Paloma y Leña Priv.*[20÷3]*+ ©️ 658 906 816 network* hostel set back from the road *'an oasis of peace and tranquillity.'* 20 beds €10 + priv. rooms from €38. All modern facilities with dinner and breakfast available. *¿porque no acqui?* Why not indeed!

For **alternative route ❷** via Samos turn <left at option point in Triacastela down past the pilgrim and over the river to join the main road [!]. This a dangerous stretch of road – use the margins behind the crash barriers wherever possible. Continue alongside the road and cross over to take the access road down into:

3.6 km San Cristobo traditional village occupying a lovely position on the bank of the river Oribio with its ancient weir and mill buildings. Cross over the river onto a delightful track that winds its way through mixed woodland following the meandering course of the río Oribio to **optional detour [0.5 km]** Detour Lusío ●●●●● path left for 400m detour to new albergue in beautifully restored monastery building in Lusío. •**Albergue** *Casa Grande Xunta.[60÷4]* ©️ 659-721 324 well restored house with 60 beds €5 in this ancient hamlet. Return to option point to continue s/o along the woodland path before turning <left (path continues to Lastires) and over bridge by chapel up to the main road in:

1.7 km Renche continue back down and over the river and up steeply to *Capela de Freituxe* **[1.6 km]** to take a track back down and over the river again into **San Martiño** [1.2 km] with chapel and up steeply under main road through tunnel [0.5 km] over secondary road onto track above Samos (good viewpoint here over the monastery) and down steeply again into Samos with the town hall over the river. For the monastery albergue turn right along the river and over the next bridge to:

4.5 km **Samos** the town wraps itself around the enormous monastery in this peaceful river valley where time seems to stand still and the only thing in a hurry are the waters of the río Oribio rushing to join the río Miño. •**Albergue** ❶ *Monasterio de Samos Conv.[70÷1]* ℭ 982-546 046 Benedictine hostel located to rear of the main monastery building (entrance by petrol pumps).

Open all year with 70 beds € *donativo* in one stark dormitory corridor. Basic facilities only with no kitchen or lounge area. The simple austerity matches the surroundings and regular services take place throughout the day with Vespers at 19:30 in the chapel. Regular tours of the monastery take place during the day. This is one of the oldest monasteries in the whole of the western world with one of the largest ground plans and cloisters in Spain. •**Albergue** ❷ *Albaroque Priv.[10÷1]*+ ℭ 982-546 087 opp. the monastery, open all year with 10 beds €9 + priv. rooms and all meals available. Adjacent are: •**Victoria** HsR* ℭ 982-546 022 and •**Domus Itineris** HsR* ℭ 982-546 088. At the other end of town is •**Albergue** ❸ *Val de Samos Priv.[48÷7]* ℭ 982 546 163 with 48 beds €11 and all facilities. We now follow the main road out of town (signposted Sarria) passing [0.9 km] •**A Veiga** Hr* ℭ 982-546 052 along track by the road to picnic area and continue to another picnic site by the river [1.4 km] and roadside chapel in Tequin *Teixos* and shortly after cross the main road right [0.4 km] [!]

2.7 km **Cruce** Cross main road onto side road (signposted Pascais) further up we turn off <left onto path and <left again by church and then back down to:

2.5 km **Gorolfe** with wayside chapel a short stretch of track joins to a quiet country road which we follow over the river (twice) through Veiga into:

2.8 km **Sivil** continue s/o up through woodland and the hamlet of Perros before emerging through tunnel under the road into Hospital and bar •*Taberna do Camino* where the other route joins and we continue to:

2.7 km **San Mamed del Camino** to connect with the San Xil route.

The path now follows a track parallel to the road through the hamlets of San Pedro do Camiño [0.9 km] and Carballal [0.5 km] passing Camping Vila de Sarria and •*Café* [0.8 km] and finally to the outskirts of Sarria [0.7 km].

2.9 km **Vigo de Sarria** ❶*Oasis Priv.[27÷4]* ℭ 982-535 516 newly renovated building with all mod cons. ❷ *APedra Priv.**[15÷3]+ ℭ 982-530 130 network* hostel with 15 beds €9 + priv. rooms - meals in bar adj. *Turismo* ℭ 982-530 099 with pilgrim advice and maps of the town and list of accommodation and activities in the area if you plan to stay an extra day. To get to the central pilgrim hostels and the old quarter proceed over the busy Calvo Sotelo by •**Il Fiorino** Pr* ℭ 982-535 400 Italian restaurant and pension, into rúa do Peregrino with luxury hotel (right) •**Alfonso IX** H*** ℭ 982-530 005 turning right> in c/Benigno

Quiroga (or left for the more affordable hotel) •**Oca Villa** H** © 982-533 873 and then <left by •*Peregrinoteco* © 982-530 190 where we can browse maps and equipment exclusive to pilgrims. Climb the ancient granite steps *Escalinata Maior* into the bottom end of **c/Maior** to **Nº76** by waymark [km. 111,5] is pension •**Escalinata** Pr* © 982-530 259 and **Albergues ❶ – ❿**

1.0 km **Sarria** *Centro* ❶*Casa Peltre [22÷3]* © 606 226 067 with 22 beds €10. **Nº64 c/ Maior** ❷*Mayor Priv.[16÷3]* ©685 148 474 with 16 beds €10. **Nº79** ❸*Xunta.[40÷2]* © 660 396 813 with 40 beds €5 in sympathetically restored period town house (see photo right). Further up at **Nº44** ❹*O Durmiñento Priv. [43÷6]+* © 982-531 099 with 43 beds €10 + massage room *sala de masajes* (no kitchen) but meals available. **Nº57** ❺*Internacional*

Albergue ❷ *Xunta*

Priv.[44÷4]+ © 982-535 109 with 44 beds €10 + priv. rooms modern facilities (no kitchen) café/restaurant and roof-top terrace. **Nº31** ❻*Los Blasones Priv.*[42÷4]+* © 600-512 565 with 42 beds from €8 + priv. rooms and rear patio. **Nº10** ❼*Don Álvaro Priv.[40÷4]* © 982-531 592 with 40 beds €9 + pilgrim reading room and open fireplace and patio garden. Just behind in rúa Conde de Lemos, 23 is ❽*Dos Oito Marabedís Priv.[24÷7]* © 629 461 770 mod. terraced house with 34 beds €10 and all facilities. Down rua da Calexa is ❾*San Lázaro Priv.[30÷4]+* © 982-530 626 c/San Lázaro,7 with 30 beds €10 + priv. room and at the top of town ❿*Monasterio de la Magdalena* Av. de la Merced, © 982 533 568 with 90 beds €10 + garden also ●*Barbacoa del Camino Priv.[14÷2]+* © 982 531 524 c/ Esqueiredos (Campo de la Feria) €10. **Other accommodation:** •**Camino Francés** Pr* © 982-532 351 Praza da Constitución (c/Maior). •**Casa Matías** Pr** © 982-532 680 Calvo Sotelo,39 and at the far end of by the railway station •**Roma** Hr* © 982-530 570 also nearby in rúa Formigueiros is pensión •**Mar de Plata** © 982-530 578.

❏ **Historical monuments: ❶** *Iglesia de Santa Mariña XIX* •*credencial* ❷ *Iglesia de San Salvador XIII* ❸ *Hospital de San Anton XVI antiguo hospital de peregrino* ❹ *Fortaleza y Torres XIII* ❺ *Mosteiro de Santa María Madalena XIII* ❻ *Ponte Áspera medieval.*

SARRIA: with its Celtic origins was a major medieval centre for pilgrims with several churches, chapels, monasteries and 7 pilgrim hospitals. The ancient atmosphere can still be felt in the attractive old quarter that climbs along the main street *rúa Maior* past Igrexa de Santa Mariña (*credenciales*) with its evocative pilgrim mural – on up to the ruined castle at the top *Fortaleza de Sarria*. The ancient convent *Mosteiro da Madalena* (*credenciales*) has a fine plasteresque façade and leads down to the medieval bridge over the río Celerio (see next stage). The advent of the railway in the 19th century pulled the town centre eastwards leaving the ancient *camino real* largely intact. Sarria is a bustling modern town with a population of 13,000. It has become a major starting point for pilgrims with limited time but anxious to pick up a *compostela* at Santiago – starting from here will cover (just) the requisite 100 km to the cathedral (hence the profusion of pilgrim hostels in town). Pilgrims arrive via the bus and rail stations and from this point the route becomes crowded with the new arrivals. Many hostels provide a backpack *mochila* transport service. *Note:* Beware for any sign of resentment at such intrusion on 'my' camino – remember that many of the new arrivals may be nervous starting out and the last thing they need is aloofness built on a false sense of superiority. A loving pilgrim welcomes all they meet along the path – without judgement.

SALIDA
Ponte Áspera **6**
rio Celeiro
Camiño Francés

San Roque
Cementerio
10 *Albergue Conv.*
5 *Mosteiro da Madalena*
•credencial

9 San Lázaro
Estación Ferrocarril
rúa José Antonio
Roma **H**

Campo da Feira
Fortaleza (Ruinas)
Barbacoa **Torre 4**
rúa do Castelo
Parque Do Bosque
rúa Calexa
Cruceiro
Sarmiento
rúa Ponvir

Casa Matías **P**
Mar de Plata **P**
rúa Calvo Sotelo

Dos Oito **8** *Marabedís*
3 ■ San Anton
2 ✝ El Salvador
Don Álvaro **7** **P** Camiño Francés
• Taberna Lopez
Matias Locanda Italiana
6 *Los Blasones*
Concello •credencial
5 *Internacional*
O'Durmiñento **4**
✝■ Santa Mariña **1** •credencial
rúa Nova
rúa Matías López
Estación de Autobuses (Santiago via Lugo) 🚌

Mayor **2**
3 *Xunta*
Casa Peltre **1**
rúa Maïor
Escalinata
Escalinata Maïor→
rúa Benigno Quiroga
■ *Peregrinoteca (equipamiento)*
© 982-530 190
rúa Matías López

SARRIA
(Pop. 13,000 – Alt. 455m)

Oca Villa **H**
Ferreiro
rúa Diego Pazos
Malecón

Río Sarria
Rúa do Peregrino
H Alfonso IX***
Campo do río
Río Sarria

rúa Calvo Sotelo

O
Puesta del Sol
S ———— N
Salida del Sol
E

IL Fiorino **P**
© 982-535 516 *Oasis* **A**
VIGO DE SARRIA
Turismo © 982-530 099
i **A** A Pedra
ENTRADA ↗

❐ **To err is human, to forgive, divine.** *Alexander Pope*

29 115.2 km (71.6 miles) to Santiago

SARRIA – PORTOMARÍN

⅏⅏⅏	Path / Track	--- ---	10.3	--- *46%*
▬▬	Quiet Road	--- ---	12.1	--- *54%*
▬▬	Main Road	--- ---	0.0	
Total km	**Total distance**		**22.4 km** (13.9 ml)	

▰▰ Adjusted for climb   23.9 km (accrued ascent 300m = 1.5 km)
Alto ▲ High Point: Cruce / Mominetos 660m (2,165 feet)

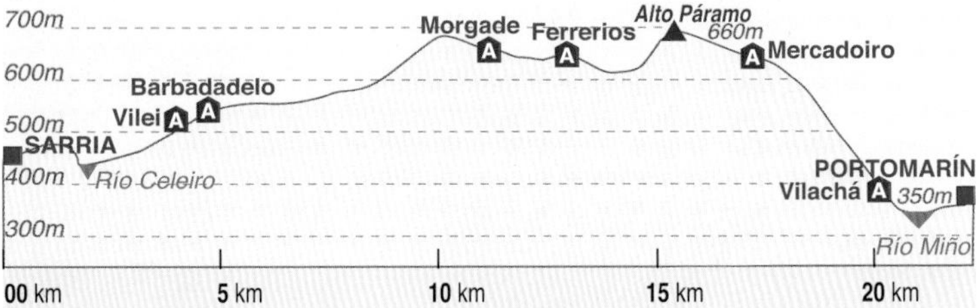

The Practical Path: Today's stage is spread equally between quiet country roads and natural pathways. Apart from the bare flanks around the Peña do Cervo at Momientos (above Portomarín) much of this stage is along tree-lined roads and pathways. So we have good shade from the sun or shelter from the driving rain. We will pass through many small hamlets that seem to blend seamlessly one into the next but few offer any facilities so bring some provisions. **Intermediate accommodation:** *distances from albergue* ❶ *in Sarria:* Barbadelo **4.2** km – Morgade **12.0** km – Ferrerios **13.3** km – Mercadoiro **16.8** km.

❐ **The Mystical Path:** Two ancient Orders occupied opposite sides of this river but their strongholds are long gone – buried under the flood waters created by the dam to serve the insatiable demands of a new generation. We cannot live in the past and we try in vain to live with the idea of some future golden age. The only place we can truly inhabit is the present. The rest is fantasy – some painful, some pleasurable – both deceptive.

❐ **Personal Reflections:** *"… I reflect on the extraordinary revelation of the third secret of Fátima. We are all fallen angels struggling to find our wings so that we can fly back home to the Divine. If God is my Father what does that make me and, by extension, all my fellow brothers and sisters? We each share the same Identity and the same Inheritance. And so I come full circle, back to the place where I began and to the realisation that the only way out – is in. The only way off the mortal coil is through the total forgiveness of self, other and the world. That is why external authority must collapse. The Voice for God is within and urges each one of us, as children of one God, to become the authors of own awakening …"*

0.0 km **Sarria** *Centro* from albergue ❶ in Sarria head up c/Mayor past the church of Santa Mariña (right – provides *credencial*) with its sombre medieval pilgrim murals and past the town hall (left) *Casa do Concello* with (some) tourist information. Next we come into the intimate *Praza da Constitución* with various albergues. cafes and restaurants and towards the top of the street (left) is the Church of St. Saviour *Igrexa de San Salvador XIII[th]C* that has a lovely

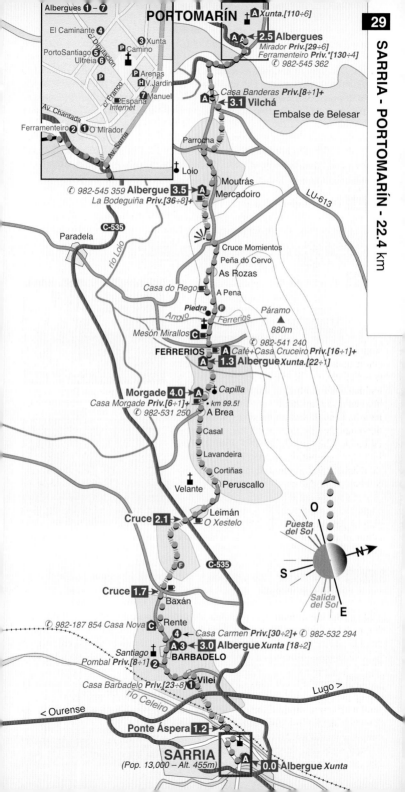

Albergues ❶ – ❼

PORTOMARÍN ✝ Ⓐ Xunta.[110÷6]

El Caminante ❹

c Digitacion

PortoSantiago ❺
Ultreia ❻

P Camino
❸ Xunta

P Arenas
H V.Jardin
c Franco
❼ Manuel

España
Internet
Av. Chantada

Ferramenteiro ❷ ❶ O Mirador

Ⓐ Ⓐ **2.5 Albergues**
Mirador Priv.[29÷6]
Ferramenteiro Priv.*[130÷4]
☎ 982-545 362

Ⓐ ⦁ Casa Banderas Priv.[8÷1]+
3.1 Vilchá

Embalse de Belesar

Parrocha

✝ Loio

☎ 982-545 359 **Albergue 3.5** Ⓐ Moutrás
La Bodeguiña Priv.[36÷8]+ Mercadoiro

LU-613

Paradela

C-535

rio Loio

Cruce Momientos
Peña do Cervo
As Rozas

Casa do Rego ⦁ A Pena

Piedra Ⓕ Páramo
Arroyo Ferreiros ▲ 880m

Mesón Mirallos Ⓒ
☎ 982-541 240
FERREIROS ⦁ Ⓐ Café+Casa Cruceiro Priv.[16÷1]+
Ⓐ **1.3 Albergue** Xunta.[22÷1]

Morgade 4.0 Ⓐ ⦁ Capilla
Casa Morgade Priv.[6÷1]+ ⦁ km 99.5!
☎ 982-531 250 A Brea

Casal

Lavandeira

Cortiñas
Velante ✝ Peruscallo

Cruce 2.1 Leimán
⦁ O Xestelo

Ⓕ
C-535

O
Puesta
del Sol

S N

Salida
del Sol
E

Cruce 1.7
Baxán

☎ 982-187 854 Casa Nova Ⓒ Rente

❹ Casa Carmen Priv.[30÷2]+ ☎ 982-532 294
Ⓐ ❸ **3.0 Albergue** Xunta [18÷2]
Santiago ✝ **BARBADELO**
Pombal Priv.[8÷1] ❷
Casa Barbadelo Priv.[23÷8]+ ❶ ⦁ Vilei

rio Celeiro Lugo >

< Ourense
Ponte Áspera 1.2

SARRIA
(Pop. 13,000 – Alt. 455m) Ⓐ **0.0 Albergue** Xunta

Romanesque tympanum over the main door. Adjacent was St. Anthony's pilgrim Hospice *Hospital de San Anton* (now courts of Justice) and here we turn right> to pass the ruins of the Sarria castle *Fortaleza de Sarria* (left) only one of the 4 original towers remains. The castle was destroyed during the uprising of the peasantry against the aristocracy in the 15th century known as the *Irmandiños*. We pass a stone *cruceiro* (right) with fine views back over the town and up past the country market *Campo da Feira* (left) which has existed here since the 14th century and down to the plasteresque façade of the *Mosteiro da Madalena* [**0.7 km**] (also provides *credencial*) originally instituted in the 13th century, later coming under the Augustinian rule. We finally head down past the cemetery and *Capela de San Lázaro* to cross the road and río Celeiro [**0.5 km**] at:

1.2 km **Ponte Áspera** 'Rough Bridge' which describes its coarsely cut stone. A path now winds between river and railway before crossing the line in *Santi Michaelis* under road viaduct to cross a stream and climb up through delightful ancient woodland to join the road in **Vilei [2.5 km]** **Albergue** ❶ *Casa Barbadelo Priv.[23÷8]* © 982-531 934 with 23 beds €9–12. •Café 108 *km* [**0.5 km**] to:

3.0 km **Barbadelo** ❷ *Xunta.[18÷2]* © 660 396 814 former school house with 18 beds €5 and all facilities. ❸ *O Pombal Priv.[8÷1]* © 686 718 732 in field below the church 8 beds €10 all facilities. *Igrexa de Santiago XII[th]C* Romanesque with a fine tympanum over the entrance door and statue of St. James. Pilgrim mass at 19:00. The area is known locally as Mosteiro in reference to a monastery founded here as early as the 9th century. Behind the Xunta albergue is a summer cantina and at the top of the lane (200m) ❹ *Casa de Carmen Priv.[28÷3]*+ © 982-532 294 with 28 beds €10 + priv. rooms in restored 17th c farmhouse with terrace and private chapel *Capela de San Silvestre*.

Xunta Albergue ❶ *(above)*

Igrexa de Santiago (below)

Continue on road through woodland to **Rente** [**1.1 km**] •**Casa Nova** CR © 982-187 854. We continue along woodland paths through ancient oak and chestnut groves and cross road [**0.7 km**] in:

1.7 km **Cruce** *Baxán* with roadside •*Café* continue on country lane passing [F] to crossover main road:

2.1 km **Cruce** *Leiman* •*Café O Xestelo* s/o in Peruscallo •*Café* [**0.9 km**] *[off route (1 km left) is Romanesque Church at Velante]* continue on path through straggling hamlets with no clear boundaries to pass through the 100 km barrier! (km 100,5) into *A Brea* [**2.1 km**] pass (km 99,5) into Morgade [**1.0 km**]:

4.0 km **Morgade** •**Casa Morgade & Albergue** *Priv.[6÷1]*+ © 982-531 250 with 6 beds €10 + priv. rooms from €28 and popular Bar-restaurant. Pass stone chapel (right) and continue on rough track down (through!) the Ferreiros stream. This is rural Galicia at her best; green and wet underfoot with the earthy

smell of cow dung. Narrow laneways with granite stepping-stones raised above normal flood levels and another gentle climb up to:

1.3 km **Ferreiros** traditional *Mesón Casa Cruceiro* and ultra mod (2012) **Albergue ❶** *Casa Cruceiro Priv.[16÷1]*+ ✆ 982-541 240 with 16 beds from €10 + priv. €35. **❷***Xunta. [22÷1]* ✆ 686 744 940 with 22 beds €6 in former schoolhouse set in a leafy glade (see photo). *[Ferreiros translates as blacksmith].*  Continue past •**Mesón Mirallos** CR café-inn adjoining the Romanesque Church of Santa María and just beyond (also on the left) the ancient •*Chalice Stone* and up steeply merging from road to track passing **A Pena** •*Casa do Rego* bar-café with plans for future albergue ✆ 982 167 812. Couto, Rozas [F] and the high point *Pena dos Corvos 660m* with fine views over the reservoir as we begin our descent into the río Miño valley:

3.5 km Mercadoiro Albergue *La Bodeguiña Priv.[36÷8]*+ ✆ 982-545 359 with 32 beds €10 + priv. rooms €40. Popular café-restaurant adjoining (see photo) with pilgrim menu in this delightful hamlet with an official population of – one! Continue through the hamlets of Moutras and A Parrocha. *[off route left is the remote and beautiful valley of Loio with the ruins of the Monastery of Santa María de Loio – birthplace of the Order of*  *Santiago in the 12th century].* The route crosses over several country lanes to drop down steeply on rough asphalt lane into:

3.1 km Vilachá between KM marker 92 and 91.5 is **Albergue** *Casa Banderas Priv.[8÷1]*+ ✆ 982-545 391 with 8 beds €10 + priv. room €30 all meals available from South African owner. Now we follow the road and make our way over the modern bridge over the deep Miño basin into Portomarín. The original bridge was of Roman origin and joined the southern district of San Pedro (with links to the Knights of Santiago) with the northern district of San Nicolás (headquarters of the Knights of Saint John). The river formed a major strategic boundary and consequently the area had a turbulent past. The steep staircase in front is part of the original medieval bridge across the river Miño. These lead up to the arch and *capela de Santa María de las Nieves* which, along with several other historic monuments, were all removed to the high ground around Portomarín when the dam was built across the river to create the Belesar reservoir in 1962. Climb the stairs and turn <left for the lower 2 albergues with fine views over the river.

2.5 km **Portomarín** Albergue **❶** *O Mirador Priv.[29÷6]* ✆ 982-545 323 the first hostel as we enter the town with 29 beds €10. meals available in the popular *mirador* bar and restaurant above with views over the rio Miño. Adjoining it •**Albergue ❷** *Ferramenteiro Priv.***[130÷4]* ✆ 982-545 362 network* hostel with 130 beds €10 and excellent modern facilities in this purpose built hostel overlooking the river.

Albergue ❶ *O Mirador*

The centre of the town (and action) is at the top end ½ kilometre further on.

Continue up the cobbled main street *rúa Xeral Franco* with its handsome stone colonnades into the main square *Praza Conde de Fenosa* in the centre of which is austere Romanesque church of San Nicolás *XIIthC*, sometimes referred to as San Juan or San Xoán due to its links with the Knights of Saint John. It was painstakingly rebuilt from its original site now submerged under the reservoir and is ascribed to the workshop of Master Mateo who carved the Portico de Gloria in Santiago. At the back of the square are the handsome *Casa do Concello* and *Correos*.

A variety of cafés, restaurants hotels and pensiones surround the square. Just behind the church is: **Albergue ❸** *Xunta.[110÷6]* ℂ 982-545 143. The original hostel (recently renovated) with 110 beds €5 and all modern facilities with washing and drying machines at the rear. Up to the left of the church (from the main street) are: **Albergue ❹** *El Caminante Priv.[12÷1]+* ℂ 982 545 176 located on c/ Rúa Sánchez Carro. 12 beds €10 + ind. rooms from €28 + bar/ restaurant. Just below on c/

Albergue ❸ *Xunta*

Diputación **Albergue ❺** *Ultreia Priv.[14]+* ℂ 982-545 067 private hostel with 14 beds €10 + priv. rooms – adjacent is **Albergue ❻** *Porto Santiago Priv.*[14÷2]+* ℂ 618 826 515 network* hostel 14 beds €10 + ind. rooms €20. Down below the main square on c/Rua Miño **Albergue ❼** *Manuel Priv.[16÷1]+* ℂ 982-545 385 with 16 beds €10 + adjoining pension with 4 rooms from €25.

Other accommodation: in the central square *Praza Condes Fenosa* •**Posada del Camino** ℂ 982-545 081 with restaurant also •**Arenas** Pr** ℂ 982-545 386. Nearby •**Villajardín H**° ℂ 982-545 200 Rúa do Miño, 14. and at the top end of town and price bracket: •**Pousada de Portomarín H***** ℂ 982-545 200 adjacent to the attractive Parque Antonio Sanz and nearby Church of Saint Peter *Iglesia San Pedro* with fine Romanesque doorway. *[Next albergue: Gonzar – 8.2 km].*

Posada del Camino

REFLECTIONS:

❏ **The foolish man seeks happiness in the distance; the wise man grows it under his feet.** *J R Oppenheimer*

---

30 **92.8** km (57.7 miles) to Santiago

PORTOMARÍN – PALAS DE REI

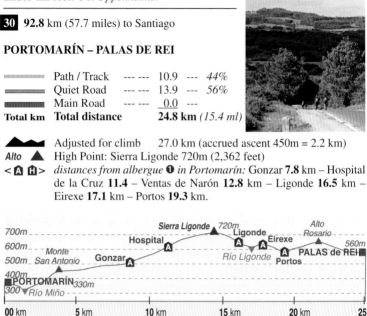

▦ Path / Track	--- ---	10.9	--- *44%*
▦ Quiet Road	--- ---	13.9	--- *56%*
▦ Main Road	--- ---	0.0	---
Total km **Total distance**		**24.8 km** *(15.4 ml)*	

◣ Adjusted for climb 27.0 km (accrued ascent 450m = 2.2 km)

Alto ▲ High Point: Sierra Ligonde 720m (2,362 feet)

< 🅰 🅷 > *distances from albergue* ❶ *in Portomarín:* Gonzar **7.8** km – Hospital de la Cruz **11.4** – Ventas de Narón **12.8** km – Ligonde **16.5** km – Eirexe **17.1** km – Portos **19.3** km.

The Practical Path: A day of varied terrain as we start by skirting the reservoir *Embalse de Belesar* climbing up through woodland to join the main road which we have to cross and re-cross on several occasions before leaving it to climb the ridge beyond Ventas de Narón *Sierra Ligonde*, descending to Portos which offers us the detour to Vilar de Donas. Then comes a gentler climb around the side of Rosary Heights *Alto Rosario* to drop down finally to Palas de Rei. Prepare for an early start if you intend to take the detour to Vilas de Donas.

❏ **The Mystical Path:** Will you make time to detour to this mystical resting place of the Knights of Saint James? Here effigies of the knights in their armour are watched over by the beautiful frescoes that adorn the walls of this sacred temple dedicated to Saint Saviour. A pilgrim must travel on two paths simultaneously. The tourist will look for the stone altar – the pilgrim an altered state. The one seeks sacred sites – the other in-sight. Will you make time today to detour into the inner mystery?

❏ **Personal Reflections:** *"... The incessant rain pounds down as heavy as when it started a week ago. The country is awash; roads have turned to rivers – rivers to torrents. I sat for a while at the base of the ancient oak and felt its solid support and in the same instant knew that my period of silence was ended. I don't know how long I been in this altered state, induced as much by physical exhaustion as any ecstatic revelation. And I don't know how long they had been there but they helped me to my feet and we embraced in love and respect for the experiences we had each invoked; 3 pilgrims from 3 different countries with 3 different languages but part of one family. I found it hard to speak after such a long spell of silence but I managed to say 'bless you' realising that with every breath I send out positive or negative vibrations. Regardless of outer conditions I can choose to send out love. Until that moment I had not noticed the ancient wayside cross silently witnessing this loving meeting of fellow pilgrims ..."*

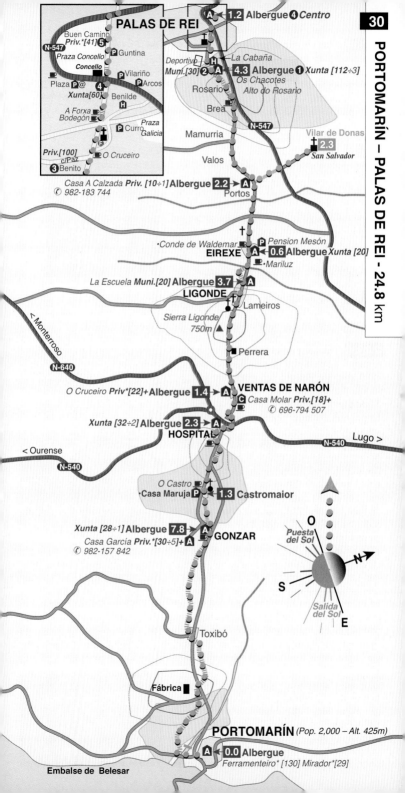

PALAS DE REI

Buen Camino *Priv.**[41] **5**
N-547
Praza Concello
Concello
P Guntina
P Vilariño
Plaza P@ **4**
Xunta[60]
P Arcos
Benilde
H
A Forxa
Bodegón
P Curro
Praza Galicia
Priv.[100]
c/Paz
O Cruceiro
3 Benito

A ←**1.2** Albergue **4** *Centro*

Deportivo ☐ **2** A ←*La Cabaña*
Muni.[30]
←**4.3** Albergue **1** *Xunta* [112÷3]
Rosario
Os Chacotes
Alto do Rosario
Brea
N-547
Vilar de Donas
2.3
San Salvador
Mamurria
Valos

Casa A Calzada Priv. [10÷1] Albergue **2.2** →A
☎ 982-183 744
Portos

†
·Conde de Waldemar·
P Pension Mesón
A ←**0.6** Albergue *Xunta* [20]
EIREXE
·*Mariluz*·

La Escuela Muni.[20] Albergue **3.7** →A
LIGONDE
†
Lameiros
Sierra Ligonde 750m ▲
Perrera

< Monterroso
N-640

O Cruceiro Priv*[22]+ Albergue **1.4** →A **VENTAS DE NARÓN**
C *Casa Molar Priv.*[18]+
☎ 696-794 507

Xunta [32÷2] Albergue **2.3** →A
HOSPITAL
N-540 Lugo >

< Ourense
N-540

O Castro ☐ †
·*Casa Maruja* P ←**1.3** Castromaior

Xunta [28÷1] Albergue **7.8** →A GONZAR
Casa García Priv.*[30÷5]+ A
☎ 982-157 842

O
Puesta del Sol
N
S
Salida del Sol
E

☐ Toxibó

Fábrica ■

PORTOMARÍN (Pop. 2,000 – Alt. 425m)

A ←**0.0** Albergue
Ferramenteiro* [130] Mirador*[29]

Embalse de Belesar

`0.0 km` **Portomarín** from albergue ❶ return to the *Escalinata N. S das Nieves* and turn right> to pass the petrol station and <left on bridge over the río Torres. We now make our way up through dense woodland around St. Anthony's height *alto San Antonio* to join the pilgrim track *senda* by the main road at San Mamed-Belad **[2.5 km]** cross over opposite tile factory *Fábrica de Ladrillos* and re-cross by Coren fertilizer plant in Toxibo **[1.6 km]** after which we have a brief and delightful respite through woodland past [F] to Gonzar **[3.7 km]**.

`7.8 km` **Gonzar** busy •*Café Descanso del Peregrino* on the main road and •**Albergue** ❶ *Xunta [28÷1]* ℂ 982-157 840 noisy location but recently refurbished with 28 beds €5. Around the corner (100m) is •**Albergue** ❷ *Casa Garcia* **Priv.** *[30÷5]+* ℂ 982-157 842 traditional village house with covered courtyard (see photo) in quiet location off main road with 30 beds €10 + priv. rooms €35 and •*Café-restaurant* Continue and turn off <left onto minor road and then right> onto track before joining road into:

`1.3 km` **Castromaior** •**Casa Maruja** P* ℂ 982-189 054 •*Café O Castro* (originally a Celtic castro) with its tiny Romanesque church of Santa María. Continue through the village hopping over the main road and back to:

`2.3 km` **Hospital de la Cruz** where the N-540 cuts rudely through this ancient village – its medieval pilgrim hospice no longer visible, but hospitality awaits at •**El Labrador** Pension and restaurant and just beyond •**Albergue** *Xunta.[32÷2]* ℂ 982-545 232 another conversion of a school building by the main road with 32 beds €5. The main road is on a blind bend at this point (N-540 Ourense – Lugo) take the minor road across to the next village.

`1.4 km` **Ventas de Narón** •**Albergue** ❶ *Casa Molar Priv.[18]+* ℂ 696-794 507 attractively renovated rural house with 18 beds €10 + priv. rooms €30. Good facilities (no kitchen) but restaurant and bar (see photo right). •**Albergue** ❷ *O Cruceiro Priv.*[22]+* ℂ 658-064 917 with 22 beds €10 + priv. rooms from €30. No kitchen but restaurant and bar.

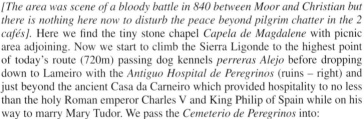

[The area was scene of a bloody battle in 840 between Moor and Christian but there is nothing here now to disturb the peace beyond pilgrim chatter in the 2 cafés]. Here we find the tiny stone chapel *Capela de Magdalene* with picnic area adjoining. Now we start to climb the Sierra Ligonde to the highest point of today's route (720m) passing dog kennels *perreras Alejo* before dropping down to Lameiro with the *Antiguo Hospital de Peregrinos* (ruins – right) and just beyond the ancient Casa da Carneiro which provided hospitality to no less than the holy Roman emperor Charles V and King Philip of Spain while on his way to marry Mary Tudor. We pass the *Cemeterio de Peregrinos* into:

`3.7 km` **Ligonde** ancient hamlet long associated with the camino with its *Cemeterio de Peregrinos* and humble hospitality at •**Albergue** *Fuente del Peregrino* **Priv.** *[20÷2]* ℂ 687 550 527 offered by religious organisation with 20 beds € *donativo* (summer only) and basic facilities but communal meal

offered.
•**Albergue** *Escuela Muni.[20]* © 679 816
061 skilfully restored hostel with all facilities.
Ligonde was formerly a significant medieval
stop on the way. Charlemagne reputedly
stayed here and other royal personages and it
had a pilgrim hospice. The church is dedicated
to Santiago and has a Romanesque porch.

Opposite the Albergue is a short track down and over the río Ligonde passing
café-restaurant •*Casa Mari Luz* up past church and cruceiro into:

0.6 km Eirexe •**Albergue** *Xunta.[20÷2]* © 982-153 483 ex-school building
at village crossroads with 20 beds €5 and all facilities. Also around the village
green are: • **Mesón Eirexe** © 982-153 475 pension and bar-restaurant and also

•*Conde Valdemar*. Continue on quiet country
road passing splendid 17th century wayside
cross (left) by gnarled oak tree and the ancient
hamlet of Lameiros with its diminutive capela
San Marcos we climb gently to cross of 5 roads
with fine views of the surrounding countryside
before dropping down again over stream
through Portos to:

2.2 km A Calzada *Detour* •**Albergue** *A
Calzada Priv.[10÷1]* © 982-183 744 private
hostel with 10 beds €10 in separate stone
pavilion at the rear (see photo right). No kitchen
but meals available at the café-restaurant with
peaceful garden and picnic area.

Detour: Vilar de Donas recommended
detour (4.6 km there and back) to this national
monument and ancient seat of the Knights
of Santiago. Closed Mondays and holidays
(check in A Calzada for opening times before
proceeding). The Church of El Salvador is
primarily 14th century but its origins go back
to the formation of a nunnery here in the 10th
century (hence the appellation Donas). The
stone effigies of the knights and its unique

frescoes (see photo under reflections) and are hauntingly expressive. ***Directions:***
Turn right off the camino (opposite A Calzada) along quiet country lane across
the main road [1.1 km] (N-547 Palas de Rei – Lugo) passing rest area *área de
descanco* (right) for remaining [1.2 km] to:

2.3 km Vilar de Donas – Igrexa San Salvador. Take time to soak in its ancient
history and to savour its treasures lovingly attended by the knowledgeable
guardian and recently restored. Return the same way.

From *A Calzada* continue along pathways into and through the hamlets of
Lestedo [0.6 km] •**Rectoral de Lestedo** CR © 982-153 435 Converted from
an original pilgrim hospital, then priests house *casa rectoral* and finally to
this modernised gem with rooms from €57. Dinner available. We pass village
cemetery and then Valos, Mamurria and on to *A Brea* [1.8 km] •*Mesón A Brea*

on the main N-547. A short woodland path at the back of the restaurant takes us up to *Alto Rosario* [**0.9** km]. Here (before the trees were planted) you could see the sacred peak above Santiago *Pico Sacro* and on entering the hamlet of Rosario pilgrims would start to recite the Rosary, hence the name. We now pass through the hamlet (which adjoins the main road) before entering the suburbs of Palas de Reis and its delightful municipal parkland [**1.0** km]:

4.3 km Palas de Rei *Pavillón* •Albergue ❶ *Os Chacotes Xunta.[112÷3]* ✆ 607 481 536 with 3 cavernous dormitories packed tightly with bunk beds €5. The design is so modern they even invented a new description *Pavillón de Peregrinos*. Directly opposite is a pilgrim assistance centre and a new (more traditional) municipal hostel •Albergue ❷ *Muni.[30]* with basic facilities only and likewise surrounded

Albergue ❶ Os Chacotes

by the wide recreation area. Here also we find the hotel •La Cabana ✆ 982-380 950 with chalet style rooms and restaurant. Continue past sports stadium into town passing c/Paz (left 50m) to •Albergue ❸ *Mesón de Benito Priv. [100÷7]* ✆ 636 834 065 with100 beds €10 and modern restaurant. Continue into town passing *Café O Cruceiro* and the parish church of San Tirso first built in the 11th century now only retaining its original Romanesque doorway. [F]. Continue over the road down into the town centre:

1.2 km Palas de Rei •Albergue ❹ *Xunta [60÷7]+* ✆ 660 396 820 prominently located at main road junction directly opposite the Town Hall *Casa Concello* the original pilgrim hostel still providing 60 beds €5 with all basic facilities, somewhat neglected but popular on account of its central position. Just over the road on rua do Peregrino (backing on to praza Concello) is •Albergue ❺ *Buen Camino Priv.*[41÷8]* ✆ 982-380 233 network* hostel with 41 beds €10 in renovated town house with all facilities. *[Next albergue: Mato Casanova – 6.3 km].*

Albergue ❹ Xunta Central

Other accommodation: •Casa Curro P* ✆ 982-380 044 Av. Ourense. •Casa Benilde Hr** ✆ 982-380 717 c/del Mercado. Pensión Bar •Guntina Pr* ✆ 982-380 080 on Travesia do Peregrino (opp. Buen Camino). The main N-547 goes through the town centre as *Av. de Compostela* on which we find: •Vilariño Hs* ✆ 982-380 152 and •Plaza P ✆ 982-380 109 with internet café.

Palas de Rei stands directly on the way but little remains to remind us of its illustrious past. The Church of San Tirso has a Romanesque portal and scallop shell motifs are visible in the town. Today, it is an administrative centre with good modern facilities serving a population of 2,000. The regular Lugo – Santiago bus stops here and if you didn't take the detour to Vilar de Donas you can always share a taxi there from this point (see mural right).

REFLECTIONS:

❐ **Walking, I am listening to a deeper way. Suddenly all my ancestors are behind me.** *'Be still, they say. Watch and listen. You are the result of the love of thousands'.* Linda Hogan

31 **68.0** km (42.3 miles) to Santiago

PALAS DE REI – RIBADISO (ARZÚA)

	Path / Track	--- ---	14.8	---	57%
	Quiet Road	--- ---	10.2	---	40%
	Main Road	--- ---	0.8	---	3%
Total km	**Total distance**		**25.8 km** (16.0 ml)		

Adjusted for climb   26.7 km (accrued ascent 180m = 0.9 km)
Alto ▲   High Point: O Coto 515m (1,670 feet)
< 🅐 🄷 >   San Xulián **3.5** km – Casanova **5.8** km – O Coto **8.5** km –
       Melide **15.0** km – Boente **20.5** km – Castañeda **22.8** km.

560m
■PALAS de REI   Coto   515m
500m 🅐   Casanova 🅐 ▲   MELIDE   Boente   Portela
400m - - - Río Pambre - - - - - - - - - - 🅐 - - - 🅐🅐 - - RIBADISO
300m - - - - - - - - - - - - - - - - - Río Furelos - - - Río Boente - 230m■
                                              Río Iso
00 km   **5 km**   **10 km**   **15 km**   **20 km**   **25**

The Practical Path: Today we cross 6 shallow river valleys and half is on pathways mostly through woodland that helps to stifle the noise from the busy N-547 which we cross and re-cross all the way to Arzúa. Melide makes a good half way stop where we can sample the renowned octopus *pulpo Galega*. If you intend to detour off the route to visit Pambre Castle or the famous Pazo Ulloa you need to leave early in the morning.

❐ **The Mystical Path:** Will you see the tiny representation of Santiago in the flyover? He appears at the entrance and the exit, welcoming us and blessing us on our way. What does he represent to you and why do we follow his way? Is it to revere his relics that may lie in a silver casket two days ahead? Is that what brought you this far? Do you believe he chose to martyr his earthly body so we could venerate it? He has many names, but who was he really and what significance does he play in our story? What unknown hand beckons us to follow in the way of the true Master? Where will we find Him?

❐ **Personal Journal:** *"... In each passing moment I sense my guides setting up situations for me to learn the next lesson. I have an image of adoring angels urging me to learn through grace rather than grit. But the lesson will be integrated in perfect timing and with exquisite precision for the exact amount of sand required to produce the pearl. Not one grain too many, but, alas, not one grain too few. So my angelic escort set me up Toshio, just when I had lost my inner way and was confused as to my motivation. And he asks me three questions: each one a reminder of my reason for doing this pilgrimage and an invaluable aid to its accomplishment. How, in heaven's name, did they conceive of a Japanese Shinto grandfather to place on the earthly path of a lost Christian soul? ..."*

0.0 km **Palas de Rei** *Centro* from albergue ❹ continue over the N-547 down rua do Peregrino and over the N-547 past the monument and field of the pilgrims *Campo dos Romeiros* where medieval pilgrims gathered for the

ARZÚA (Pop. 7,000 – Alt. 390m)

© 981-500 554 •El Retiro **H**

Túnel

N-547

RIBADISO

© 647-020 600 •Los Caminantes **Priv.[52]+ ❷ ⊞Ⓐ❶ 3.0** Albergue *Xunta* [70÷4]

Manuel

Portela
© *Casa Garea* © 981-500 400
© Casa Milia

© 605 787 382 •La Calleja
Albergue **2.3** Ⓒ Ⓐ **Castañeda**
© 981-501 711 •Santiago **Priv.[6÷1]** Ⓑ

río Boente

Boente 3.2 →❶†
Os Albergues **Priv.[28÷8]** ❶Ⓐ
Boente **Priv.[22÷5]** ❷

Raído

Penas

río Boente

A Coruña >
C-540

Carballal

San Lázaro

2.7 Puente

S.María

6

MELIDE (Pop. 8,000)

C-540
1.5 Centro
†■ San Pedro

Furelos †■Ⓕ❶Ⓗ Carlos
4.6 Puente

río Furelos

Polígono
Industrial
Gándarra

N-547

Ⓕ

Disicabo
†Sta.María XIII

Lobreiro

Río Seco

Ramil

O Coto 2.7
Ⓒ *Casa de Somoza* © 981-507 372
Cornixa

Remonde

A CORUÑA

Castillo Pambre 🏰

LUGO

© 609 124 717 •A Bolboreta Ⓒ Ⓐ

N-547

Ⓐ ◂ **2.3 Mato-Casanova** *Xunta.[20÷]*

Pazo Ulloa 🏛

© 982-163 226 Casa Domingo **Priv.*[14]** Ⓐ

Ponte Campaña Mato

N-547

San Xulián
Albergue 3.5 →Ⓐ
© 676 596 975 O Abrigadoiro **Priv.[18]**

Carballal

© 982-380 132 •Ponterroxan Ⓟ
Ⓕ

Centro 0.0 ◂Ⓐ **PALAS de REI**
Albergue **4** (Pop. 4,500 – Alt. 575m)

Inset map (MELIDE):

Río Iso

Ⓐ Ⓐ

O

Puesta
del Sol

S

Salida
del Sol

E

6 Xunta
H Chiquitin

Pereiro
3

5
Apalpador **4** Vilela

MELIDE

Estilo
Ⓟ

❷ Cruceiro
Ⓟ Berenguela

† Crucero
■ S.Pedro

Pulpería ❶❶
Pulpería ❶❶

❶ Alb.Melide
H Carlos   Ⓟ Xaneiro

journey to Santiago and onto a path to cross the N-547 again past [F] and back down to the N-547 with pensión •**Ponterroxan** P ℰ 982-380 132 and cross the river Ruxián and up into Carballal with its raised granaries *Horreos* and back down to re-cross the N-547 onto woodland path into:

3.5 km San Xulián (*Xiao*) do Camiño classical camino village with its tiny 12th century church dedicated to Saint Julian and •**Albergue** *O Abrigadoiro Priv.[18÷3]* ℰ 676 596 975 with 18 beds €10. No kitchen but dinner and breakfast available. The path continues down to the Rió Pambre that we cross at Ponte Campaña-Mato [**1.0** km] and •**Albergue** *Casa Domingo Priv.*[14÷3]* ℰ 982-163 226 network* hostel with 18 beds €10 and occupying a tranquil rural setting on the river. No kitchen but communal meals available. The route now climbs gently through ancient oak woods for [**1.3** km] to Mato-Casonova:

2.3 km Casanova •**Albergue** *Xunta.[20÷2]* ℰ 982-173 483 the last Xunta hostel in Lugo before we enter into A Coruña. 20 beds €5 in this quiet rural location surrounded by woodland. We proceed up the country lane to junction (left) for *off route* (2 km) albergue and casa rural •**A Bolboreta** *Priv.[8÷2]*+ ℰ 609 124 717. Traditional house in Vilar de Remonde with 8 beds €13 incl. + ind. rooms

Albergue *Casanova*

from €27 and all meals available. A good place from which to detour as below.

Detour: Castillo de Pambre and **Pazo de Ulloa**. 3 km along the quiet country road we have just joined is the impressive 14th century Castillo de Pambre. Strategically situated on the río Pambre it has survived the advances of time and the Irmandiños revolt (the war in which the aristocracy were fighting the peasants rather than each other) but is currently engaged in a dispute between private ownership and public access. Unlike its counterpart in Sarria, the four corner towers and inner keep are still proudly standing. 2 km further still is the Palacio Villamayor de Ulloa one of the best-preserved Galician manor houses *Pazos* and setting for the novel *Los Pazos de Ulloa* by Emilia Pardo Bazán (only available in Spanish).

Continue up the Pass of the Oxen *Porto de Bois [scene of a bloody battle between warring nobility]* and then up to Campanilla the high point of this stage at 515m before crossing over the provincial border at an unsightly car scrap yard in Cornixa to:

2.7 km O Coto hamlet at the crossroads with •Casa de Somoza CR ℰ 981-507 372 also •**Die Zwei Deutschen** *Los dos Alemanes* P ℰ 981-507 337. We now follow a delightful undulating track through woods to cross a medieval bridge into the quintessential camino village of ***Leboreiro*** [**0.7** km] *field of hares* no facilities (a former hostel no longer appears open) but with the 13th century Romanesque Church of Santa María with a lovely carved stone tympanum of Virgin and Child over the main door. The house opposite with armorial shield was formerly a pilgrim hostel donated by the wealthy Ulloa (*pazo*) family. We now cross the medieval Magdalena Bridge over the río Seco into ***Disicabo*** [**0.5** km]. The path continues up towards the main road and over a footbridge to join a stretch of senda separating the N-547 from an industrial estate *polígono industrial Gándara* [F] [**1.6** km]. Here the *Orde de Caballeros y Damas del Camino de Santiago* have erected a monument to themselves and a huge sword of Santiago leads us back through woodland down to:

4.6 km Furelos *Ponte Velha* medieval bridge into Furelos where a traditional village house has been turned into a museum. Church of *San Juan* but no trace remains of the pilgrim hospice that used to adjoin the church (a replacement hostel is planned). Bar taberna •*Farruco*. [F] From here we begin the climb up to Melide through modern suburbs to join the main road opposite the Romanesque Church of *San Pedro & San Roque* beside its famous 14thc stone cross reputed to be the oldest in Galicia *Crucero do Melide* – Christ in majesty facing us and Christ crucified on the reverse. We now make our way up past the main square (left) to the busy cross roads and roundabout *Ronda de la Coruña*.

1.6 km Melide *Centro* Albergue ❷ *O Cruceiro Priv.[72÷10]* © 616 764 896 opened in 2013 right in the centre with its neo-classical facade. 72 rooms €10 with all facilities. *Note:* ❶ *Melide Priv.[42÷2]* is down at the far end of Av. Lugo (Nº92) with 42 beds €10 – opp. Hotel **Carlos** © 981-507 633. ❸ *Pereiro [45÷4]* c/Progreso, 43 © 981-506 314 opened in 2013 with 45 rooms €10. ● From the central roundabout a route continues via the old town into rua Principal or the main route down rua San Antonio with access to the remaining albergues as follows: ❹ *Vilela Priv.[24÷3]* © 616 011 375 with 24 beds €10. ❺ Albergue *O Apalpador Priv.[30÷3]* © 679 837 969 with 30 beds €12 and finally at the end of the street (and the town) ❻*Xunta.[156÷7]* © 660-396 822 with 156 beds €6. All with modern facilities. **Other Accommodation: Berenguela** Pension © 981-505 417 rúa San Roque,2 (by roundabout) single rooms from €30. •**Xaneiro II** Hs** © 981-506 140 Av. de la Habana. Cafe/Pension •**Estilo** c/del Progreso and in the old opposite the main albergue is chic pousada •**Chiquitín** Hr*** © 981-815 333 with restaurant, roof terrace and rooms from €30.

MELIDE a prosperous administrative centre with a population of 8,000. The old part follows its medieval layout with narrow winding streets with shops, bars and restaurants serving the regional speciality, octopus *pulpo*. For a genuine experience try *pulpería Exequiel* on Av.de Lugo on the way into town. In *Plaza del Convento* we find the austere parish church, Sancti Spiritus, formerly a 14thc Augustinian monastery. Opposite was the hospice de Sancti Spiritus that served the Jacobean pilgrimage. This is the point where pilgrims travelling down from Oviedo on the original pilgrim route *camino Primitivo* join the *camino Francés*. In the Casa Municipal is an interesting museum and displays of the traditional life of this part of Galicia *Museo Etnográfico*.

We leave Melida via the western suburbs past the cemetery across the N-547 (sign San Martiño) past the Romanesque church *Igrexa Santa María de Melide XII (see photo)* where we finally leave the busyness of Melide behind and make our way into woodland to the arroyo San Lázaro (the remains of the leprosy hospice long disappeared).

1.6 km Arroyo San Lázaro we cross this small river via a stone causeway

[We cross several shallow river valleys during these final stages so our path is more arduous than the contour plans might suggest. Ultreya!] Our way is now by path that winds through shaded forest, oak and chestnut increasingly giving way to eucalyptus and pine. Continue through Carballal and the river beyond **[1.6 km]** through Parabispo over the río Raído with picnic area **[2.2 km]** passing Peroxa and Boente de Arriba back down to the N-547 **[1.1 km]** at:

5.5 km **Boente** *Igrexa Santiago* with image of the Saint above the altar and convivial parish priest who offers a blessing to passing pilgrims. A welcoming new (2012) **Albergue ❶** *Boente Priv.[22÷5]* ℂ 981 501 974 with 22 beds €10 + menú. **Albergue ❷** *Os Albergues Priv.[28÷8]* ℂ 629 146 826 with 28 beds €10. Also bar •*Os Mesón.* We leave past Cruceiro and [F] and through underpass down into the Boente valley with shaded rest area (right) the delightful riverside setting somewhat marred by the noise of traffic. Up the other side we join minor road (N-547 in a cutting below) into Castañeda past café •*No Camino* and the parish Church of Santa María to:

2.3 km Castañeda •**Albergue** *Priv.[6÷1]+* ℂ 981-501 711. Private hostel located on the corner with 6 beds €10 + priv. rooms from €30. No kitchen but attractive terrace bar and restaurant. It was here in Castañeda that the pilgrims would deposit the limestone rocks they had brought from Triacastela to be fired for the lime used in the building of the

Cathedral at Santiago. Just beyond the albergue we pass the popular casa rural •**La Calleja** ℂ 605 787 382 rooms from £25 and down over river with shaded rest area **[0.6 km]**. From here we go around a wooded hill with track (right) **[0.5 km]** to N-547 casa rurales •**Garea** ℂ 981-500 400 and •**Milía** ℂ 981-515 241 (400m *off* route). We now climb to alto (440m) and cross a raised pass over the N-547 **[1.0 km]** through woodland to pick up minor road with café-bar •*Manuel* **[0.6 km]** down to the fine medieval bridge over the río Iso **[0.3 km]** at:

3.0 km Ribadiso •**Albergue ❶** *Xunta. [70÷4]* ℂ 981-501 185 idyllic location on the river Iso adjoining the medieval bridge. 70 beds €5 (toilets located in a separate block) and all facilities. Pleasant space to relax on the river bank (weather permitting). This is a wonderful reconstruction of one of the oldest pilgrim hospitals still in existence with an award for environmental architecture. Adjoining bar and restaurant (see photos). In 2011 an adjoining pilgrim hostel was opened •**Albergue ❷** *Priv.[52÷4]+* ℂ 647-020 600 52 beds €10 + priv. rooms.

[Next albergue: Arzúa – 2.0 km]. Also modern casa rural •**Vaamonde** ℂ 981 500 364 off route in Traseirexe and on the way into Arzúa (directly en route) the refurbished •**O Retiro** P** ℂ 981-500 554 with restaurant (1.8 km but up steeply).

REFLECTIONS:

_____

_____

_____

_____

_____

_____

_____

_____

_____

_____

_____

_____

_____

_____

_____

_____

_____

_____

_____

_____

_____

_____

_____

_____

_____

❏ **Let no one ever come to you without leaving better and happier.** *M.Teresa*

32 **42.2** km (26.2 miles) to Santiago

RIBADISO – O PEDROUZO *(ARCA / O PINO)*

▥▥▥ Path / Track --- ---	14.6	---	66%
▬▬▬ Quiet Road --- ---	2.7	---	12%
▬▬▬ Main Road --- ---	4.8	---	22%
Total km Total distance	**22.1 km** (13.7 ml)		

◣◢ Adjusted for climb   22.9 km (accrued ascent 160m = 0.8 km)
Alto ▲ High Point: Santa Irene 420m (1,378 feet)
< Ⓐ Ⓗ > Arzúa **3.1** km – Salceda 14.2 km – Santa Irene **19.4** km.

[elevation profile]
Alto de Santa Irene
400m Arzúa Pereiriña   Salceda 405m ▲ S. Irene
RIBADISO Ⓐ   Calle   Ⓐ   ARCA
300m   Río Ladrón   Río Languello   290m
200m   Arroyo Burgo
00 km   5 km   10 km   15 km   20 km

The Practical Path: 2/3rds of today we walk on natural pathways with good shade offered by the ubiquitous eucalyptus. We start with a steep climb up into Arzúa and end with a climb around the alto de Santa Irene. In between we have a largely level path with just 3 shallow river valleys.

❏ **The Mystical Path:** The beautiful memorial to Guillermo Watt is timely. What plans have *we* made for our onward journey? Or are we too preoccupied with the dramas of this life to consider the next? To contemplate the impermanence of our earthly form can be revitalising, urging us to make every step a prayer for understanding, every breath a song of gratitude, every moment a chance to awaken from the dream that keeps us separate from our eternal Source.

❏ **Personal Reflections:** *"... The debate became heated, the only seeming accord being that the problems that beset our world were real and worsening. She had remained silent but now took the rare moment of quiet to state with utter conviction, 'There is only one solution'. Her words made us attentive – 'Allah'. The response was so unexpected. We had been looking for solutions on the level of the problem – our human condition of fear. She was a Sufi devotee. I laugh at the paradox that it took a Muslim woman walking an outwardly Christian path to point out to us the deeper truth that lay beyond. Whatever name we choose to describe the ineffable is immaterial. The only way out of our dilemma, is inward through Love ..."*

0.0 km **Ribadiso** from the albergue proceed up to and through the tunnel under the N-547 and veer right> on the far side back onto track parallel to the main road which we follow all the way into Arzua passing café-hostal **[1.8 km]** •El Retiro ✆ 982-500 554 and another **[0.6 km]** to •**Albergue ❶** *Don Quijote Priv.*[50÷3] ✆ 981-500 139 network* hostel in modern terraced building on the left as we enter Arzúa on c/Lugo – 50 beds €10 no kitchen but bar/ café. Adjoining is •**Albergue ❷** *Ultreia Priv.*[39÷2] ✆ 981-500 471 another network* hostel in same modern block with

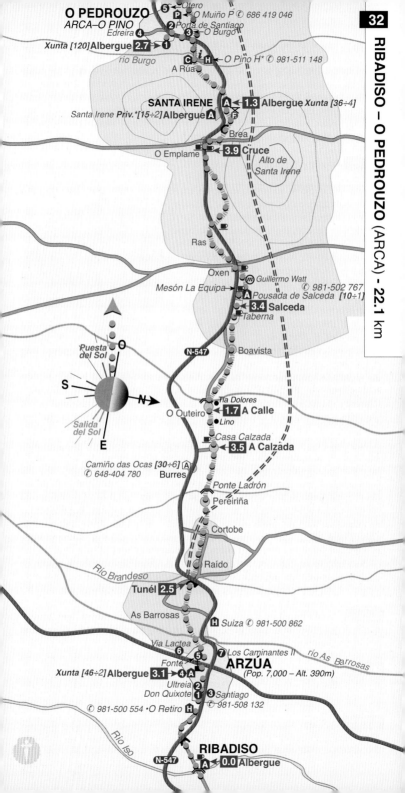

O PEDROUZO
ARCA–O PINO

⑤ *Otero*
Ⓟ *O Muiño P* ℂ 686 419 046
② *Porta de Santiago*
Edreira ④
③ *O Burgo*

Xunta [120] Albergue **2.7** →①

río Burgo
Ⓒ ⓘ Ⓗ — *O Pino H** ℂ 981-511 148
A Rúa

SANTA IRENE
Ⓐ ←**1.3** Albergue *Xunta [36÷4]*
✕
Santa Irene Priv.*[15÷2] Albergue Ⓐ
Ⓕ
Brea

O Emplame **←3.9** Cruce
Alto de Santa Irene

Ras

Oxen
ⓜ *Guillermo Watt*
℃ 981-502 767
Mesón La Equipa→ Ⓐ *Pousada de Salceda [10÷1]*
3.4 Salceda
Taberna

N-547
Boavista

Puesta del Sol
O
S ⟵ N
E
Salida del Sol

Tía Dolores
O Outeiro ←**1.7** A Calle
Lino

Casa Calzada
3.5 ← A Calzada

Camiño das Ocas [30÷6] Ⓐ
℃ 648-404 780
Burres

Ponte Ladrón
Pereiriña

Cortobe

Raído

Río Brandeso
Tunél **2.5**

As Barrosas
Ⓗ *Suiza* ℃ 981-500 862

Vía Lactea
⑥ Fonte ⑤ ⑦ *Los Caminantes II*
río As Barrosas
Xunta [46÷2] Albergue **3.1** →④ Ⓐ
②
Ultreia
Don Quixote ① ③ *Santiago*
ARZUA
(Pop. 7,000 – Alt. 390m)
℃ 981-508 132
℃ 981-500 554 • *O Retiro* Ⓗ

Río Iso

RIBADISO
N-547
Ⓐ **0.0** Albergue

39 beds €10 with all facilities and café. Directly opposite is •**Albergue ❸** *Santiago Apostol Priv.[84]* © 981-508 132 with 84 places and every modern convenience (including a lift to all floors!) and restaurant with pilgrim menu. Proceed towards the centre of town and the Plaza Mayor **[0.5 km]** *Turismo* and hostal •**Teodora** © 981-500 083 (despite the sign this is not a pilgrim hostal but does have cheap rooms and overflow in another building elsewhere). Turn <left into rúa Cima do Lugar and adjoining the *Iglesia de Santiago y capela da Madalena* **[0.2 km]** in the centre of town:

3.1 km Arzúa •**Albergue ❹** *Xunta.[46÷2]* © 660 396 824 hostel in restored town house in convenient central location. 46 beds €5 and all facilities. 50m beyond we come to a crossroads ❖ where alternative albergues (all within a

few hundred meters) compete for the lucrative pilgrim trade. The camino continues s/o down rúa do Carme with the traditional •**Albergue ❺** *da Fonte Priv.[20÷5]* © 659 999 496 with 20 beds €10-12 in this quiet 'backwater'. ❖Turn left for •**Albergue ❻** *Vía Láctea Priv. [60÷5]* © 981-500 581 on main road c/Neira Vilas. 60 beds €10 and all facilities. ❖ Turn right into the square off Av. de Lugo (N-547) and turn left along it for •**Albergue ❼** *Los*

Albergue ❹ Xunta

Caminantes II Priv.[28÷1] © 647 020 600 all facilities (no kitchen) in this modern building directly on main road with 28 beds €10. Other accommodation not already mentioned: •**Rúa** Hsr** © 981-500 139 on Av.Lugo (on the way in). Centrally located in more traditional accommodation on rúa Ramón Franco •**Casa Frade** © 981-500 019 and adjacent •**Casa Carballeira** © 981-500 094. Close by •**Mesón do Peregrino** Hs* © 981-500 830, while on the outskirts on the main road *carratera Santiago* is the modern •**Suiza** H** © 981-500 862.

ARZÚA is the last major centre of population (7,000) before we enter Santiago. The untidy development of the modern town is mirrored in the haphazard layout of the older central part and waymarking is also irregular. Off the central square (with variety of bars, cafés and restaurants) is the modern parish church dedicated to St. James with image of Santiago as both Moorslayer and pilgrim and just behind is the original 14th century Augustinian *Capilla de La Magdalena*. The town is known for its local cheese and the cheese fair *festa do queixo* held in March. The camino continues out through the old quarter of town down c/del Carmen (left of the main road) past fountain and over stream (site of San Lázaro hospice) onto a delightful track through ancient oak woods in *As Barrosas* meandering back to the main road (close to Hotel Suiza) and over several small streams passing Preguntoño to take path through tunnel:

2.5 km N-547 **Túnel** we now alternate between track and country lanes through the tiny hamlets of Raído, Fondevila, Cortobe, Pereiriña and Ponteladrón whence we cross the arroyo Ladrón and up the far side into:

3.5 km A Calzada •*Casa Calzada* popular track side café. *[Note: ½ off route on the main N-547 in Burres is a new (2012) •albergue Camiño das Ocas Priv. [30÷6]* © 648-404 780 € 10].* Continue into:

1.7 km A **Calle** quaint village with traditional houses (*Bar Lino* and cafe *Tia Dolores* adjoining the river now closed). [F]. The camino wends its way over the stream and through Boavista and Alto down to the main road at:

3.4 km **Salceda** along the N-547 with bar •*Taberna Salceda* and •*Mesón La Equipa / Bar Verde* and •**Albergue** *Pousada de Salceda* ***Priv.[10÷1]*** Ⓒ 981-502 767 with 10 rooms €7-10 and bar/restaurant. Continue on woodland path with a poignant monument (right) to fellow pilgrim *Guillermo Watt* who died at this spot only a day away from his earthly destination. Take care as we now crisscross the N-547 [!] continuing through ***Xen*** **[1.3 km]** (bar 50m right on main road), ***Ras*** where a pedestrian underpass brings us safely into ***Brea*** **[1.0 km]** (pension-mesón •*Brea* off route) and now its back over the N-547 past 'rest' area (no respite from the noise) up to crossroads **[1.6 km]**.

3.9 km **Cruce** *O Emplame* bar-restaurants with pilgrim menus •*O Ceadoiro* and •*Andenna*. We cross here to take track that runs between the N-547 and the woods around *Alto de Santa Irene* down into Santa Irene passing tunnel (direct to private hostel left) and s/o passing pilgrim rest [F] to:

1.3 km **Santa Irene** •**Albergue** ❶ *Xunta.[36÷4]* Ⓒ 660 396 825 with 36 beds €5 and all facilities but directly on the busy main road (noisy) ❖. On the opposite side of the road is: **Albergue** ❷ *Santa Irene Priv*.[15÷2]* Ⓒ 981-511 000 network* hostel with 15 beds €13 in small refuge set back from the main road with rear garden (see photo) and basic meals available. Named after the nearby 18th century Chapel of Santa Irene, an early Christian martyr. ❖ We

continue down on woodland paths through *túnel* **[0.8 km]** down into *A Rúa* **[0.6 km]** and pilgrim information centre with hotel booking service (accommodation becomes increasingly busy). Just off route right (200m) is •*O Pino H*** Ⓒ 981-511 148 on the main road while the traditional village offers pension •**Casa da Gallega** P Ⓒ 981-511 463 opposite •**O Acivro** CR Ⓒ 981-511 316 with bar-cafeteria and meals available. We now cross arroyo Burgo to climb steeply up through eucalyptus back to the N-547! **[0.7 km]** *Option:* ● ● ● ● To continue directly to Santiago cross the main road here [!] s/o into the eucalyptus woods ahead and continue into ***San Antón*** where the route below re-joins. To access the albergues turn <left along the main road up to ***Correos*** **[0.6 km]** in:

2.7 km **O Pedrouzo** •**Albergue** ❶ *Xunta.* *[120÷4]* Ⓒ 660-396 826 purpose-built hostel 120 beds €5 and all facilities ('hidden' down behind the supermercado /Correo on the busy Av. de Lugo (N-457). Opp. side of main road ❷ *Porta de Santiago Priv.*[56÷3]* Ⓒ 981-511 103 network* hostel in modern building with 56 beds €10 no kitchen but café and rear garden. Also on Av. de Lugo ❸ *O Burgo*

Albergue ❶ Xunta

Priv.[14÷1]*+ Ⓒ 630 404 138 network* hostel with 14 beds €10 + priv. rooms from €35 also bar-restaurant. 250m down Rua Fonte (an extension of rua Minas) ❹ *Edreira Priv.*[52÷4]* Ⓒ 981 511 365 network* hostel with 52 beds €10 and the new (2012) puropse-built hostel ❺ *Otero Priv.[36÷2]* Ⓒ 671 663 374 with 36 beds €10 on c/Forcarei, 2. **Other accommodation:** •**BuleBic** P Ⓒ 981 511 222 on Av. de Lugo•**O Muiño** P* Ⓒ (Maika) 686-419 046 adj. bar O Muiño. 100m further on (left) rua Os Mollaos •**Maribel** Pr* Ⓒ 981-511 404 and •**Arca** P Ⓒ 981-511 437. *Pedrouzo (town), Arca (parish) O Pino (municipality)* modern satellite town of Santiago straddling the busy N-547 with variety of shops and restaurants. *If you intend to make the Cathedral for 12 noon pilgrim mass you need to leave early.*

❏ **He went up into the mountain to pray... and the fashion of his countenance was altered, and his raiment was white and glistening.** *Luke IX, 29.*

33 **20.1** km (12.5 miles) to Santiago

O PEDROUZO (ARCA) – SANTIAGO

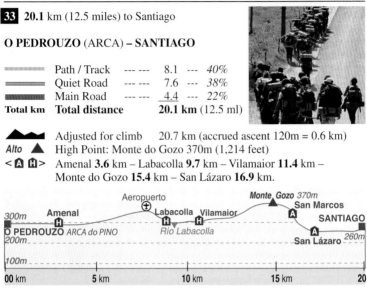

	Path / Track	--- ---	8.1	---	*40%*
	Quiet Road	--- ---	7.6	---	*38%*
	Main Road	--- ---	4.4	---	*22%*
Total km	**Total distance**		**20.1 km** (12.5 ml)		

Adjusted for climb   20.7 km (accrued ascent 120m = 0.6 km)
Alto ▲ High Point: Monte do Gozo 370m (1,214 feet)
< 🅰 🏠 > Amenal **3.6** km – Labacolla **9.7** km – Vilamaior **11.4** km –
Monte do Gozo **15.4** km – San Lázaro **16.9** km.

The Practical Path: The first part of this last stage is through tall stands of the ever-present eucalyptus. Make the most of their shade and the peace they exude. As we get nearer the city, asphalt and crowds begin to take over as busloads of pilgrims join the route for this one-day into Santiago. If you are making for the pilgrim mass at 12 noon be prepared for large crowds and try and create an air of compassionate detachment – be patient and prepare for the long slog up to Monte Gozo which, while surrounded by eucalyptus, is all on asphalt.

❏ **The Mystical Path:** Will you stay awhile and lose yourself in the tiny grove of holm oak, itself almost lost amongst the mass of alien eucalyptus? Will you stop in Lavacolla, whose waters were used in the ritual cleansing of pilgrims prior to entering the City of Saint James? Today the water is putrid but it is the symbolic purification that we seek so that we might glisten with the pure white light of Christ consciousness.

❏ **Personal Reflections:** *"... I had walked the equivalent of one day for each year Christ spent on earth. Here I was on the 33rd day but I could find no joy on this hill amongst the crowd of pilgrims huddled against the driving rain ... As I entered the cathedral I realised I had failed in my purpose. But in that same instant I realised I had been searching in the wrong place. A sudden rush of joy enveloped my soaking body. I knew the answer lay where the world of things ended and the unseen world began and I knew I had to go there. Not tomorrow, but now. I hurried down the steps and out the city gate. I was alone but I had company. I did not know where I was going but I felt completely guided ..."*

0.0 km **Pedrouzo** *Arca O Pino* from albergue ❶ turn <left on main road and take first right> **[0.3 km]** *Casa Concello* up to the social centre and sports hall *polideportivo* **[0.3 km]** where the alternative direct route (that bypasses the hostels in Arca) joins from the right. Continue past bar and turn <left into dense eucalyptus forest and through the village of San Antón and head down into the río Amenal valley over river and through tunnel under N-547 **[3.0 km]:**

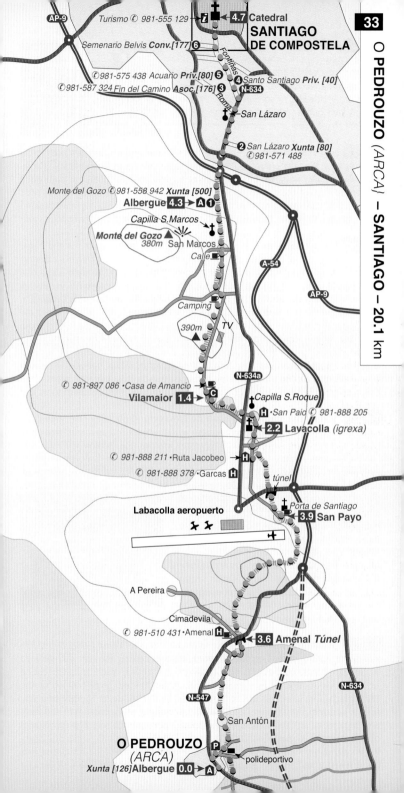

Turismo ℂ 981-555 129 ℹ ✝ ◀ **4.7** **Catedral**
SANTIAGO
DE COMPOSTELA

Seminario Belvis **Conv.[177]** 6

ℂ 981-575 438 Acuario **Priv.[80]** 5 4 Santo Santiago **Priv. [40]**
ℂ 981-587 324 Fin del Camino **Asoc.[176]** 3 N-634

✝ San Lázaro

2 San Lázaro **Xunta [80]**
ℂ 981-571 488

Monte del Gozo ℂ 981-558 942 **Xunta [500]**
Albergue 4.3 ▶ Ⓐ 1

Capilla S.Marcos ✝
Monte del Gozo ▲
380m San Marcos
Calle

A-54

AP-9

Camping

390m TV
▲

N-634a

ℂ 981-897 086 •Casa de Amancio Ⓒ
Vilamaior 1.4 ▶ ✝ Capilla S.Roque

Ⓗ •San Paio ℂ 981-888 205
◀ **2.2** **Lavacolla** *(igrexa)*

ℂ 981-888 211 •Ruta Jacobeo Ⓗ
ℂ 981-888 378 •Garcas Ⓗ

túnel

✝ Porta de Santiago
◀ **3.9** San Payo

Labacolla aeropuerto

✈ ✈

A Pereira

Cimadevila

ℂ 981-510 431 •Amenal Ⓗ
◀ **3.6** **Amenal** *Túnel*

N-634

N-547

San Antón

O PEDROUZO
(ARCA) Ⓟ
Xunta [126] Albergue 0.0 ▶ Ⓐ polideportivo

3.6 km Amenal *Túnel* new (2011) popular
Hotel-Restaurant •**Amenal** Ⓒ 981-510 431
up through Cimadevila and the forestry area
around Santiago airport. A dedicated pilgrim
track alongside the motorway takes us down
into a deep cutting at the end of the runway
(see photo) to cross over an access road into:

3.9 km San Paio ancient hamlet with popular bar and restaurant •*Casa Porta de Santiago*. We now enter the last recognisable stretch of the medieval 'Royal Way' *Real Camino* as we head uphill veering right> onto a natural path lined with remnants of the native deciduous woodland that once covered this area before eucalyptus was imported to fuel the pulp industry. Head downhill passing rear entrance to •**Ruta Jacobea** H***Ⓒ 981-888 211 (special pilgrim price) to:

2.2 km Lavacolla *Igrexa*. Lavacolla is recognised today more for the name of the international airport than the place where medieval pilgrims came to wash *lavar* and purify themselves before entering the city. Modern Lavacolla now caters more for the business traveller than the pilgrim with variety of restaurants, bars and hotels •**San Paio** P* Ⓒ 981-888 205 on Lugar de Lavacolla. *[**Short detour** ● ● ● ● ● **Capela San Roque (300m)**: If you continue down the steps past the bandstand you come to the little chapel dedicated to the pilgrim saint San Roque (right) and while it may be closed it has a covered portico and sits in a shaded grove of trees. A good place to shelter from the rain or sun and here you can perform your own purification ritual in relative peace].* The path now continues around the side of the parish church to cross over the access road to the airport (N-634a) and over a small stream to head steeply uphill to:

1.4 km Villamaior casa rural •**Casa de Amancio** Ⓒ 981-897 086 with café. Continue on pilgrim track across a stream with rest area and up to our high point of this stage at 396m which is not Monte de Gozo but the studios of TV Galicia (a sign of how TV has come to dominate our lives). **[1.6 km]**. We turn <left at Camping •*Café* **[0.6 km]** and pass down the side of RTVE into San Marcos with several bars and cafés ahead **[1.2 km]**. We turn <left past •*Café Calle* and a short paved pathway now brings us to the charming *capilla de San Marcos* **[0.5 km]**
sitting in a small glade of trees and where, if it
was not raining, medieval pilgrims first espied
the cathedral towers giving rise to the name,
Mount Joy *Monte do Gozo – Mon Xoi* in
Galego. Today, a monument commemorating
the visit of Pope John Paul II stands sentinel
atop the hill and the view is now dominated by
the sprawling suburbs of Santiago. Continue
downhill **[0.4 km]** to:

4.3 km Monte del Gozo •**Albergue ❶** *Monte do Gozo* Xunta.*[400]* Ⓒ 660 396 827 prominently located on this elevated site overlooking the city. 400 beds €5 in separate blockhouses containing rooms with 8 beds in each room (reception in N°29). Good modern facilities with bar, restaurant and large canteen on the main plaza. The hill itself has been reshaped by the bulldozer to provide a vast leisure complex for the city. The sprawling dormitory and recreational buildings are the price of an ever-increasing demand for accommodation. The tiny chapel of San Marcos is the only thing left on the hill that gives any sense of history to this romantic sounding place. The route continues down the hill along Rua do Peregrino and down a flight of steps at the far end where we join the city traffic to pass over the railway line and past statue of *El Templario Peregrino* (left) over A-9 autopista and roundabout into the wide N-634 and the modern city suburbs with prominent monument to notable historical figures connected with the camino **[1.2 km]**. Here we have the *Palacio Congresos y Exposicións* halls (left) and on the opposite side of the road (right – not well signposted 200m from roundabout and 50m down side road (behind *Museo Pedagóxico*) •**Albergue** ❷ *Residencia de Peregrinos San Lázaro* **Xunta.**[80÷6] ℂ 981-571 488 with 80 beds €10 (€7 subsequent nights) and all facilities with garden area. Continue along the main road passing •**San Jacobo** H*ℂ 981-580 361 (Av. de San Lázaro, 101) over roundabout to pass the ancient chapel of **San Lázaro Santiago** *[witness to the leprosarium that existed here in the 12th century,*

sufficiently far outside the medieval city walls to ensure contamination didn't spread inside]. Continue over crossroads (traffic lights) to:

❖**[0.9** km] ***Option*** *(200m left–signposted):* •**Albergue** ❸ *Final de Camino (Jaime García Rodríguez)* **Asoc.**[110÷8] ℂ 981-587 324 c/Moscú, modern building behind the austere HQ *Policía Autonómica* on corner of ruas Moscú and Estocolmo. 110 beds €8 and what it lacks in character it makes up for in the range of modern shower and laundry facilities and rear patio *(bus 11 to Plaza Galicia).* ❖Continue over rua de París into rua do Valiño **[0.3 km]** to modern hostal •**Albergue** ❹ *Santo Santiago* **Priv.**[40÷2] ℂ 657 402 403 with 40 beds €10 and restaurant. Below the parque (steps down left) is: •**Albergue** ❺ *Acuario* **Priv.***[80÷7] Rúa Estocolmo, 2-b. ℂ 981-575 438. Network* hostel with 80 beds €10. Modernised and extended in 2012. Continue into rúa das Fontiñas and Fonte dos Concheiros and over ring road *Av. de Lugo* **[0.8 km]** (main bus station *estación de autobuses* – up right) and enter *Rúa dos Concheiros* named after the stall holders who used to sell pilgrim shells *conchas* and at the top we reach St. Peter's cross *Cruceiro de San Pedro* ❖**[0.5 km]** which heralds our arrival into the old city as the spires of the Cathedral now open up before us.

Option: We are now only 900m from the cathedral and the likelihood is you will want to go straight there. However you have an option at this point to go to the main pilgrim hostel at Belvis which is only 500m to our left *(signposted).*

Access from the city centre is via rua Trompas (see city plan) •**Albergue** ❻ *Seminario Menor La Asunción* **Conv.**[177]+ ℂ 881-031 768 with 177 beds €10 + ind. €15. Depending on your time of arrival and intentions for the day you might consider going directly to the hostel (opens from 13.30 with lockers for backpacks) *Directions:* Turn left and immediately right into

rua dos Lagartos to re-join alternative route (from Praza da San Pedro) in rua de Belvís and continue around the walls of the convento de Belvís to the Seminario Menor which houses the main city hostel (Parque Belvís below right).

❖Continue down rua de San Pedro past Praza San Pedro with its tiny shaded square and Church of San Pedro (left) and s/o to the famous Gate of the Way **Porta do Camiño [0.4 km]** which gives access to the wonderful old medieval city. Up on the right and overlooking this main city entrance is the *Convento de Santo Domingo de Bonaval* which houses the Pantheón and the Galician museum, with the centre for contemporary Galician art opposite. There is also a relatively quiet park behind the convent buildings to refresh mind and soul from the rigours of city life. (See city map for directions to these and other places of interest). We now proceed up Casas Reais and Rúa das Ánimas into Praza de Cervantes **[0.3 km]** (with statue to the writer atop the central pillar) now we head down rúa da Azabachería (lined with jewellers selling jet *azabache* – see later) into Praza da Inmaculada (also called Azabachería) down under the arch of the Pazo do Xelmírez **[0.3 km]** to:

4.7 km **Praza Obradoiro and Cathedral**.
Take time to just *arrive*. We each experience different emotions on entering the Cathedral that range from euphoria to disappointment. Whatever your individual reaction – honour and accept it. Gratitude for safe arrival is a frequent response but if you are overwhelmed by the crowds why not return later when you feel more composed and the Cathedral is, perhaps, quieter (open daily from 07:00 until 21:00). Whether now or later and whichever door you entered by, you might like to follow the timeworn pilgrim ritual as follows:

[1] It is no longer permitted to place your hand in the Tree of Jesse, the central column of the Master Mateo's masterpiece Door of Glory *Portico de Gloria*. But you can stop and admire the incomparable beauty of this inner portico carved between 1166 and 1188 (the exterior façade was added in 1750). The Bible and its main characters come alive in this remarkable storybook in stone. The central column has Christ in Glory flanked by the apostles and, directly underneath, St. James sits as intercessor between Christ and the pilgrim. Millions of pilgrims over the centuries have worn finger holes in the solid marble as a mark of gratitude for their safe arrival (the reason why it is now protected by a barrier). Proceed to the other side and **[2]** touch your brow to that of Maestro Mateo whose kneeling figure is carved into the back of the central column (facing the altar) and receive some of his artistic genius in the ritual known as head-butting the saint *Santo d'os Croques* – touch your forehead to his and receive some of his inspiration. Proceed to the High Altar (right) to ascend the stairs and **[3]** hug the Apostle. Perhaps lay your head on his broad shoulders and say what you came here to say. Proceed down the steps on the far side to the crypt and the reliquary chapel under the altar. **[4]** Here, you can kneel before the casket containing the relics of the great Saint and offer your prayer …

Pilgrim mass at 12 noon each day (doors may close 5 minutes before on busy days). The swinging of the giant incense burner *Botafumeiro* was originally used to fumigate the sweaty (and possibly disease-ridden) pilgrims. The ritual requires half a dozen attendants *tiraboleiros* to perform it and so became an infrequent event but is used increasingly during the mass these days. During 2004 the seating capacity was permanently extended from 700 to 1,000 so you might even find somewhere to sit but don't hold any expectations and remember – time itself is a journey.

Pilgrims arrive at the cathedral

REFLECTIONS: 'Time is the journey from ignorance to Gnosis. Time is imperfection longing to be the Good and progressively improving. Time is the relative reaching towards the Absolute.' *Jesus and the Lost Goddess.*' Freke.

4 squares surround the cathedral and provide access to it, as follows:

■ **Praza do Obradoiro**. The 'golden' square of Santiago is usually thronged with pilgrims and tourists admiring the dramatic west facing façade of the Cathedral, universal symbol of Santiago, with St. James looking down on all the activity from his niche in the central tower. This provides the main entrance to the Cathedral and the Portico de Gloria. To the right of the steps is the discrete entrance to the museum. A combined ticket will provide access to all rooms including the crypt and the cloisters and also to the 12th century palace of one of Santiago's most famous individuals and first archbishop, Gelmírez *Pazo de Xelmírez* situated on the (left).

In this square we also find the beautiful Renaissance façade of the Parador named after Ferdinand and Isabel *Hostal dos Reis Católicos* on whose orders it was built in 1492 as a pilgrim hospice. Opposite the Cathedral is the more austere neoclassical seat of the Galician government and town hall *Pazo de Raxoi* with its solid arcade. Finally, making up the fourth side of the square is the gable end of the *Colegio de S. Jerónimo* part of the university. Moving anti-clockwise around the cathedral – turn up into Rúa de Fonseca to:

■ **Praza das Praterías**. The most intimate of the squares with its lovely centrepiece, an ornate statue of horses leaping out of the water. On the corner of Rúa do Vilar we find the Dean's House *Casa do Deán* now the **pilgrim office.** Along the walls of the Cathedral itself are the silversmith's *prateros* that give the square its name. Up the steep flight of steps we come to the magnificent southern door to the Cathedral, the oldest extant doorway and traditionally the entrance taken by pilgrims coming from Portugal. The quality of the carvings and their arrangement is remarkable and amongst the many sculptured figures is one of St. James between two cypress trees. Continuing around to the right we come to:

■ **Praza da Quintana.** This wide square is readily identified by the broad sweep of steps separating the lower part *Quintana of the dead* from the upper *Quintana of the living*. Opposite the Cathedral is the high blank wall of the *Mosteiro de San Paio de Antealtares* (with museum of sacred art). The square provides the eastern entrance to the Cathedral via the Holy Gate *Porta Santa* sometime referred to as the Door of Pardon *El Perdón* that is only opened during Holy Years (the next in 2021). Adjoining it is the main entrance to the Cathedral shop that has several guidebooks (in various languages) with details of the Cathedral's many chapels and their interesting carvings and statuary and

Pilgrims during Holy Year

the priceless artefacts and treasures in the museum. Finally, we head up the broad flight of steps around the corner and back into:

■ **Praza da Inmaculada (Azabachería)** to the north facing Azabachería façade, with the least well-known doorway and the only one that *descends* to enter the Cathedral. It has the most weathered aspect, with moss and lichen covering its bleak exterior. Opposite the cathedral is the imposing southern edifice of *Mosteiro de San Martiño Pinario* the square in front gets any available sun and attracts street artists. The archbishop's arch *Arco Arzobispal* brings us back to the Praza do Obradoiro.

Check in at the •**Pilgrim Office** *Oficina del Peregrino* and pilgrim welcome centre (open every day from 09:00-21:00) adjacent to the Cathedral on Rúa Vilar, 1. The office issues the *compostela* and welcomes all pilgrims arriving with the teams of *Amigos* a volunteer initiative of the Irish Society and the CSJ in London who offer help with any queries. Here we also find toilets and backpack storage so you can explore accommodation alternatives and there is a notice board for pilgrims to leave messages. Providing you have fulfilled the criteria of a bona-fide pilgrim and have walked at least the last 100 km, you will be awarded a certificate of completion *Compostela*. This may entitle you to certain privileges such as reduced entry fees to museums and discounted travel home (but check deals that may be available elsewhere and may prove cheaper than the 'special' fares on offer and refer to the travel notes at the beginning of this guide.

Compostela

❏ **Turismo:** ❖ r/Vilar, 63 © 981-555 129 *June-Sept 09-21 / Oct-May 10-15 &*
17-20. ❖ *Kiosco* Plaza do Galicia. ❖ *TurGalicia* r/do Vilar.43 © 981 584 081.

❏*Albergues: Peregrino oficina: Rua Vilar, 1.* © *981-562 419 daily* 09:00-21:00.
❶**Monte del Gozo** *Xunta.[400÷50]* €6 ©660 396 827. ❷**San Lázaro** *Xunta.*
[80÷7] r/de San Lázaro €10 (2nd night €7) ©981-571 488. ❸**Fin del Camino**
(Rodríguez) Asoc.[110÷6] r/de Moscova €8 ©981-587 324. ❹**Santo Santiago**
Priv.[40÷1] r/do Valiña,3 €10 ©657 402 403. ❺**Acuario** *Priv.***[60]* r/Estocolmo,
2-b €10 © 981-575 438. ❻**La Estrella** *Priv.[24÷1]* c/Concheiros,36 €10 (*open*
2013) ©981-589 200.❼**Seminario Menor** *La Asunción Conv.[177÷6]+* r/de
Belvis *(via r/de Trompas)* €10 (ind.€20) ©881-031 768. ❽**La Salle** *Priv.[84]+*
c/de Tras de Santa Clara €17+ ©981-584 611. ❾**Meiga Backpackers** *Priv.*
[30÷5] c/Basquiños, 67 €13-18 ©981 570 846. **10●** **O Fogar de Teodomiro**
Priv.[20÷5] Plaza de Algalia de Arriba,3 €15+ ©981-582 920. **11●** **The Last**
Stamp *Priv.[62÷10]* r/Preguntorio,10 €15-18 ©981 563 525. **12●** **Azabache**
Priv.[20÷5] c/Azabachería,15 €16-20 ©981 071 254. **13●** **Mundoalbergue**
Priv.[34÷1] c/San Clemente, 26 €16-20 ©981-588 625. **14●** **Roots & Boots**
Priv.[48÷6] r/do Campo Cruceiro do Galo from €10 ©699 631 594.

❏ *Hoteles:* ■ *€30 – €60:* •**Hostal Moure** ©981-583 637 r/dos Loureiros.
•**Hostal Moure II** r/Laureles 12. •**Hotel Fonte de San Roque** ©981-554 447
r/do Hospitallilo, 8. •**La Campana** ©981-584 850 Campanas de San Juan,
4. •**Estrela** ©981-576 924 Plaza de San Martín Pinario, 5-2° •**Hospedería**
San Martín Pinario ©981-560 282 Praza da Inmaculada. •**Pico Sacro** r/San
Francisco, 22 y •**Pico Sacro II** ©981-584 466. •**La Estela** ©981-582 796 rua
Raxoi, 1. •**Hostal Barbantes** ©981-581 077 r/do Franco, 3. •**Santa Cruz** ©981-
582 362 r/do Vilar, 42. •**Hostal Suso** ©981-586 611 r/do Vilar, 65. •**San Jaime**
©981-583 134 r/do Vilar, 12-2°. •**A Nosa Casa** ©981-585 926 r/Entremuralles,
9. •**Hostal Mapoula** ©981-580 124 r/Entremuralles, 10. •**Hostal Alameda**
©981-588 100 San Clemente, 32 ■ *€60+:* •**Hotel Rua Vilar** ©981-557 102
r/Vilar, 12-2° •**Hotel Airas Nunes** ©902-405 858 r/do Vilar, 17. •**Entrecercas**
©981-571 151 r/Entrecercas. •**Costa Vella** ©981-569 530 Porta de Pena, 17.
•**MV Algalia** ©981-558 111 Praziña da Algalia de Arriba, 5. ■ *€100+:*•**San**
Francisco**** Campillo de San Francisco ©981 581 634. •**Hostal de los**
Reyes Católicos***** Plaza Obradoiro ©981-582

❏ *Centro Histórico:* ❶ Convento de Santo Domingo de Bonaval XIIIth *(panteón*
de Castelao, Rosalía de Castro y museo do Pobo Galego). ❷ Casa Gótica XIVth
museo das Peregrinációnes-1. ❸ Mosteiro de San Martín Pinario XVIth *y museo*
■ *Prazo Obradoiro* ❹ Pazo de Xelmirez XIIth ❺ Catedral XIIth –XVIIIth *Portica*
de Gloria, claustro, museo e tesouro da catedral ❻ Hostal dos Reis Católicos
XVth *Parador* ❼ Pazo de Raxoi XVIIIth *Presendencia da Xunta* ❽ Colexio de
Fonseca XVIth *universidade y claustro.* ❾ Casa do Deán XVIIIth *Oficina do*
Peregrino. **10●** Casa Canónica *museo Peregrinációnes-2.* **11●** Mosteiro de San
Paio de Antealtares XVth *Museo de Arte Sacra.* **12●** S.Maria Salomé XIIth.

Santiago is a wonderful destination, full of vibrancy
and colour. Pilgrims, street artists, musicians, dancers,
tourists all come and add to the life and soul of this
fabled city. Stay awhile and soak up some of her
culture or relax in the delightful shaded park *Alameda*
and climb to the *capela de Santa Susanna* hidden in
the trees or stroll up the Avenue of the Lions *Paseo*
dos Leónes to the statue of Rosalia de Castro and look
out west over her belovéd Galicia and... *Finis terre.*

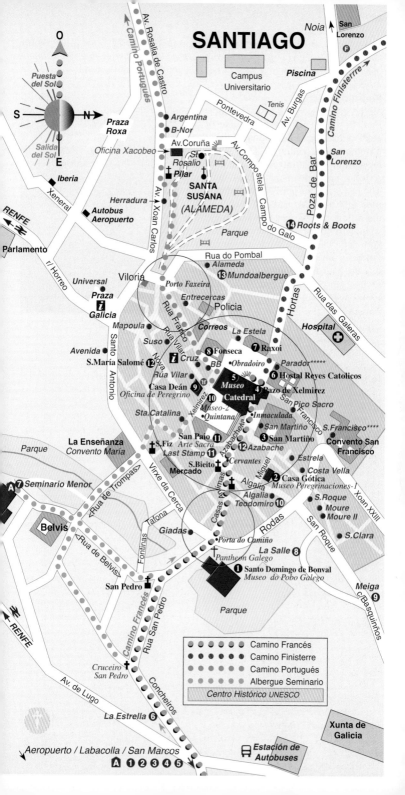

The official literature for the last compostelan jubilee year *año jubilar compostelana* stated boldly on the front cover, 'A Road with an END' *Camino que tiene META*. That may be so – but it is not the end of the road.

Finisterre. Before you leave this corner of the earth why not visit the end of it *Finis Terra*: "… Finisterre is one of the great hidden treasures amongst the many Caminos de Santiago. Only a small proportion of pilgrims arriving at Santiago continue by foot to the end of the road. The way to Finisterre truly follows *the road less travelled* and *that* may make all the difference. We need to search out the waymarks to the source of our own inner knowing. The light, while obscured, lies hidden in our memory – it is no coincidence that the path to Finisterre ends at the altar to the sun *Ara Solis* and a lighthouse." From *A Pilgrim's Guide to the Camino Finisterre*.

USEFUL PILGRIM CONTACTS:

You may be able to obtain further information of the route and a pilgrim passport, record or *credencial*, subject to membership from one of the English speaking organisations listed below. Allow several weeks to process postal applications.

UK: **The Confraternity of St. James**, 27 Blackfriars Road, London SE1 8NY (0044-[0]2079 289 988) e-mail: office@csj.org.uk / *www.csj.org.uk* the pre-eminent site in English with an on-line bookshop.

IRELAND: **The Irish Society of the Friends of St. James**. Based in Dublin, contact through their web site: *www.st.jamesirl.com*

U.S.A. **American Pilgrims on the Camino**. *www.americanpilgrims.com* *also:* Friends of the Road to Santiago *www.geocities.com/friends_usa_santiago*

CANADA: Canadian Company of Pilgrims Canada. *www.santiago.ca*

SOUTH AFRICA: Confraternity of St. James of SA *www.geocities.com/csjofsa*

TRANSLATIONS: *www.freetranslation.com/* or: *www.babelfish.altavista.com*

There are a number of additional web sites (in English) loosely connected with the Way of St. James or with the theme of pilgrimage as spiritual journeying that you may find helpful. These sites provide links with other organisations so you can explore and, hopefully, find information that resonates with you:

Latest News from Santiago and the Caminos (formerly *santiago-today) the pilgrims 'FaceBook'* **www.caminodesantiago.me**

Alternatives of St. James *www.alternatives.org.uk* exploration of ways of living that honour all spiritual traditions. Based at St. James Church, London.

The Gatekeeper Trust devoted to personal and planetary healing through pilgrimage. *www.gatekeeper.org.uk*

The Beloved Community *www.emissaryoflight.com* on-line courses in spiritual peacemaking and peace pilgrimages based in the USA.

Findhorn Foundation dedicated to personal and planetary transformation *www.findhorn.org* with daily reflections from 'Opening Doors Within.'

Lucis Trust incorporating the Arcane School of spiritual education and meditation and World Goodwill *www.lucistrust.org*

Paulo Coelho *www.warrioroflthelight.com* with on-line news and reflections from Brazilian author of 'The Pilgrimage.'

Peace Pilgrim *www.peacepilgrim.com* audio and visual reflections of Peace Pilgrim's life and work.

The Quest A Guide to the Spiritual Journey. A practical home-study course for personal and spiritual discovery *www.thequest.org.uk*

BIBLIOGRAPHY:

Some reading with waymarks to the inner path include:

A Course In Miracles (A.C.I.M.) *Text, Workbook for Students and Manual for Teachers*. Foundation for Inner Peace.

The Art of Pilgrimage *The Seeker's Guide to Making Travel Sacred*, Phil Cousineau. Element Books

Anam Cara *Spiritual wisdom from the Celtic world,* John O'Donohue. Bantam Books

A New Earth *Awakening to Your Life's Purpose*, Eckhart Tolle. Penguin Books

A Brief History of Everything *Integrating the partial visions of specialists into a new understanding of the meaning and significance of life*, Ken Wilber.

Care of the Soul *How to add depth and meaning to your everyday life*, Thomas Moore. Piatkus

Conversations with God *Books One, Two and Three*. Neale Donald Walsch. Hodder & Stoughton

From the Holy Mountain *A Journey in the Shadow of Byzantium*, William Dalrymple. Flamingo

Going Home *Jesus and the Buddha as brothers*, Thich Nhat Hanh. Rider Books

Loving What Is *Four Questions That Can Change Your Life*, Byron Katie. Rider

Handbook for the Soul *A collection of wisdom from over 30 celebrated spiritual writers*. Piatkus

The Hero with a Thousand Faces *An examination, through ancient myths, of man's eternal struggle for identity,* Joseph Campbell. Fontana Press

How to Know God *The Soul's Journey into the Mystery of Mysteries*, Deepak Chopra. Rider

Jesus and the Lost Goddess *The Secret Teachings of the Original Christians*, Timothy Freke & Peter Gandy. Three Rivers Press

The Journey Home *The Obstacles to Peace*, Kenneth Wapnick. Foundation for A Course In Miracles

The Mysteries *Rudolf Steiner's writings on Spiritual Initiation*, Andrew Welburn. Floris Books

Mysticism *The Nature and Development of Spiritual Consciousness,* Evelyn Underhill. Oneworld

Nine Faces of Christ *Quest of the True Initiate*, Eugene Whitworth. DeVorss

No Destination *Autobiography (of a pilgrimage), Satish Kumar*. Green Books

Paths of the Christian Mysteries *From Compostela to the New World*, Virginia Sease and Manfred Schmidt-Brabant. Temple Lodge

Pilgrimage *Adventures of the Spirit*, Various Authors. Travellers' Tales

The Pilgrimage *A Contemporary Quest for Ancient Wisdom*. Paulo Coelho

Peace Pilgrim *Her Life and Work in Her Own Words*, Friends of Peace Pilgrim. Ocean Tree Books

Pilgrim in Aquarius, David Spangler. Findhorn Press

Pilgrim Stories *On and Off the Road to Santiago*. Nancy Louise Frey.

Pilgrim in Time *Mindful Journeys to Encounter the Sacred*. Rosanne Keller.

The Power of Now *A Guide to Spiritual Enlightenment*, Eckhart Tolle. New World Library

Peace is Every Step *The path of mindfulness in everyday life*, Thich Nhat Hanh. Rider Books

Phases *The Spiritual Rhythms in Adult Life*, Bernard Lievegoed. Sophia Books

Sacred Contracts *Awakening Your Divine Potential*, Caroline Myss. Bantam

Sacred Roads *Adventures from the Pilgrimage Trail*, Nicholas Shrady. Viking

Secrets of God *Writings of Hildegard of Bingen*. Shambhala

Silence of the Heart *Dialogues with Robert Adams*. Acropolis Books

The Gift of Change *Spiritual Guidance for a Radically New Life*, Marianne Williamson. Element Books

The Reappearance of the Christ. Alice Bailey. Lucis Press.

The Road Less Travelled *A new Psychology of Love*, M. Scott Peck. Arrow Books

The Soul's Code *In Search of Character and Calling*, James Hillman. Bantam

The Prophet. Kahlil Gibran. Mandarin

Wandering Joy *Meister Eckhart's Mystical Philosophy*. Lindisfarne Press

Wanderlust *A history of Walking*. Rebecca Solnit. Verso

Who Dies? *An Investigation of Conscious Living and Conscious Dying*, Stephen and Ondrea Levine. Anchor Books

Whispers of the Beloved *The mystical poems of Rumi*. HarperCollins

RETURNING HOME:
Reflections ...

When, after a prolonged absence, friends and family remark, *'you haven't changed at all'* I am hopeful they are either blind or following some meaningless social convention. I have spent the last 20 years of my life with the primary intention to do just that – to change myself. One of the more potent aspects of pilgrimage is the extended time it requires away from the familiar. This allows an opportunity for the inner alchemy of spirit to start its work of transformation. It's not just the physical body that may need to sweat off excess baggage – the mind needs purifying too. Our world is in a mess and we are not going to fix it with more of the same. We need a fresh approach and a different mind-set to the one that created the chaos in the first place. Hopefully, this re-ordering of the way we see the world will quicken apace as we open to lessons presented to us along the camino and begin to understand that... life itself is a classroom.

A purpose of pilgrimage is to allow time for old belief systems and outworn 'truths' to fall away so that new and higher perspectives can arise. We may also need to recognise that colleagues and partners at home or at work may feel threatened by our new outlook on life. Breaking tribal patterns, challenging the status quo or querying consensus reality is generally considered inappropriate at best or heretical at worst. The extent to which we hold onto any new understanding is measured by how far we are prepared to *walk our talk* and live our 'new' truth in the face of opposition, often from those who profess to love us. Christ was crucified for living The Truth.

These guidebooks are dedicated to awakening beyond human consciousness. They arose out of a personal existential crisis and the urgent need for some space and time to reflect on the purpose of life and its direction. Collectively we live in a spiritual vacuum of our own making where the mystical and sacred have been relegated to the delusional or escapist. Accordingly, we live in a three dimensional world and refuse to open the door to higher dimensions of reality. We have impoverished ourselves in the process, severely limiting our potential. Terrorised by the chaotic world we have manifested around us, we have become ensnared in its dark forms. We have become so preoccupied with these fearful images we fail to notice that we hold the key to the door of our self-made prison. We can walk out any time we choose.

Whatever our individual experiences, it is likely that you will be in a heightened state of sensitivity after walking the camino. I strongly recommend that you do not squeeze your itinerary so you feel pressurised to rush back into your work and general lifestyle immediately on your return. This is a crucial moment. I have often witnessed profound change, in myself and others, only to allow a sceptical audience to induce fear and doubt in us so that we fall back to the starting point – the default position of the status quo. Be careful with whom you share your experiences and stay in contact with fellow pilgrims who can support new realisations and orientation. Source new friends and activities that enhance and encourage the on-going journey of Self-discovery.

If you feel it might be helpful, please feel free to email me any time at *jb@ caminoguides.com* – I cannot promise to answer all emails in writing but be assured they will all be noted and a blessing sent in return. I have developed great empathy and respect for my fellow pilgrims who have placed themselves on the path of enquiry. We are embarking together on a journey of re-discovery of our essential nature and opening up to knowledge of Higher Worlds. We have, collectively, been asleep a long time and while change can happen in the twinkling of an eye it is often experienced as a slow and painful process. It is never easy to let go of the familiar and to step into the new. How far we are prepared to go and how resolute in holding onto our newfound reality is a matter of our own choosing. There is little point in garnering peace along the camino if we leave it behind in Santiago. We need to bring it back into our everyday life. After the camino comes the laundry!

Whichever choice you make will doubtless be right for you at this time. I wish you well in your search for the truth and your journey Home and extend my humble blessings to a fellow pilgrim on the path. The journey is not over and continues, as you will have it be, dedicated to the sacred or the mundane, to waking or sleeping. To help remind us of our true identity, I leave you with the following words of Marianne Williamson, distilled from A Course In Miracles and immortalised in Nelson Mandela's *freedom speech*.

Our deepest fear is not that we are inadequate.
Our deepest fear is that we are powerful beyond measure.
It is our Light, not our darkness, that most frightens us.

We ask ourselves, who am I to be brilliant, gorgeous, talented and fabulous?
Actually, who are you not to be? You are a child of God.
Your playing small doesn't serve the world.
There's nothing enlightened about shrinking,
So that other people won't feel insecure around you.

We were born to make manifest the Glory of God that is within us.
It's not just in some of us; it's in everyone.
And as we let our Light shine,
We unconsciously give other people permission to do the same.
As we are liberated from our own fear,
Our presence automatically liberates others.

Before a new chapter is begun, the old one has to be finished.
Stop being who you were, and change into who you are.
Paulo Coelho – www.warriorsoflight.com

Stay in Touch:

The evolution of human consciousness is gathering apace, one manifestation of this is the increasing interest in taking time out to go on pilgrimage and nowhere is this more apparent than along the camino where facilities struggle to keep up with demand. Information garnered in one month may be out of date the next as old hostels close and new ones open up. Paths are realigned to make way for new motorways and budget airlines suddenly announce new routes (or with the advent of 'peak oil' – closing some). Whilst great care has been taken in gathering the information for this guide it also requires feedback from pilgrims who have recently walked the route to enable it to stay fresh and relevant to those who will follow on after us. Your comments and suggestions will be gratefully received and used to provide up-to-date advice on the free 'updates' page on **www.caminoguides.com** so if you would like to offer something back to the camino or simply stay in touch please e-mail me at:

jb@caminoguides.com

A tithe of all royalties from the sale of this book will be distributed to individuals and organisations seeking to preserve the physical and spiritual integrity of the Camino de Santiago.

12 · **Ways of St. James** *weeks [ ]*
12 · Caminos de Santiago

❶ Camino Francés 790 km *[5]*
St. Jean / Roncesvalles – Santiago

❷ Chemin de Paris 1000 km *[6]*
Paris – St. Jean via Orléans & Tours
Alt. route from Chartres -
Soulac – Tarnos 170km *[1]*

❸ Chemin de Vézelay 900 km *[5½]*
Vezélay – St. Jean via Bazas
Ext. to Namur (B) & Maastricht (NL)

❹ Chemin de Le Puy 740 km *[4½]*
Le Puy-en-Velay – St. Jean
Ext. to Geneva, Konstanz, Prague

❺ Chemin d'Arles 750 km *[4½]*
Arles – Somport Pass
Camino Aragonés **160** km *[1]*
Somport Pass – Óbanos

Camí San Jaume **600** km *[3½]*
Port de Selva – Jaca

❻ Camino de Levante 900 km *[5½]*
Valencia (Alicante) – Zamora
Alt. route via Cuenca – Burgos
Camino de Madrid 320km *[2]*
Madrid – Sahagún

❼ Camino Mozárabe 390km *[2½]*
Granada – Mérida
(Málaga alternative via Baena)

❽ Via de la Plata 1,000km *[6]*
Seville – Santiago

❾ Camino Portugués 241km *[1½]*
Oporto – Santiago
Camino Portugués **372**km *[2]*
Lisbon – Oporto

❿ Camino Finisterre 87km *[½]*
Santiago – Finisterre
Return via Muxía 114km *[<1]*

⓫ Camino Inglés 110km *[<1]*
Ferrol – Santiago

⓬ Camino del Norte 830km *[5]*
Irún – Santiago via Gijón
Camino Primitivo 320km *[2]*
Oviedo – Lugo – Melide